# TOMARE!

## [STOP!]

You are going the wrong way!

Manga is a completely different
type of reading experience.

To start at the *beginning*, go to the *end*!

That's right! Authentic manga is read the traditional Japanese
way—from right to left. Exactly the *opposite* of how American
books are read. It's easy to follow: Just go to the other end of
the book, and read each page—and each panel—from right side
to left side, starting at the top right. Now you're experiencing
manga as it was meant to be.

# Oh!great

TRANSLATED AND ADAPTED BY
## Makoto Yukon

LETTERED BY
## NMSG

BALLANTINE BOOKS • NEW YORK

*Air Gear,* volume 9 is a work of fiction. Names, characters, places, and incidents are the products of the author's imagination or are used fictitiously. Any resemblance to actual events, locales, or persons, living or dead, is entirely coincidental.

A Del Rey Manga/Kodansha Trade Paperback Original



Published in the United States by Del Rey Books, an imprint of The Random House Publishing Group, a division of Random House, Inc., New York.



Publication rights arranged through Kodansha Ltd.

First published in Japan in 2005 by Kodansha Ltd., Tokyo

ISBN 978-0-345-50195-0

Printed in the United States of America

www.delreymanga.com

9 8 7 6 5 4 3 2 1

Translator and Adapter—Makoto Yukon
Lettering—NMSG

# Table of Contents

# Honorifics Explained

Throughout the Del Rey Manga books, you will find Japanese honorifics left intact in the translations. For those not familiar with how the Japanese use honorifics and, more important, how they differ from American honorifics, we present this brief overview.

Politeness has always been a critical facet of Japanese culture. Ever since the feudal era, when Japan was a highly stratified society, use of honorifics —which can be defined as polite speech that indicates relationship or status—has played an essential role in the Japanese language. When addressing someone in Japanese, an honorific usually takes the form of a suffix attached to one's name (example: "Asuna-san"), is used as a title at the end of one's name, or appears in place of the name itself (example: "Negi-sensei," or simply "Sensei!").

Honorifics can be expressions of respect or endearment. In the context of manga and anime, honorifics give insight into the nature of the relationship between characters. Many English translations leave out these important honorifics and therefore distort the feel of the original Japanese. Because Japanese honorifics contain nuances that English honorifics lack, it is our policy at Del Rey not to translate them. Here, instead, is a guide to some of the honorifics you may encounter in Del Rey Manga.

**-san:** This is the most common honorific, and is equivalent to Mr., Miss, Ms., or Mrs. It is the all-purpose honorific and can be used in any situation where politeness is required.

**-sama:** This is one level higher than "-san" and is used to confer great respect.

**-dono:** This comes from the word "tono," which means "lord." It is an even higher level than "-sama" and confers utmost respect.

**-kun:** This suffix is used at the end of boys' names to express familiarity or endearment. It is also sometimes used by men among friends, or when addressing someone younger or of a lower station.

**-chan:** This is used to express endearment, mostly toward girls. It is also used for little boys, pets, and even among lovers. It gives a sense of childish cuteness.

**Bozu:** This is an informal way to refer to a boy, similar to the English terms "kid" and "squirt."

**Sempai/**
**Senpai:** This title suggests that the addressee is one's senior in a group or organization. It is most often used in a school setting, where under-classmen refer to their upperclassmen as "sempai." It can also be used in the workplace, such as when a newer employee addresses an employee who has seniority in the company.

**Kohai:** This is the opposite of "sempai" and is used toward under-classmen in school or newcomers in the workplace. It connotes that the addressee is of a lower station.

**Sensei:** Literally meaning "one who has come before," this title is used for teachers, doctors, or masters of any profession or art.

**-[blank]:** This is usually forgotten in these lists, but it is perhaps the most significant difference between Japanese and English. The lack of honorific means that the speaker has permission to address the person in a very intimate way. Usually, only family, spouses, or very close friends have this kind of permission. Known as *yobisute,* it can be gratifying when someone who has earned the intimacy starts to call one by one's name without an honorific. But when that intimacy hasn't been earned, it can be very insulting.

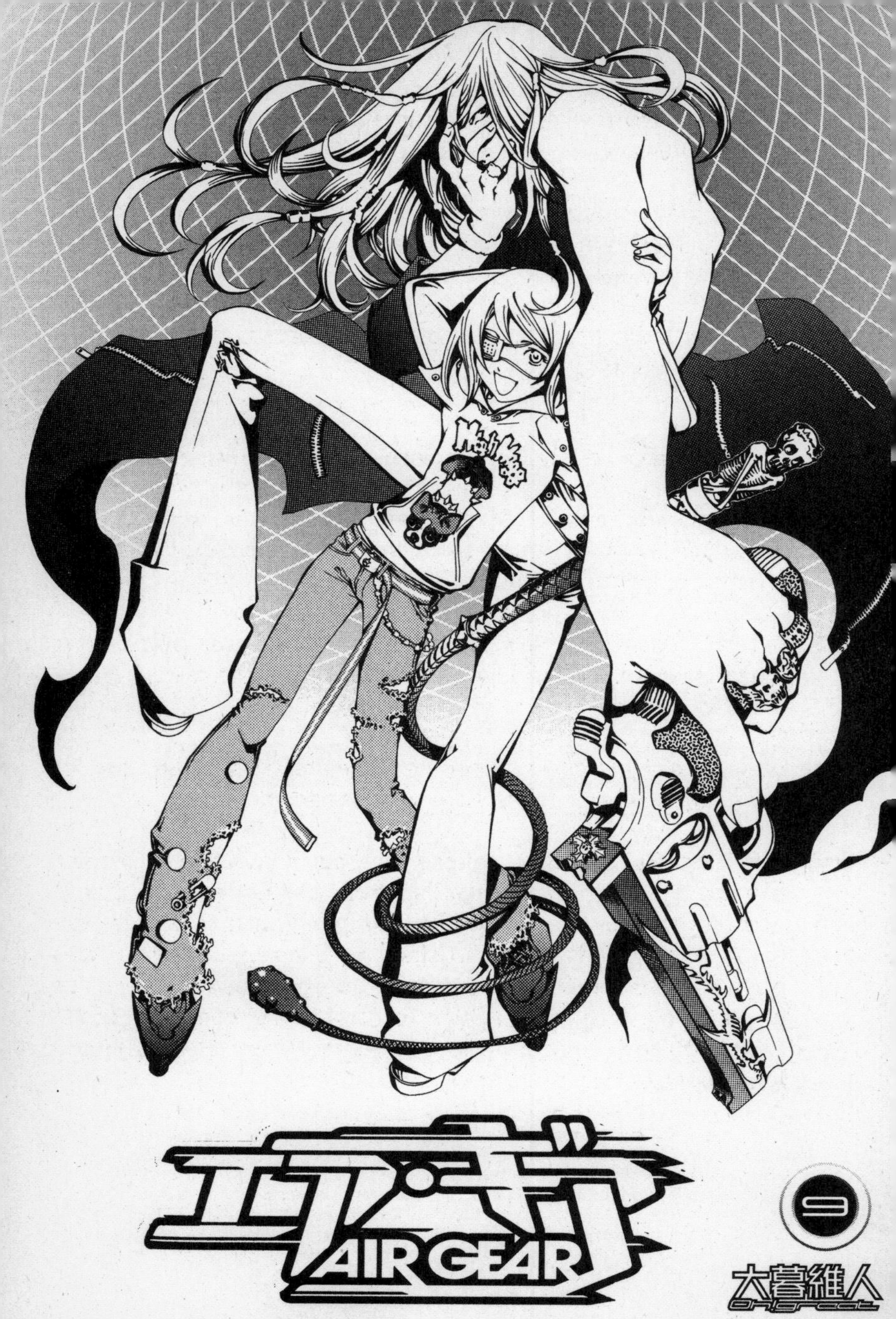

# エア・ギア
# AIR GEAR

9

大暮維人
oh!great

## Character Introductions

### BUCCHA (Issa Mihotoke)

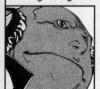

Former leader of the gang called "Night King." In the time since his battle with Ikki, he's somehow ended up on their side. Buccha is an exceptionally powerful rider, and the team's Heavy Battalion.

### IKKI (Itsuki Minami)

Our hero is fascinated with the concept of flying and the only thing on his mind lately is Air Trecks. He's called the Eastside's Greatest "Babyface," (the hero of his wrestling group). Ikki can beat anyone in a straight fight (i.e. on the ground), but in Parts War, his rank is still F.

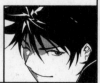

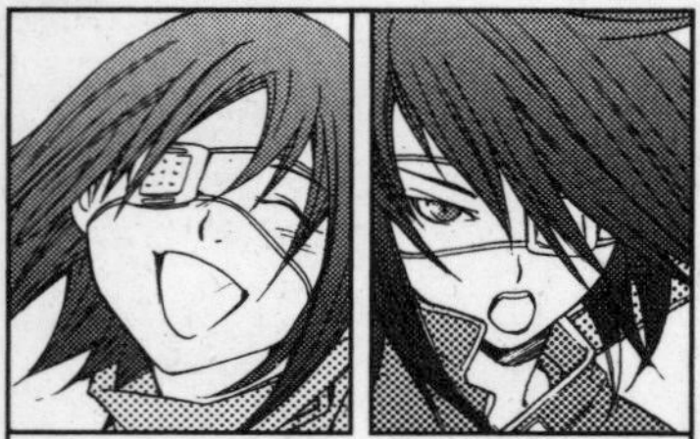

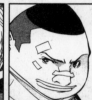

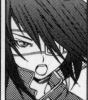

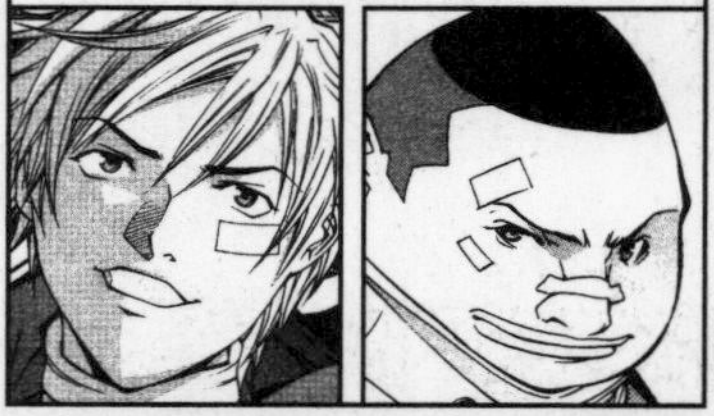

### AKITO/AGITO WANIJIMA

Recently revealed to have been the previous Keeper of the "Fang" Regalia. He has two personalities and switching the eyepatch decides which is in control. Now will this fight with Akira Udou of Behemoth seal his fate...

### KAZU & ONIGIRI

These two are Ikki's childhood friends, and also part of his previous gang, the Eastside Guns. After watching Ikki for a bit, they decided to get into Air Trecks too. As a rider, Kazu turns out to have a talent for speed. Onigiri's family owns a notoriously bad Chinese restaurant called Manchinrou. He's the Iron Hornball.

## TEAM KOGARASUMARU

### SPITFIRE

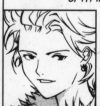

Ruling over the Flame Road, he's one of the Eight Keepers, who have Regalia. In Parts War, Spitfire is Rank A.

### SIMCA

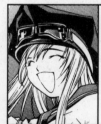

A mysterious girl on Air Trecks, she was the first to discover that Ikki had potentially "great wings," and she expects that he could become the next Keeper of the Sky.

### THE STORY SO FAR...

Now in the final battle of the Parts War match between F Class "Kogarasumaru," and the best D-Class team in history, "Behemoth." On the line: the Fang Regalia and the Kogarasumaru Emblem. With Onigiri's miraculous win, Kogarasumaru now has one win and two losses, and the final two battles were combined into one do-or-die fight, thanks to Ikki's "strategy." Together Ikki and Agito tag-team the Brute Savage Akira Udou, with combination moves that put Akira under pressure! That is until one blow from Mitsuru Bandou's Hammer roused the sleeping lion! The power of the Fang Regalia is finally revealed!

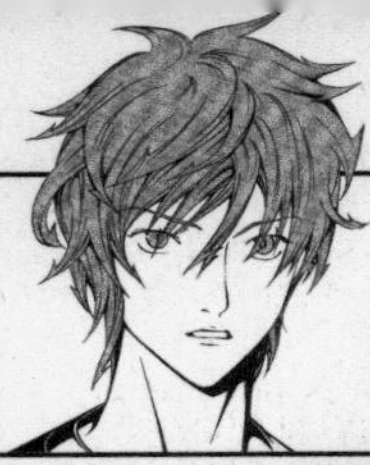

AKIRA UDOU

The leader of Team Behemoth. He must settle his fate with Agito and a battle to the death will unfold. He currently possesses the Bloody Road Regalia.

MITSURU BANDOU

Nicknamed Cyclops Hammer because he has a super-intense punch. He loves pimped-out bicycles.

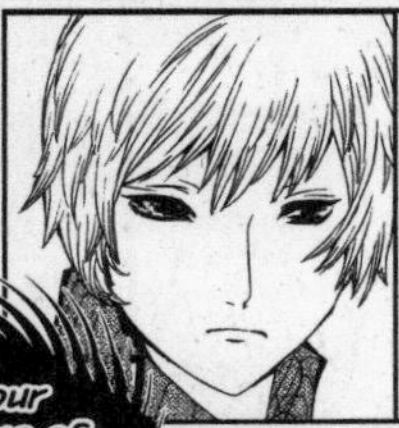

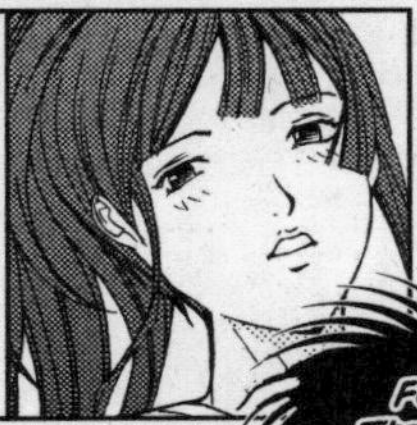

RYOU MIMASAKA

Defeated in battle by Onigiri, in spite of her sexy l v. 100 trick. She's sometimes called by her nickname, The Gorgon Shell.

Four Titans of BEHEMOTH

FUUMEI GOSHOGAWARA

Defeated Buccha by using his knockout stunt, "Digger Wasp Lock." He's also known as the "Hecatonchires Bomb."

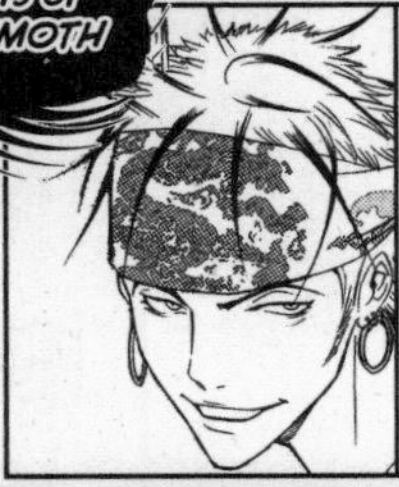

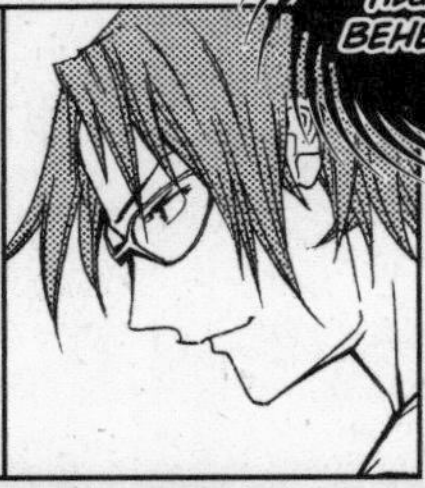

YASUYOSHI SANO

Nickname: Aeon Clock. During his battle with Kazu, Sano won with his blinding speed.

## TEAM BEHEMOTH

RINGO (Ringo Noyamano)

She's Ikki's childhood friend and roommate, and the legitimate successor of the Sleeping Forest. She appears in disguise as the Masked Swimsuit Schoolgirl whenever the team needs her help.

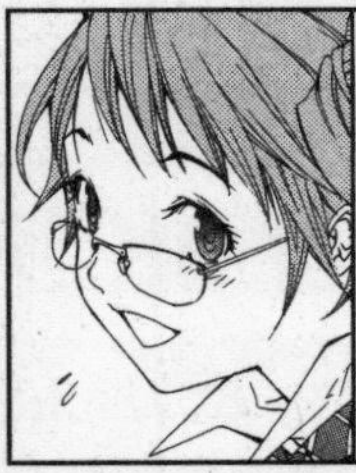

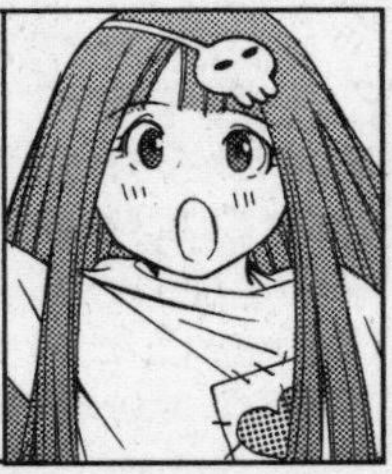

UME (Shiraume Noyamano)

Youngest of the four Noyamano sisters, Ume likes working with her hands and is especially good with mechanical things. A member of the Sleeping Forest.

MIKAN (Mikan Noyamano)

Second born of the Noyamano sisters. If one were to ask the lowly servant, Ikki, he'd say that Mikan is in charge of Discipline and Severe Ass-Kicking. A member of the Sleeping Forest.

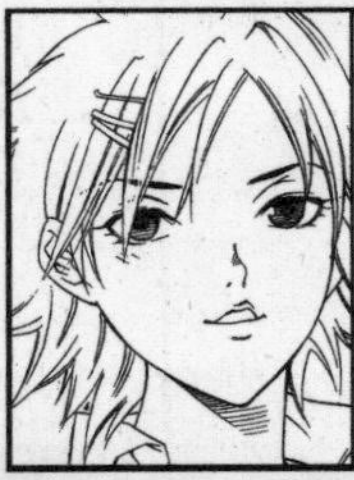

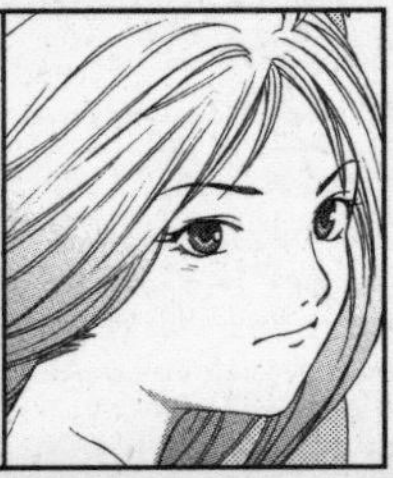

RIKA (Rika Noyamano)

The eldest of the Noyamano sisters, Rika lends a somewhat parental figure to the household. She was a member of the original Sleeping Forest.

## TEAM SLEEPING FOREST

## CONTENTS

Emblem Design by Kei Machida

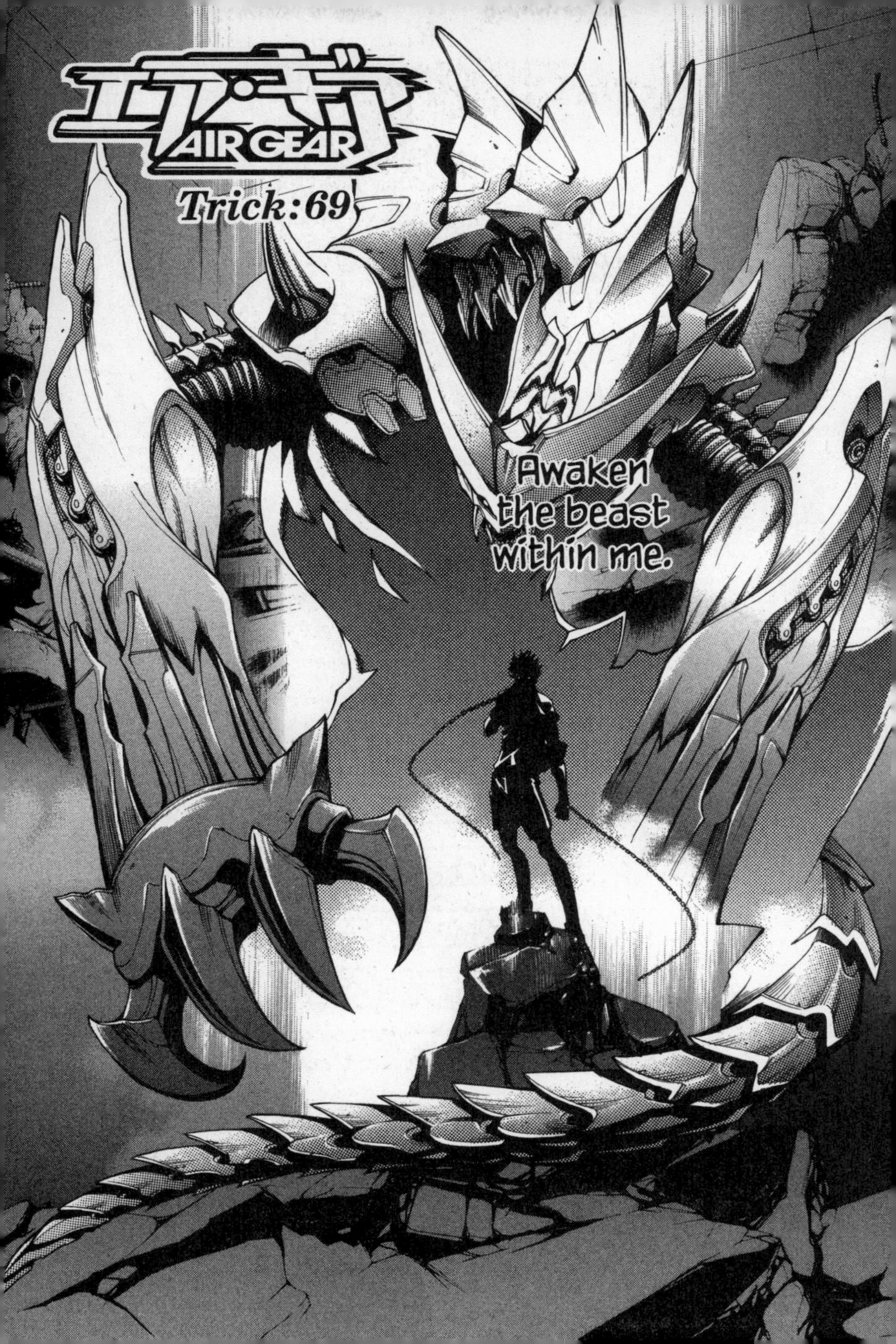
エア・ギア
AIR GEAR
Trick:69
Awaken the beast within me.

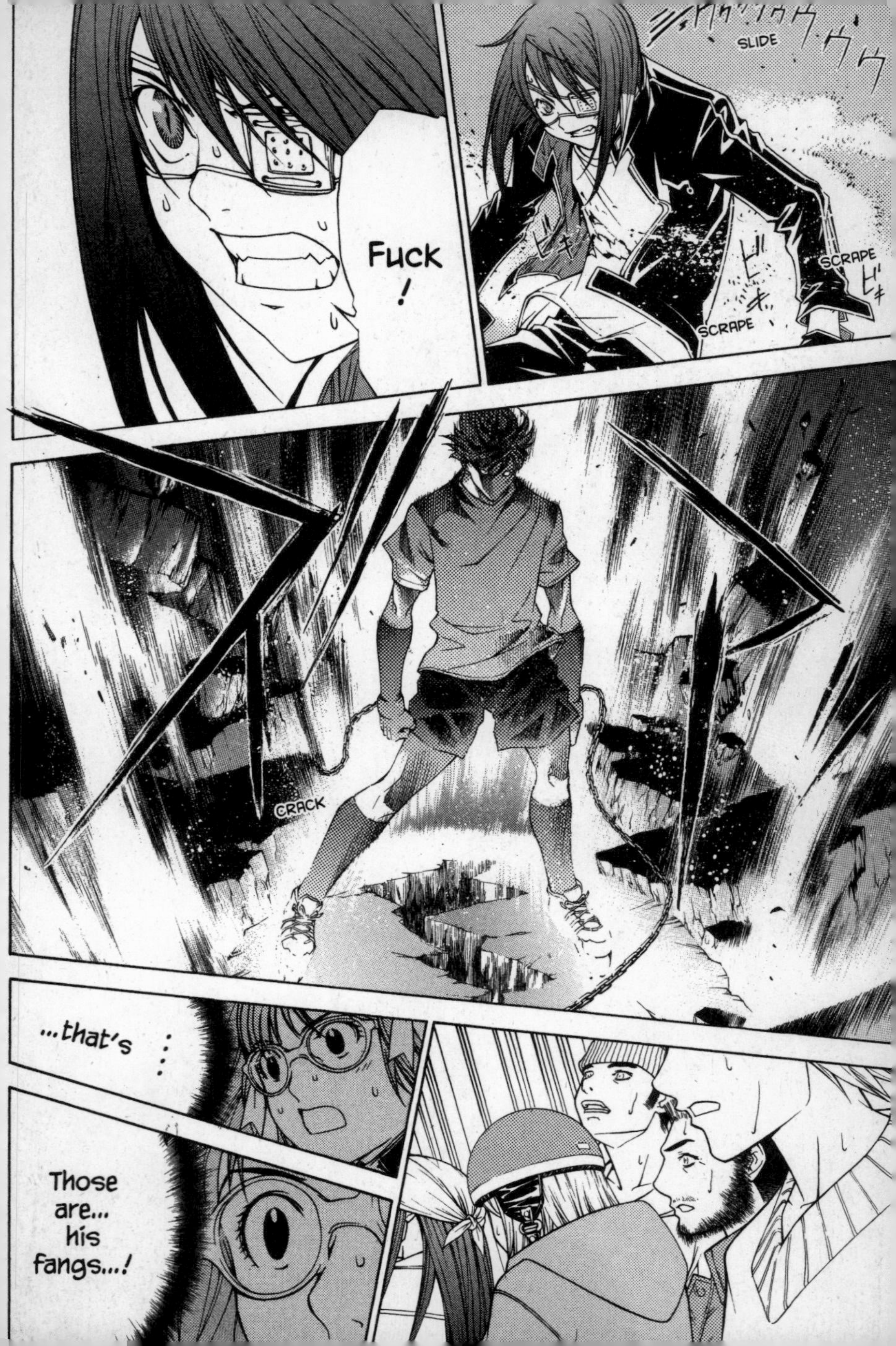
SLIDE
SCRAPE
SCRAPE
Fuck!
CRACK
...that's...
Those are... his fangs...!

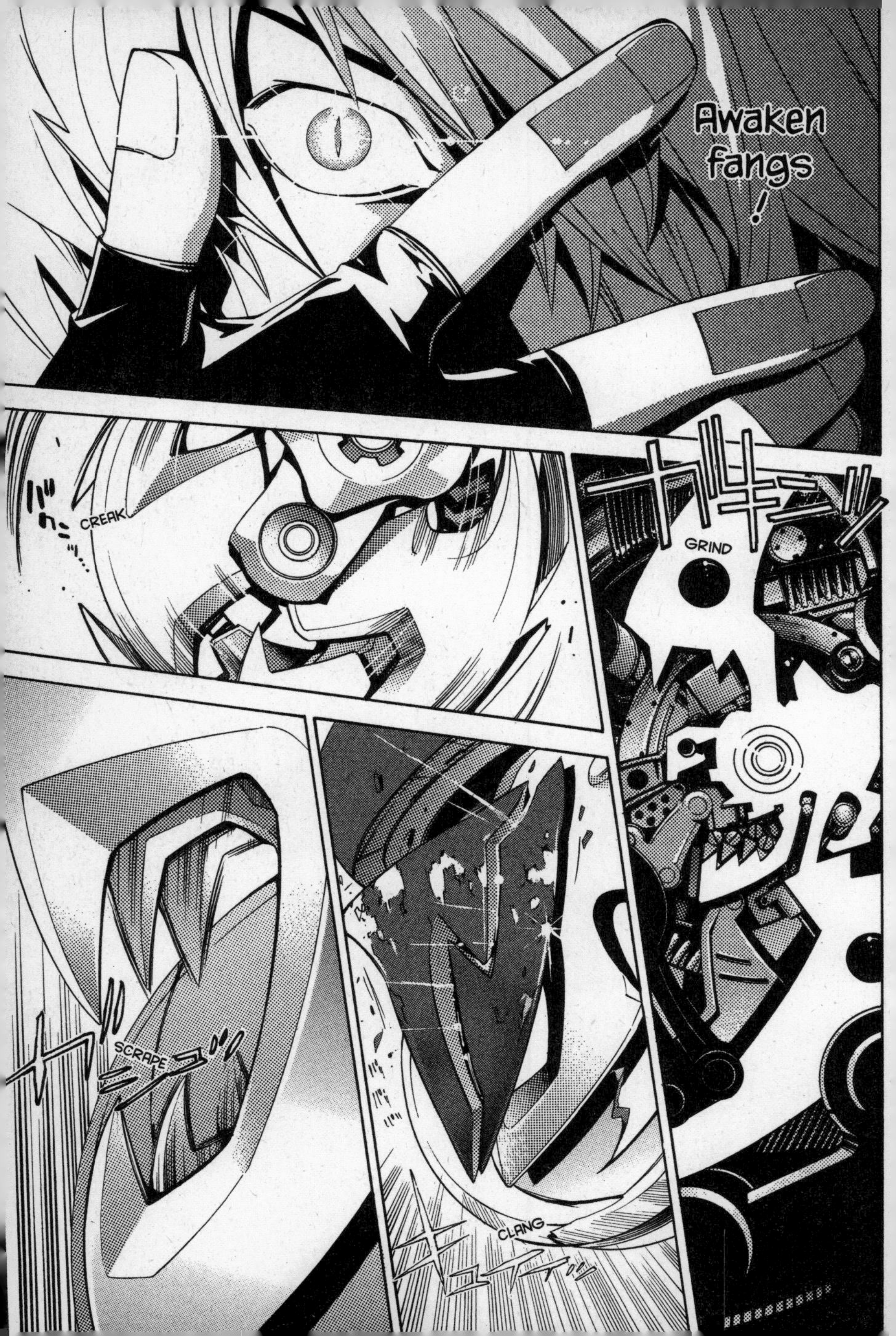
Awaken fangs!
GRIND
CREAK
CLANG
SCRAPE

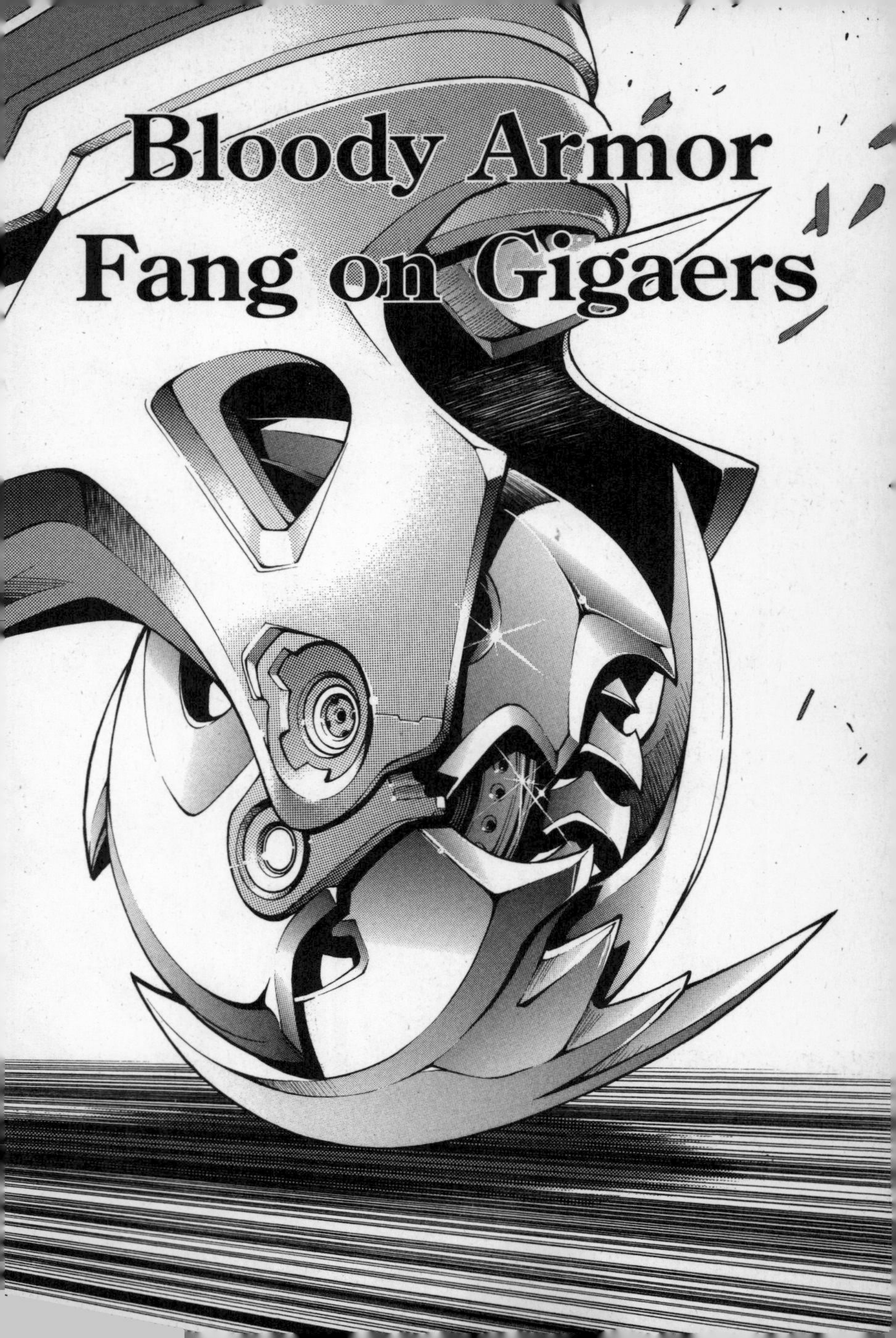
Bloody Armor
Fang on Gigaers

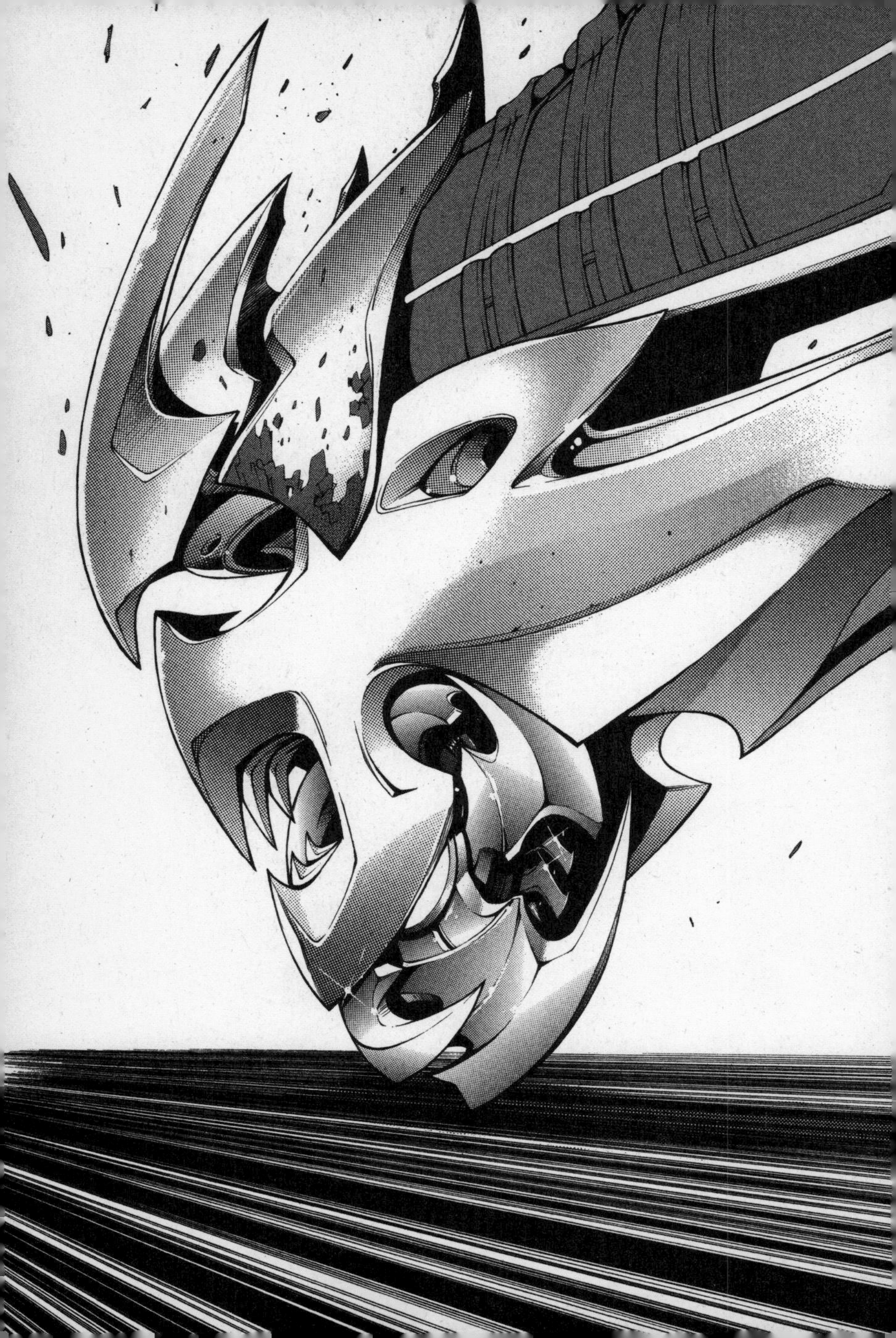

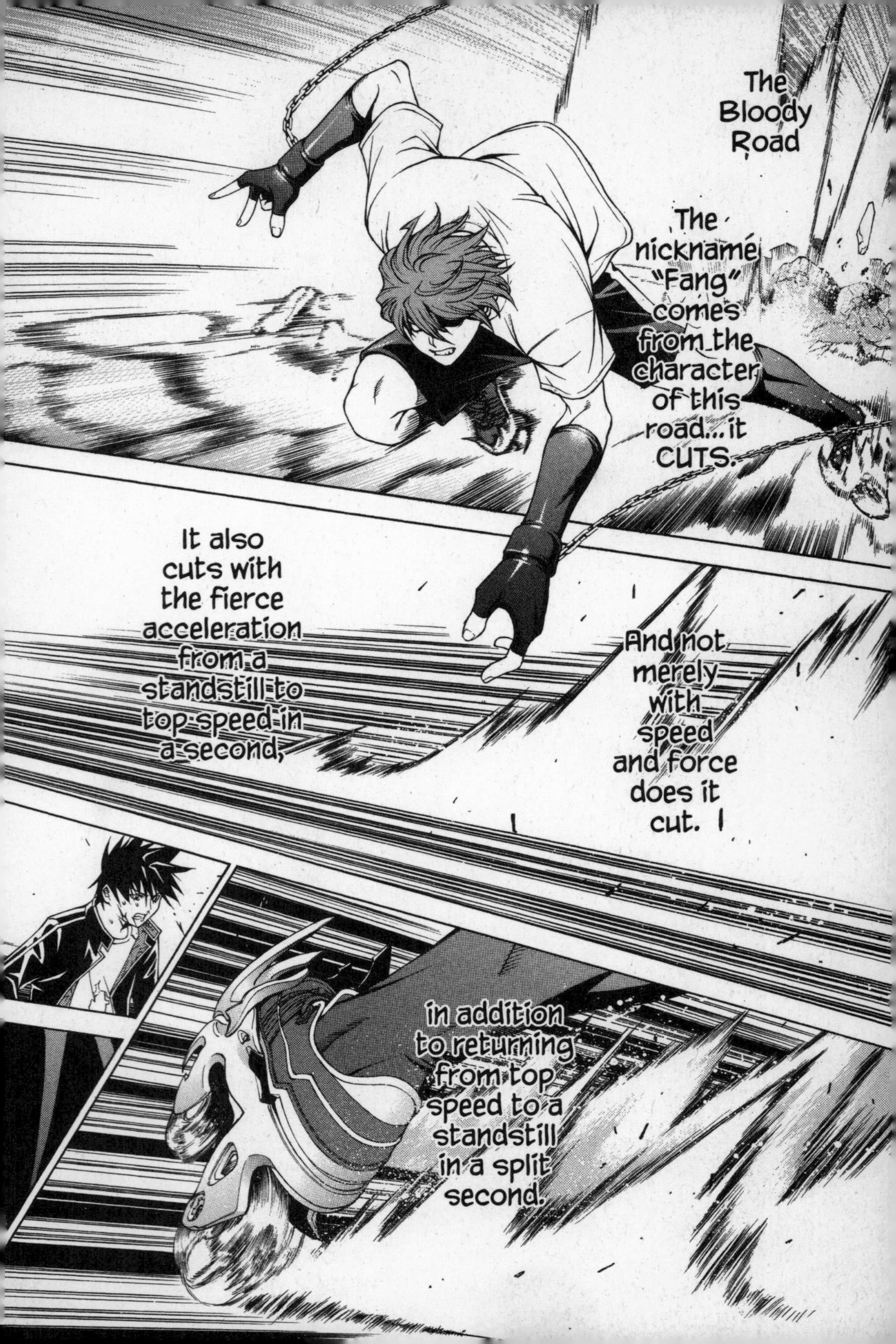
The Bloody Road
The nickname "Fang" comes from the character of this road...it CUTS.
And not merely with speed and force does it cut.
It also cuts with the fierce acceleration from a standstill to top speed in a second,
in addition to returning from top speed to a standstill in a split second.

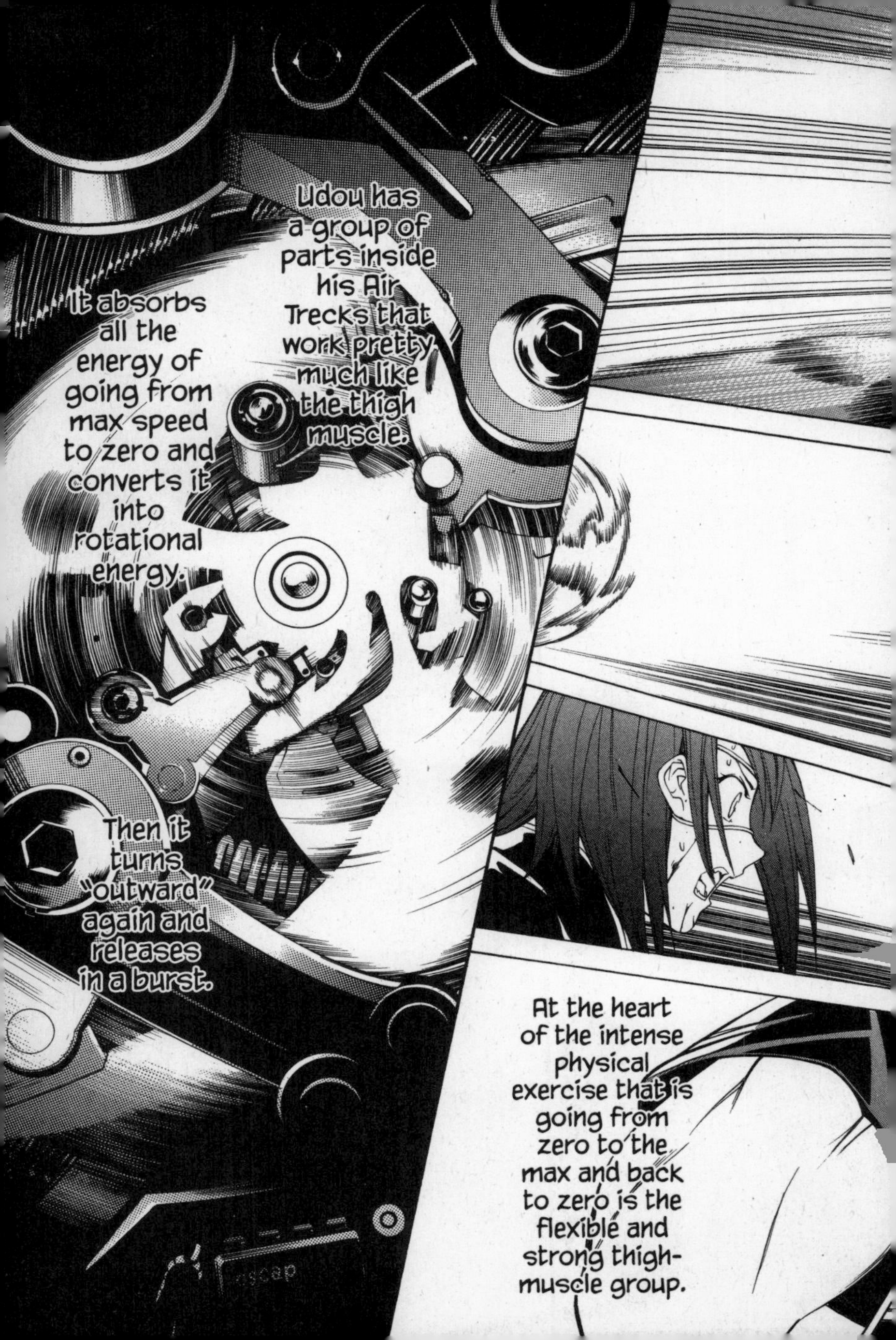
At the heart of the intense physical exercise that is going from zero to the max and back to zero is the flexible and strong thigh-muscle group.
Udou has a group of parts inside his Air Trecks that work pretty much like the thigh muscle.
It absorbs all the energy of going from max speed to zero and converts it into rotational energy.
Then it turns "outward" again and releases in a burst.

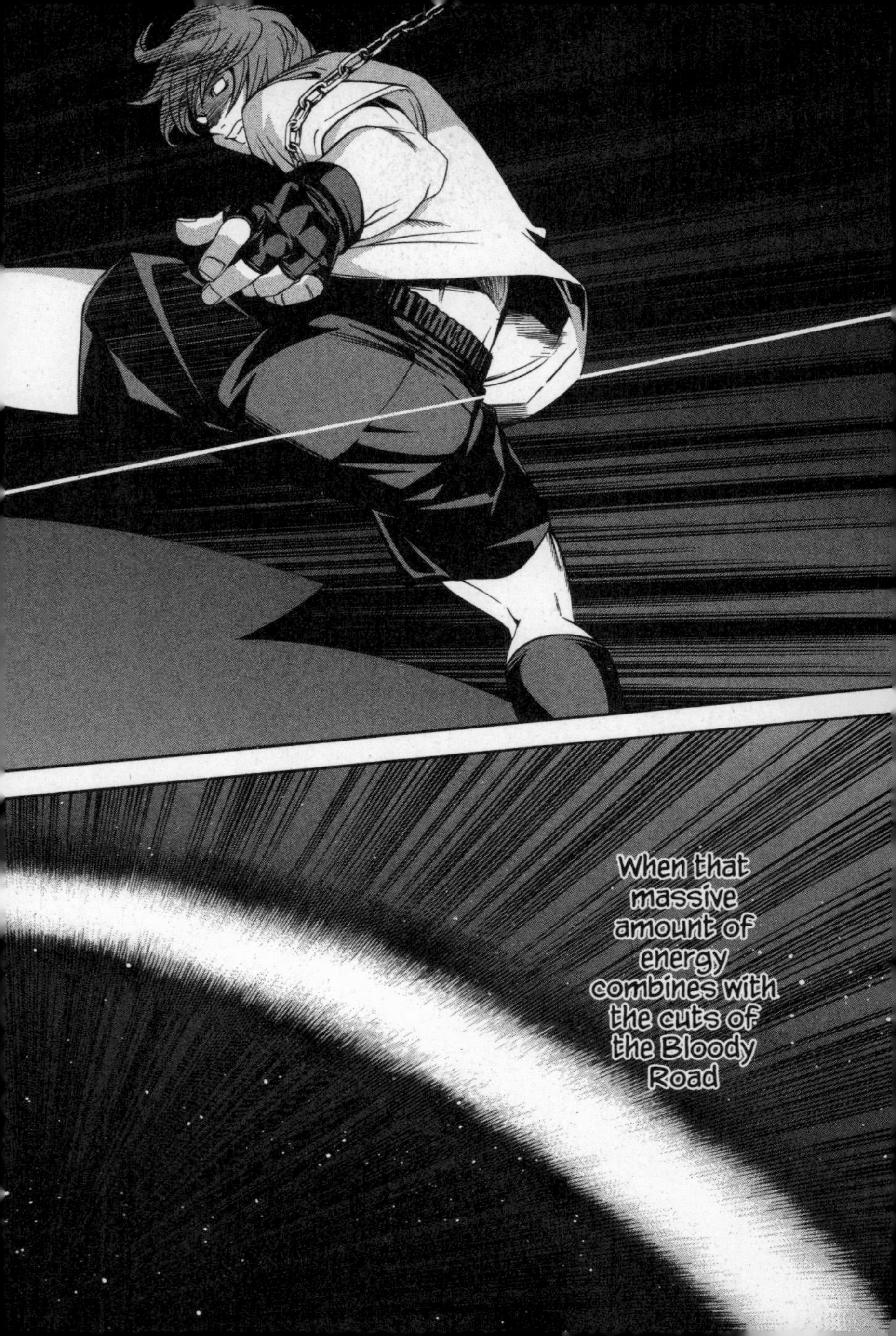
When that massive amount of energy combines with the cuts of the Bloody Road

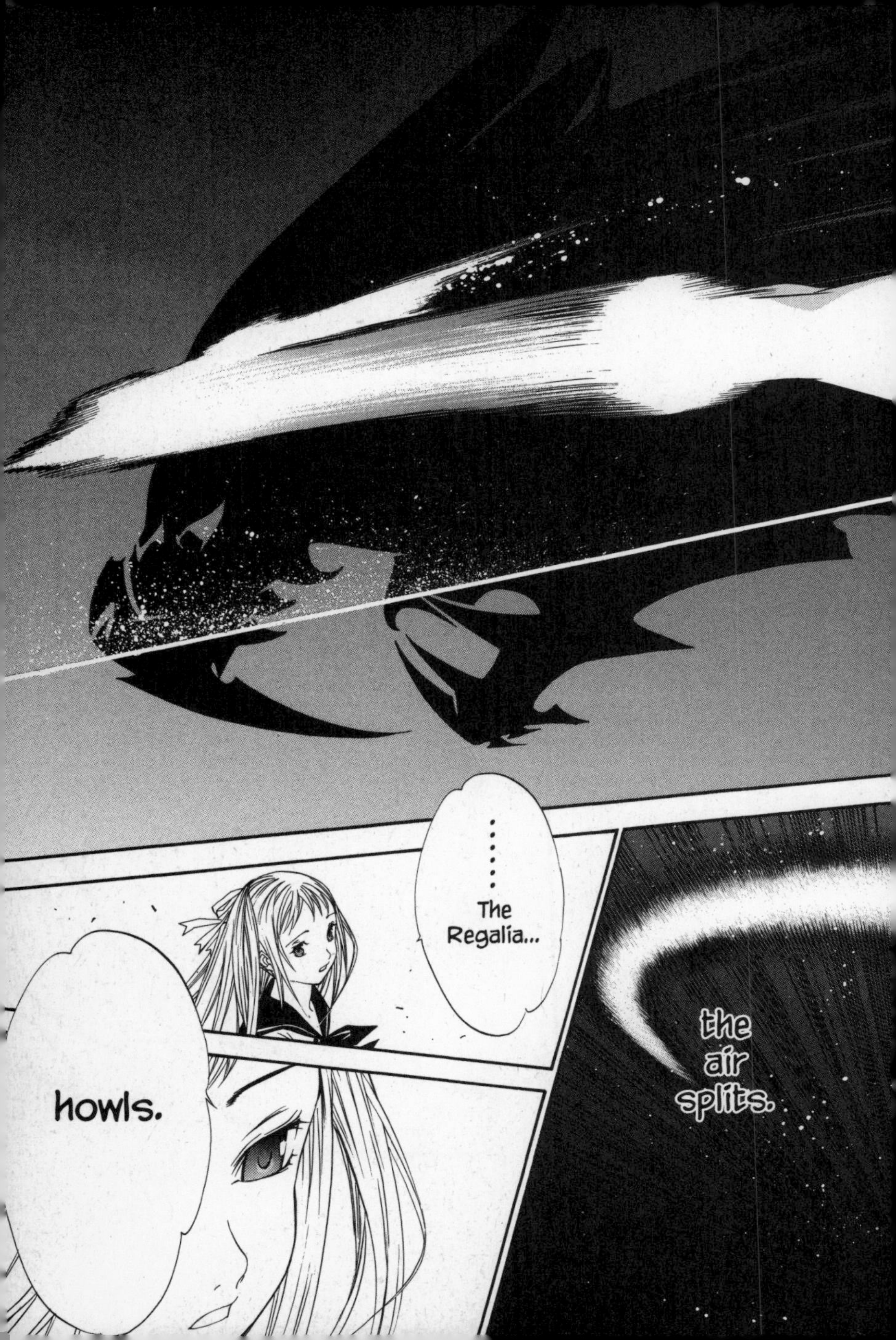
the air splits.
...... The Regalia...
howls.

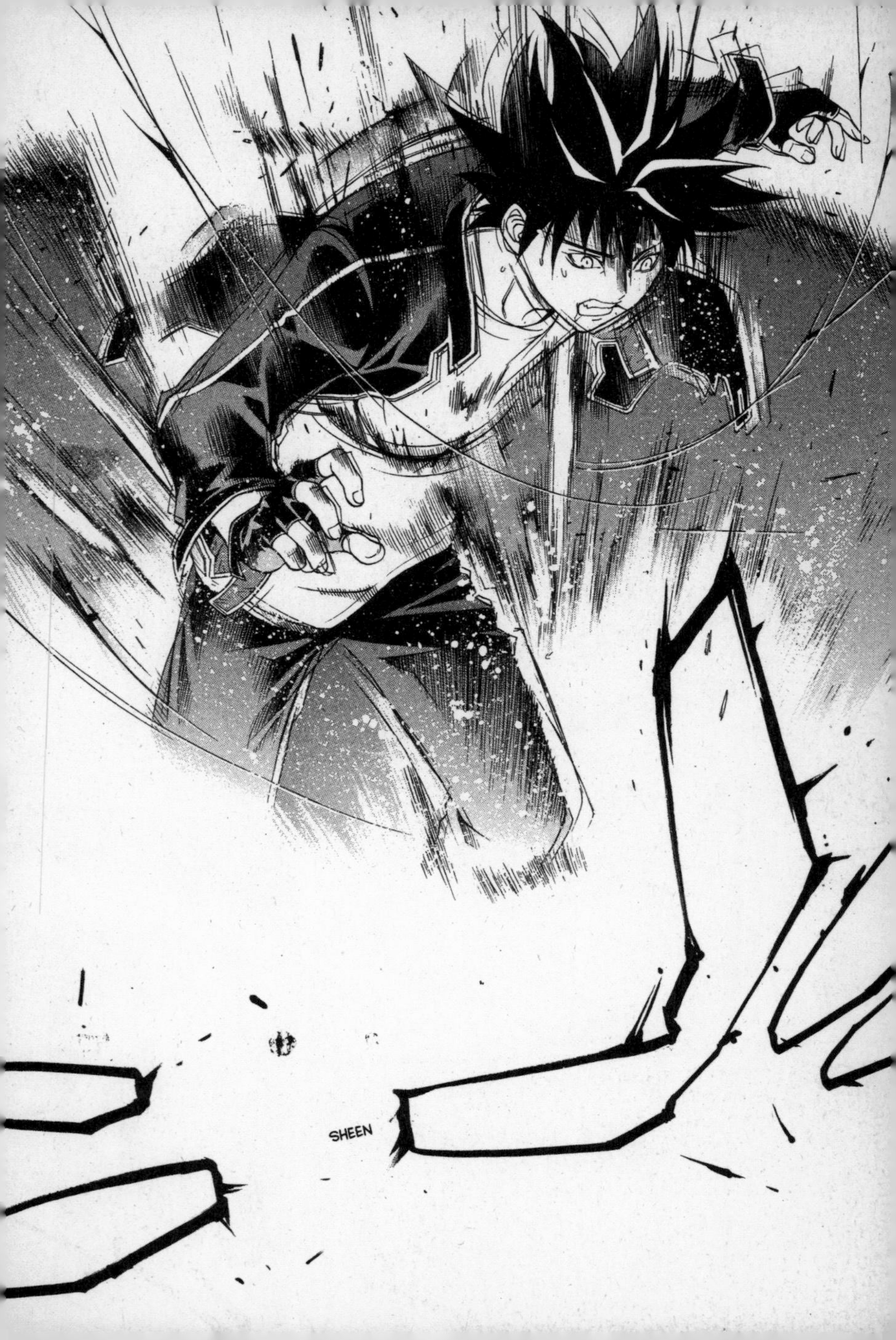
SHEEN

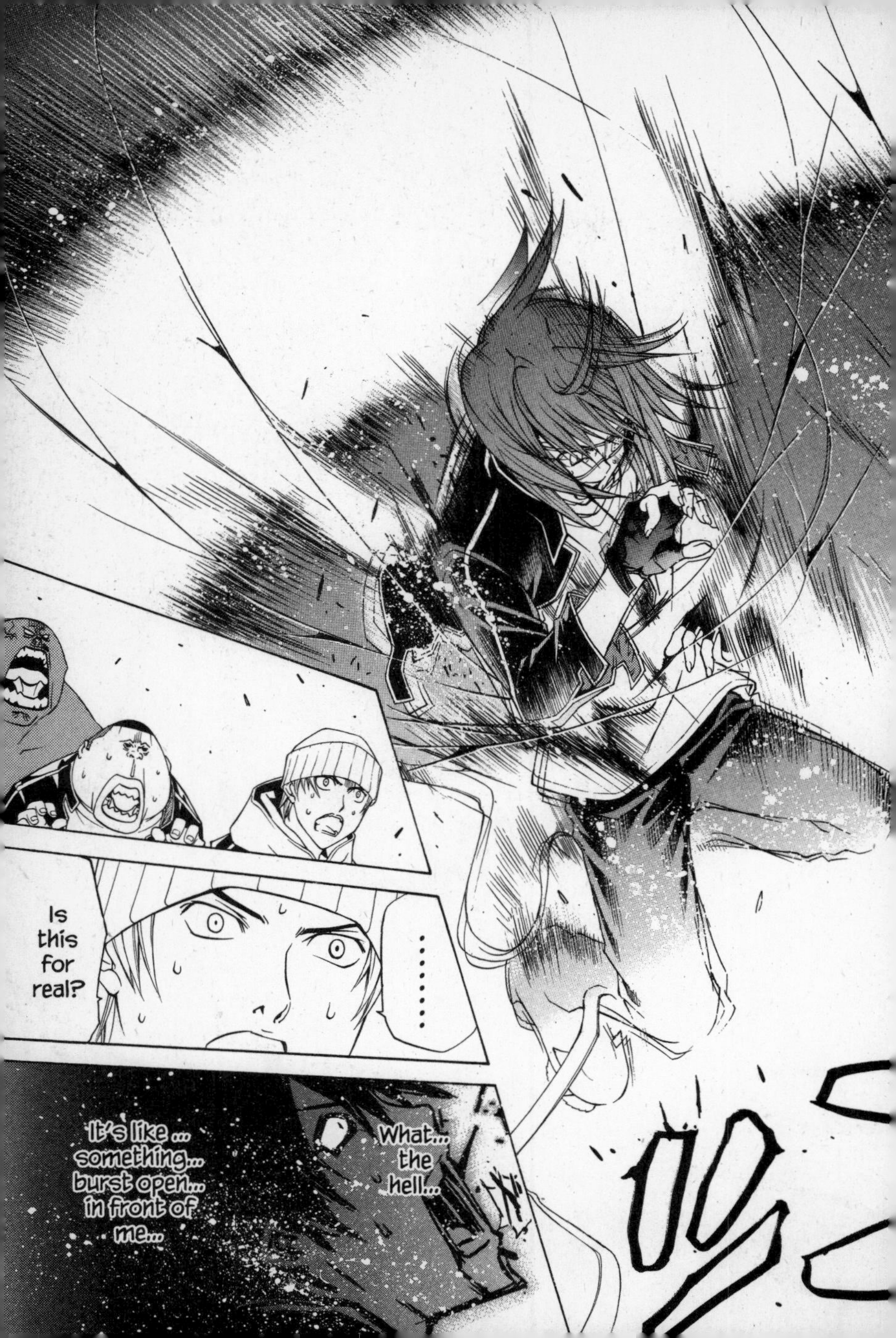
......
Is this for real?
What... the hell...
It's like ... something... burst open... in front of me...

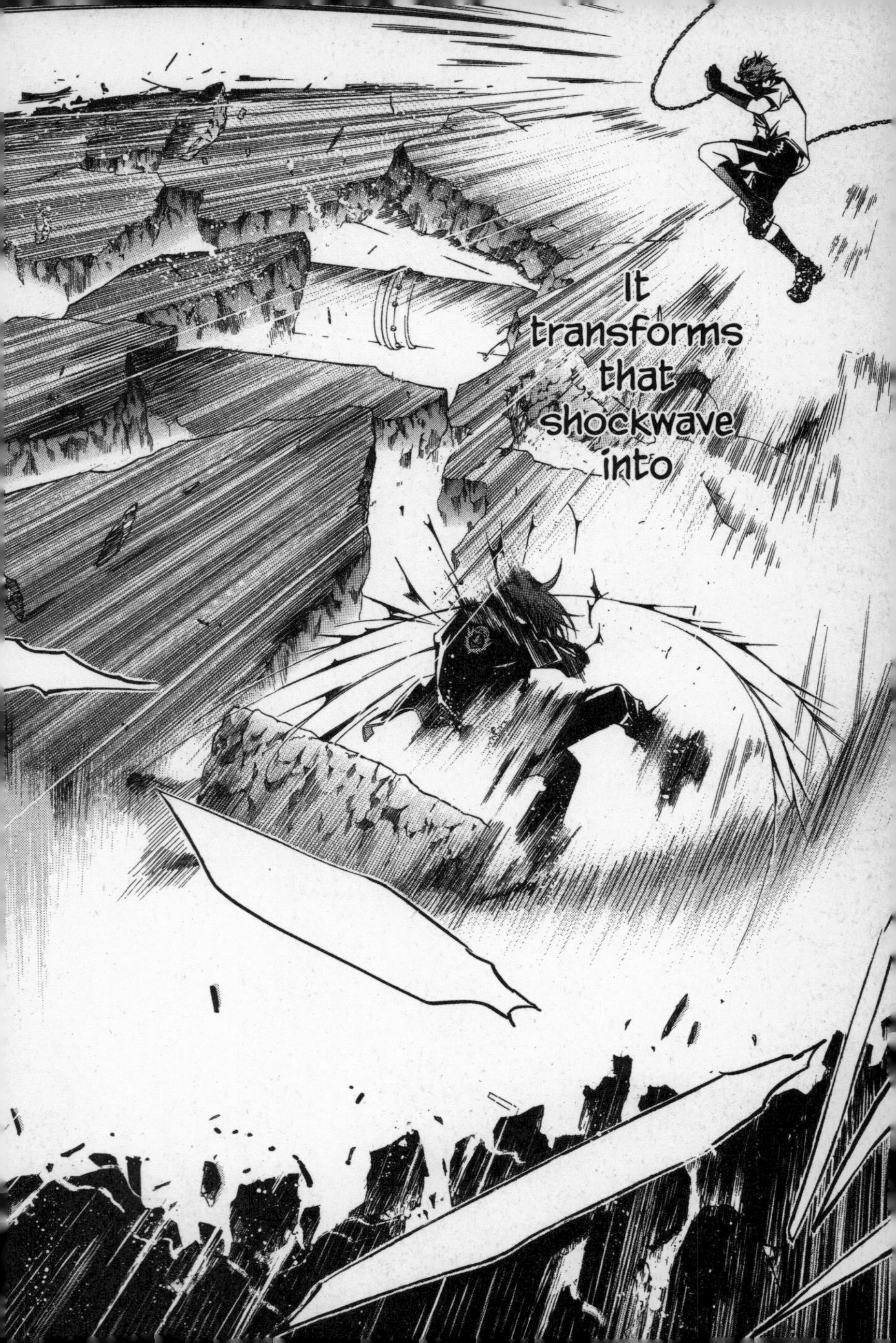
It transforms that shockwave into

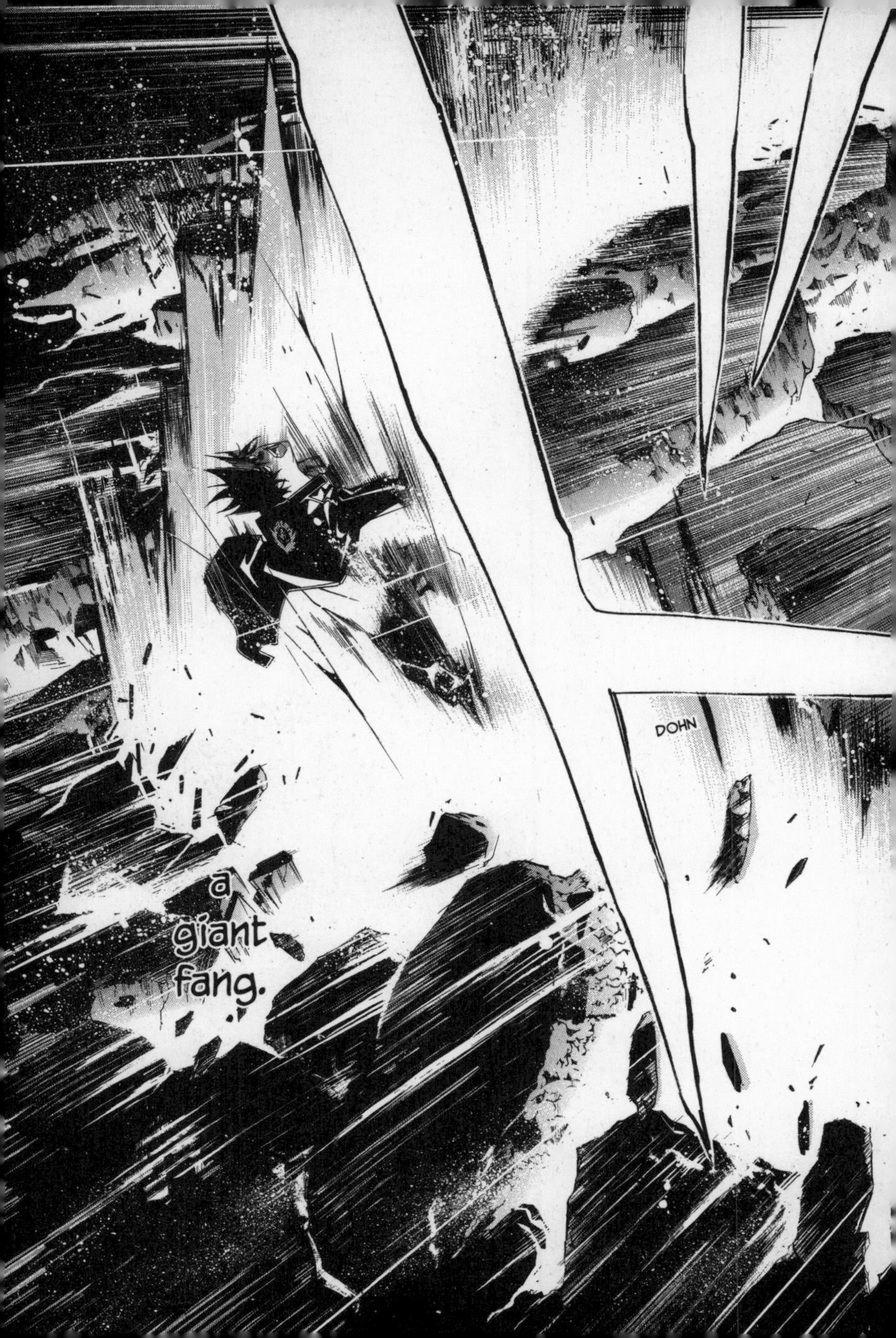
DOHN
a giant fang.

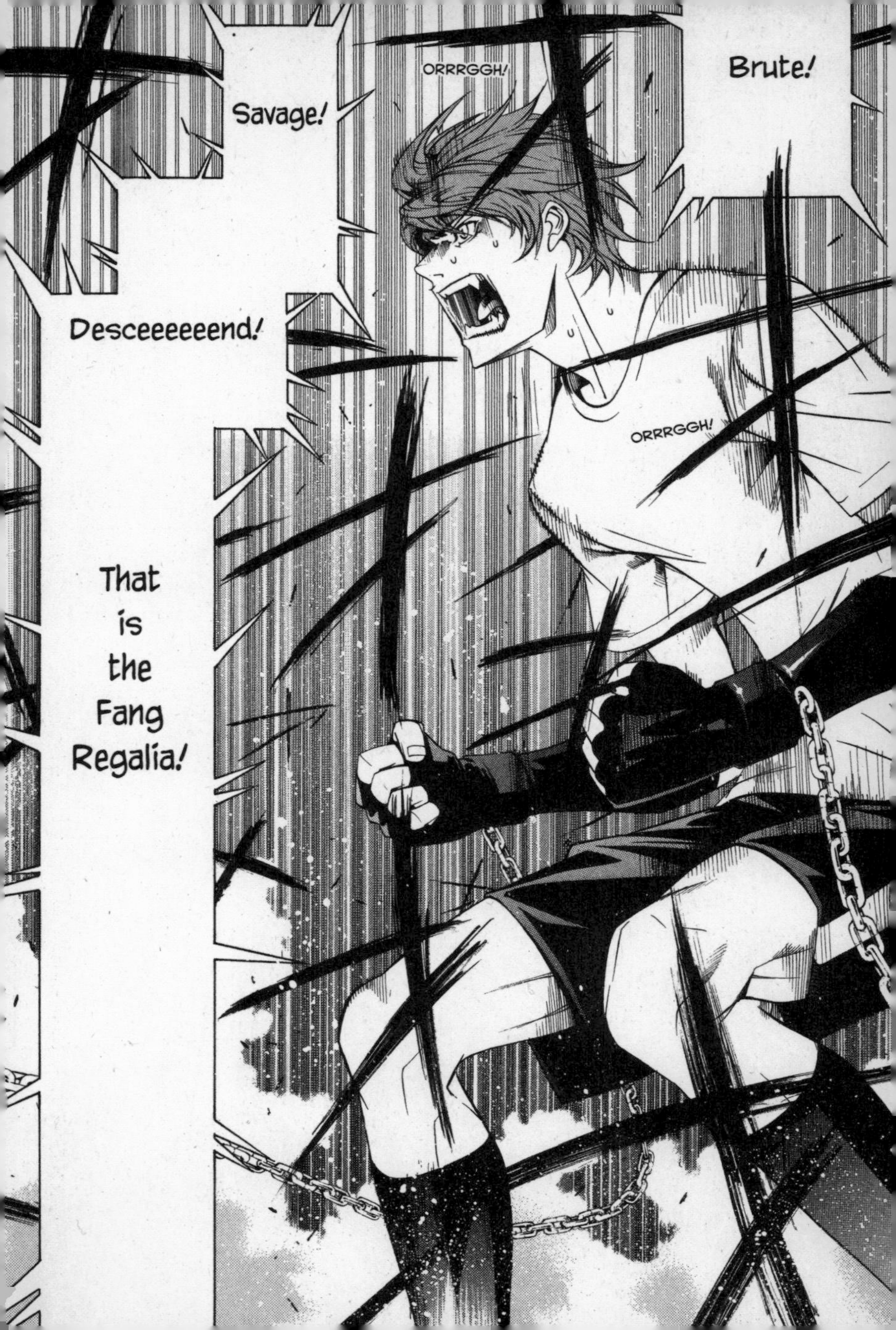
Brute!
ORRRGGH!
ORRRGGH!
Savage!
Desceeeeeend!
That is the Fang Regalia!

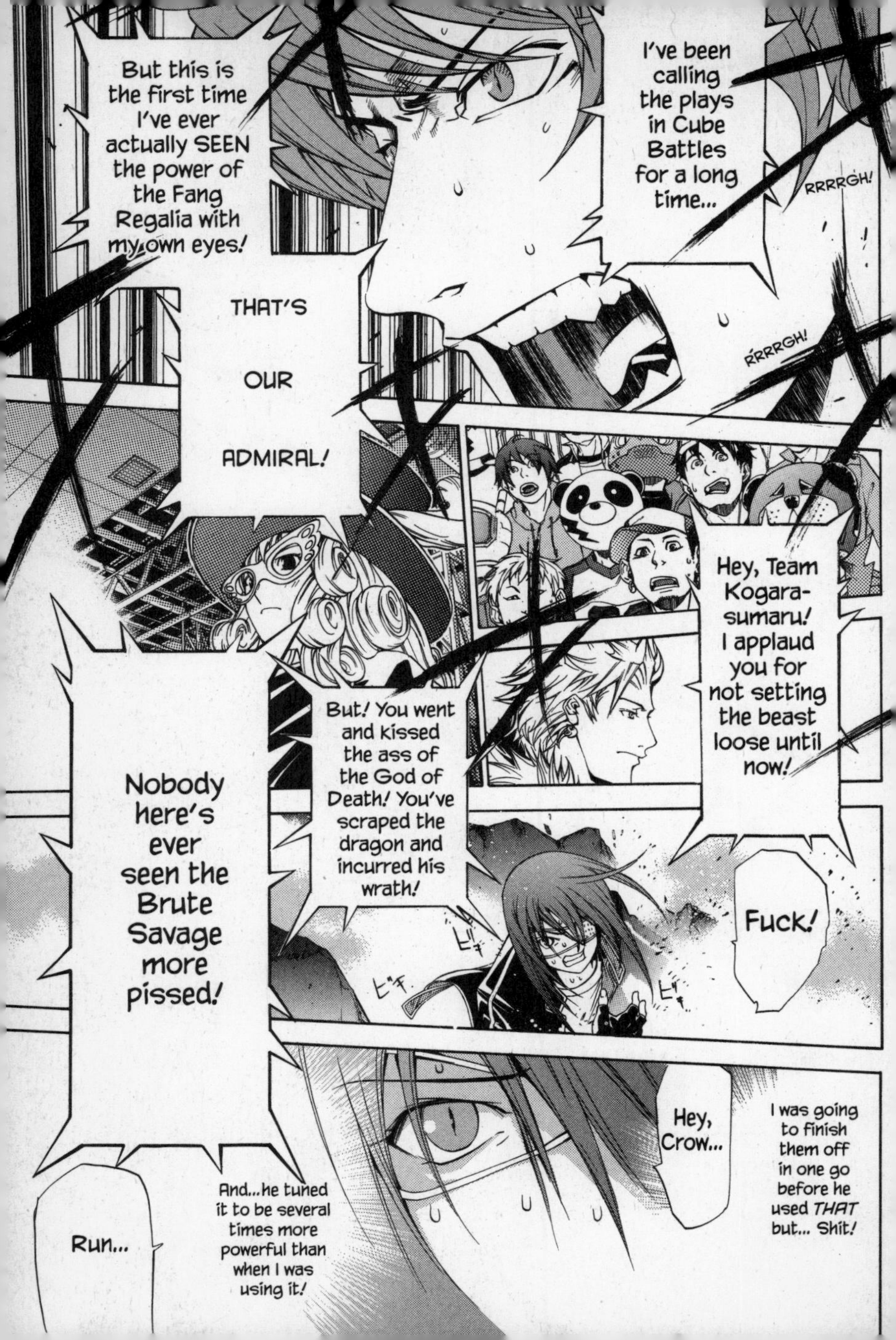
I've been calling the plays in Cube Battles for a long time...
But this is the first time I've ever actually SEEN the power of the Fang Regalia with my own eyes!
RRRRGH!
RRRRGH!
THAT'S OUR ADMIRAL!
Hey, Team Kogara-sumaru! I applaud you for not setting the beast loose until now!
But! You went and kissed the ass of the God of Death! You've scraped the dragon and incurred his wrath!
Fuck!
Nobody here's ever seen the Brute Savage more pissed!
I was going to finish them off in one go before he used *THAT* but... Shit!
Hey, Crow...
And...he tuned it to be several times more powerful than when I was using it!
Run...

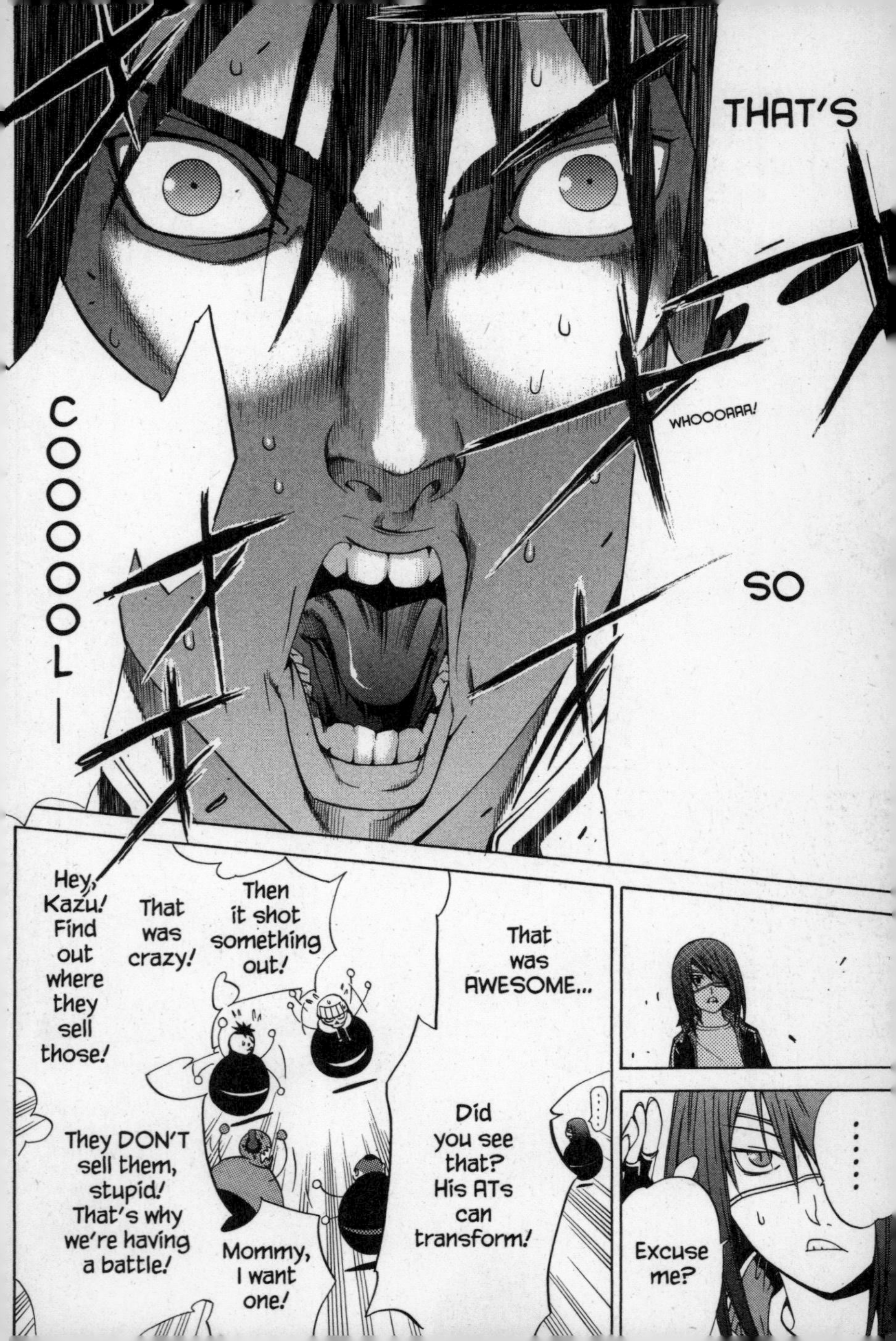
THAT'S
WHOOOAAA!
SO
COOOOOOL—
......
Excuse me?
That was AWESOME...
Then it shot something out!
That was crazy!
Hey, Kazu! Find out where they sell those!
....
Did you see that? His ATs can transform!
Mommy, I want one!
They DON'T sell them, stupid! That's why we're having a battle!

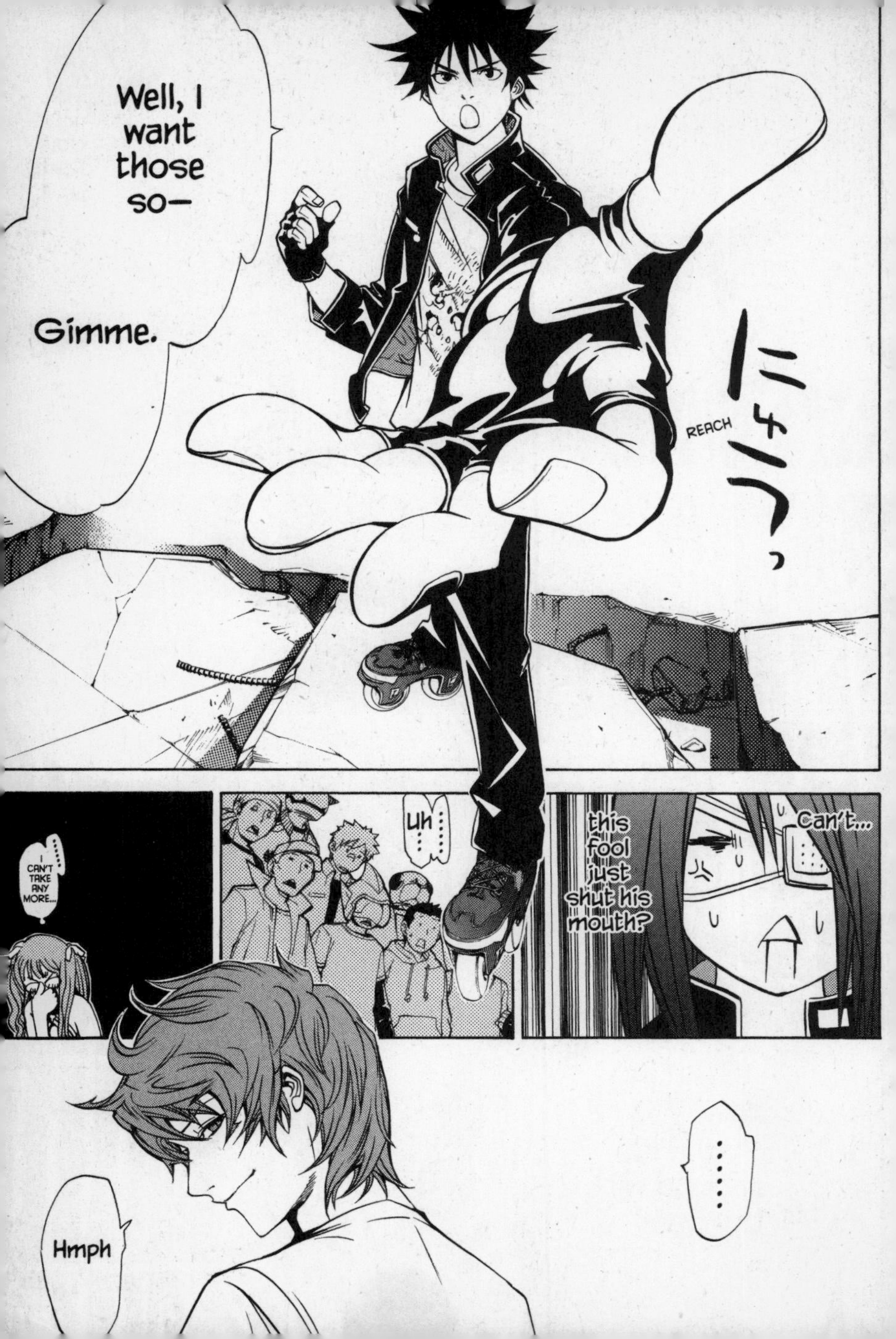
Well, I want those so—
Gimme.
ニュッ
REACH
Can't...
this fool just shut his mouth?
uh......
......
I CAN'T TAKE ANY MORE...
......
Hmph

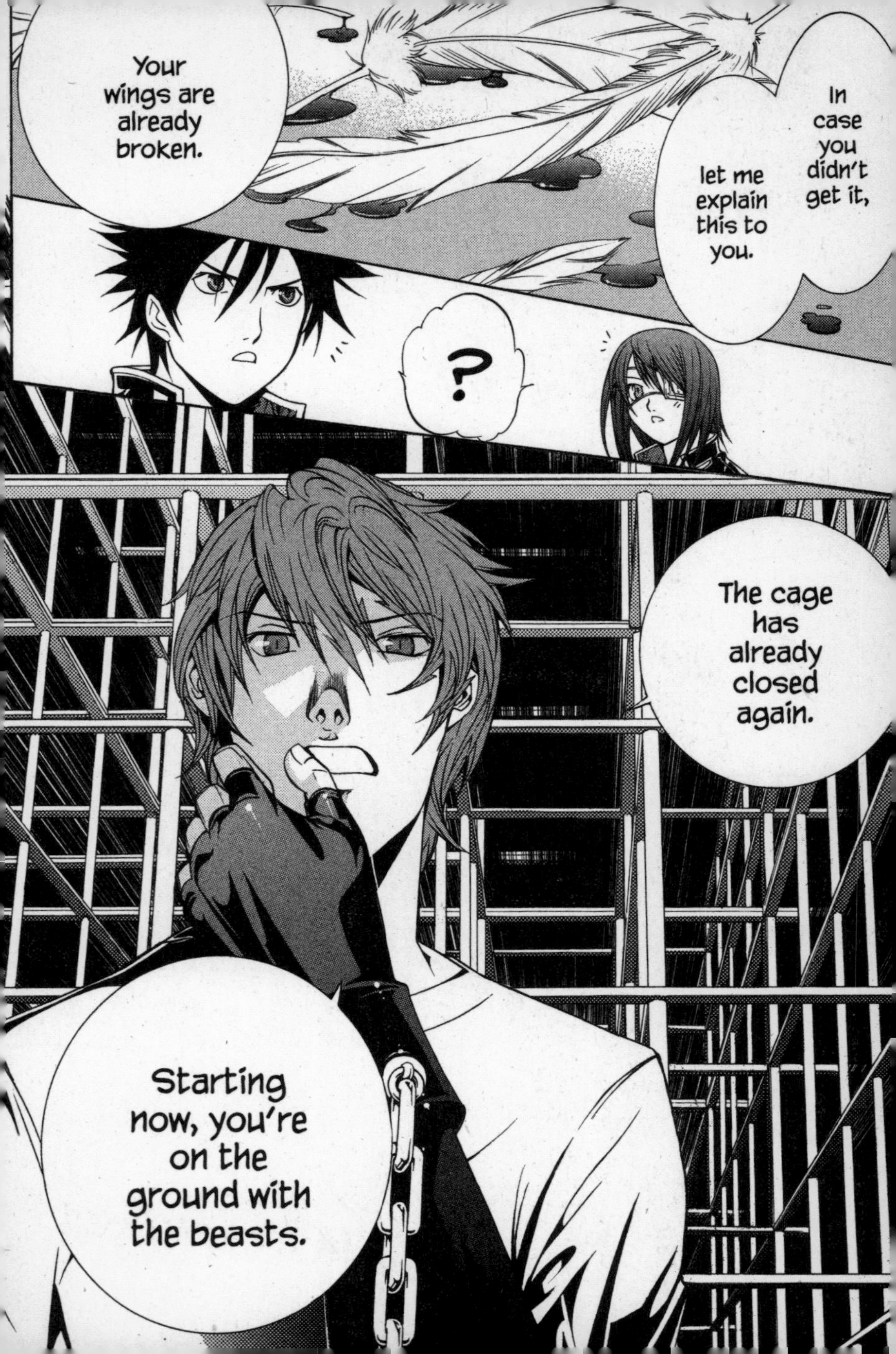
In case you didn't get it,
let me explain this to you.
Your wings are already broken.
?
The cage has already closed again.
Starting now, you're on the ground with the beasts.

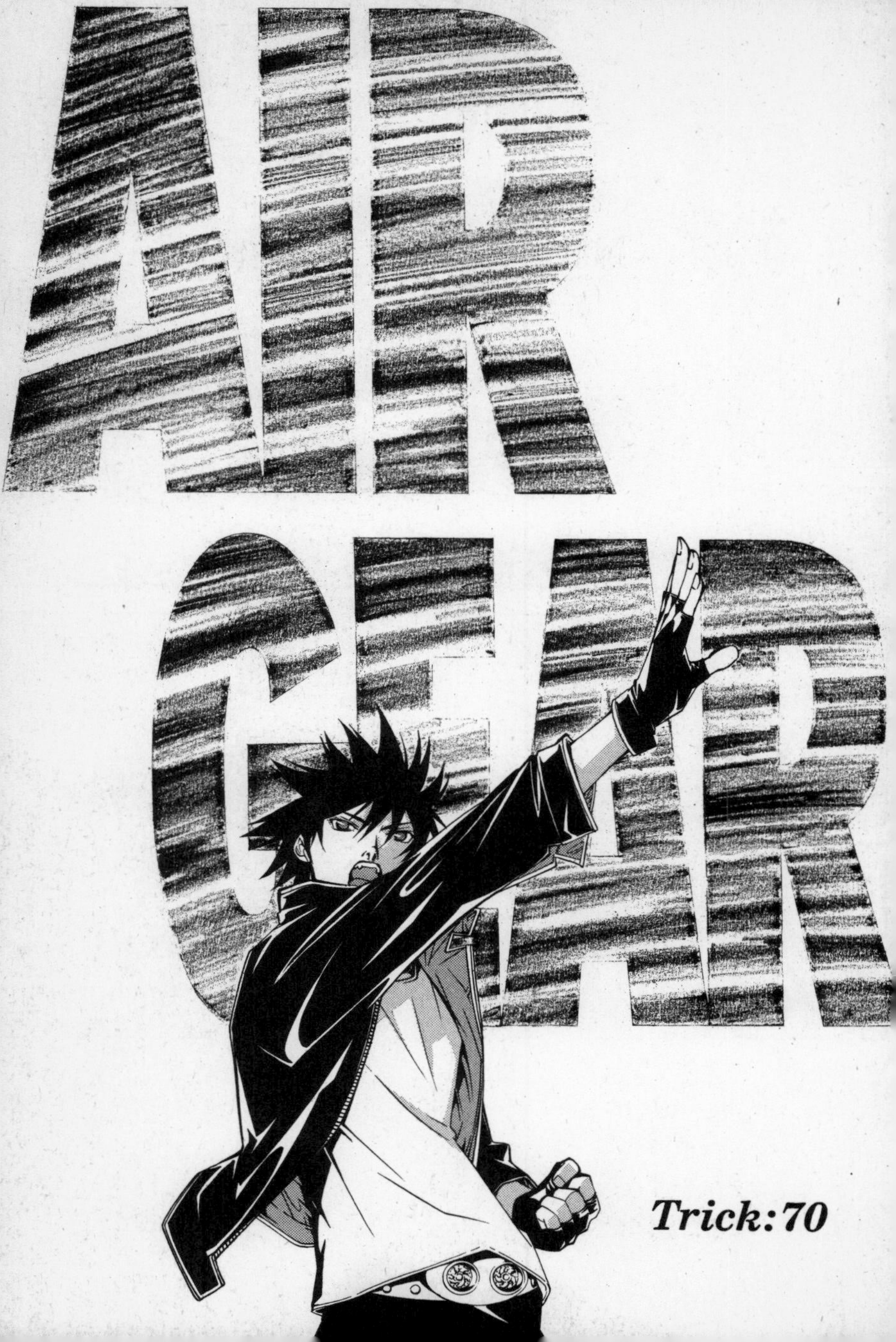
AIR
GEAR

# Trick:70

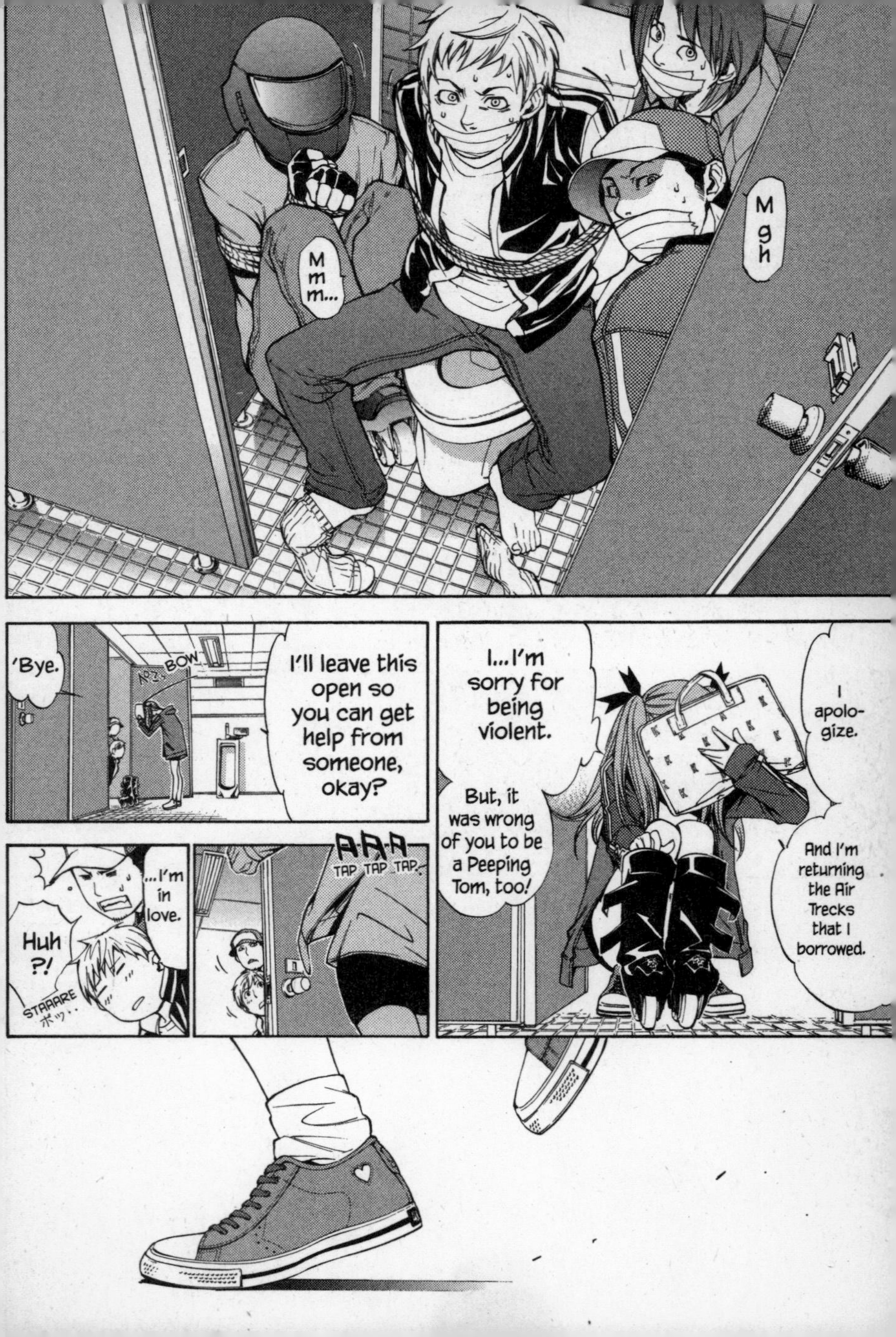
Mgh
Mmm...
I apologize.
I...I'm sorry for being violent.
And I'm returning the Air Trecks that I borrowed.
But, it was wrong of you to be a Peeping Tom, too!
I'll leave this open so you can get help from someone, okay?
BOW
'Bye.
TAP TAP TAP
...I'm in love.
Huh ?!
STAAARE
ボッ・・

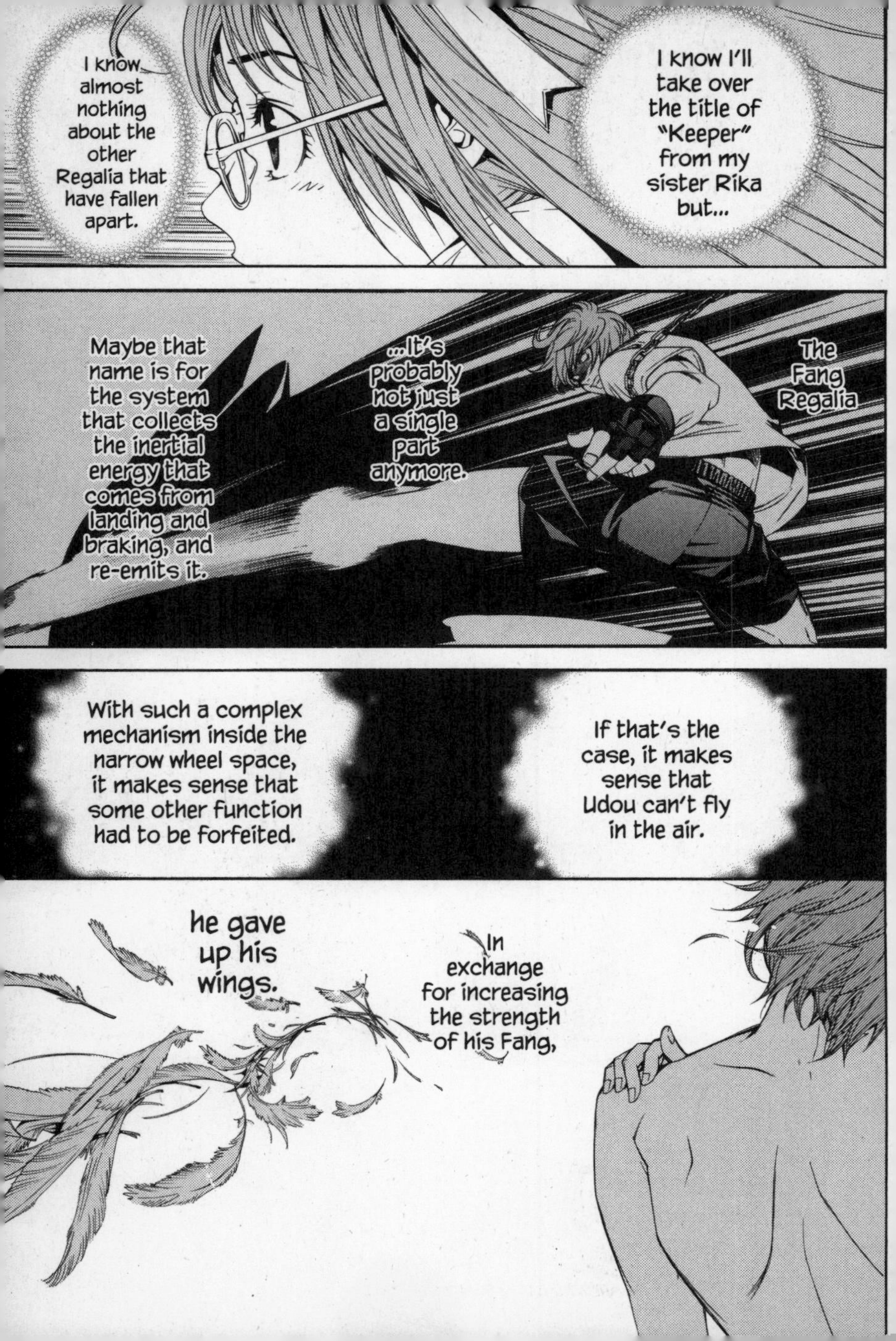
I know I'll take over the title of "Keeper" from my sister Rika but...
I know almost nothing about the other Regalia that have fallen apart.
The Fang Regalia
...It's probably not just a single part anymore.
Maybe that name is for the system that collects the inertial energy that comes from landing and braking, and re-emits it.
If that's the case, it makes sense that Udou can't fly in the air.
With such a complex mechanism inside the narrow wheel space, it makes sense that some other function had to be forfeited.
In exchange for increasing the strength of his Fang,
he gave up his wings.

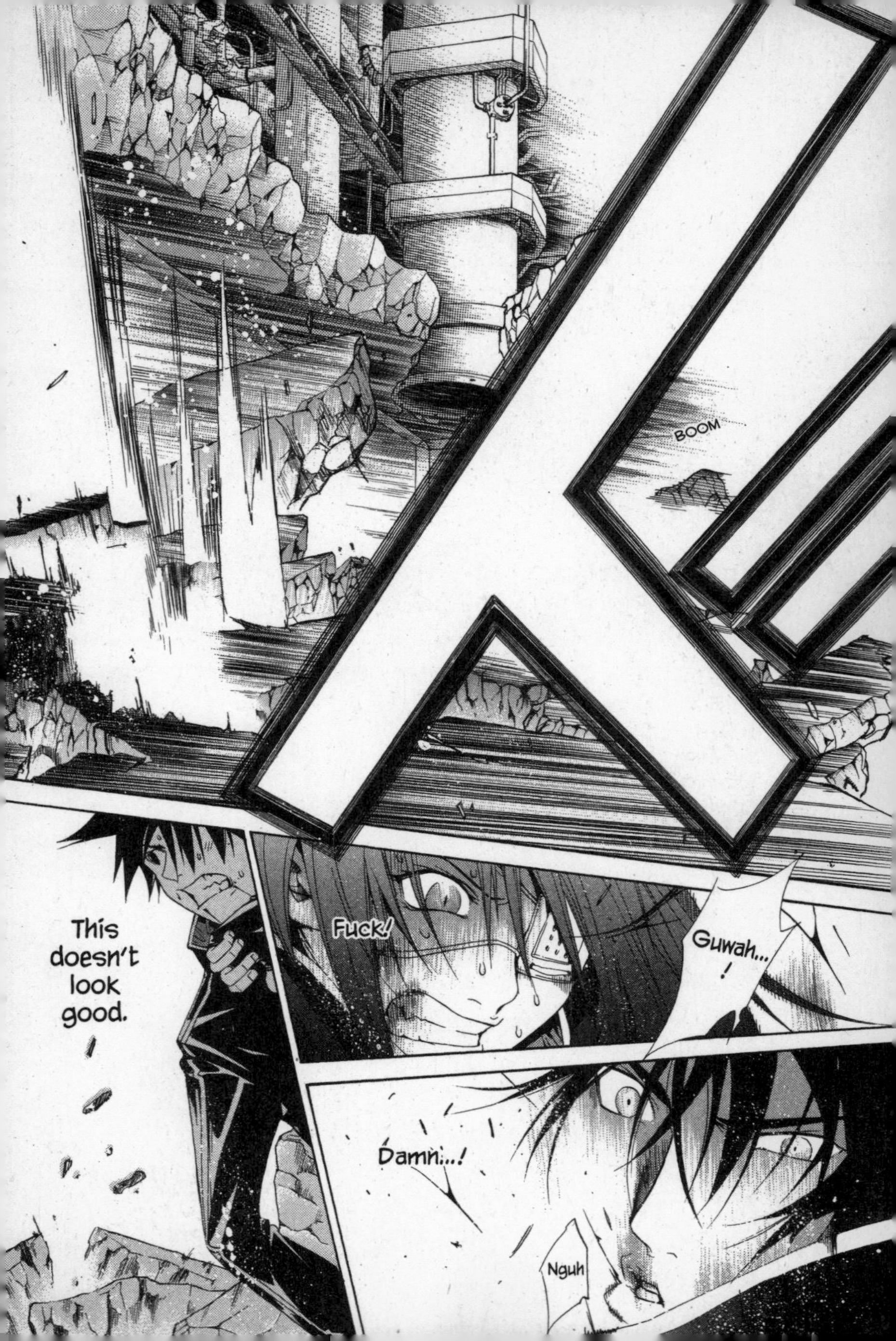
BOOM
Guwah...!
Fuck!
Damn...!
Nguh
This doesn't look good.

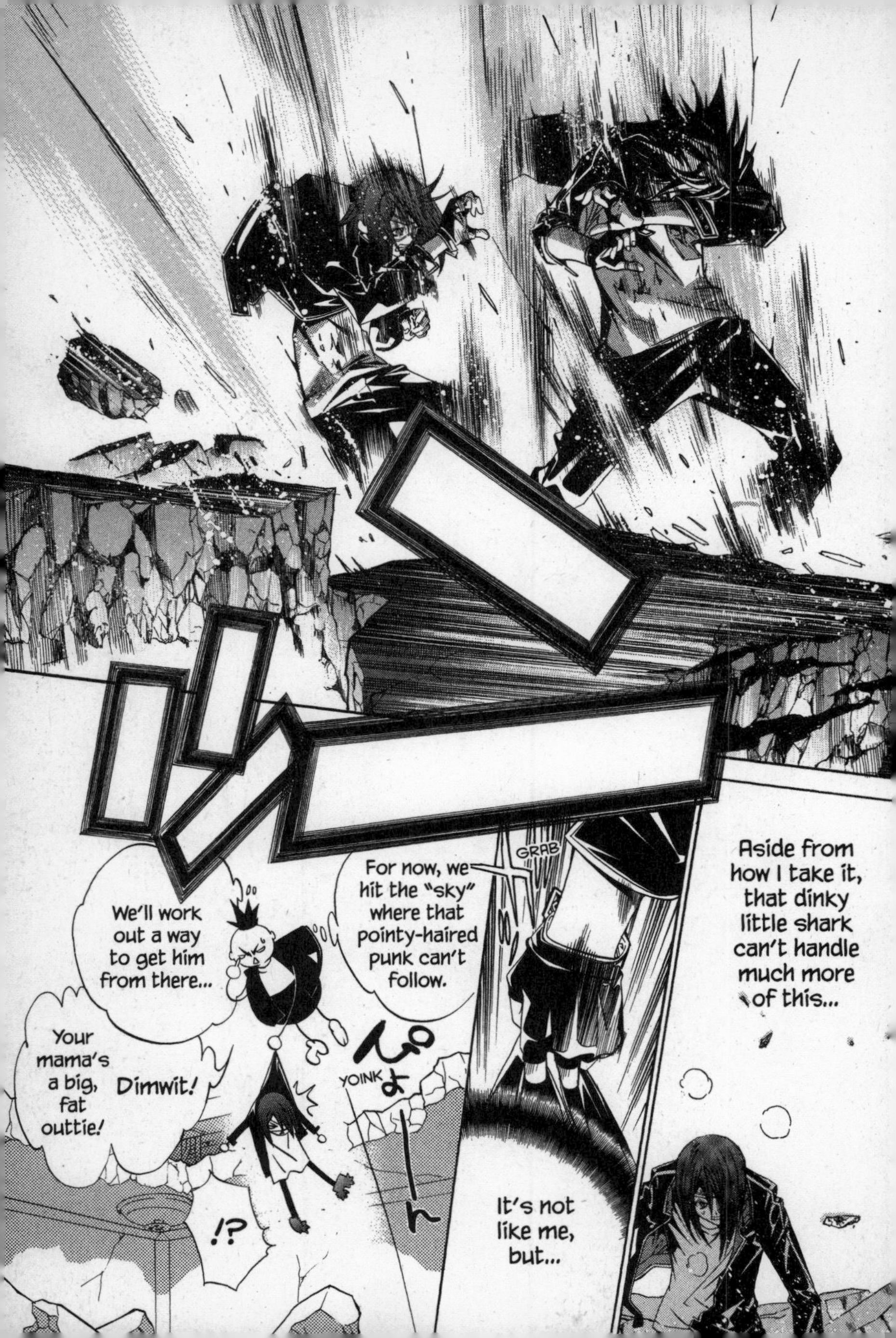
Aside from how I take it, that dinky little shark can't handle much more of this...
It's not like me, but...
GRAB
For now, we hit the "sky" where that pointy-haired punk can't follow.
We'll work out a way to get him from there...
YOINK
Your mama's a big, fat outtie!
Dimwit!
!?

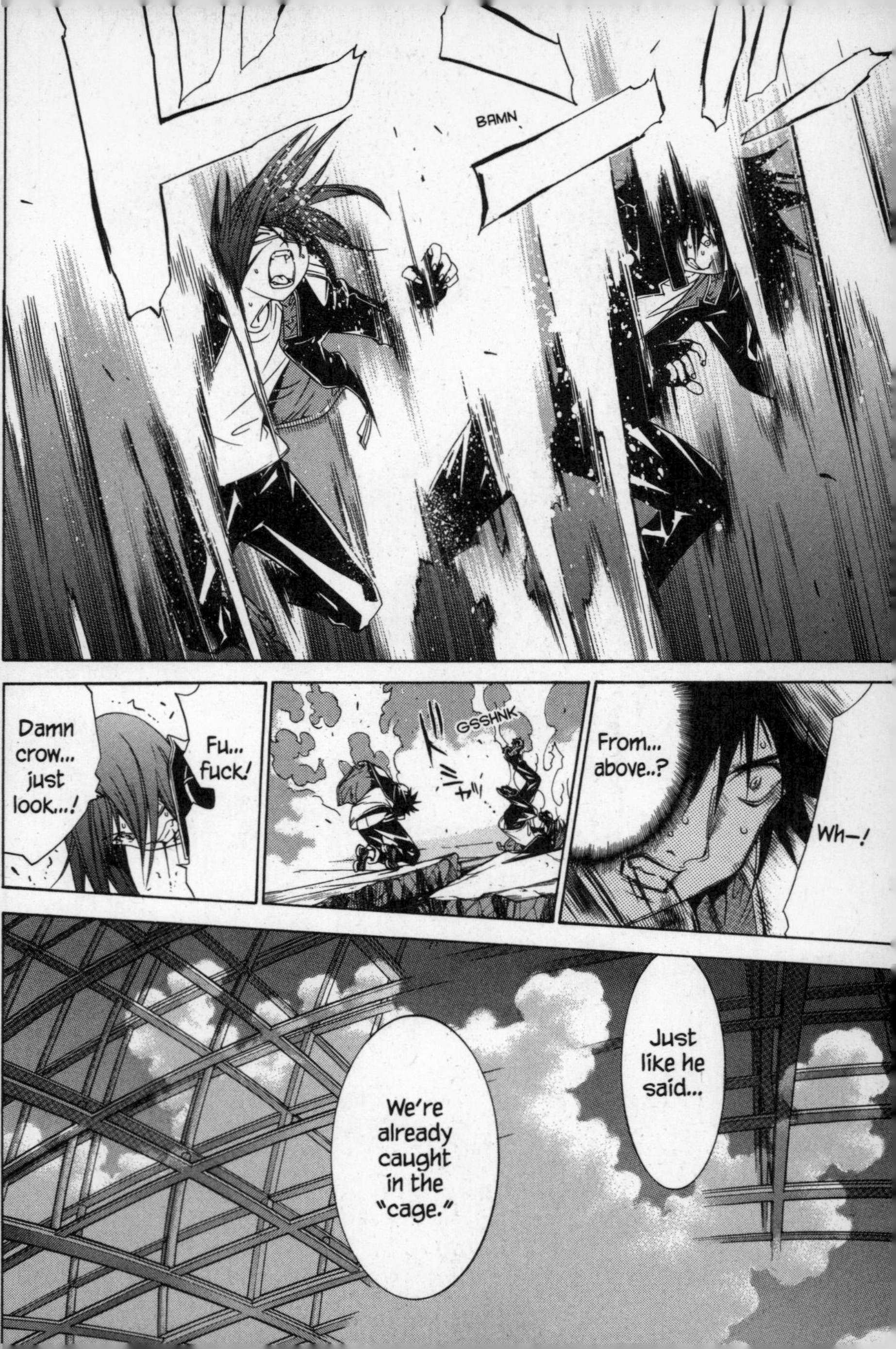
BAMN
Wh–!
From... above..?
GSSHNK
Fu... fuck!
Damn crow... just look...!
Just like he said...
We're already caught in the "cage."

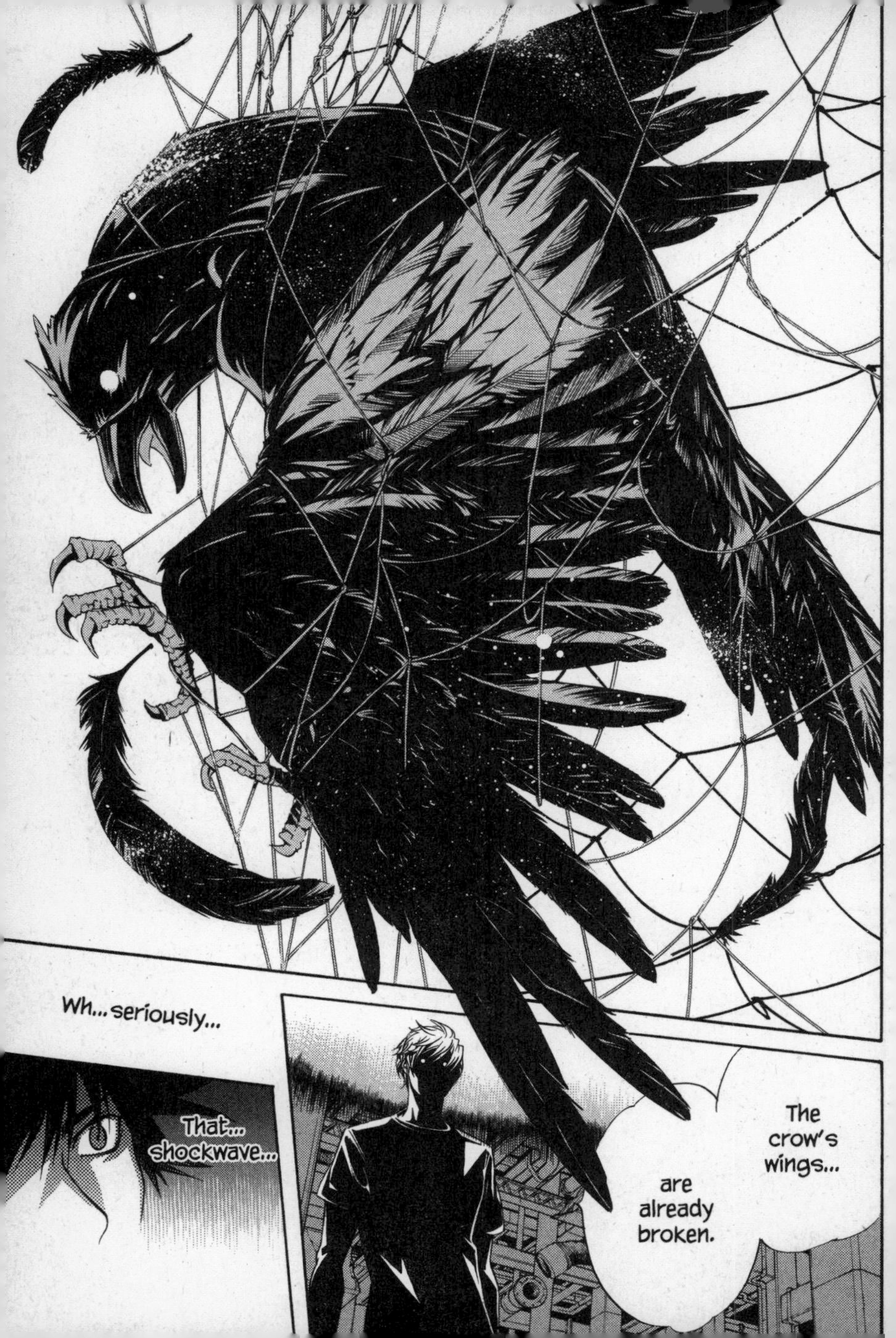
The crow's wings...
are already broken.
Wh...seriously...
That... shockwave...

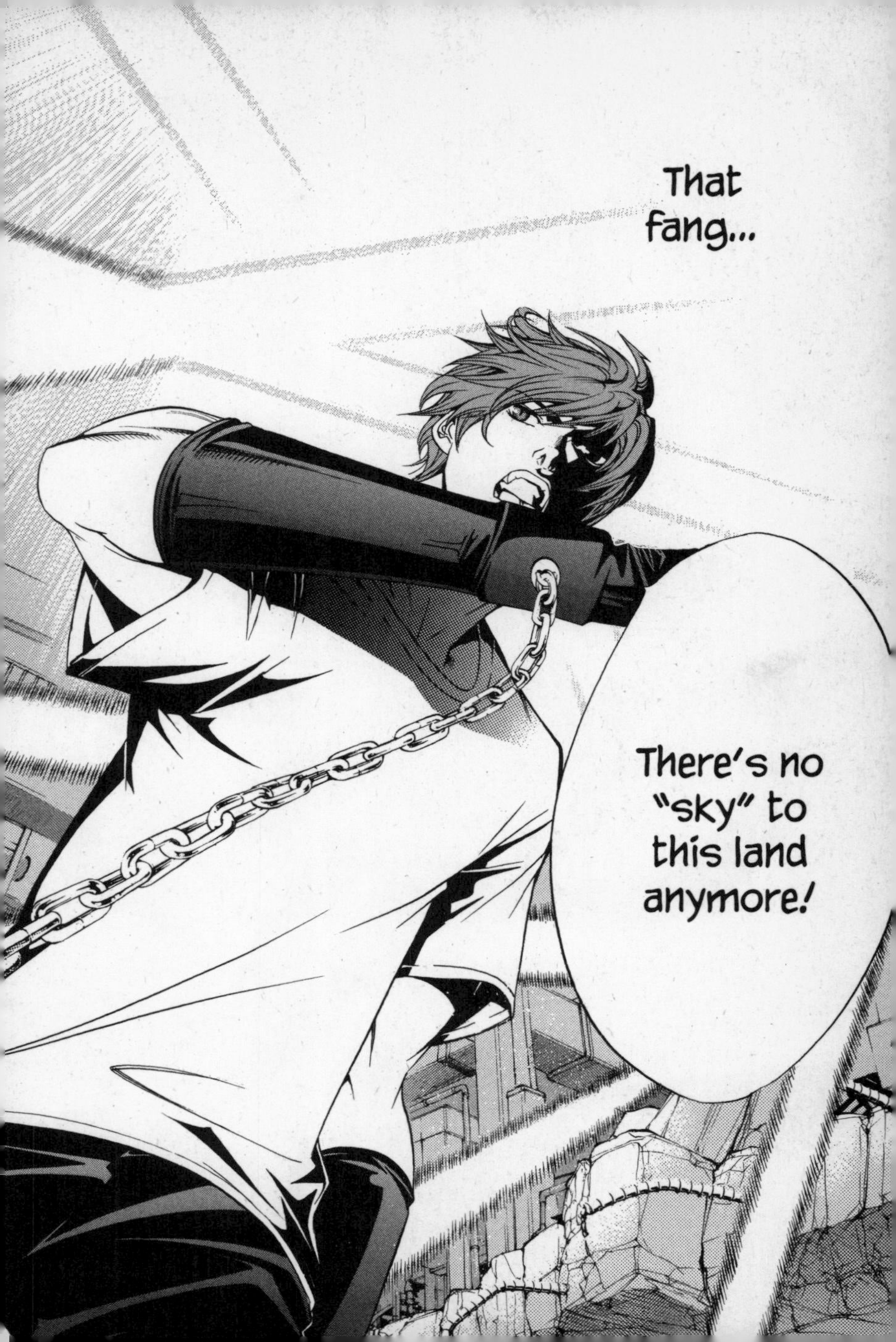
That fang...
There's no "sky" to this land anymore!

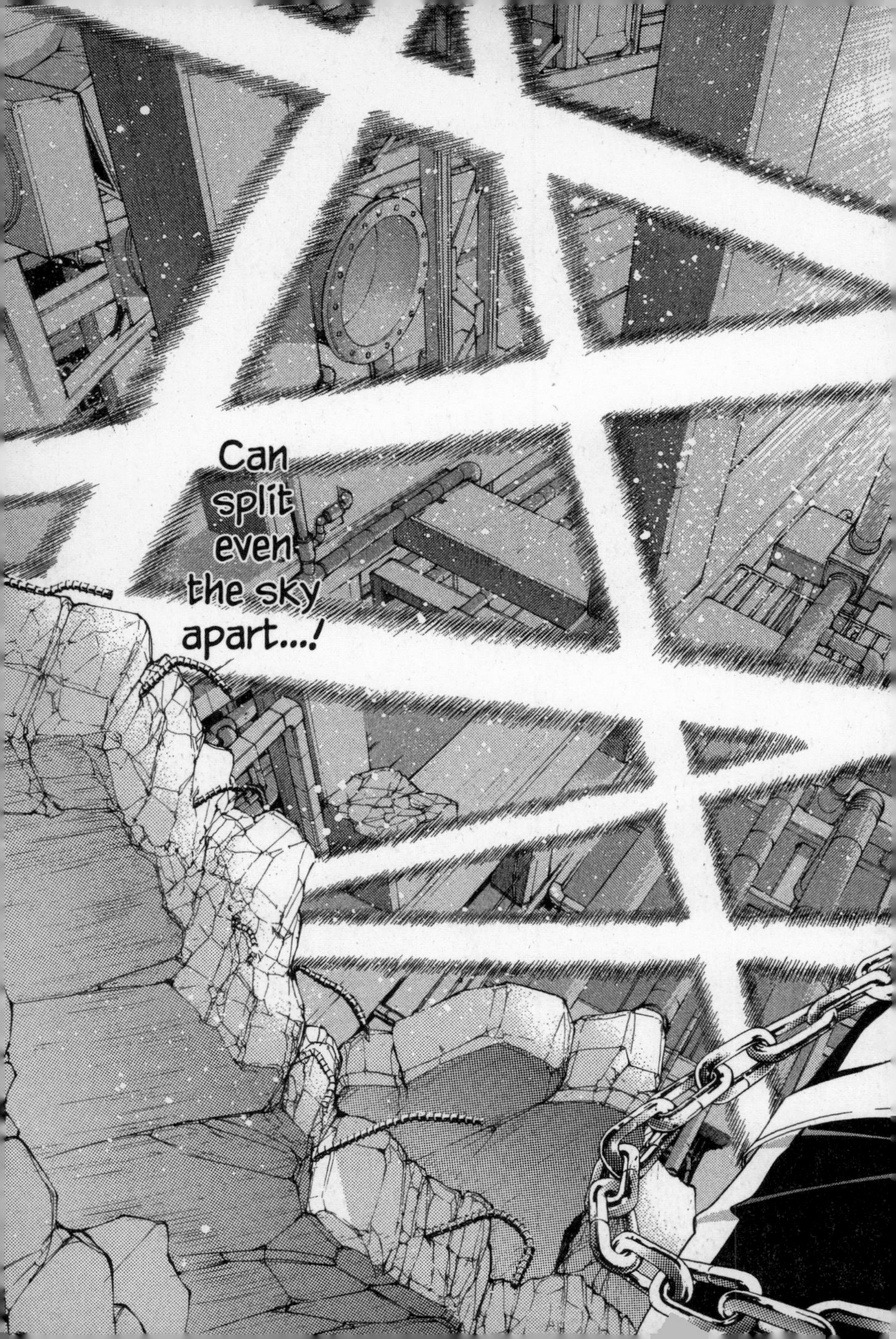
Can split even the sky apart...!

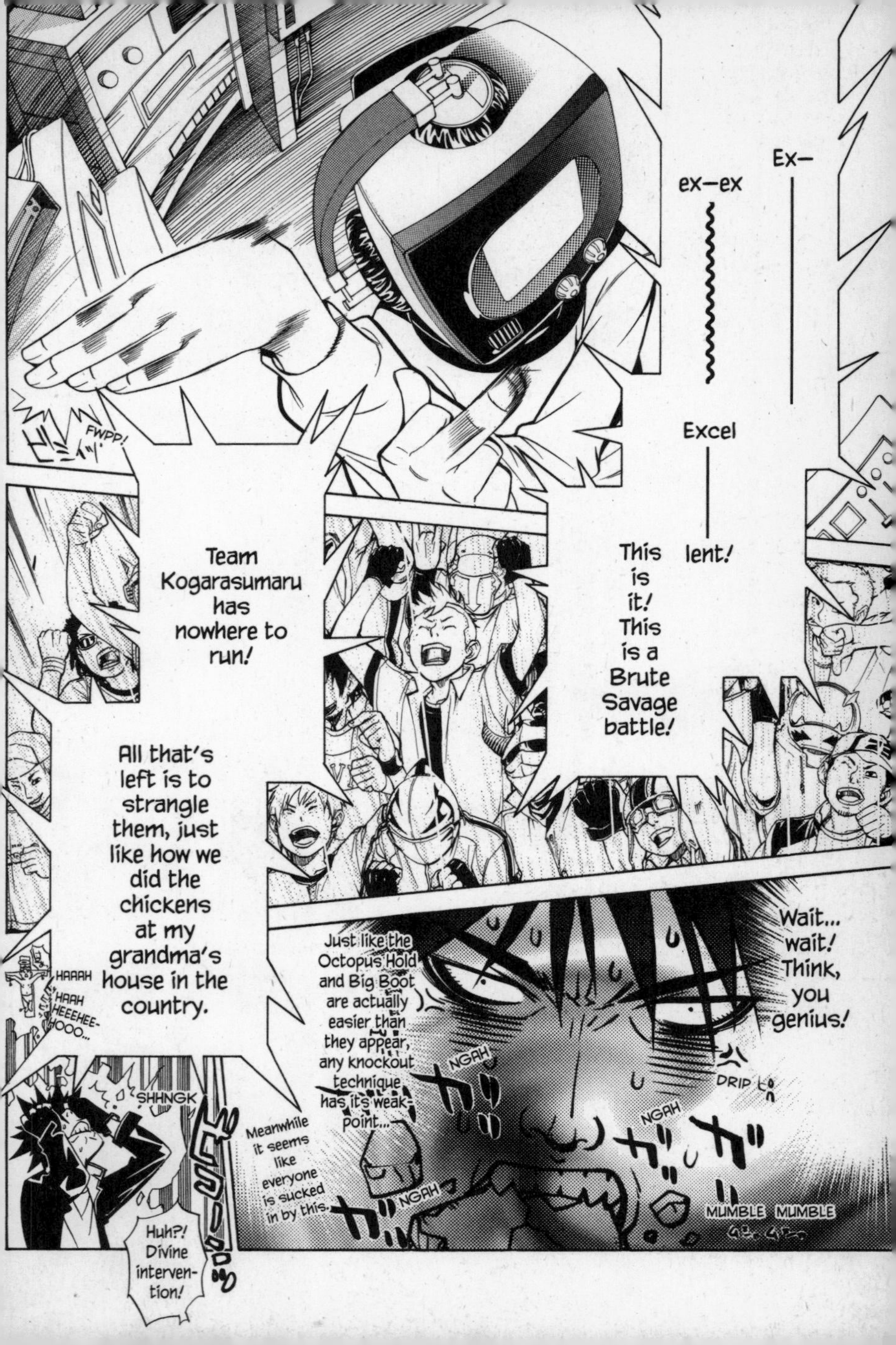
Ex—
ex—ex
Excel
lent!
FWPP!
This is it! This is a Brute Savage battle!
Team Kogarasumaru has nowhere to run!
All that's left is to strangle them, just like how we did the chickens at my grandma's house in the country.
Wait... wait! Think, you genius!
Just like the Octopus Hold and Big Boot are actually easier than they appear, any knockout technique has its weak-point...
DRIP
NGAH
NGAH
NGAH
MUMBLE MUMBLE
Meanwhile it seems like everyone is sucked in by this.
HAAAH HAAH HEEEHEE-HOOO...
SHHNGK
Huh?! Divine intervention!

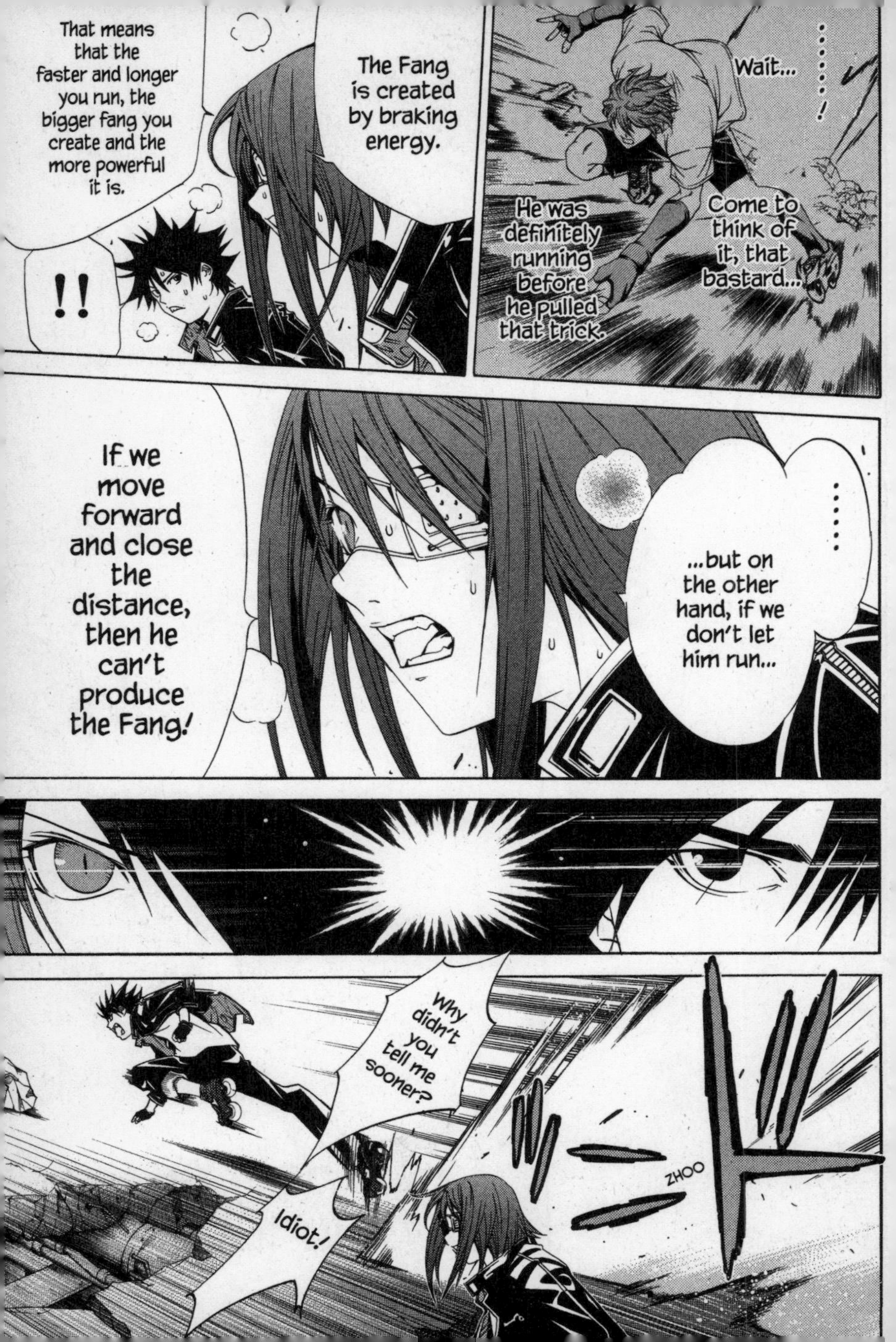
......!
Wait...
Come to think of it, that bastard...
He was definitely running before he pulled that trick.
The Fang is created by braking energy.
That means that the faster and longer you run, the bigger fang you create and the more powerful it is.
!!
......
...but on the other hand, if we don't let him run...
If we move forward and close the distance, then he can't produce the Fang!
ZHOO
Why didn't you tell me sooner?
Idiot!

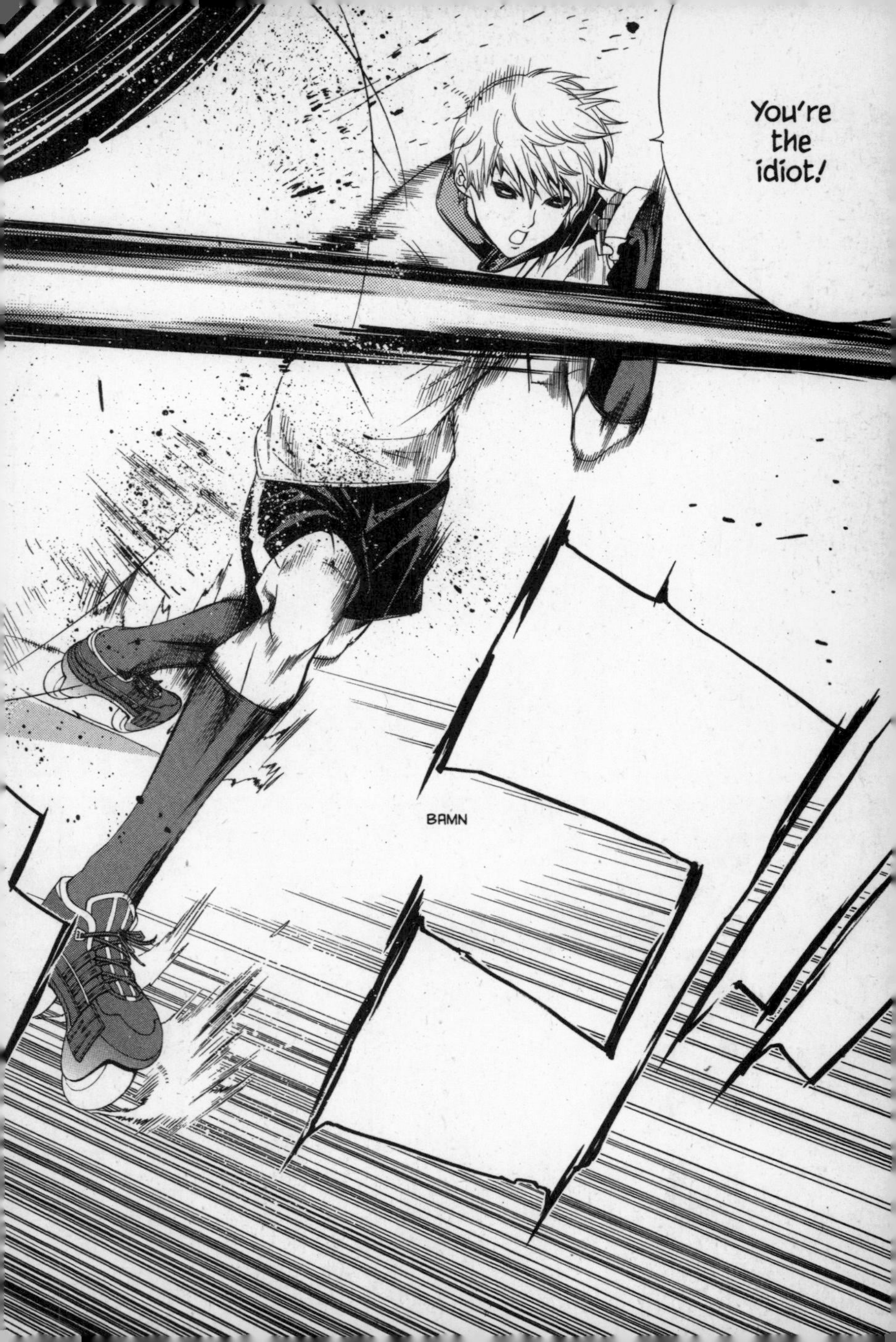
You're the idiot!
BAMN

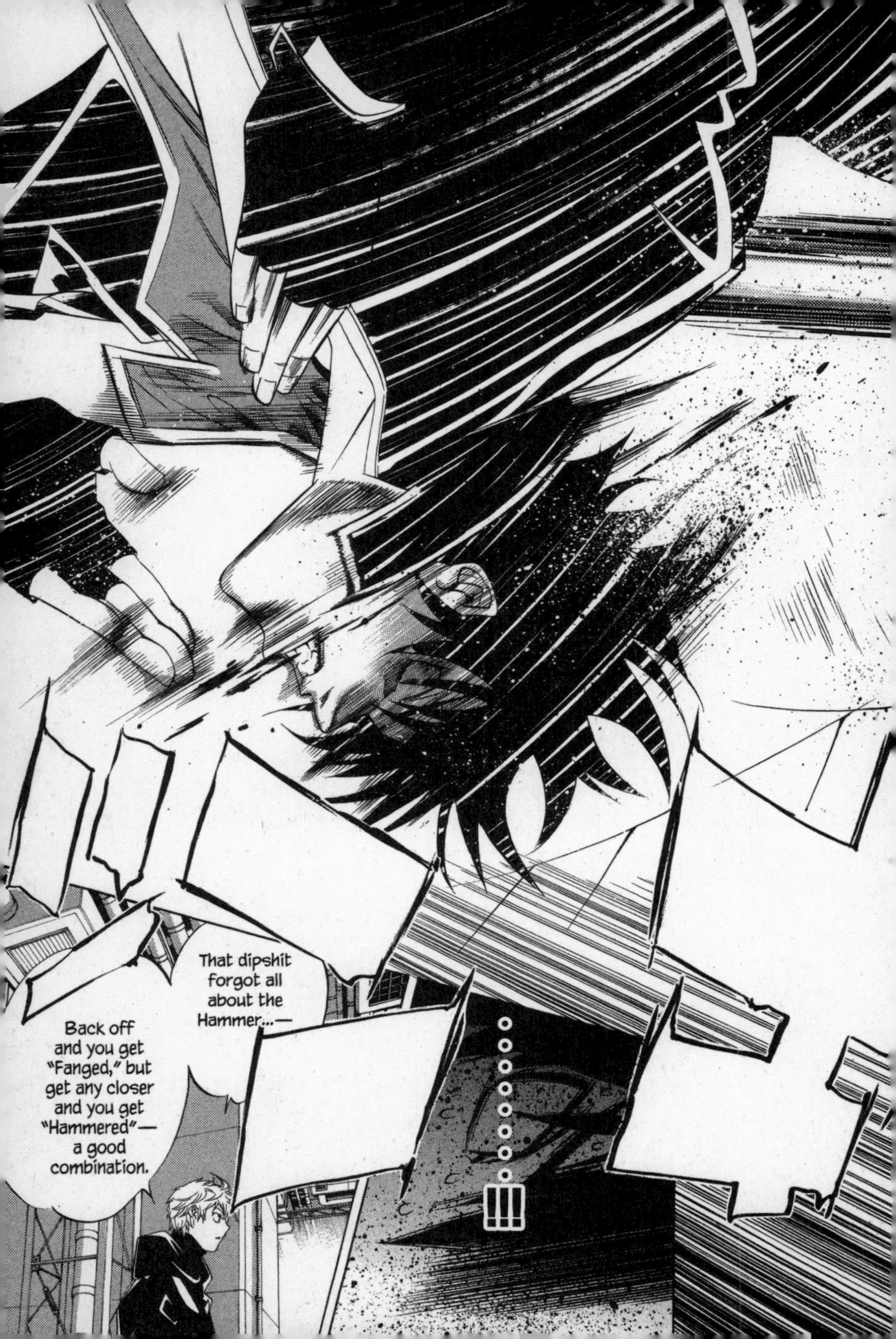
..........!!!
That dipshit forgot all about the Hammer...—
Back off and you get "Fanged," but get any closer and you get "Hammered"—a good combination.

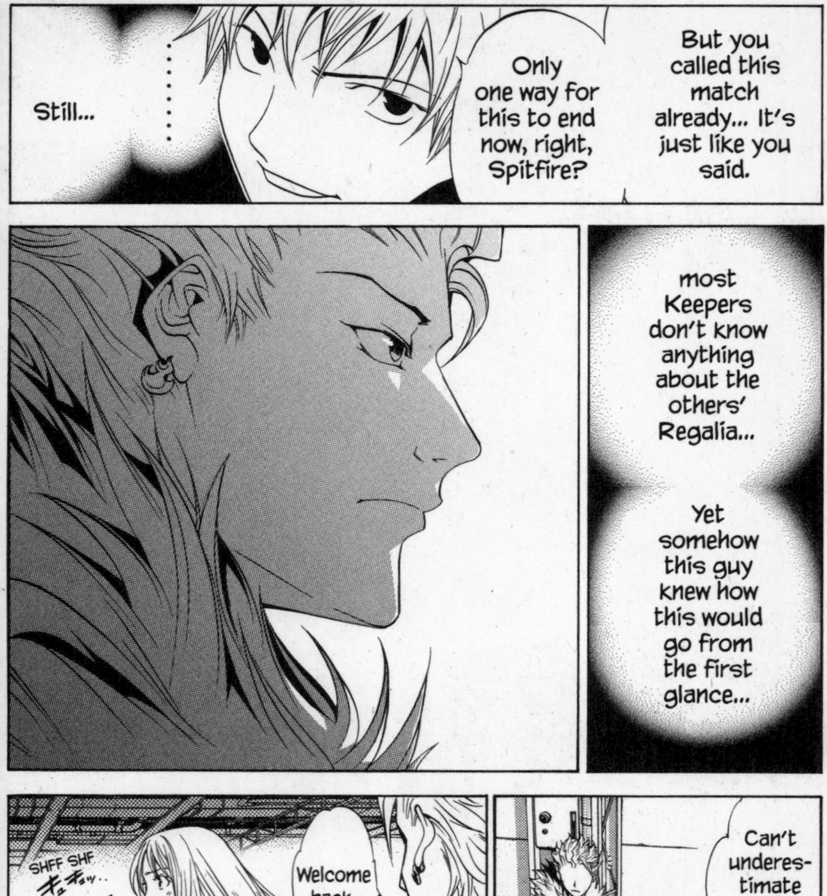

But you called this match already... It's just like you said.
Only one way for this to end now, right, Spitfire?
......
Still...
most Keepers don't know anything about the others' Regalia...
Yet somehow this guy knew how this would go from the first glance...
Can't underes-timate this guy...
!!
Welcome back.
SHFF SHF
......?
You don't look too happy.
It's no surprise really... Ikki's your favorite and he's in a tough situation...

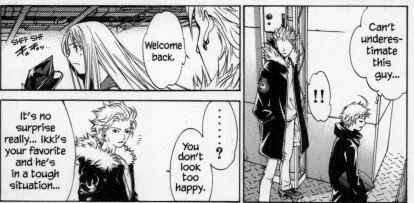

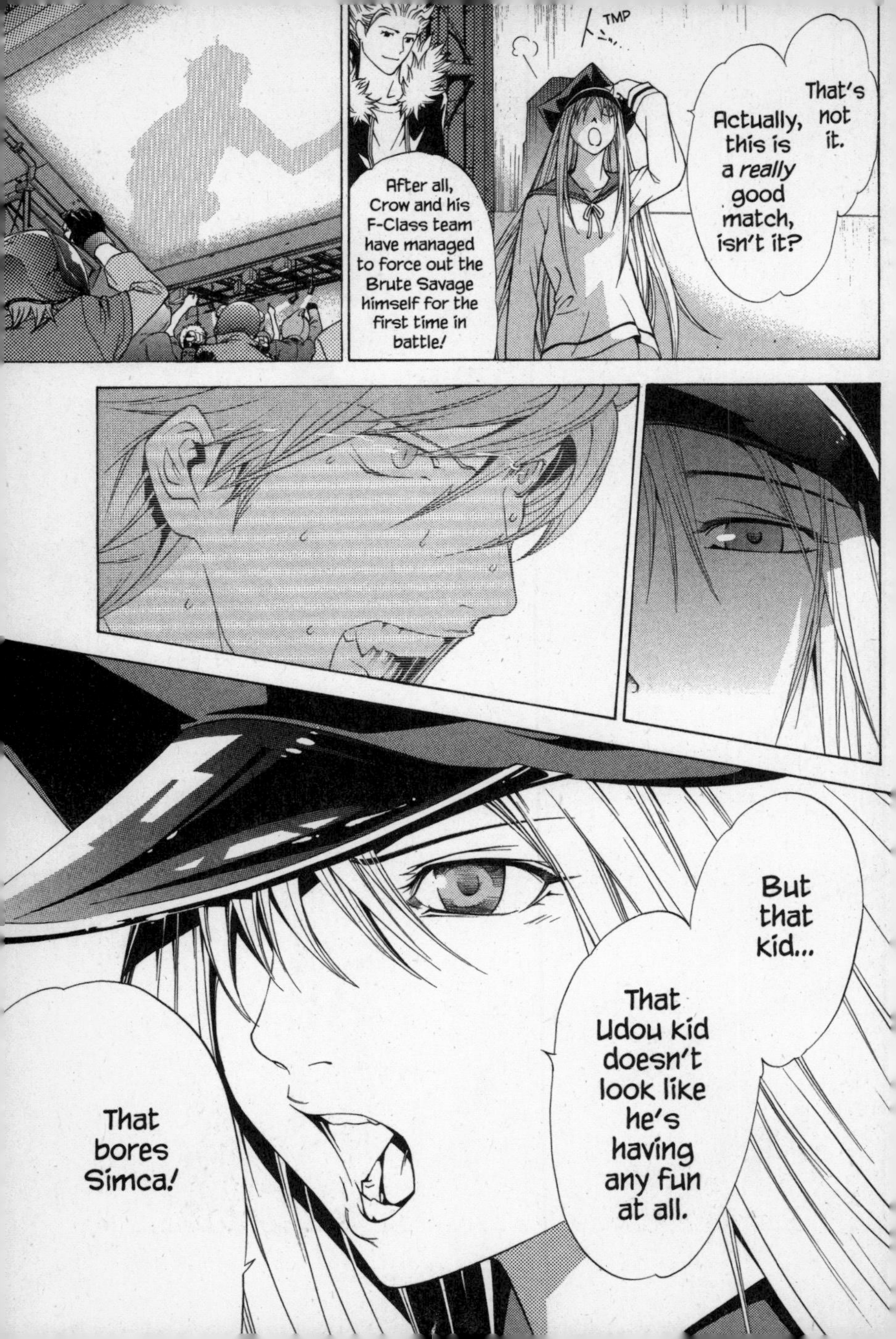
TMP
That's not it.
Actually, this is a *really* good match, isn't it?
After all, Crow and his F-Class team have managed to force out the Brute Savage himself for the first time in battle!
But that kid...
That Udou kid doesn't look like he's having any fun at all.
That bores Simca!

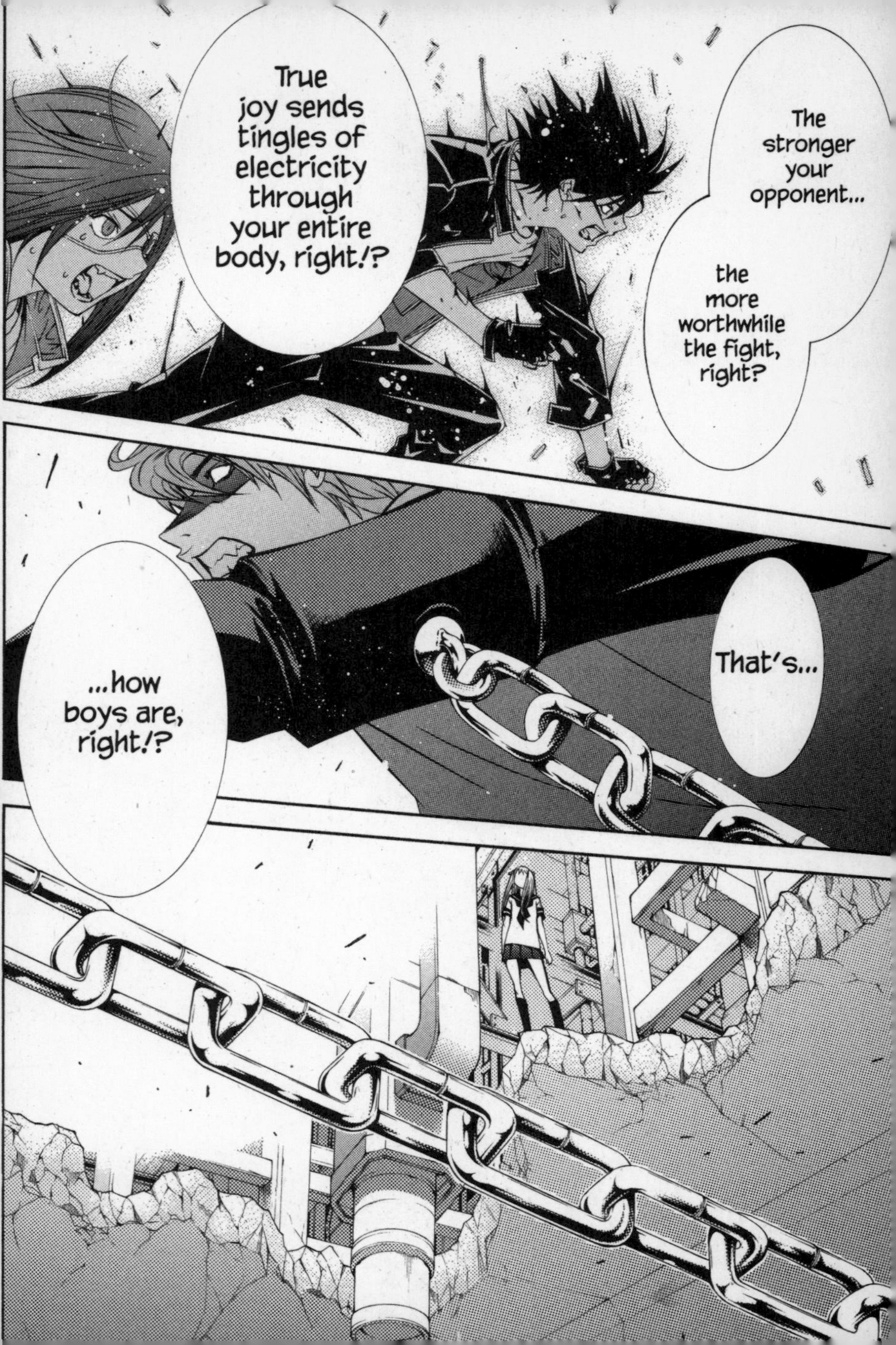
The stronger your opponent...
the more worthwhile the fight, right?
True joy sends tingles of electricity through your entire body, right!?
That's...
...how boys are, right!?

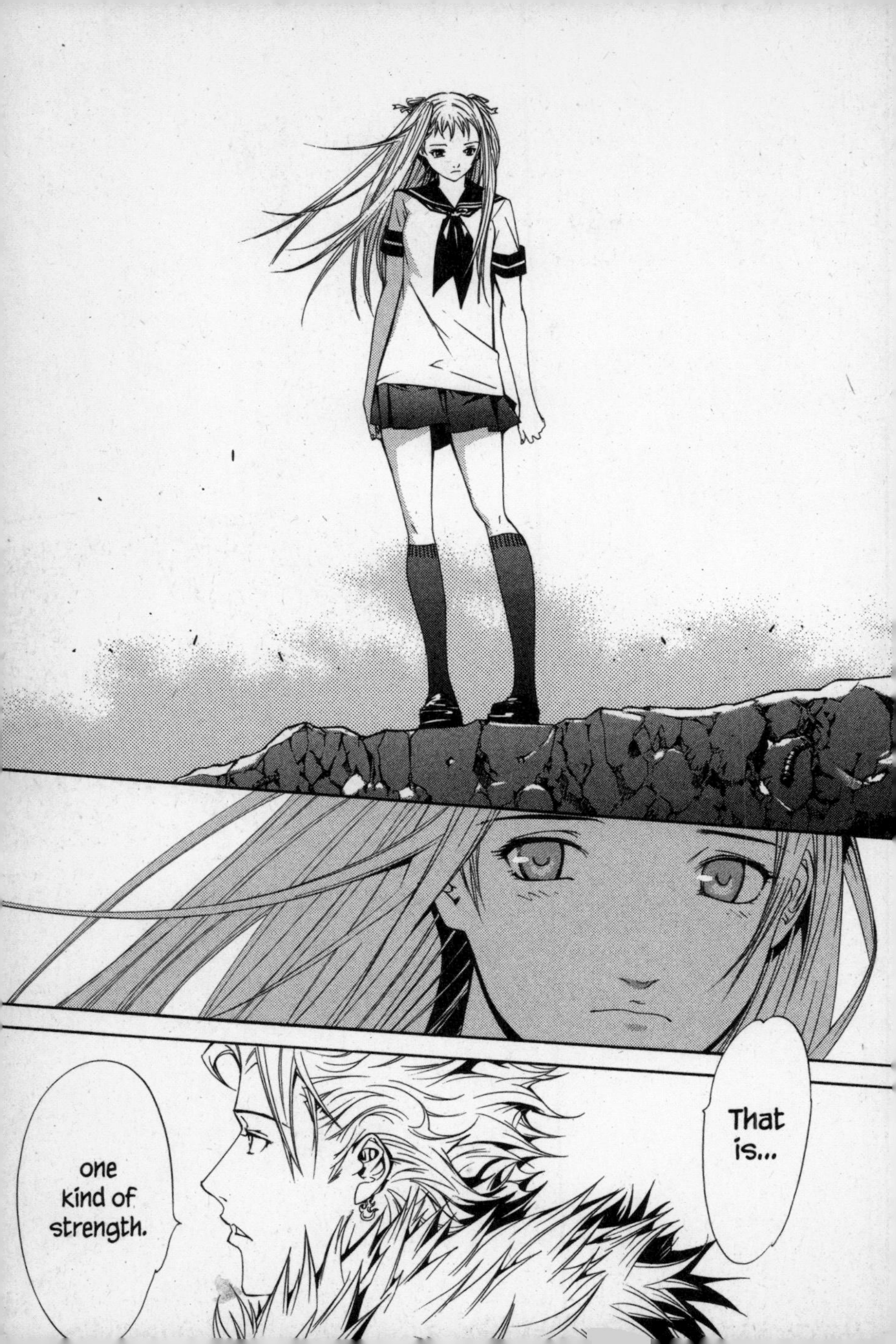
That is...
one kind of strength.

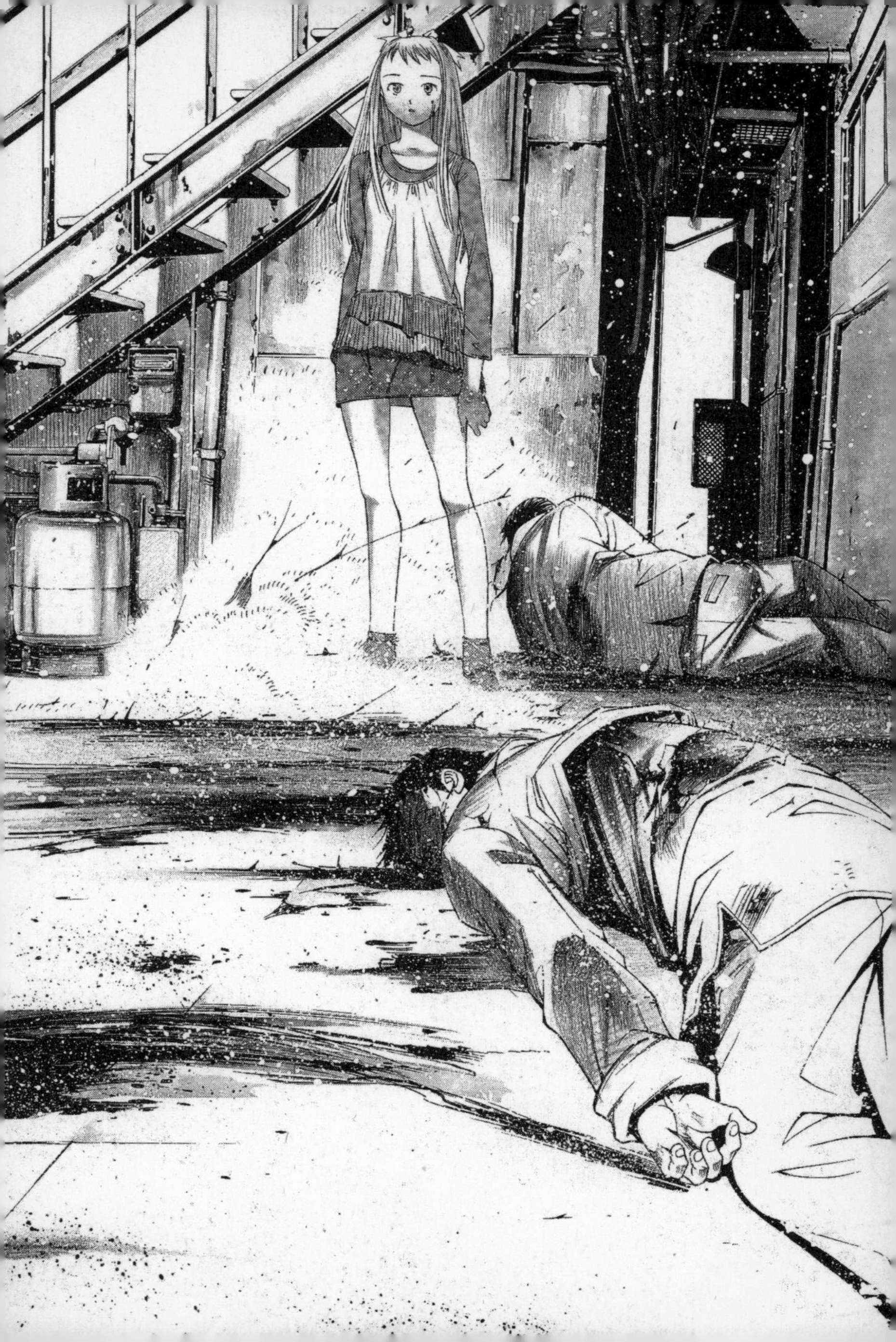

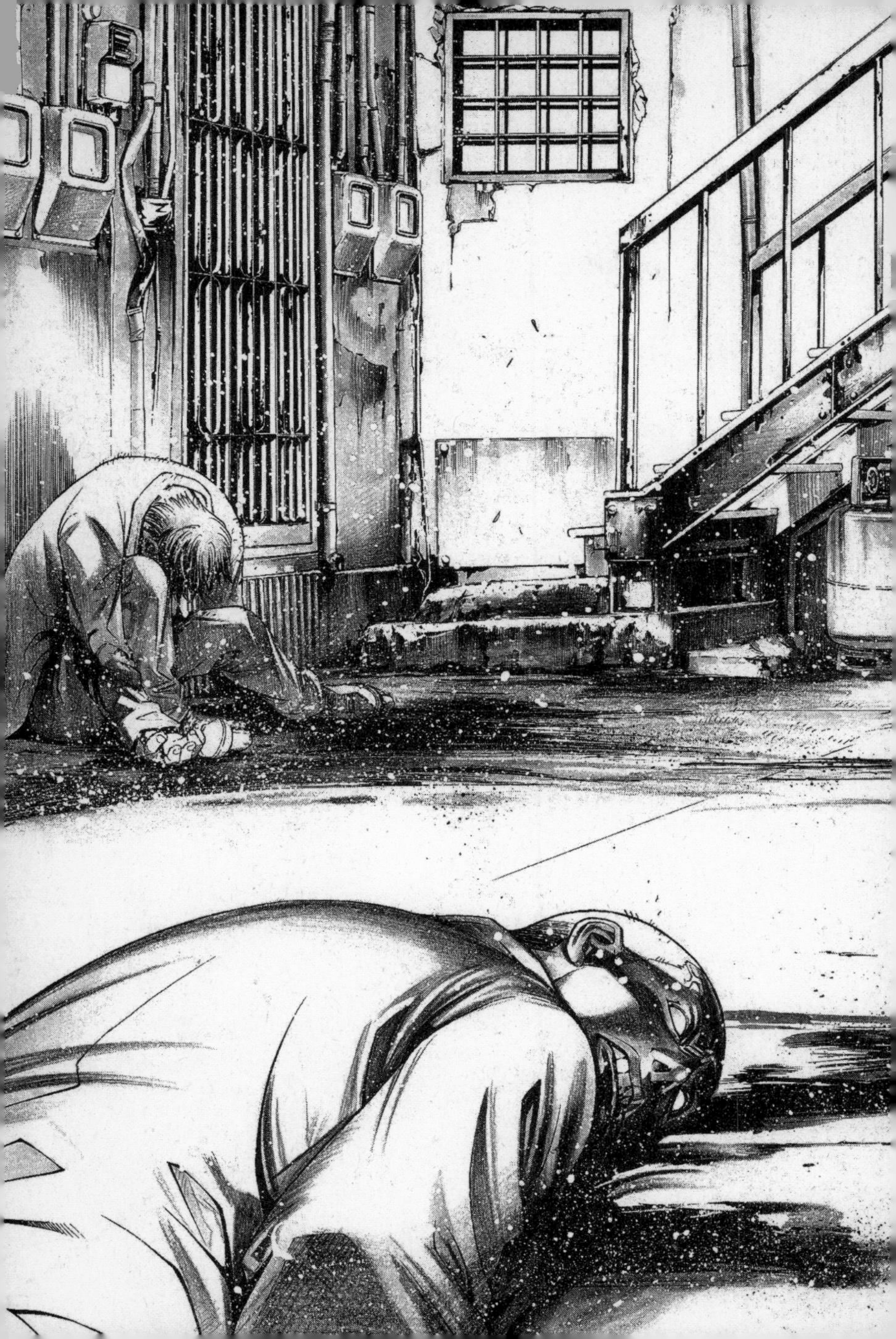

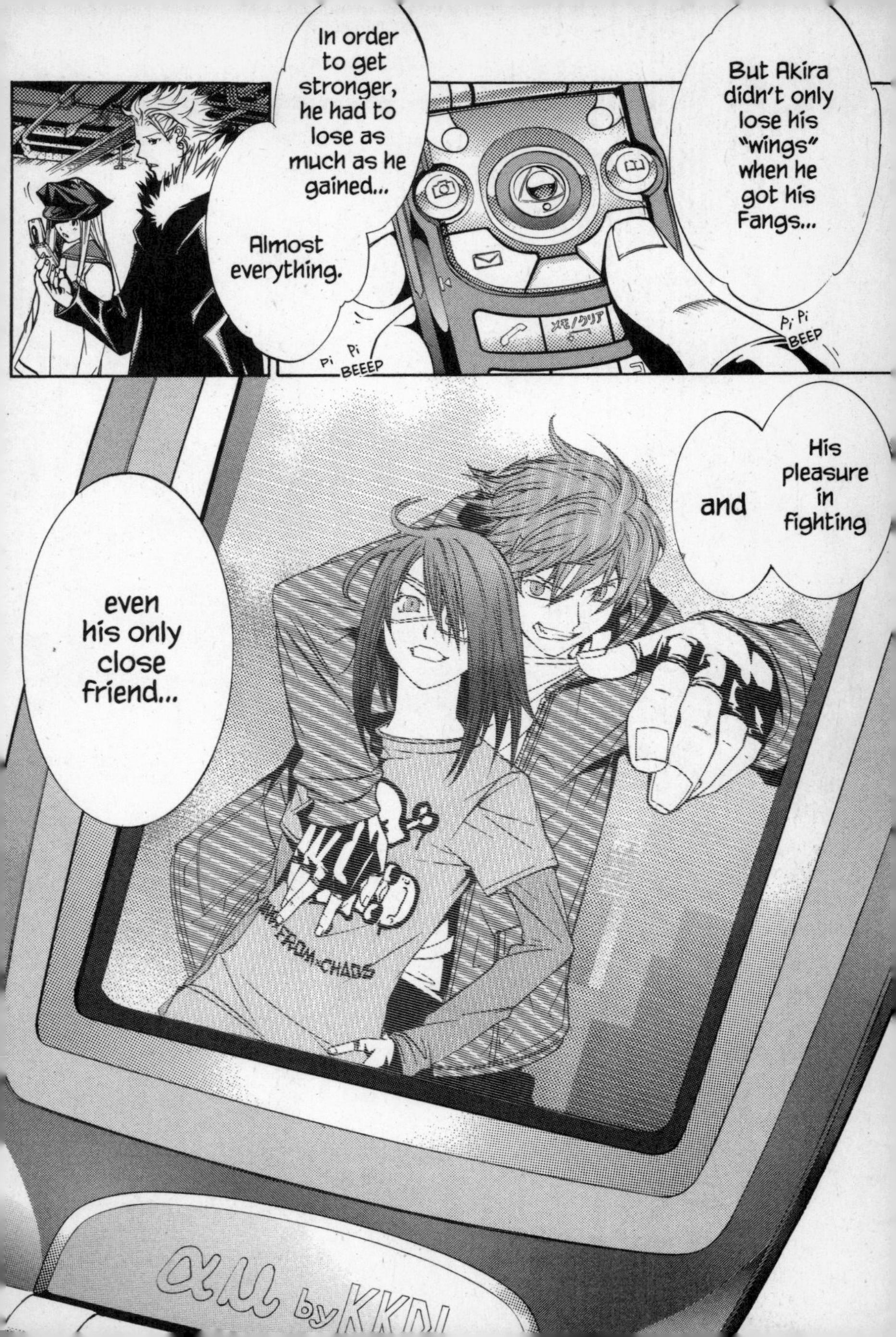
But Akira didn't only lose his "wings" when he got his Fangs...
メモ/クリア
Pi Pi BEEP
In order to get stronger, he had to lose as much as he gained...
Almost everything.
Pi Pi BEEEP
His pleasure in fighting
and
even his only close friend...

# Trick:71

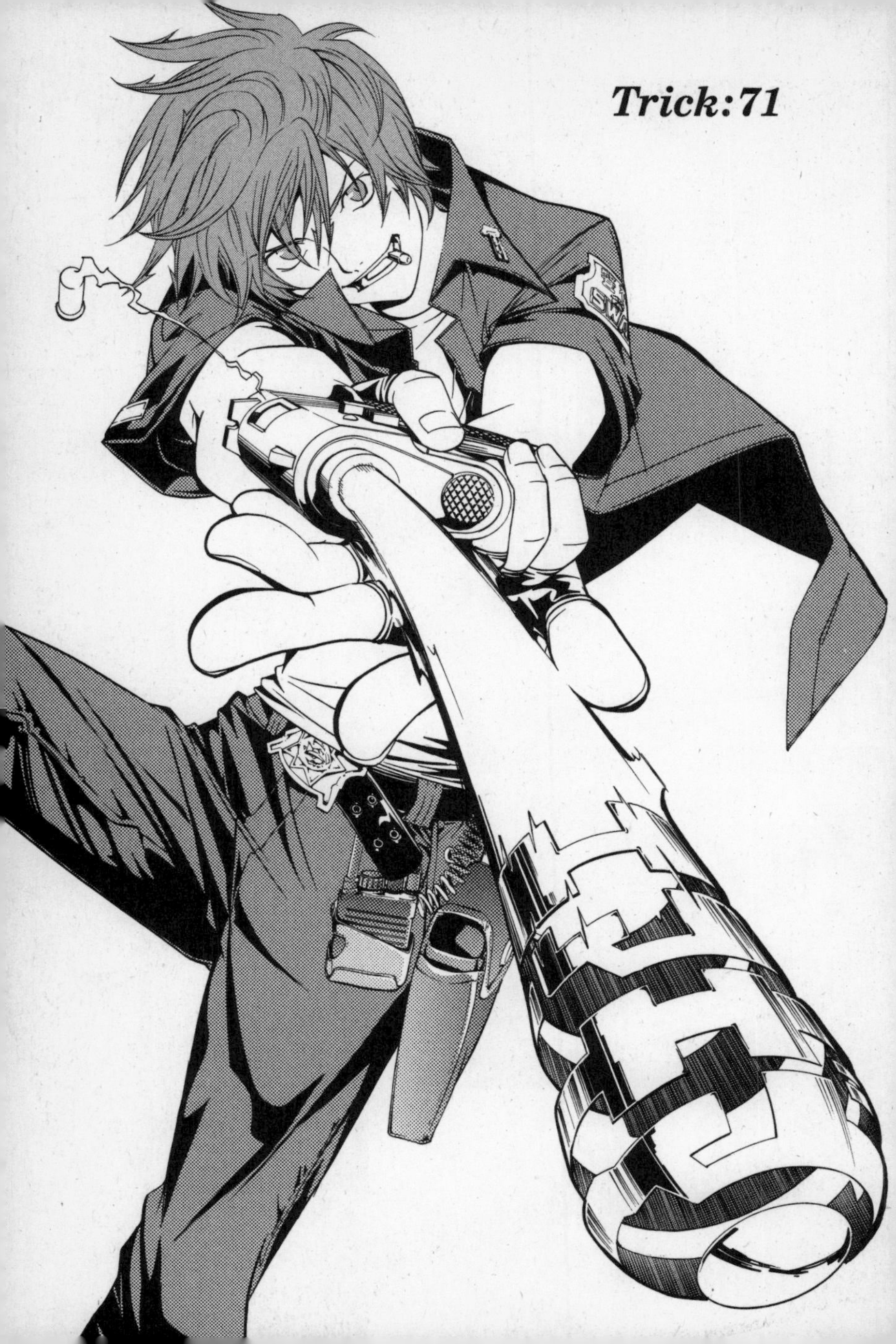

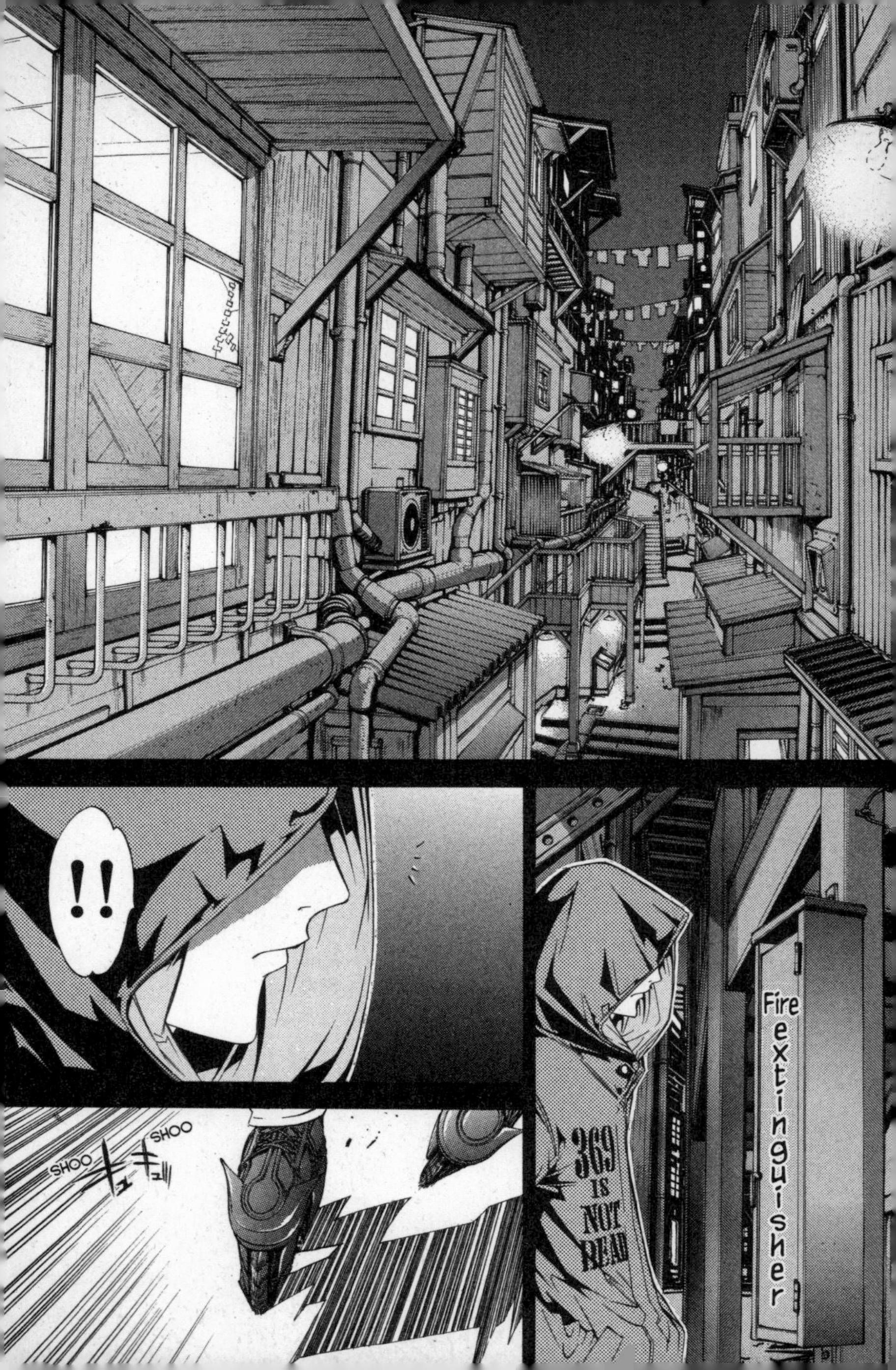
Fire extinguisher
369 IS NOT
!!
SHOO
SHOO

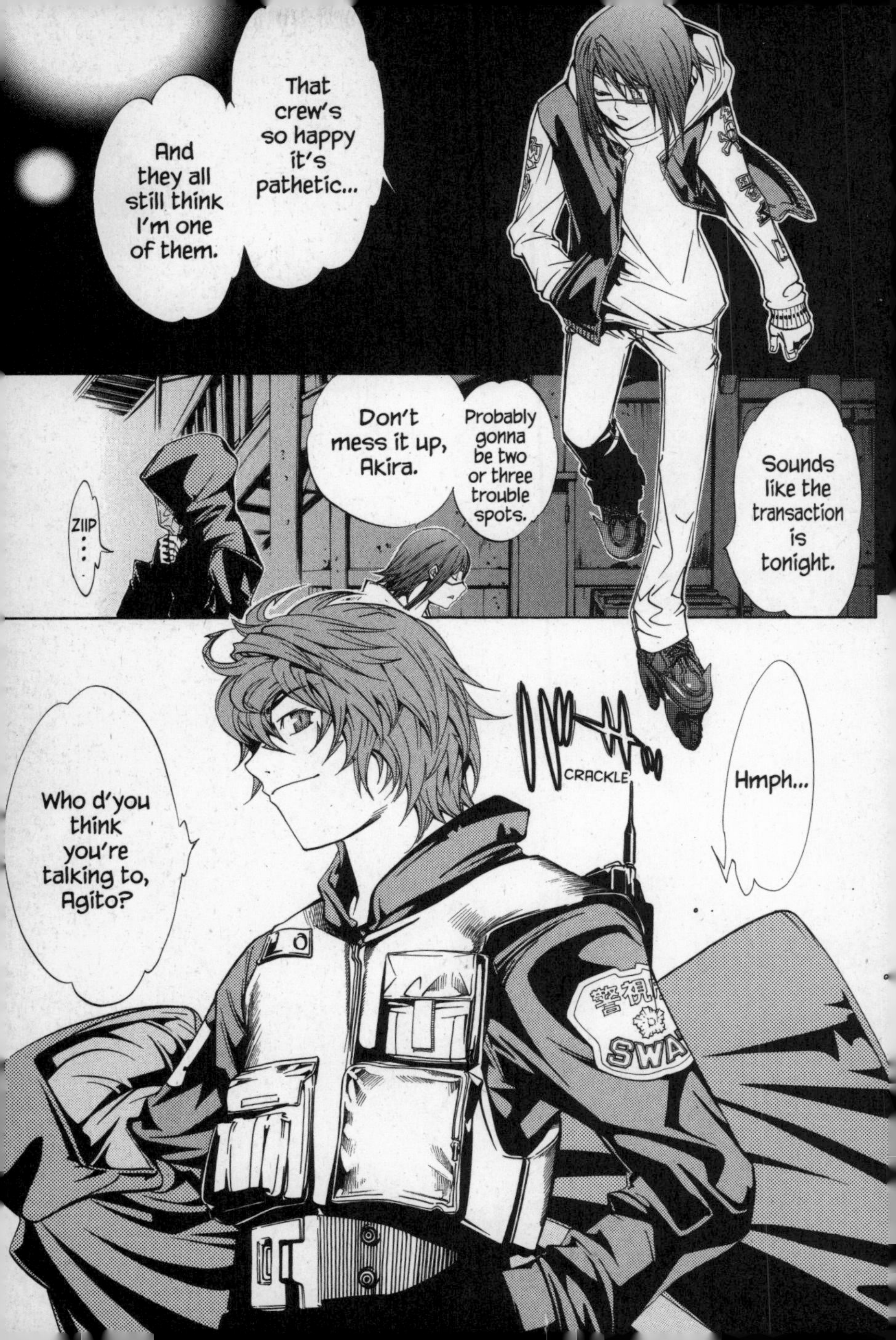
That crew's so happy it's pathetic...
And they all still think I'm one of them.
Sounds like the transaction is tonight.
Probably gonna be two or three trouble spots.
Don't mess it up, Akira.
ZIIP...
CRACKLE
Hmph...
Who d'you think you're talking to, Agito?

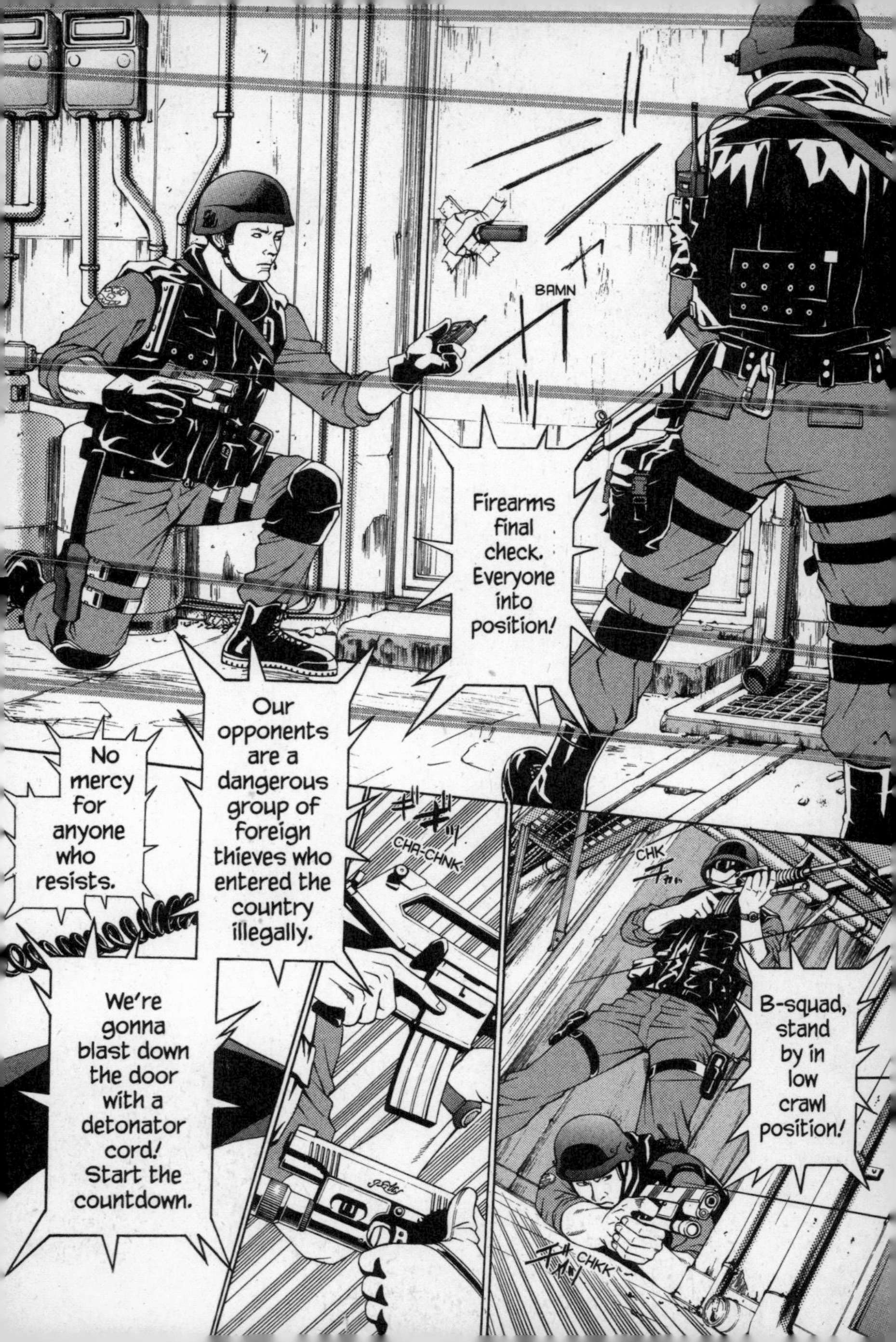

BAMN
Firearms final check. Everyone into position!
Our opponents are a dangerous group of foreign thieves who entered the country illegally.
No mercy for anyone who resists.
CHK
B-squad, stand by in low crawl position!
CHKK
CHA-CHNK
We're gonna blast down the door with a detonator cord! Start the countdown.

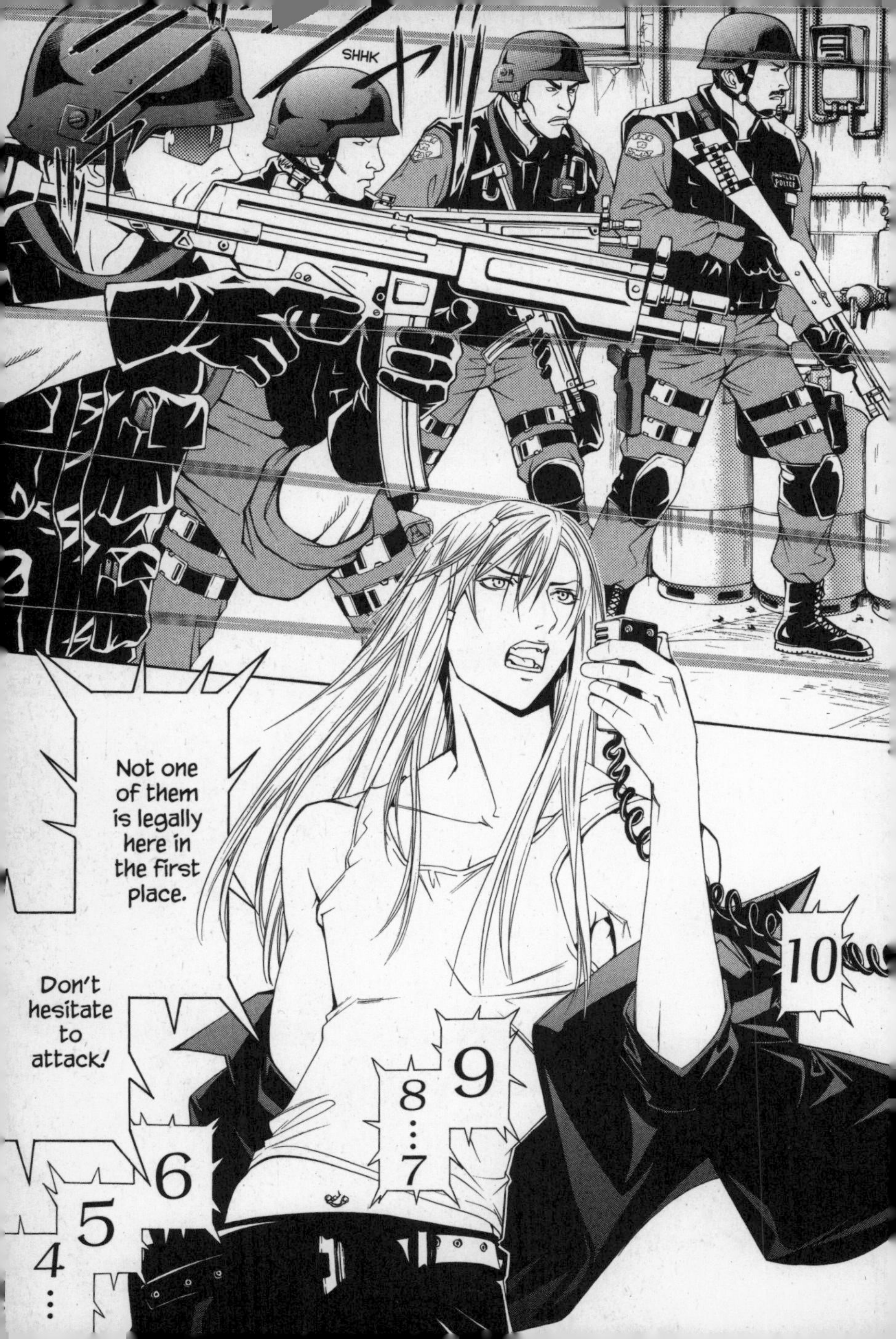
SHHK
Not one of them is legally here in the first place.
Don't hesitate to attack!
10
9
8…7
6
5
4…

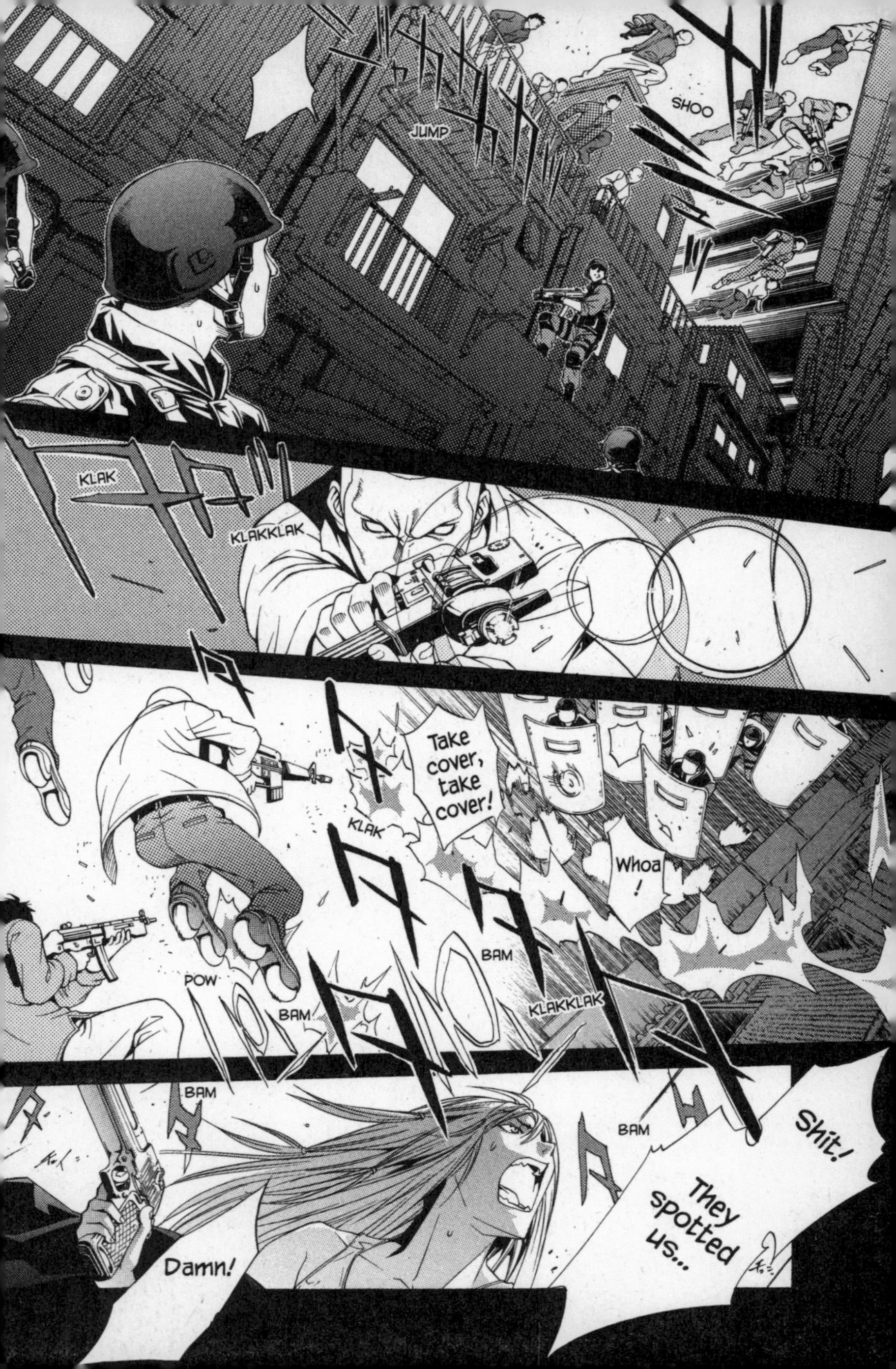
SHOO
JUMP
KLAK
KLAKKLAK
Take cover, take cover!
Whoa!
KLAK
BAM
KLAKKLAK
BAM
POW
Shit!
They spotted us...
BAM
BAM
Damn!

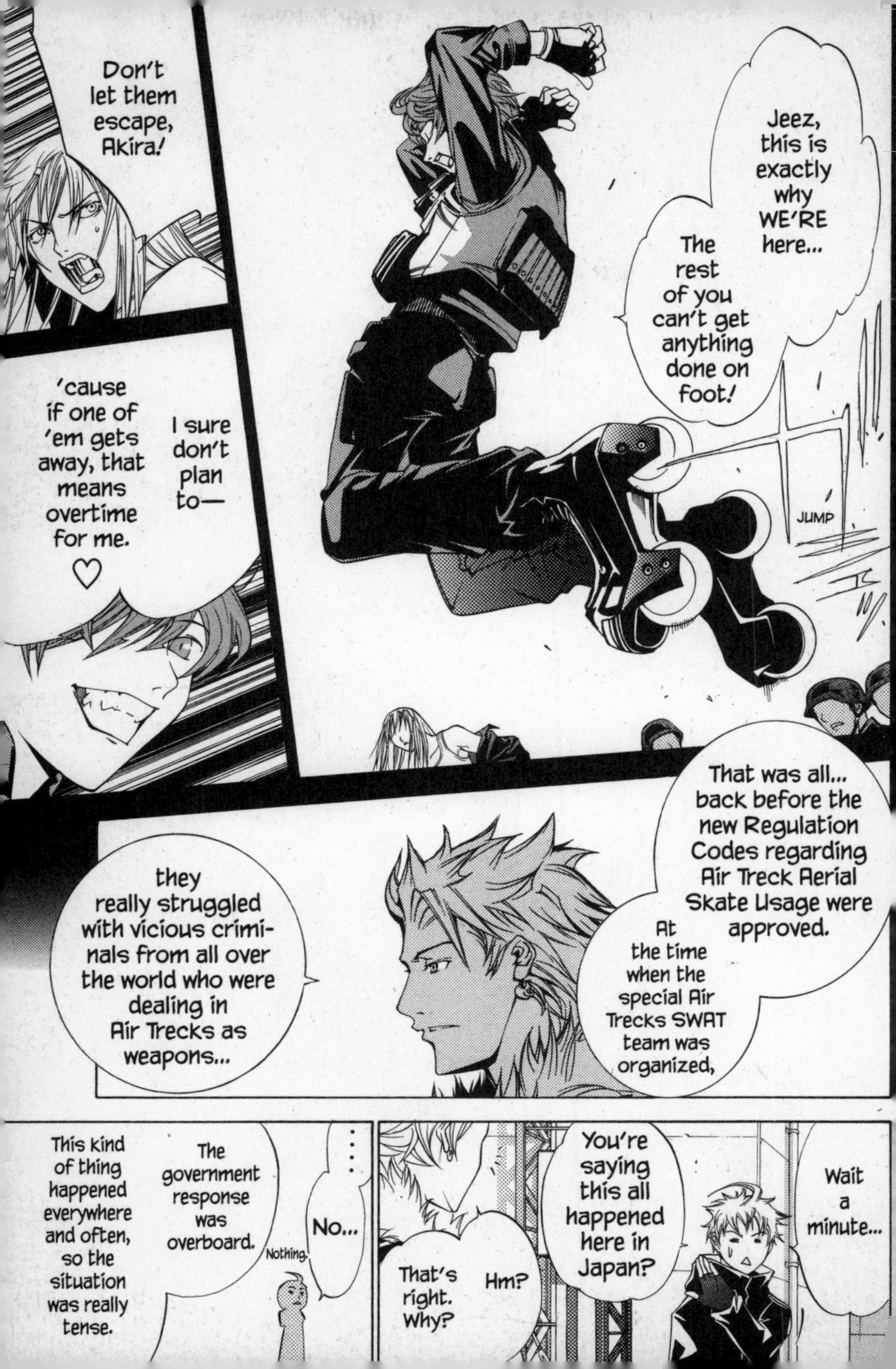
Jeez, this is exactly why WE'RE here...
The rest of you can't get anything done on foot!
JUMP
Don't let them escape, Akira!
I sure don't plan to—
'cause if one of 'em gets away, that means overtime for me. ♡
That was all... back before the new Regulation Codes regarding Air Treck Aerial Skate Usage were approved.
At the time when the special Air Trecks SWAT team was organized,
they really struggled with vicious criminals from all over the world who were dealing in Air Trecks as weapons...
Wait a minute...
You're saying this all happened here in Japan?
Hm?
That's right. Why?
....
No...
Nothing.
The government response was overboard.
This kind of thing happened everywhere and often, so the situation was really tense.

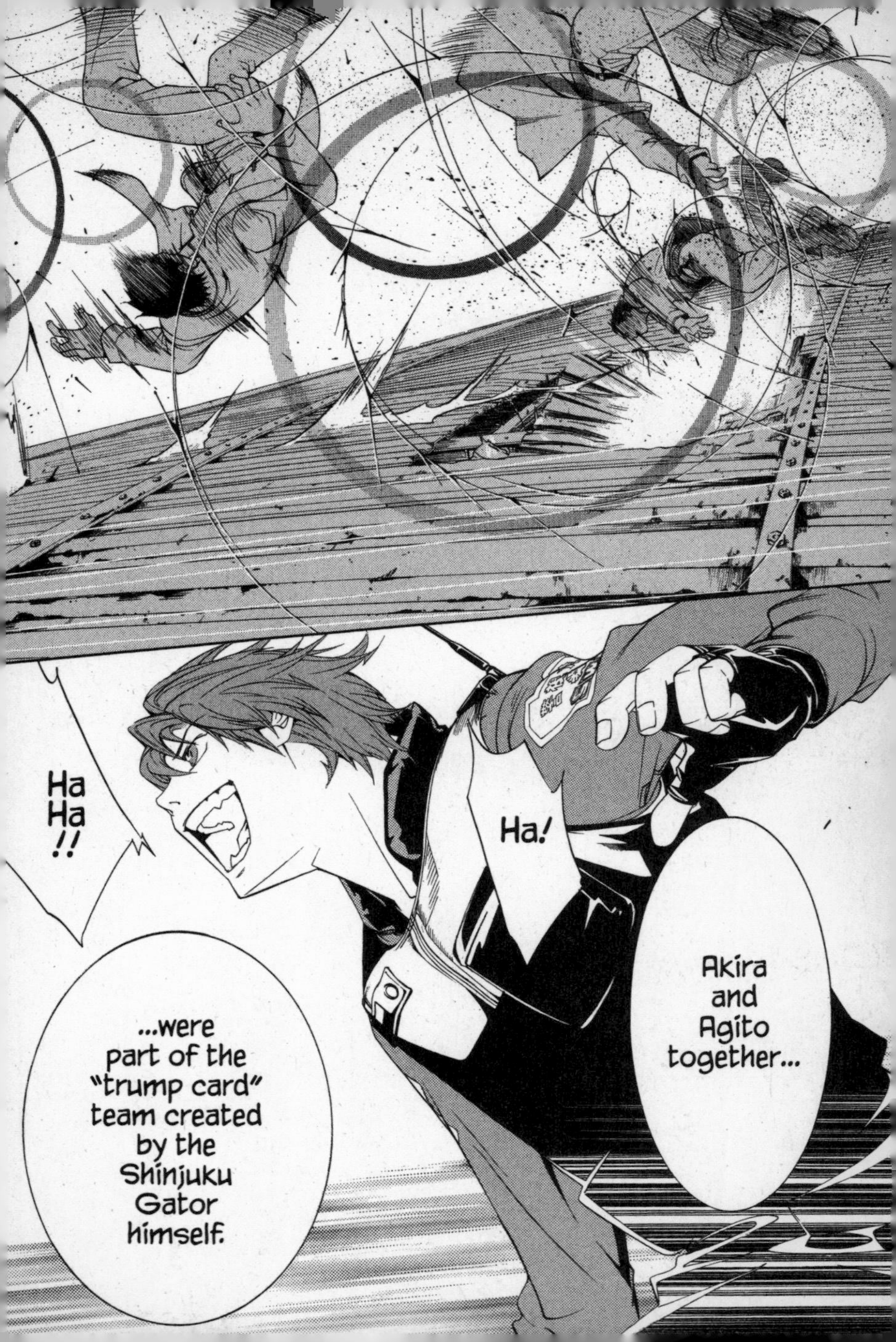
Akira and Agito together...
Ha!
Ha Ha !!
...were part of the "trump card" team created by the Shinjuku Gator himself.

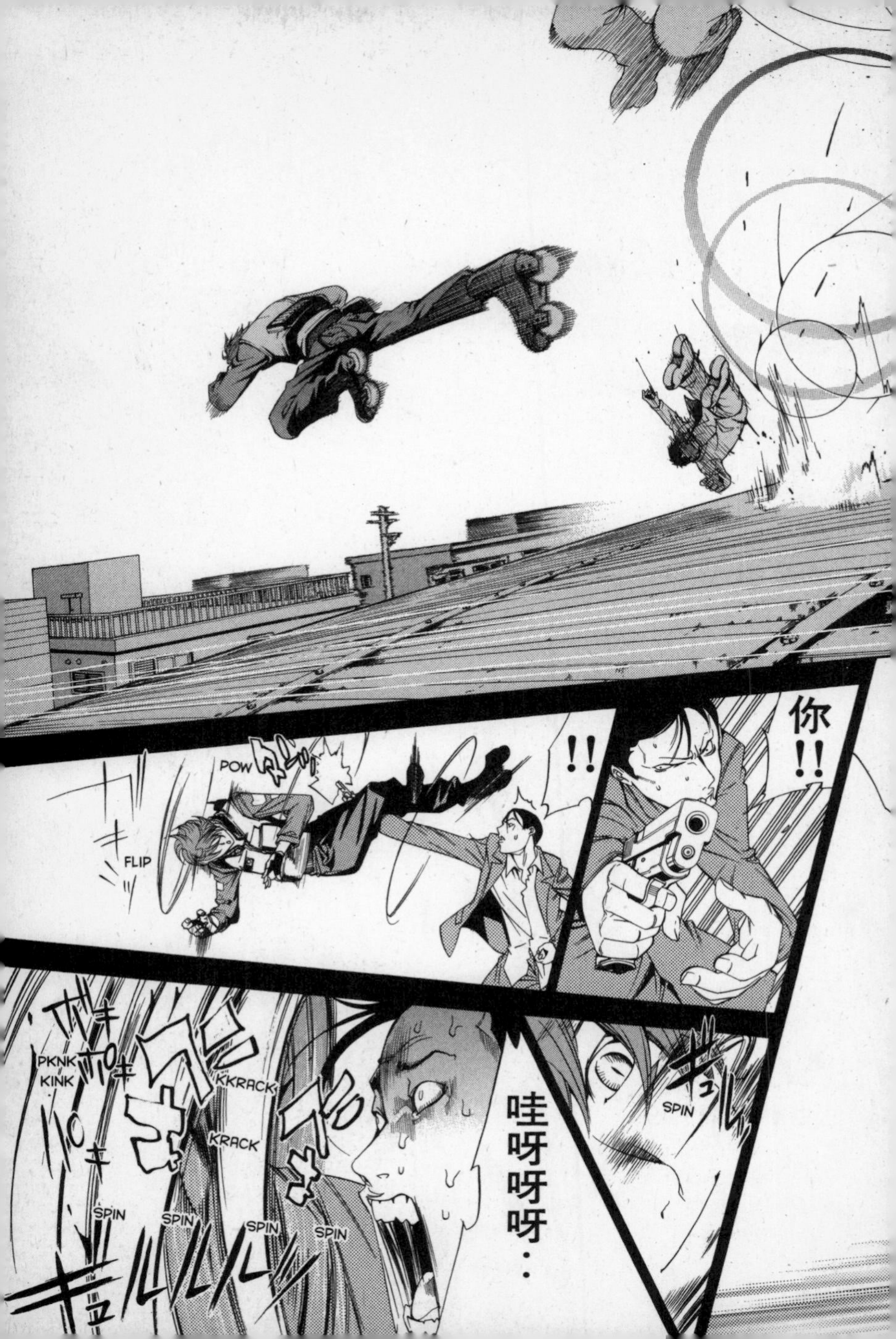
你!!
!!
POW
FLIP
SPIN
哇呀呀呀‥
KKRACK
KRACK
PKNK
KINK
SPIN
SPIN
SPIN
SPIN

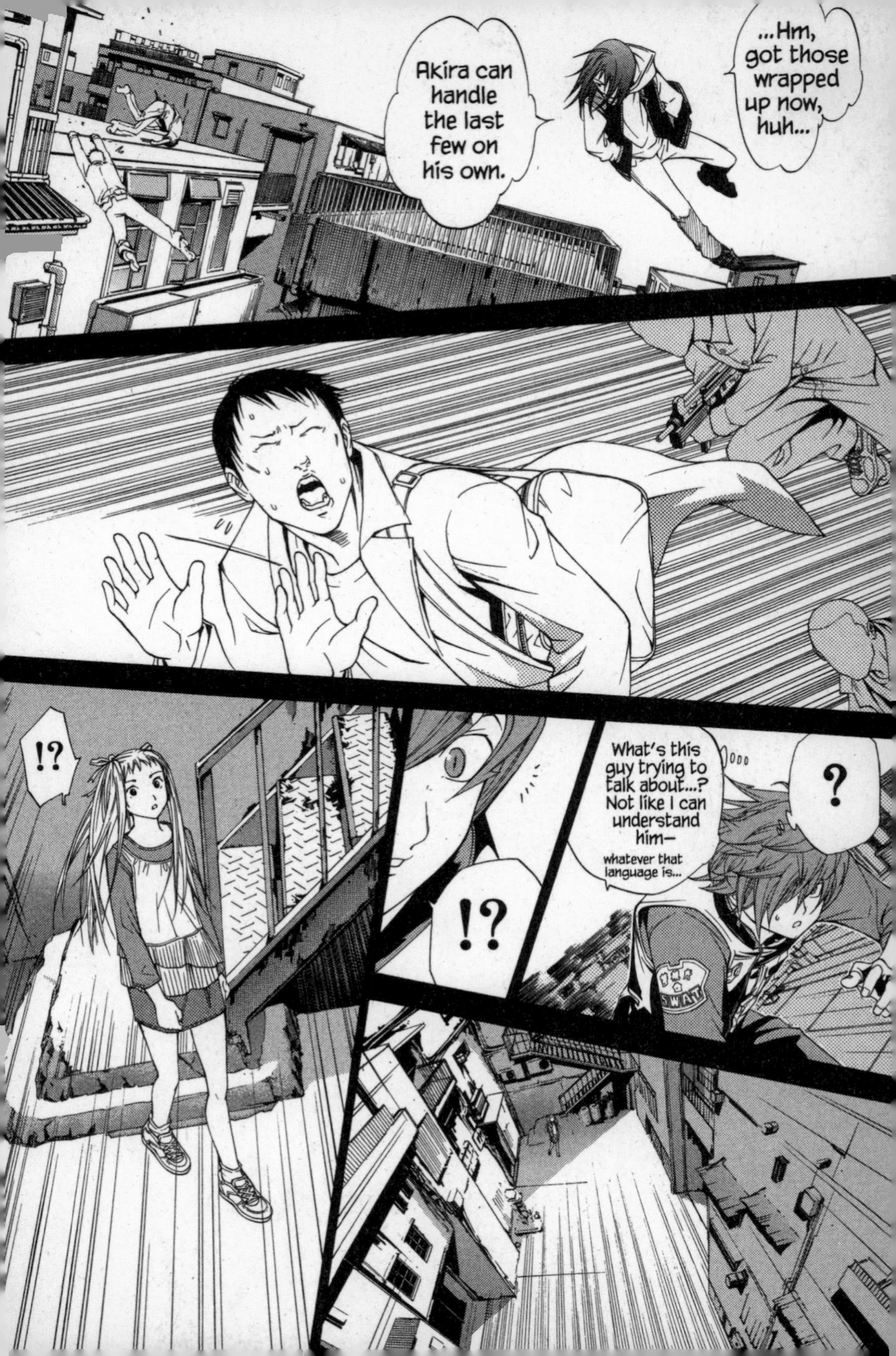
...Hm, got those wrapped up now, huh...
Akira can handle the last few on his own.
?
What's this guy trying to talk about...? Not like I can understand him— whatever that language is...
!?
!?

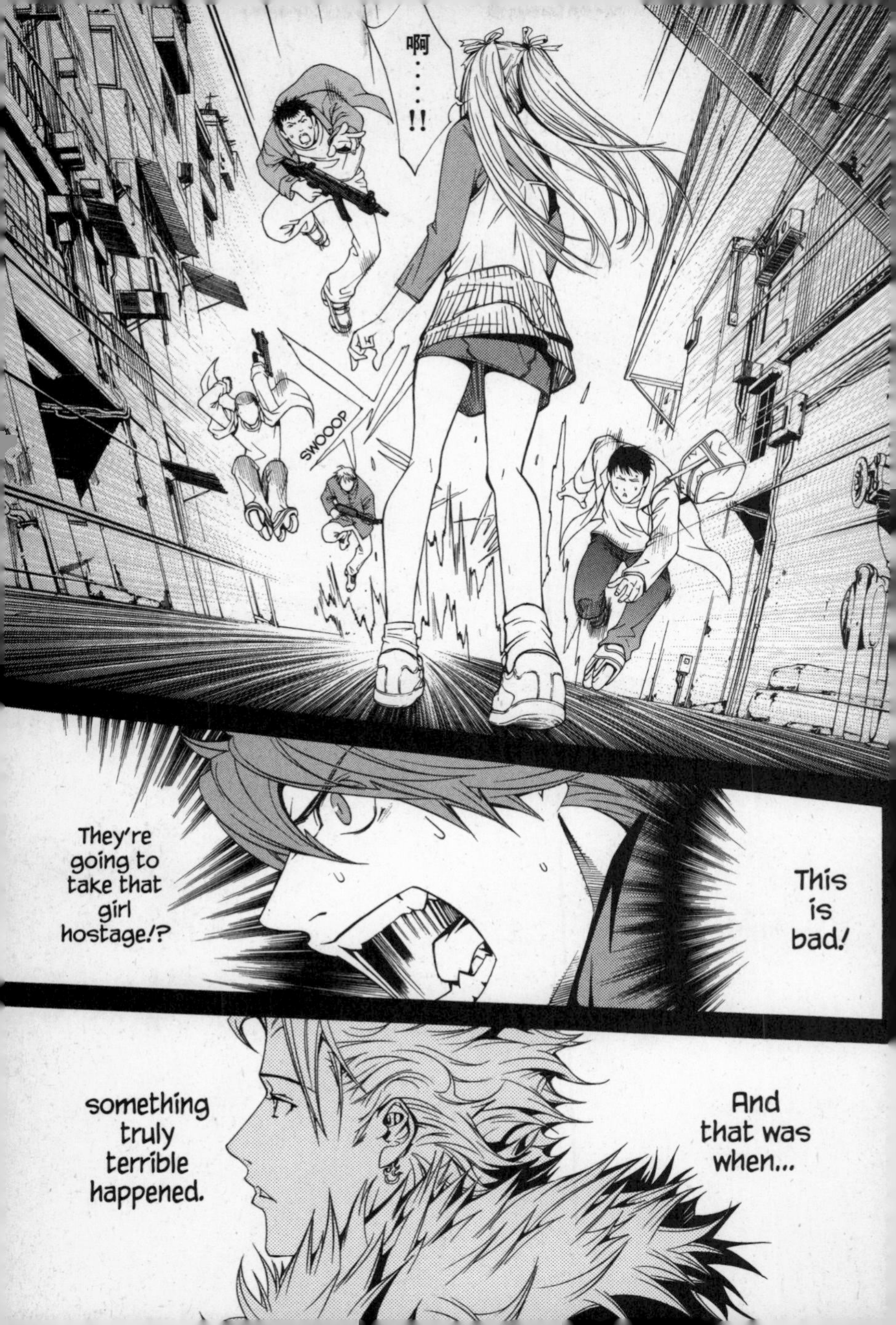
啊....!!
SWOOOP
This is bad!
They're going to take that girl hostage!?
And that was when...
something truly terrible happened.

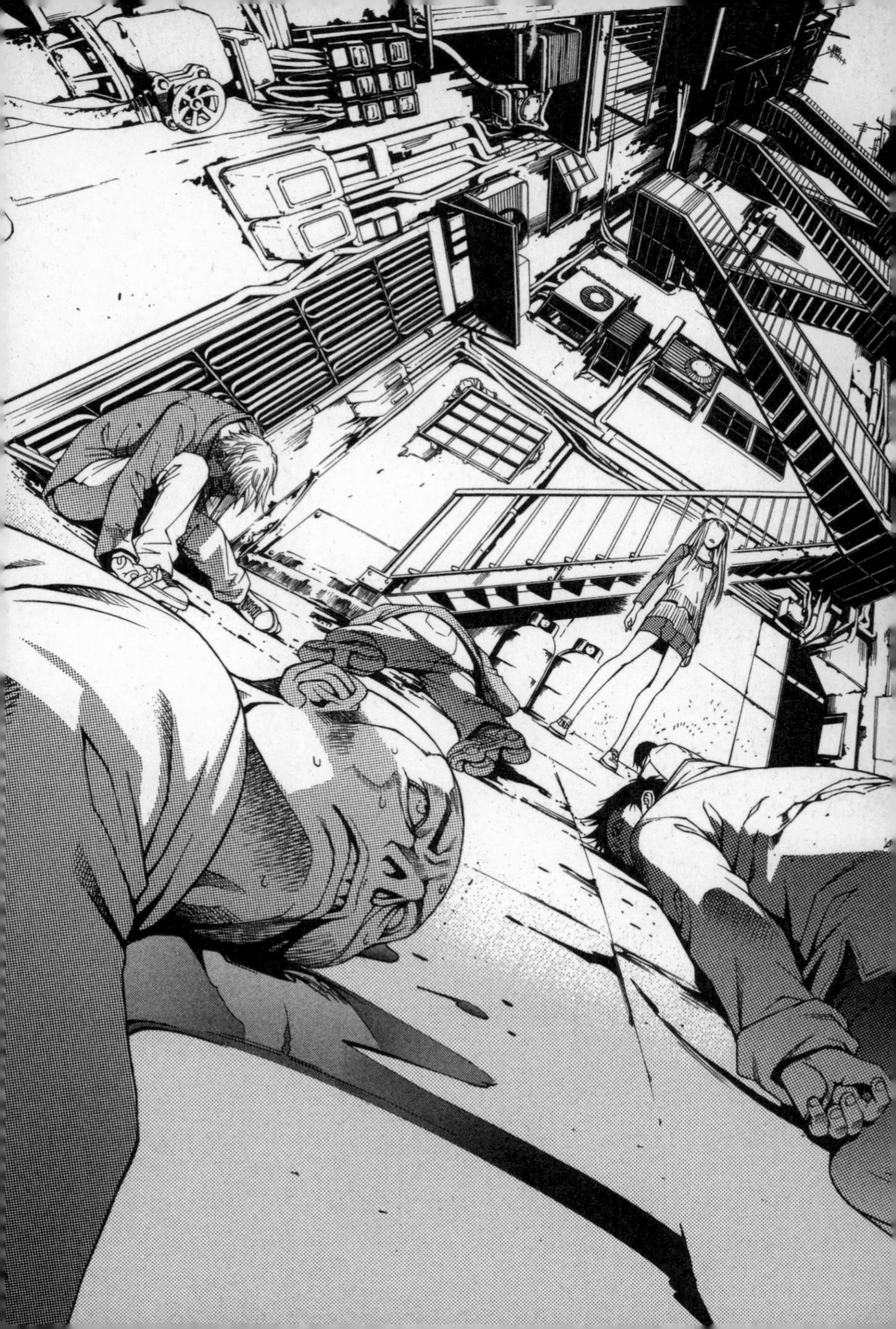

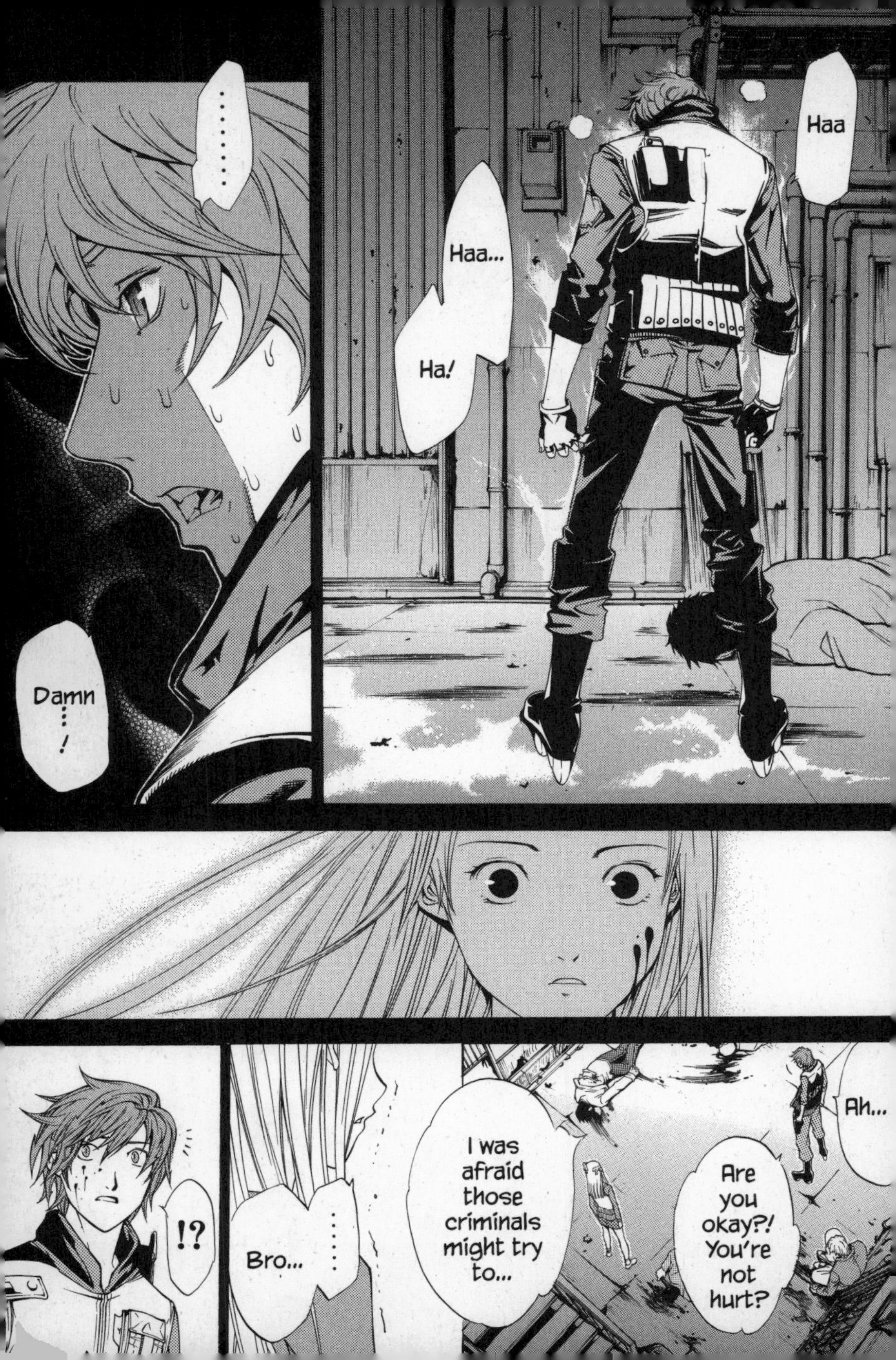
Haa
Haa...
Ha!
......
Damn...!
Ah...
Are you okay?! You're not hurt?
I was afraid those criminals might try to...
......
Bro...
!?

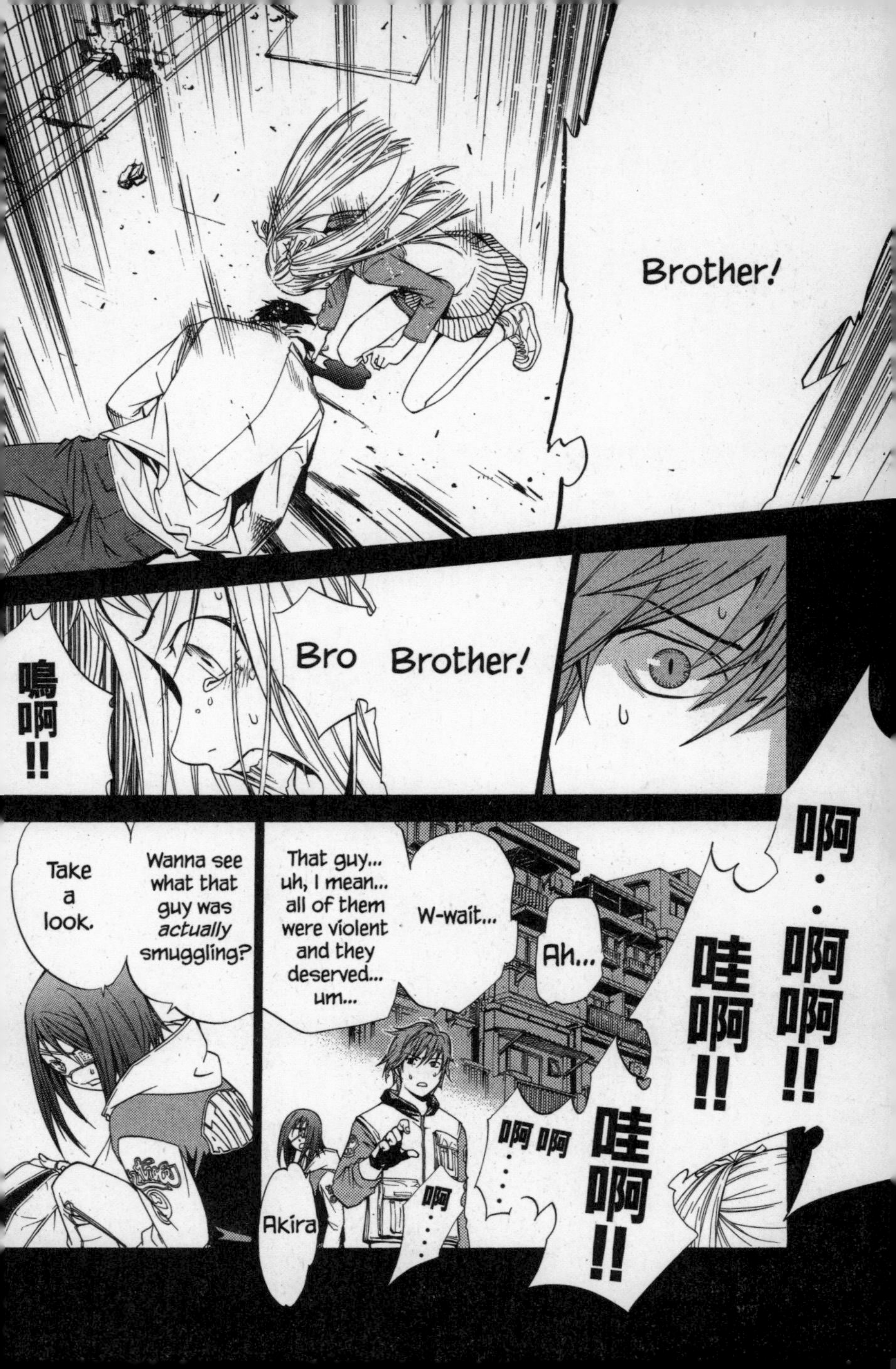
Brother!
Bro Brother!
嗚啊!!
啊··啊啊!!
哇啊!!
哇啊!!
Ah...
W-wait...
That guy... uh, I mean... all of them were violent and they deserved... um...
啊啊···
啊···
Akira
Wanna see what that guy was *actually* smuggling?
Take a look.

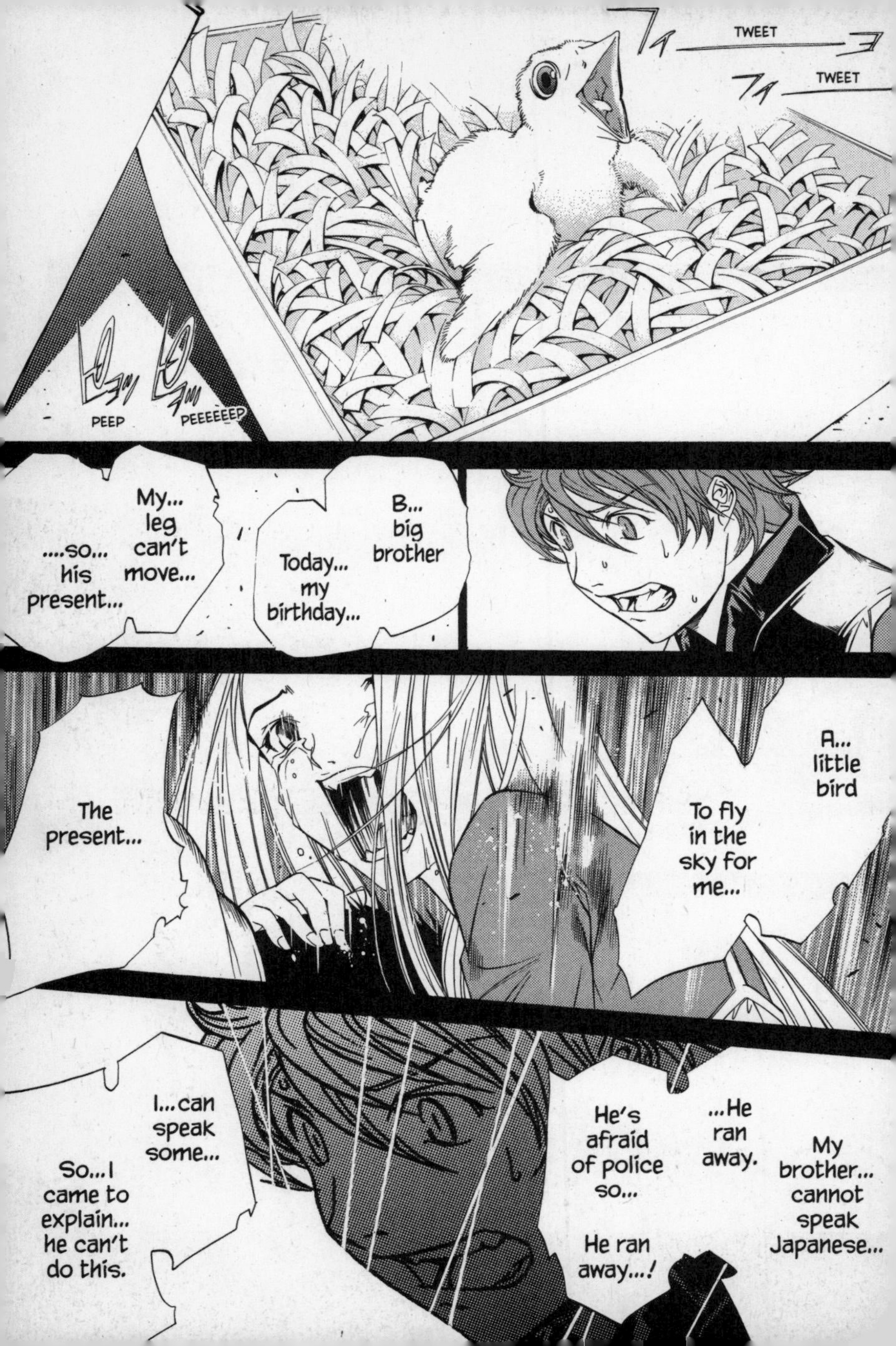
TWEET
TWEET
PEEEEEEP
PEEP
B... big brother
Today... my birthday...
My... leg can't move...
....so... his present...
A... little bird
To fly in the sky for me...
The present...
My brother... cannot speak Japanese...
...He ran away.
He's afraid of police so...
He ran away...!
I...can speak some...
So...I came to explain... he can't do this.

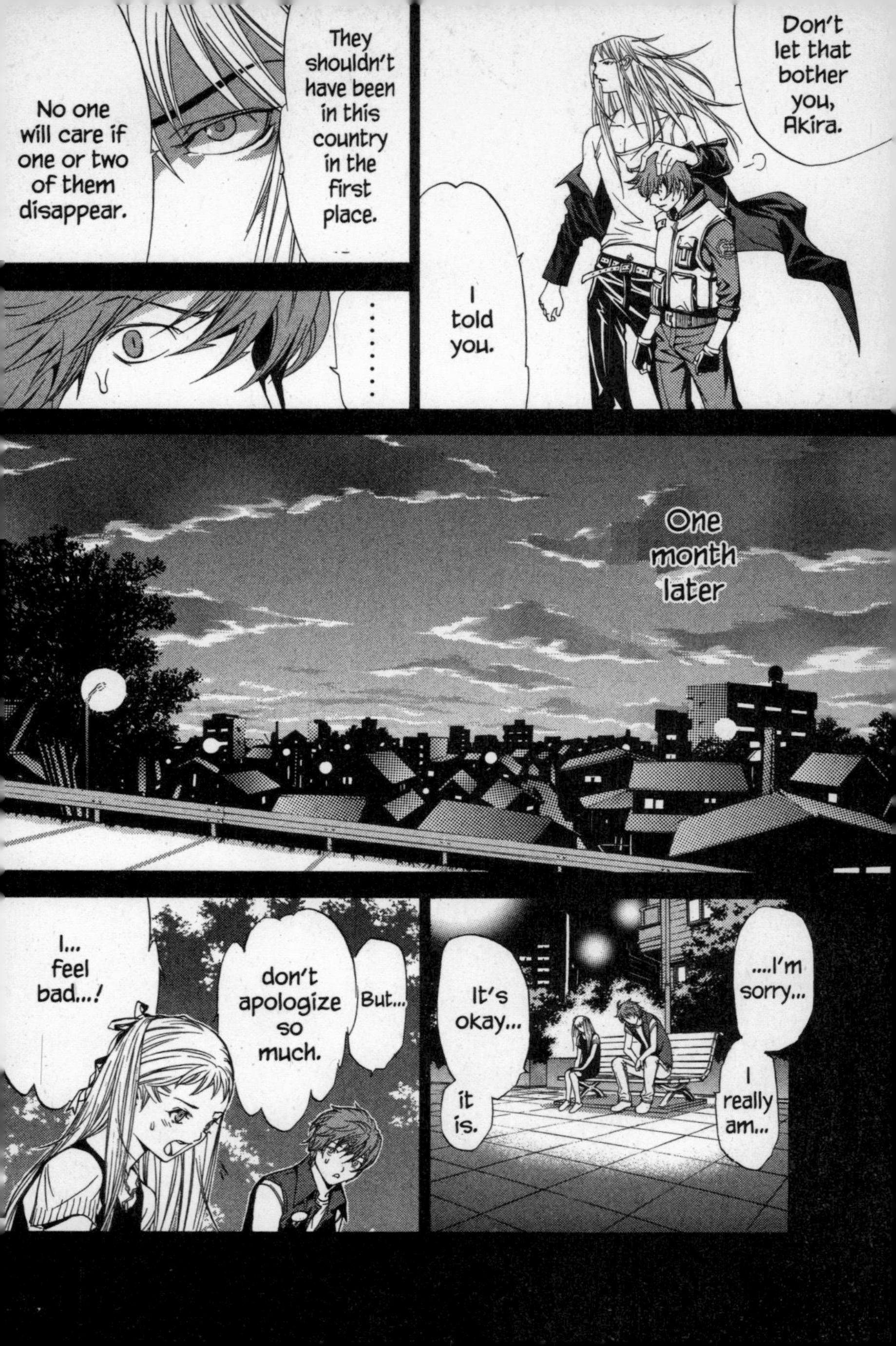
Don't let that bother you, Akira.
I told you.
They shouldn't have been in this country in the first place.
No one will care if one or two of them disappear.
......
One month later
....I'm sorry...
I really am...
It's okay...
it is.
But...
don't apologize so much.
I... feel bad...!

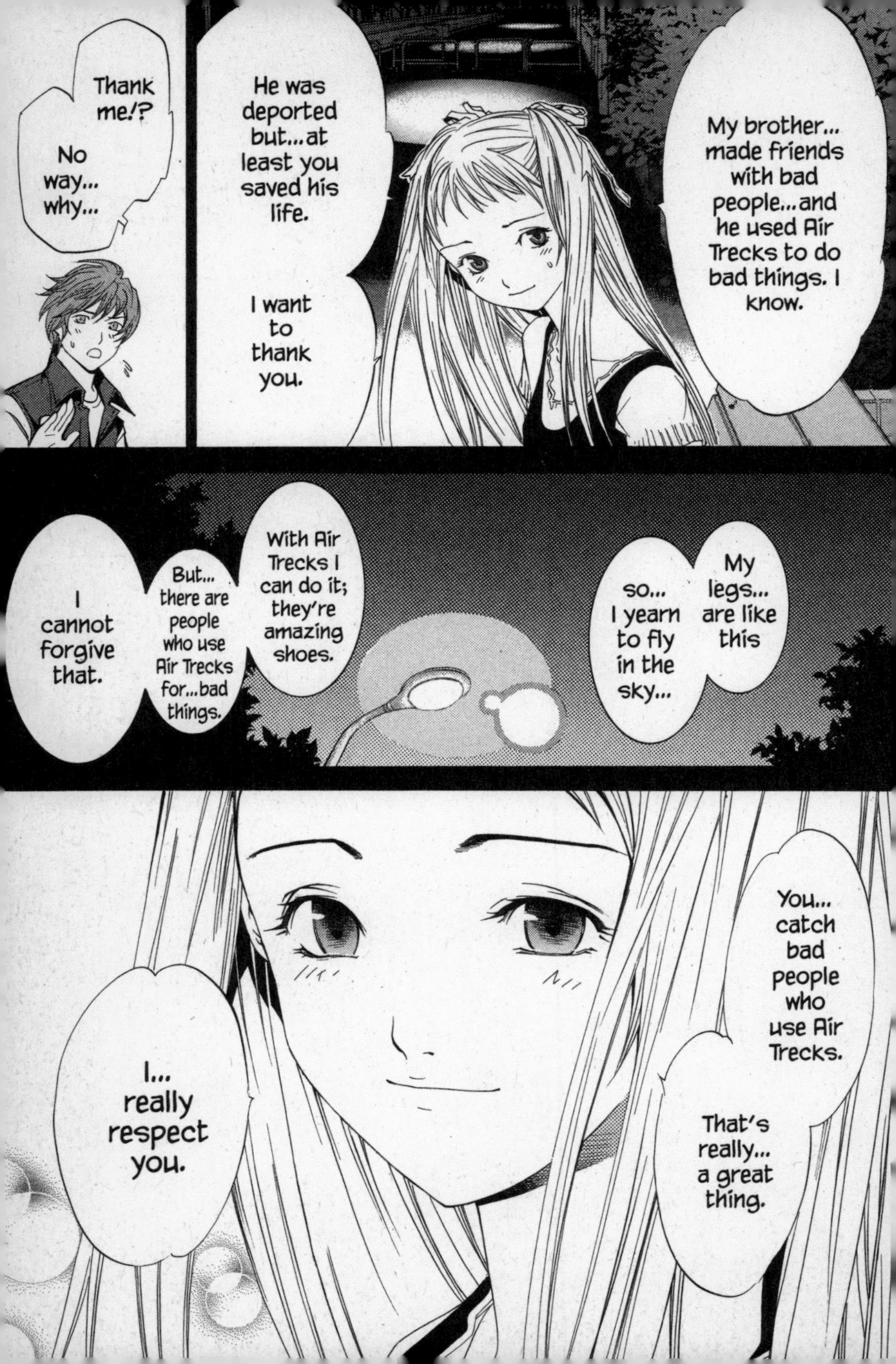
My brother... made friends with bad people...and he used Air Trecks to do bad things. I know.
He was deported but...at least you saved his life.
I want to thank you.
Thank me!?
No way... why...
My legs... are like this
so... I yearn to fly in the sky...
With Air Trecks I can do it; they're amazing shoes.
But... there are people who use Air Trecks for...bad things.
I cannot forgive that.
You... catch bad people who use Air Trecks.
That's really... a great thing.
I... really respect you.

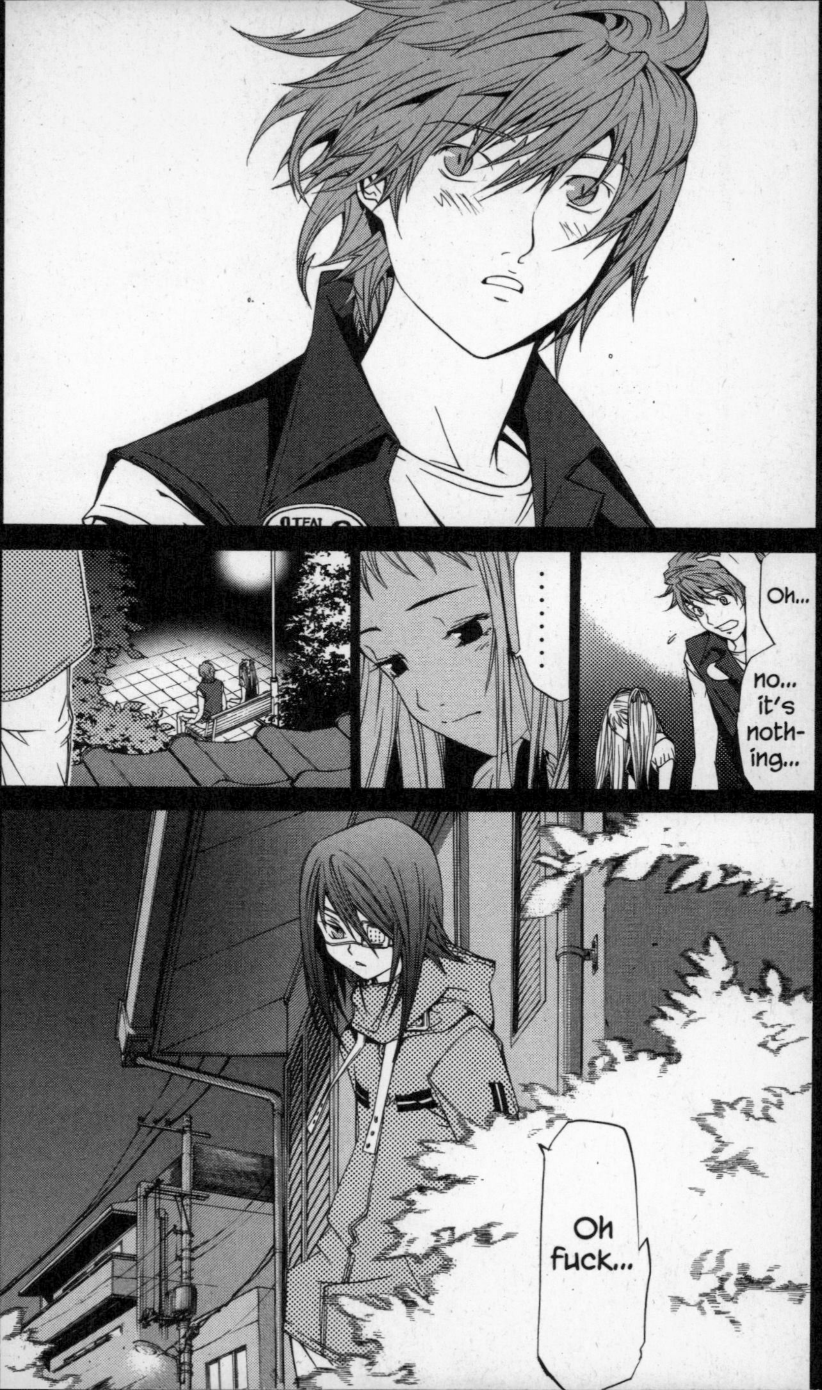
Oh... no... it's noth-ing...
......
Oh fuck...

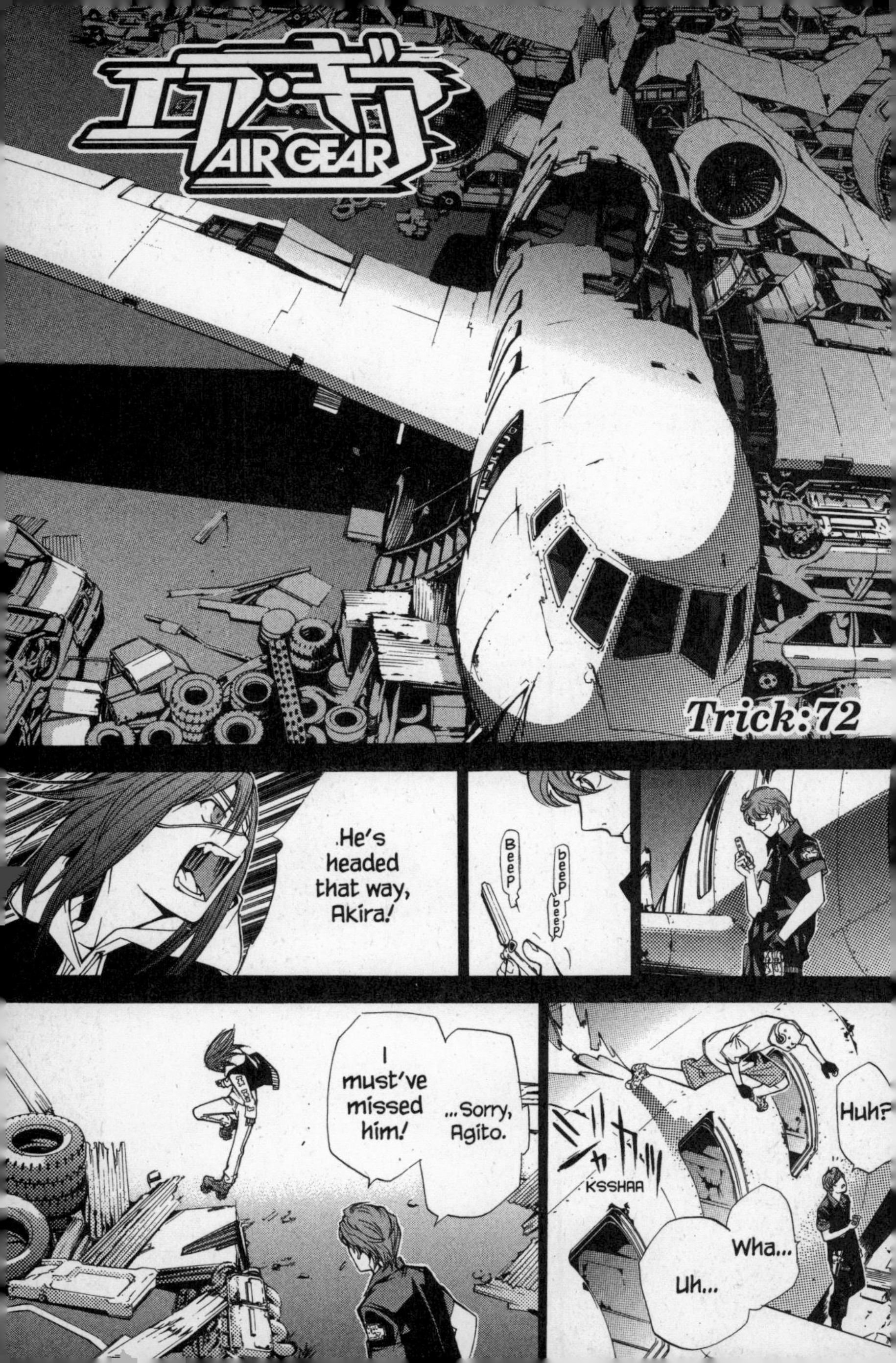

AIR GEAR
Trick:72
Beep
beep beep
He's headed that way, Akira!
Huh?
KSSHAA
Wha...
Uh...
...Sorry, Agito.
I must've missed him!

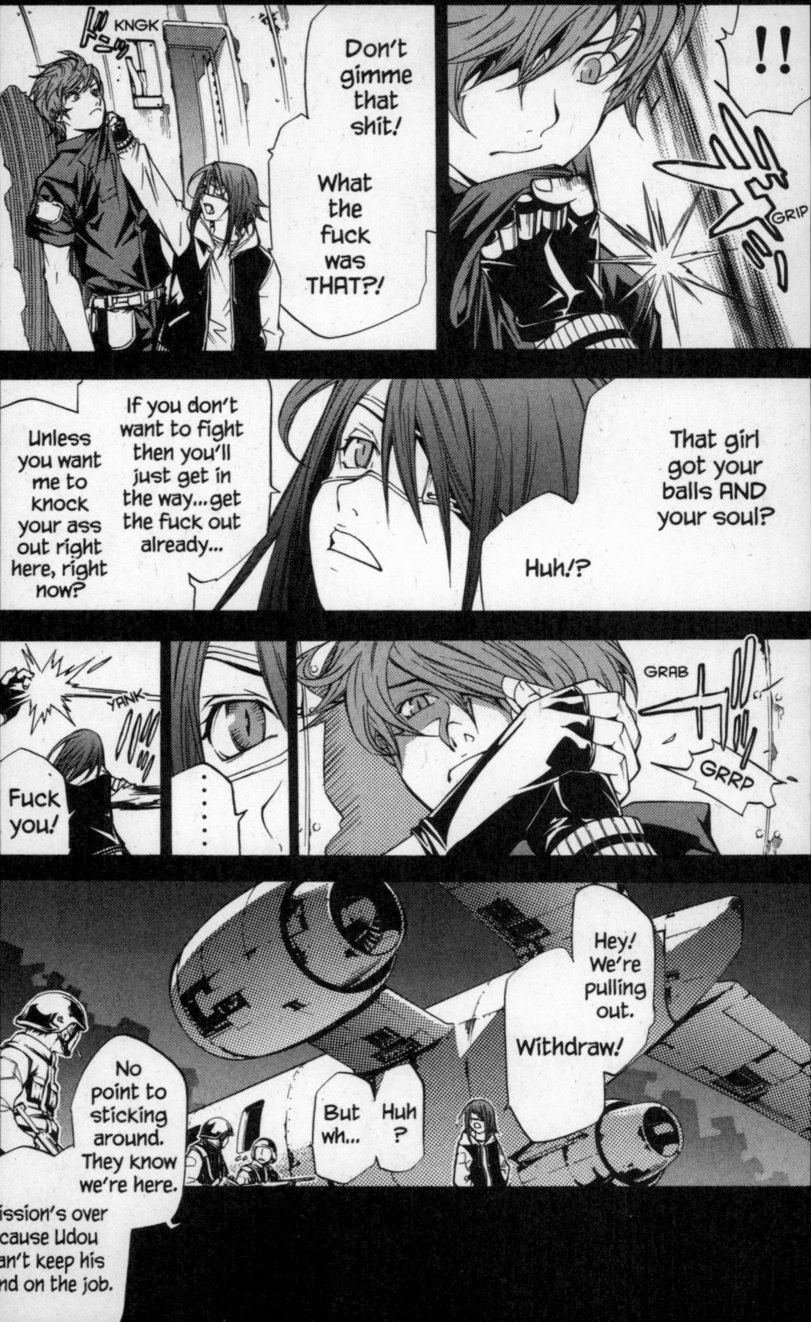
!!
GRIP
KNGK
Don't gimme that shit!
What the fuck was THAT?!
That girl got your balls AND your soul?
Huh!?
If you don't want to fight then you'll just get in the way...get the fuck out already...
Unless you want me to knock your ass out right here, right now?
GRAB
GRRP
......
YANK
Fuck you!
Hey! We're pulling out.
Withdraw!
Huh ?
But wh...
No point to sticking around. They know we're here.
ission's over cause Udou an't keep his nd on the job.

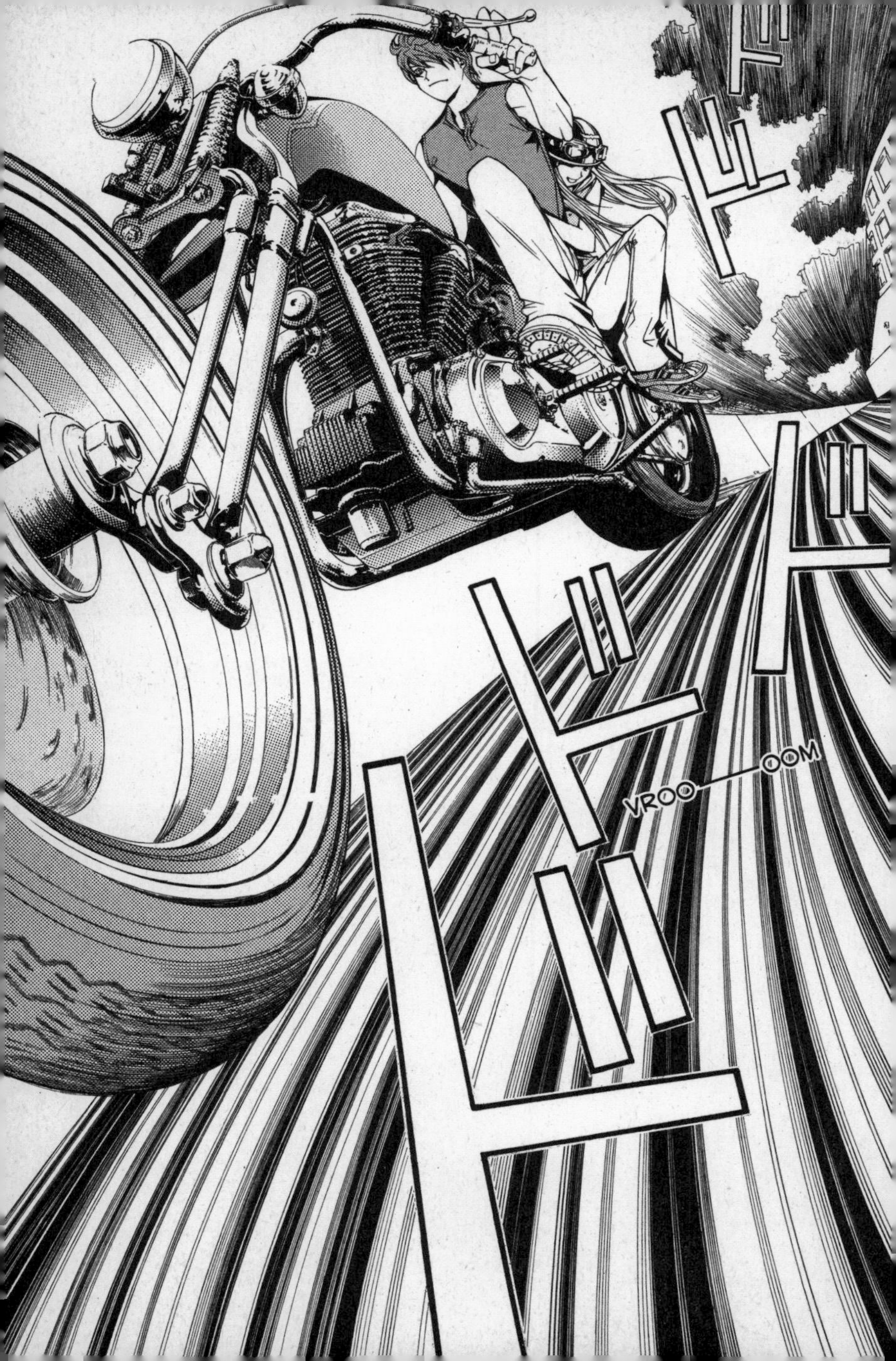
VROO——OOM

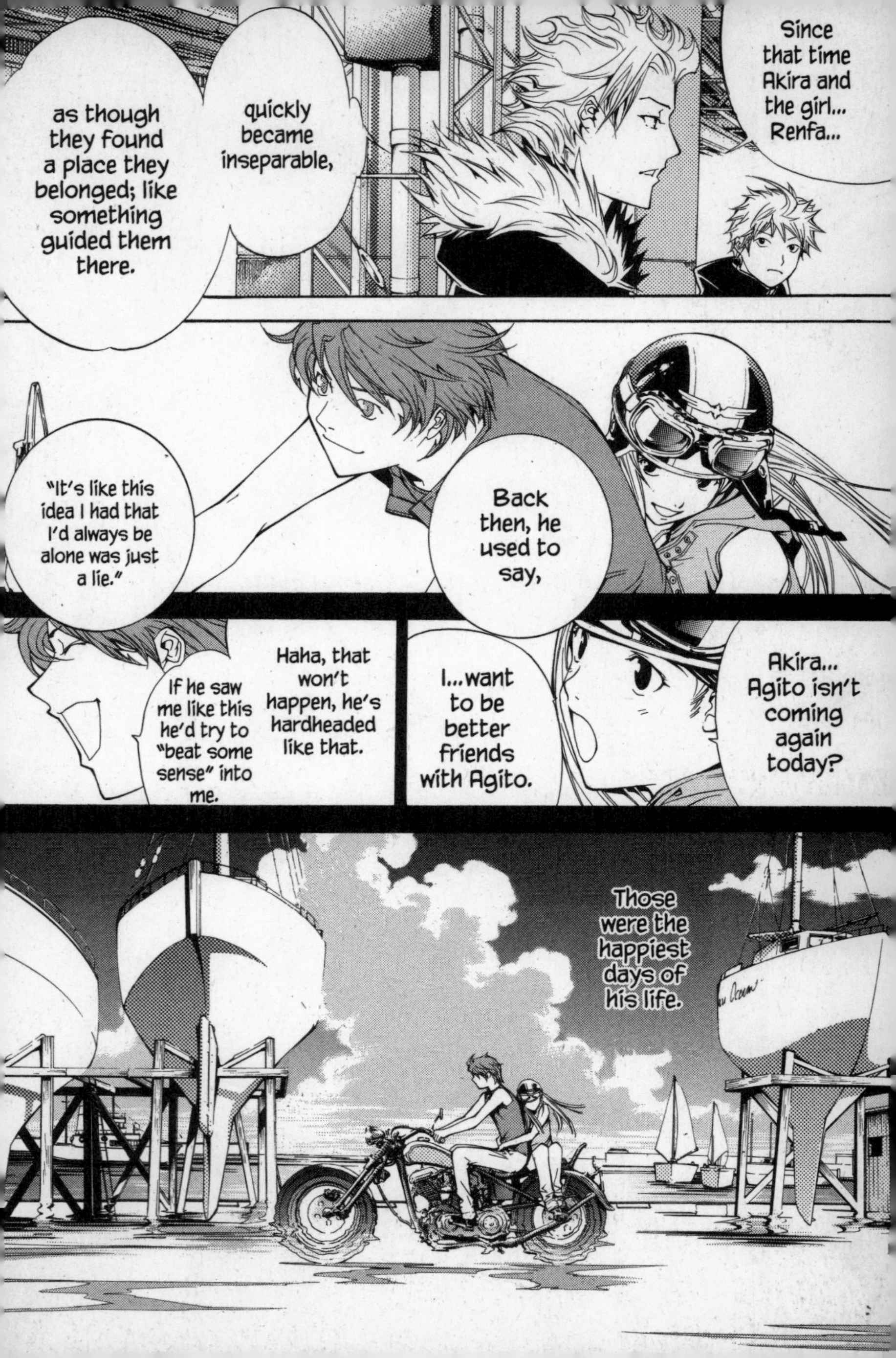
Since that time Akira and the girl... Renfa...
quickly became inseparable,
as though they found a place they belonged; like something guided them there.
Back then, he used to say,
"It's like this idea I had that I'd always be alone was just a lie."
Akira... Agito isn't coming again today?
I...want to be better friends with Agito.
Haha, that won't happen, he's hardheaded like that.
If he saw me like this he'd try to "beat some sense" into me.
Those were the happiest days of his life.

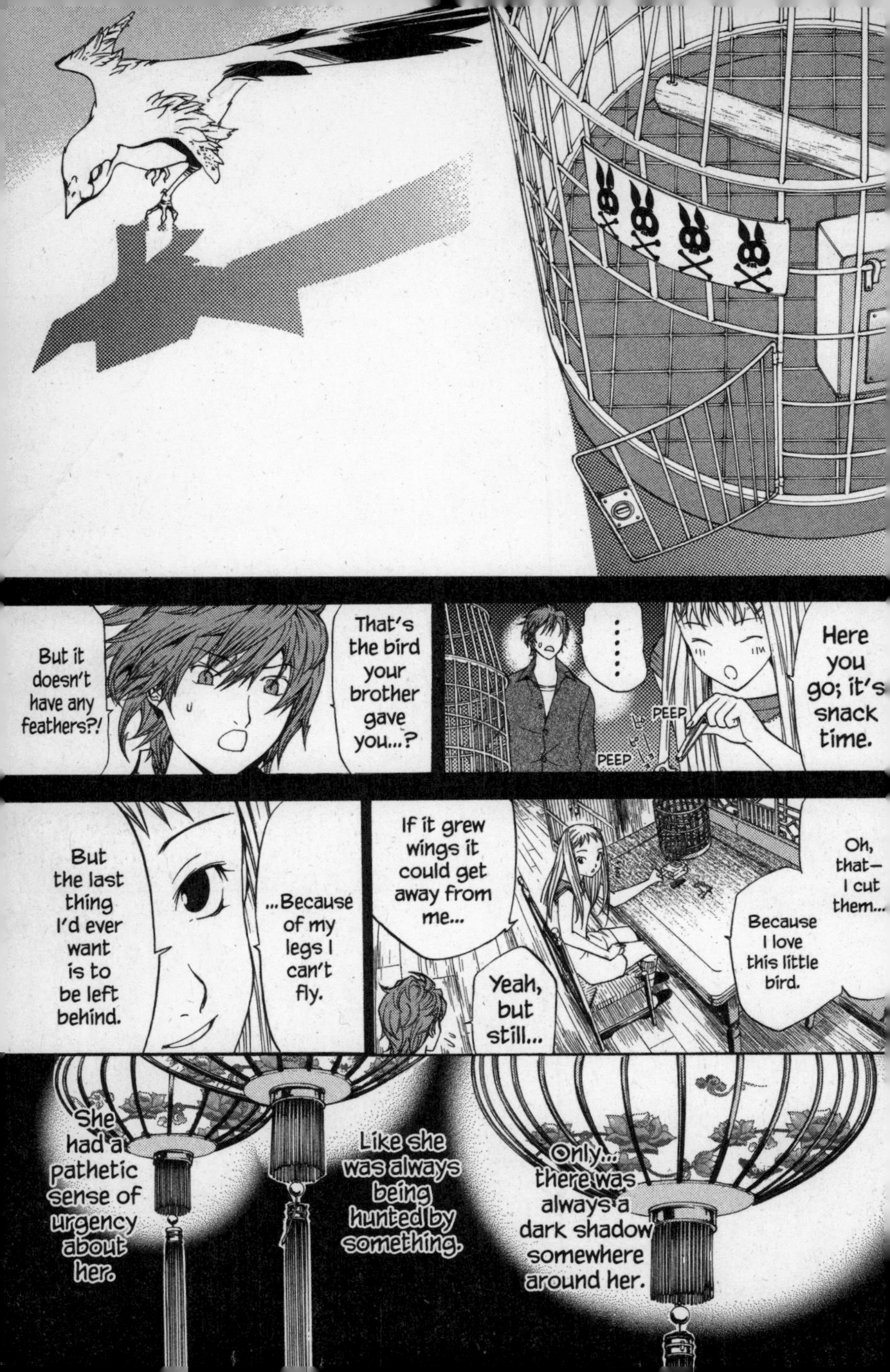
Here you go; it's snack time.
PEEP
PEEP
......
That's the bird your brother gave you...?
But it doesn't have any feathers?!
Oh, that— I cut them...
Because I love this little bird.
Yeah, but still...
If it grew wings it could get away from me...
...Because of my legs I can't fly.
But the last thing I'd ever want is to be left behind.
Only... there was always a dark shadow somewhere around her.
Like she was always being hunted by something.
She had a pathetic sense of urgency about her.

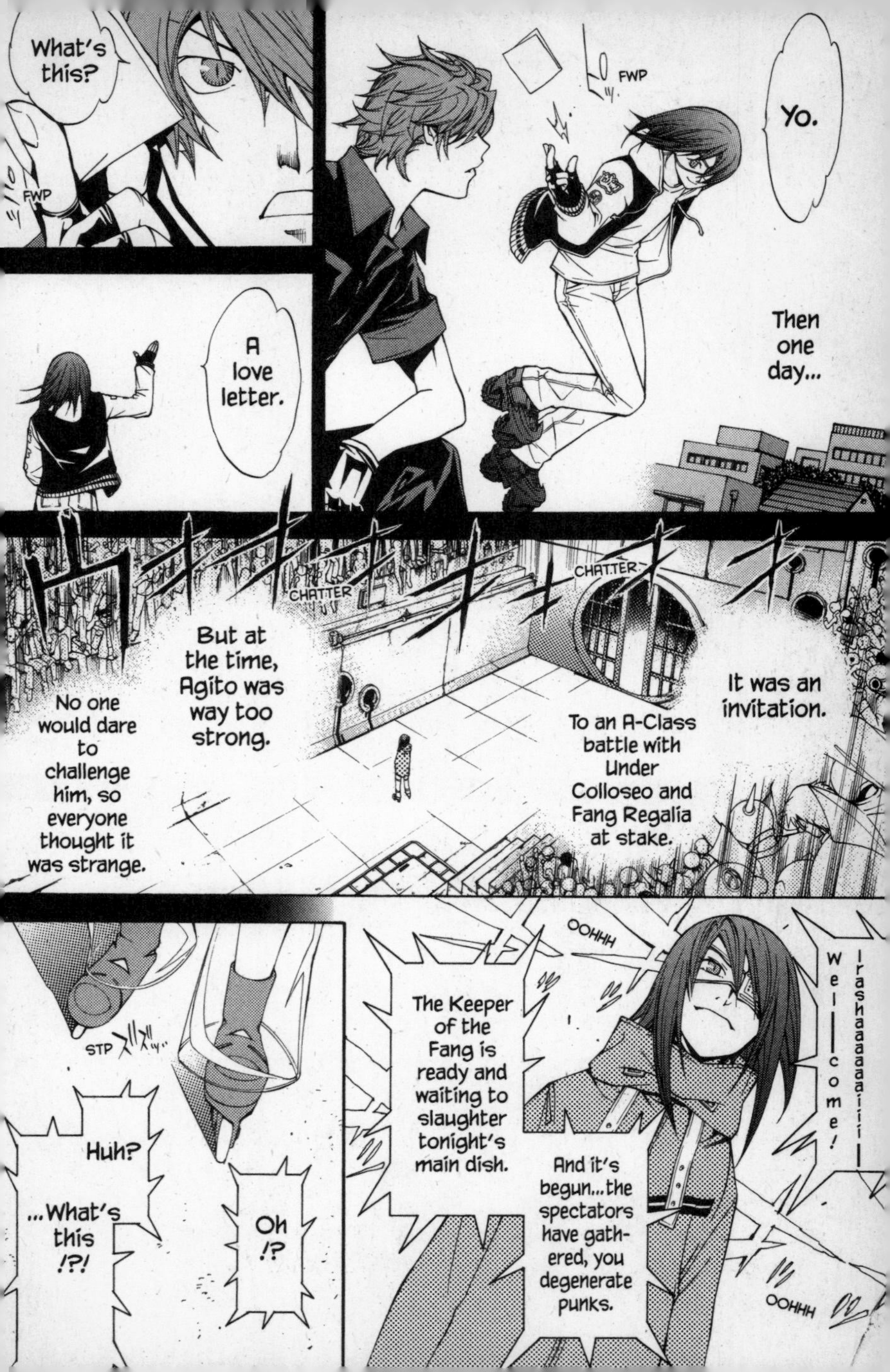
Yo.
FWP
Then one day...
What's this?
FWP
A love letter.
It was an invitation.
To an A-Class battle with Under Colloseo and Fang Regalia at stake.
CHATTER
CHATTER
But at the time, Agito was way too strong.
No one would dare to challenge him, so everyone thought it was strange.
Irashaaaaaaiiii
Wel–come!
OOHHH
The Keeper of the Fang is ready and waiting to slaughter tonight's main dish.
And it's begun...the spectators have gath-ered, you degenerate punks.
OOHHH
Oh!?
STP
Huh?
...What's this!?!

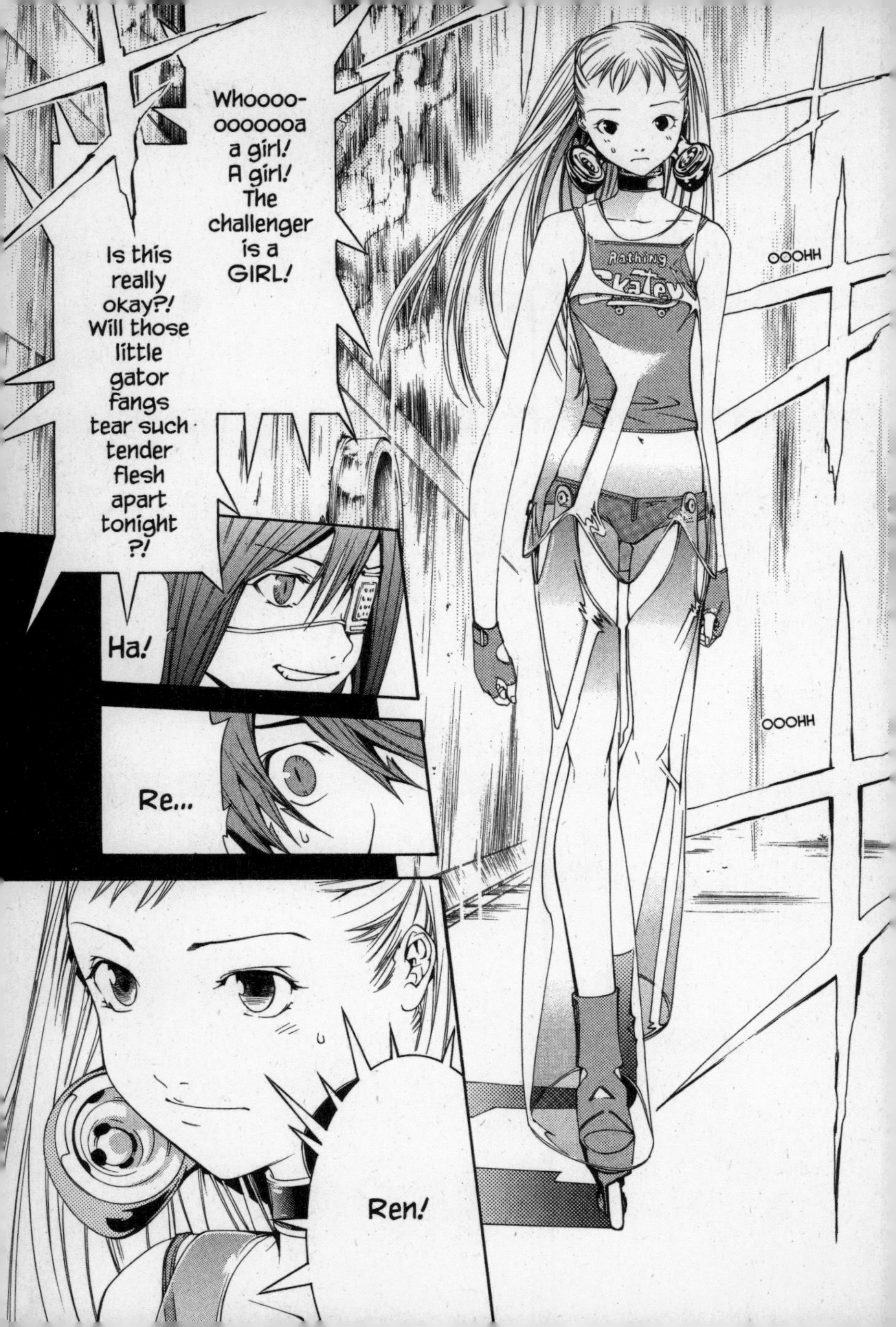
OOOHH
OOOHH
Whoooo-ooooooa a girl! A girl! The challenger is a GIRL!
Is this really okay?! Will those little gator fangs tear such tender flesh apart tonight?!
Ha!
Re...
Ren!

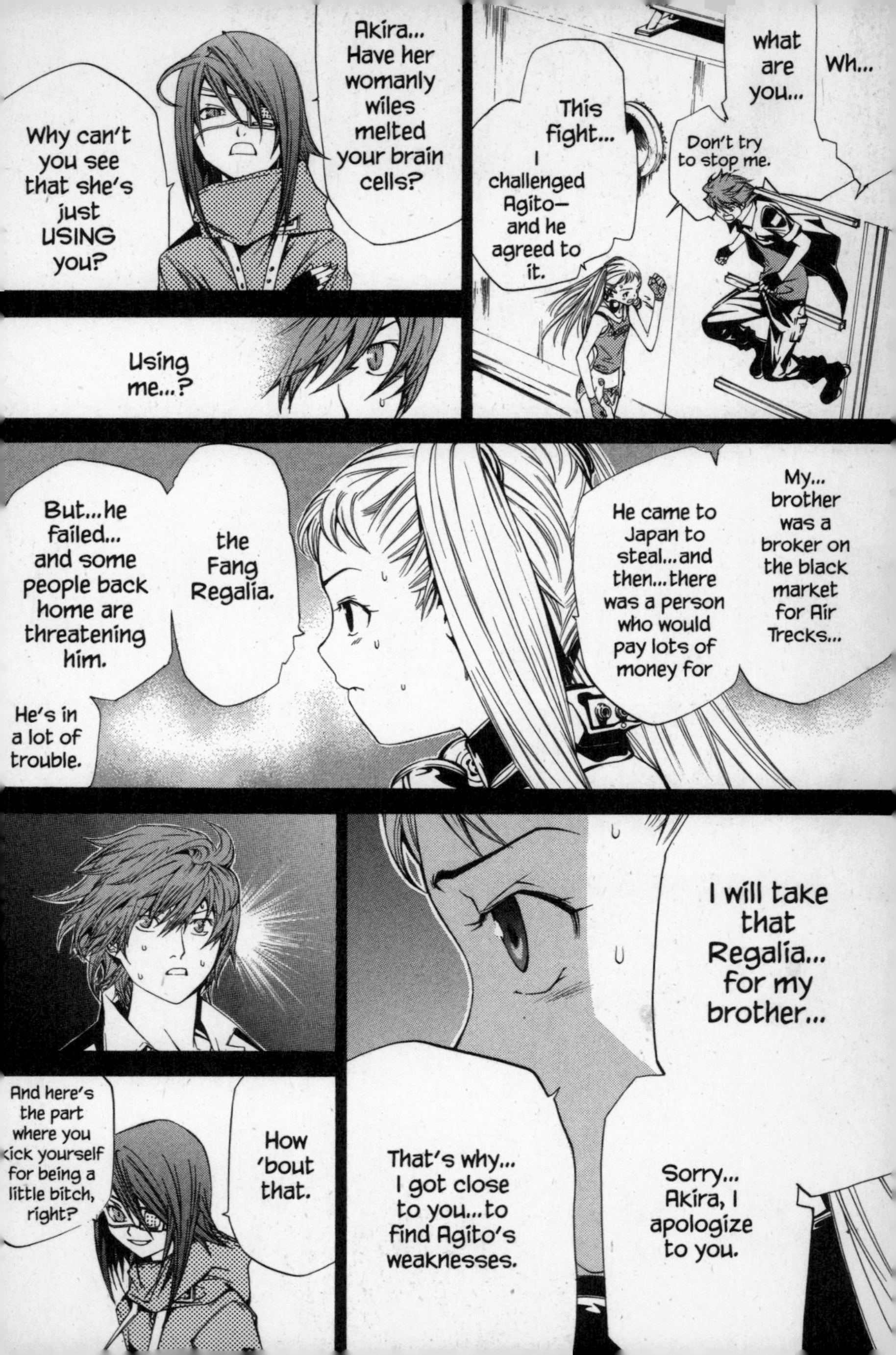
Wh...
what are you...
Don't try to stop me.
This fight...
I challenged Agito—and he agreed to it.
Akira... Have her womanly wiles melted your brain cells?
Why can't you see that she's just USING you?
Using me...?
My... brother was a broker on the black market for Air Trecks...
He came to Japan to steal...and then...there was a person who would pay lots of money for
the Fang Regalia.
But...he failed... and some people back home are threatening him.
He's in a lot of trouble.
I will take that Regalia... for my brother...
Sorry... Akira, I apologize to you.
That's why... I got close to you...to find Agito's weaknesses.
How 'bout that.
And here's the part where you kick yourself for being a little bitch, right?

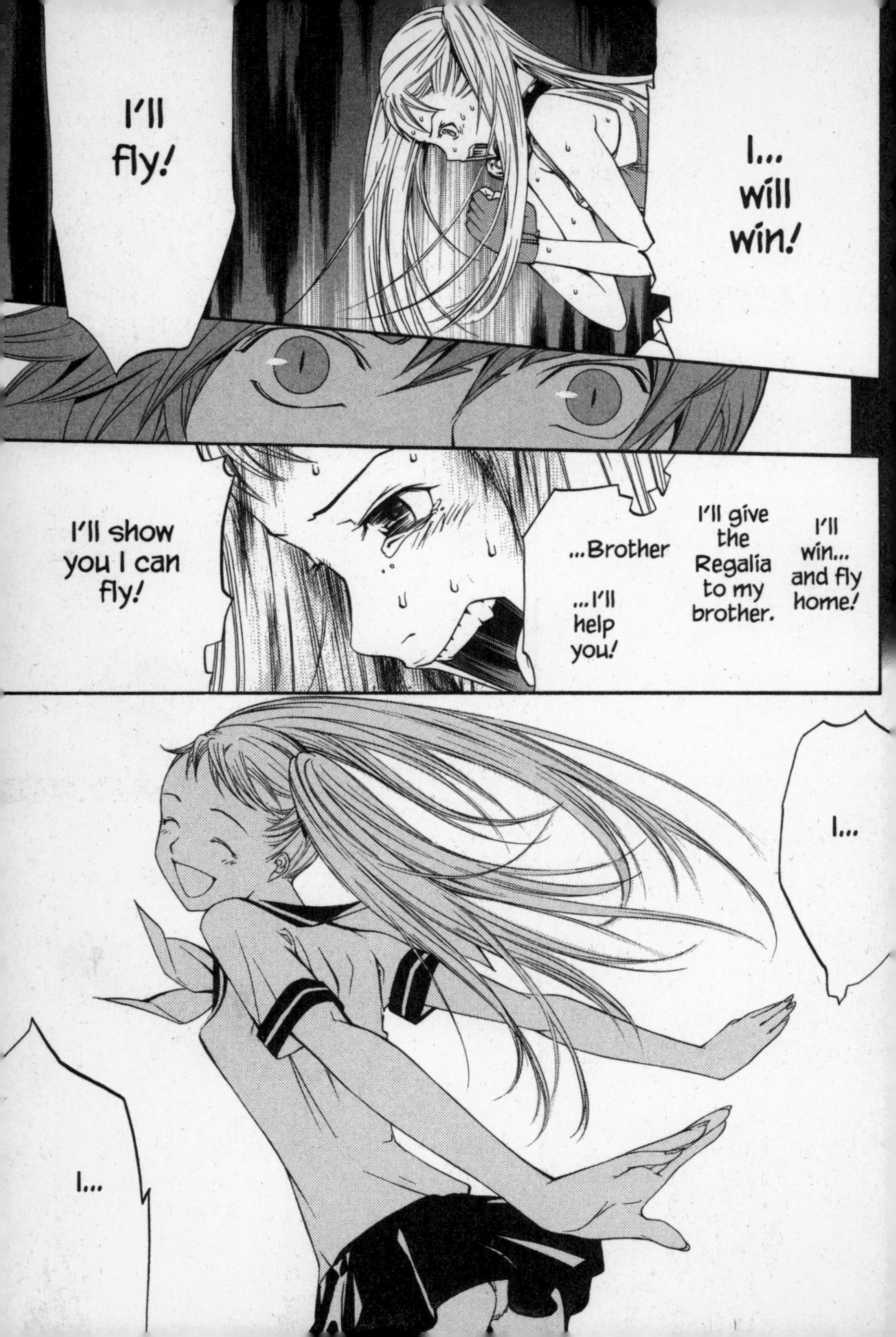

I... will win!
I'll fly!
I'll win... and fly home!
I'll give the Regalia to my brother.
...Brother
...I'll help you!
I'll show you I can fly!
I...
I...

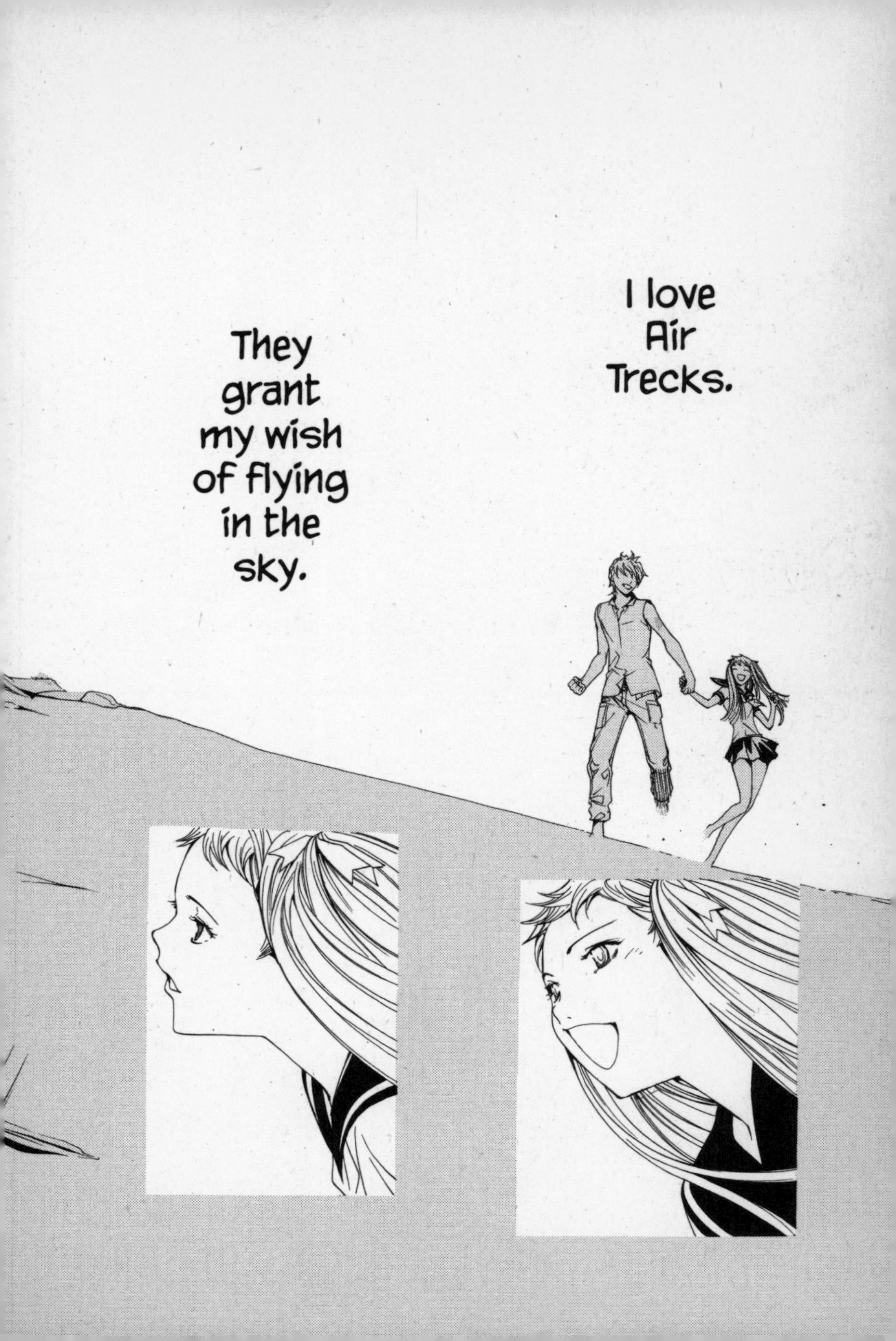
I love Air Trecks.
They grant my wish of flying in the sky.

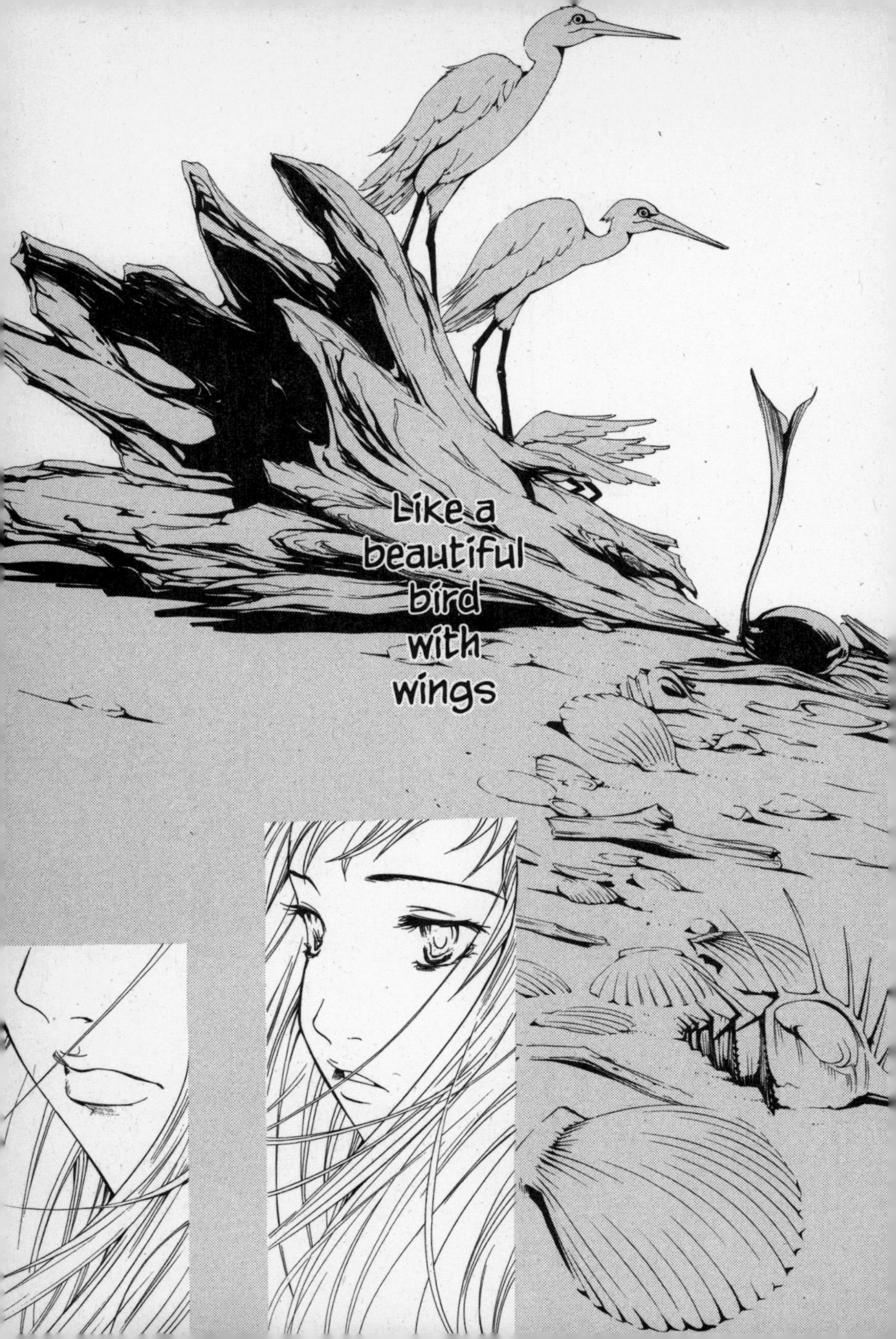
Like a beautiful bird with wings

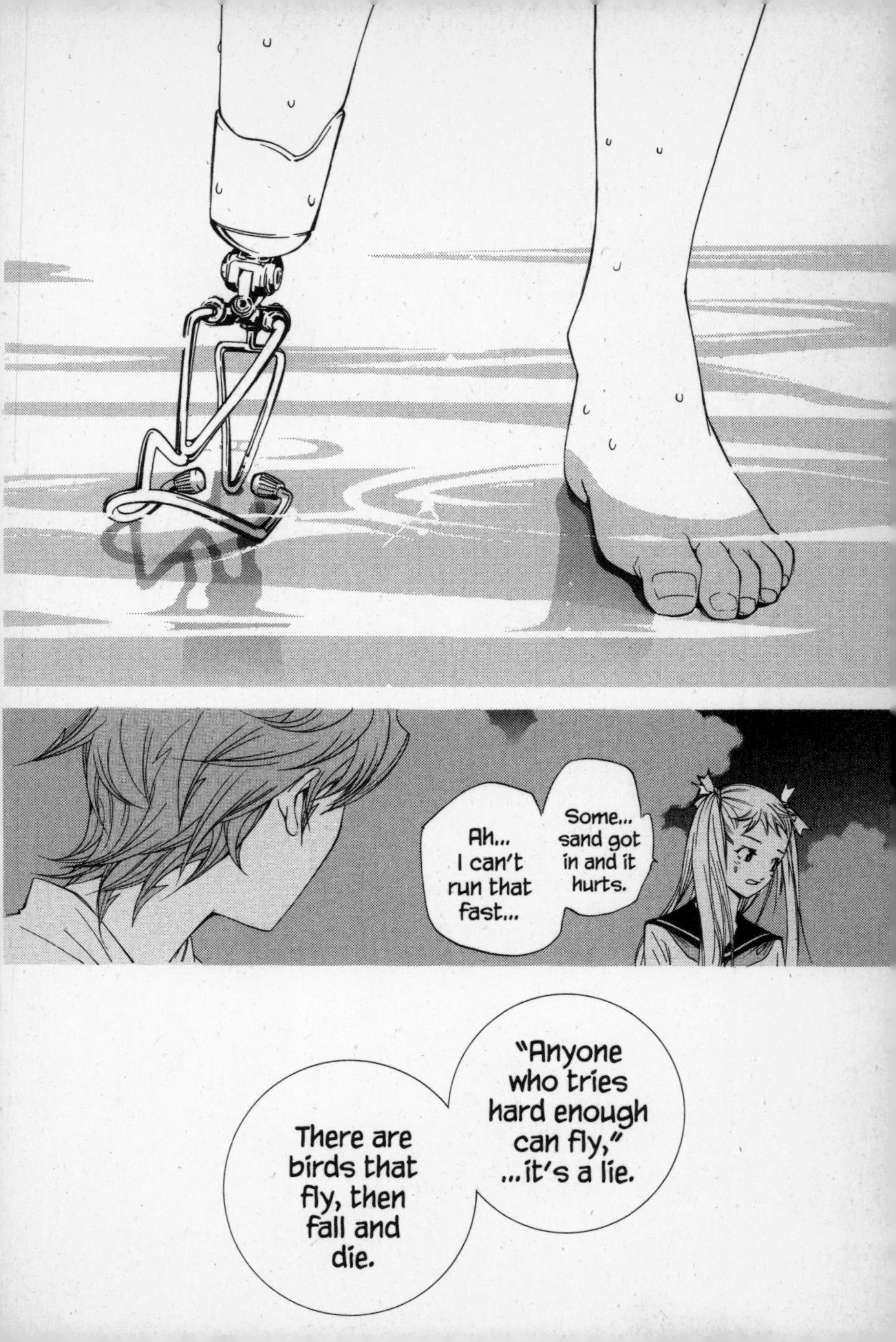
Some... sand got in and it hurts.
Ah... I can't run that fast...
"Anyone who tries hard enough can fly," ...it's a lie.
There are birds that fly, then fall and die.

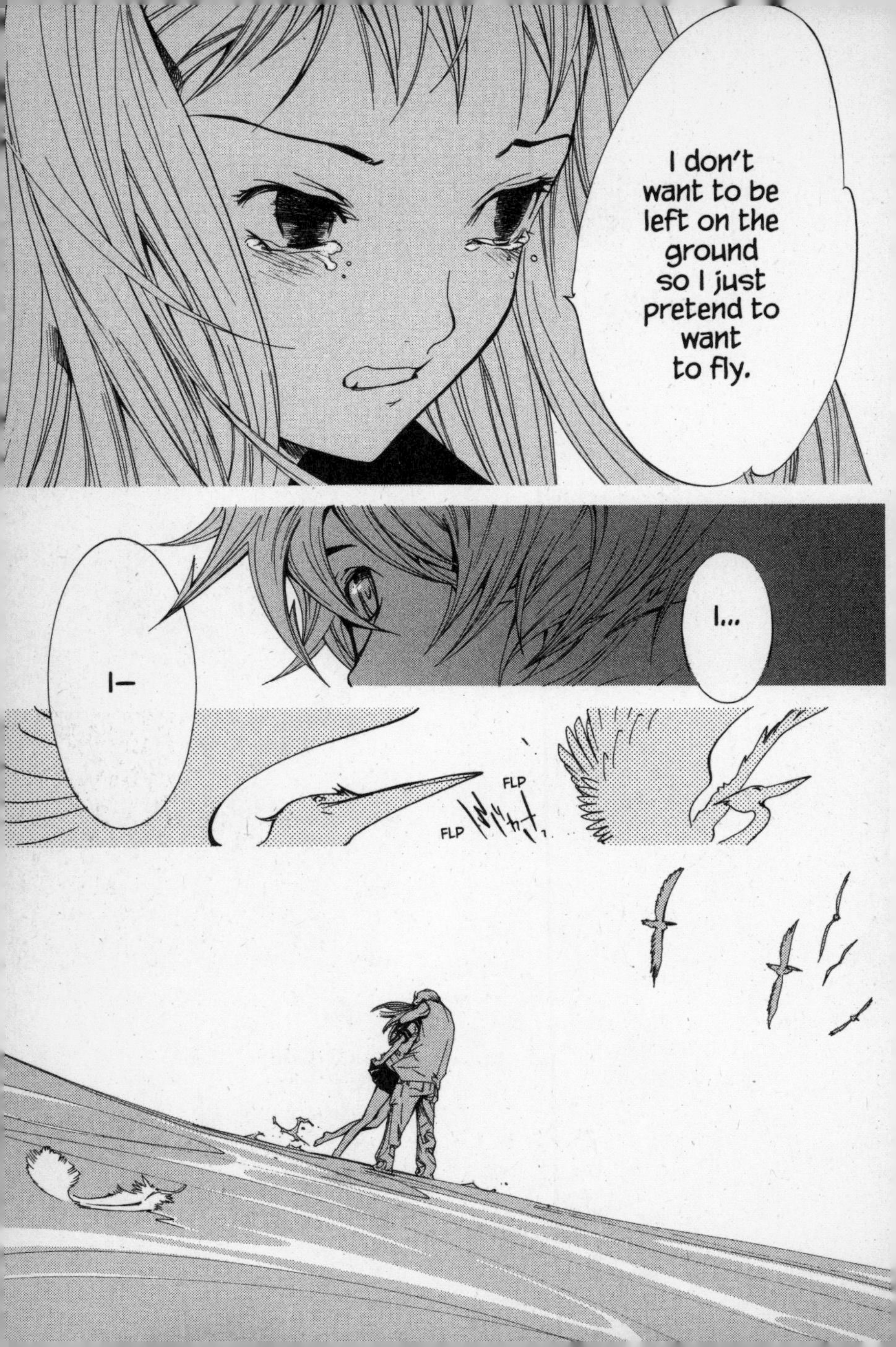

I don't want to be left on the ground so I just pretend to want to fly.
I...
I—
FLP
FLP

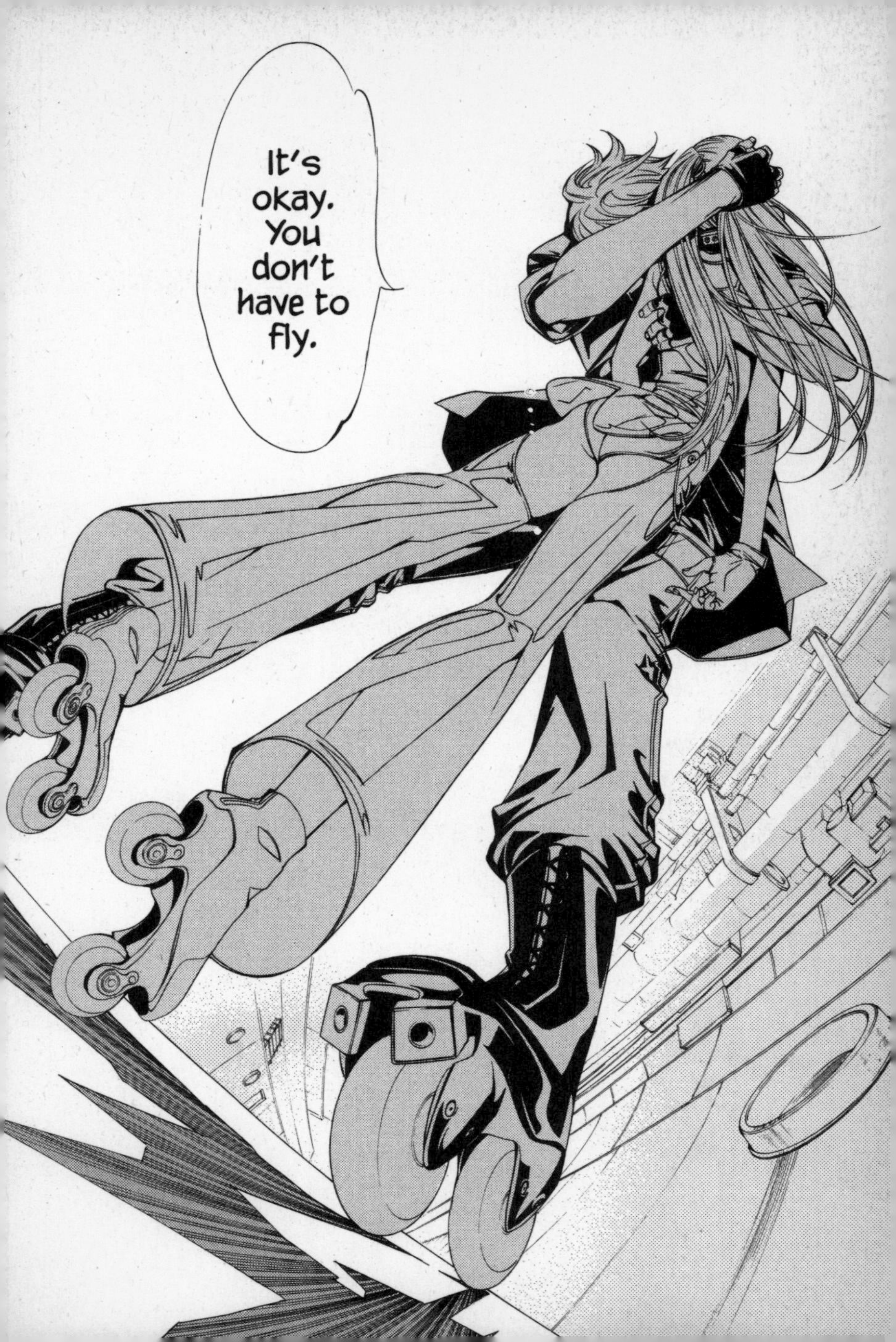
It's okay. You don't have to fly.

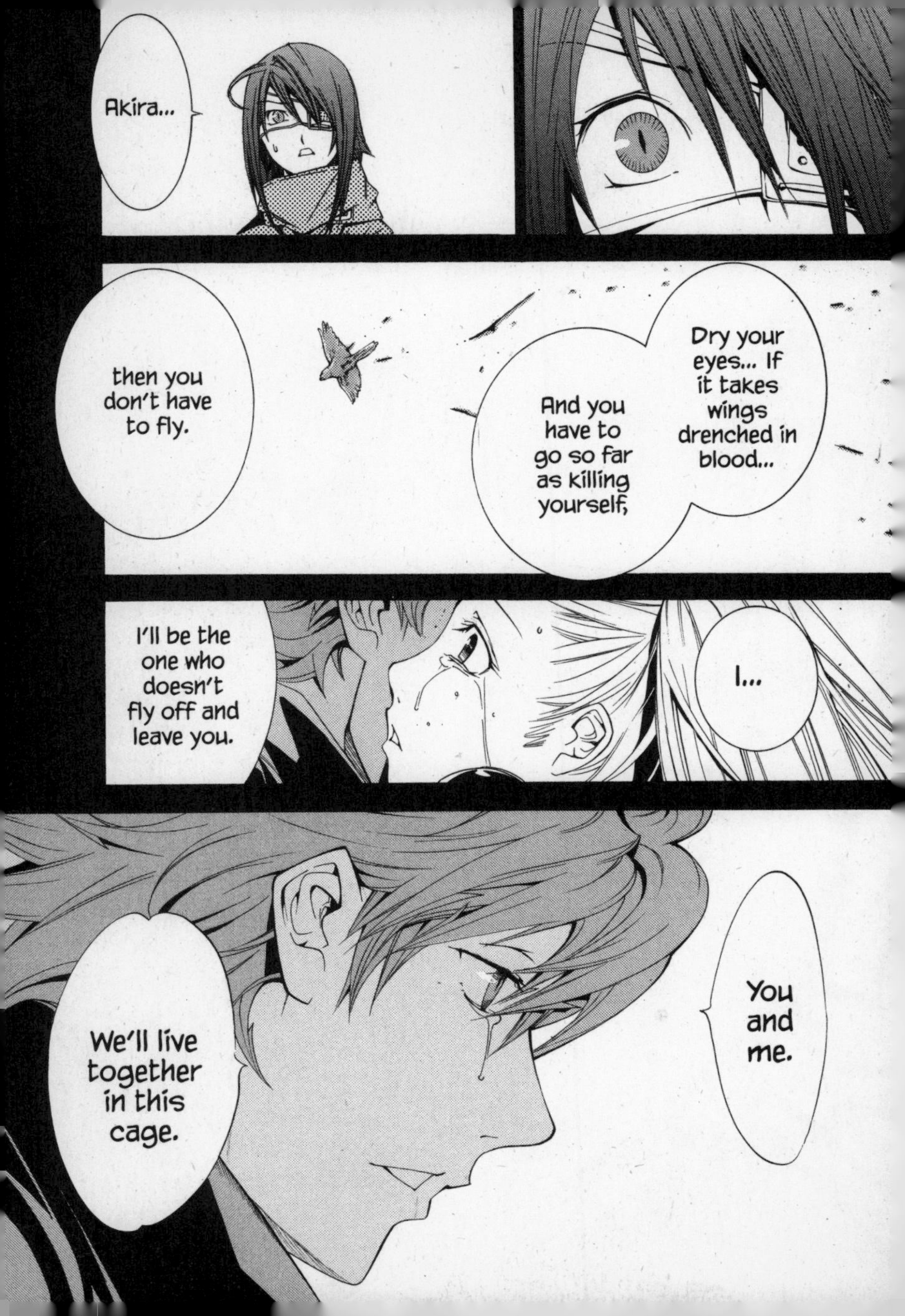
Akira...
Dry your eyes... If it takes wings drenched in blood...
And you have to go so far as killing yourself,
then you don't have to fly.
I...
I'll be the one who doesn't fly off and leave you.
You and me.
We'll live together in this cage.

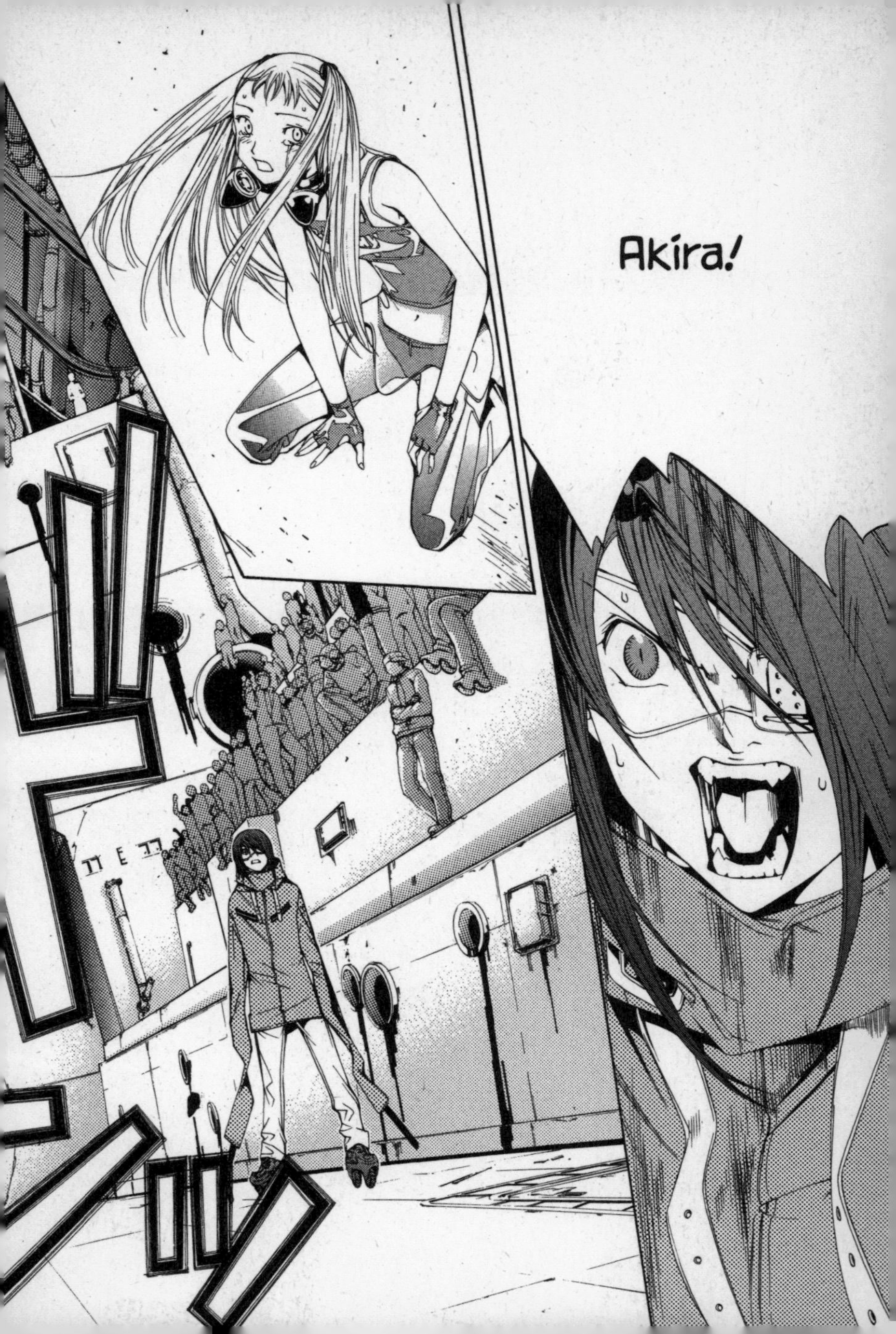
Akira!

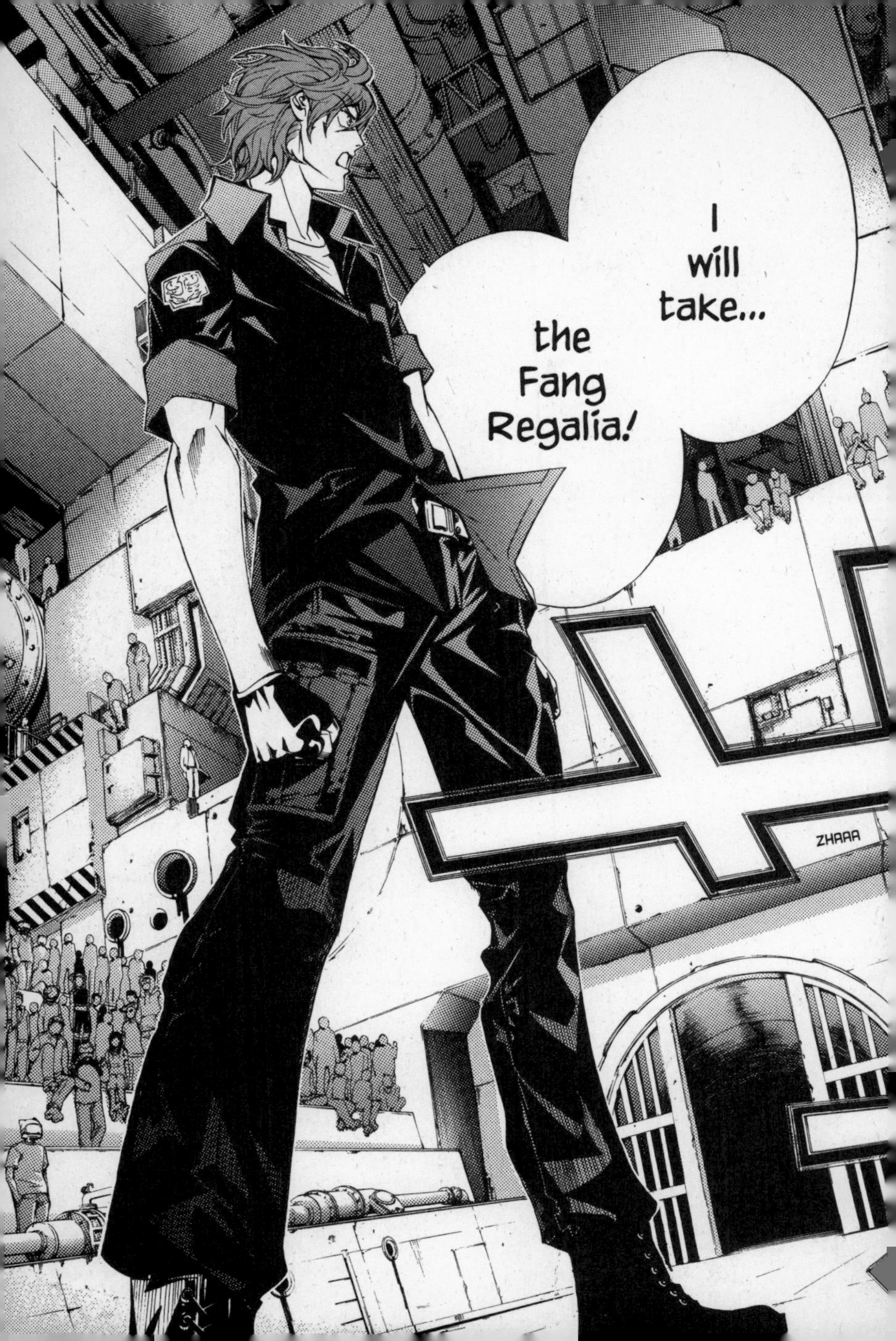
I will take... the Fang Regalia!
ZHAAA

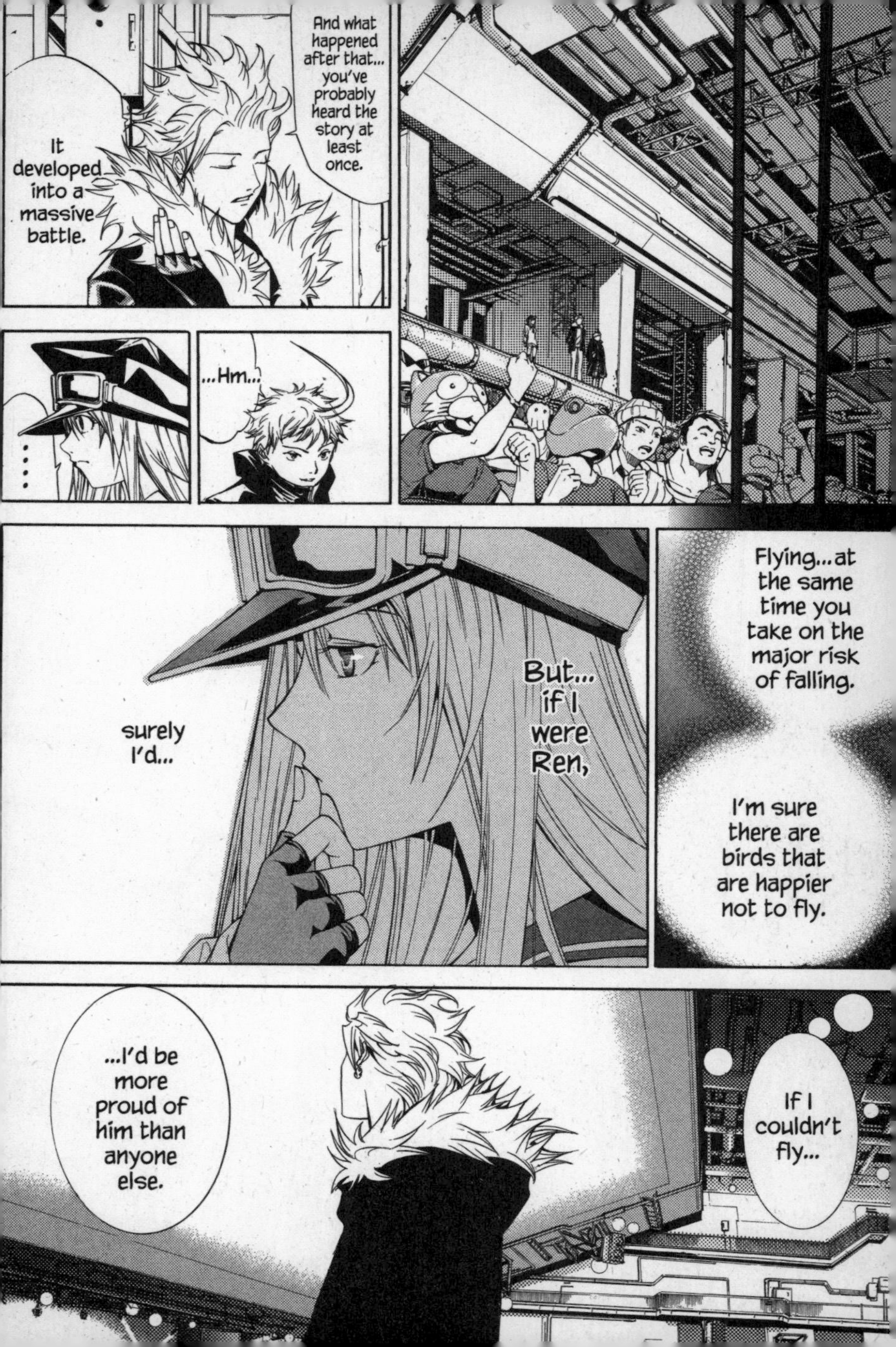
And what happened after that... you've probably heard the story at least once.
It developed into a massive battle.
...Hm...
....
Flying...at the same time you take on the major risk of falling.
I'm sure there are birds that are happier not to fly.
But... if I were Ren,
surely I'd...
If I couldn't fly...
...I'd be more proud of him than anyone else.

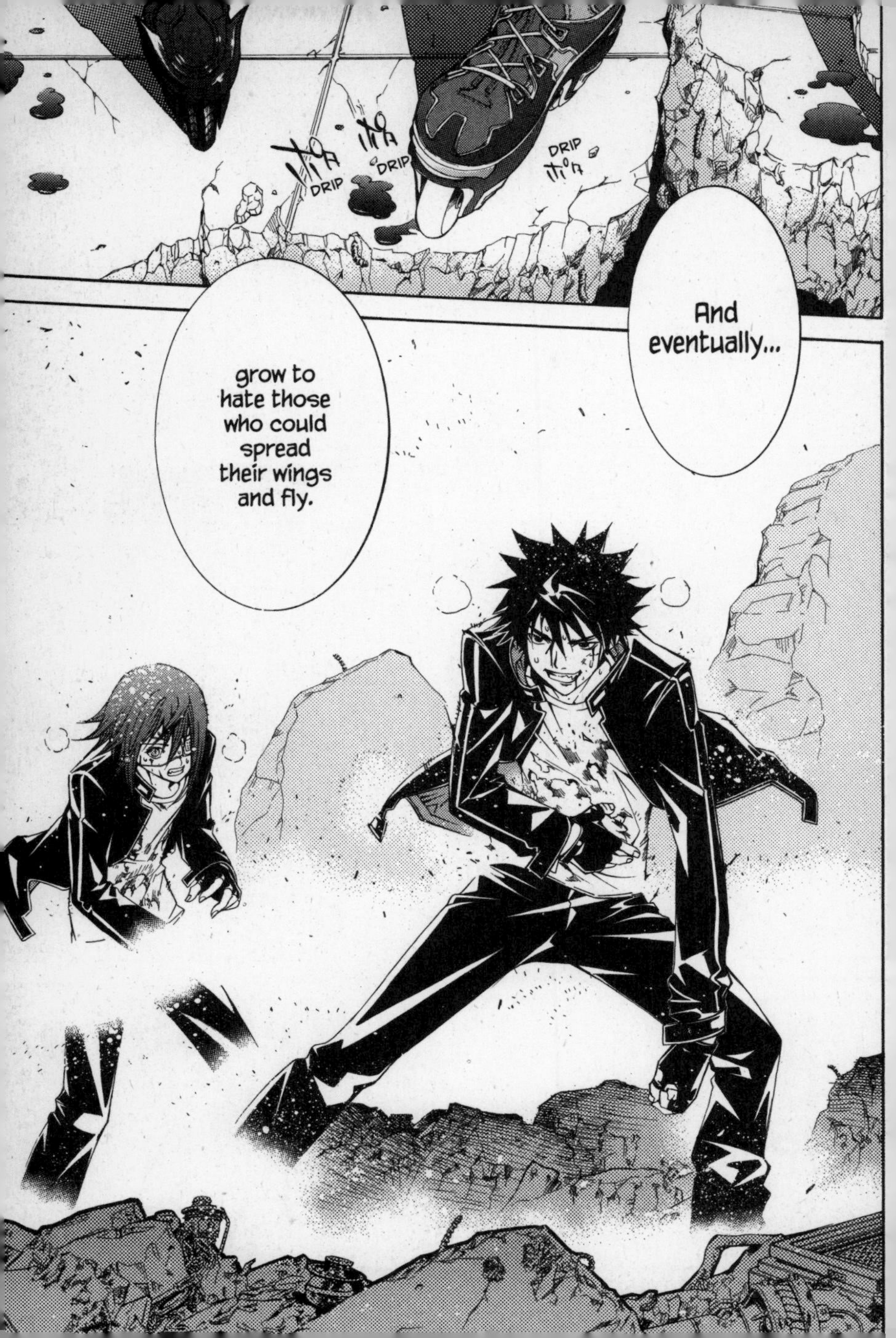
DRIP
DRIP
DRIP
And eventually...
grow to hate those who could spread their wings and fly.

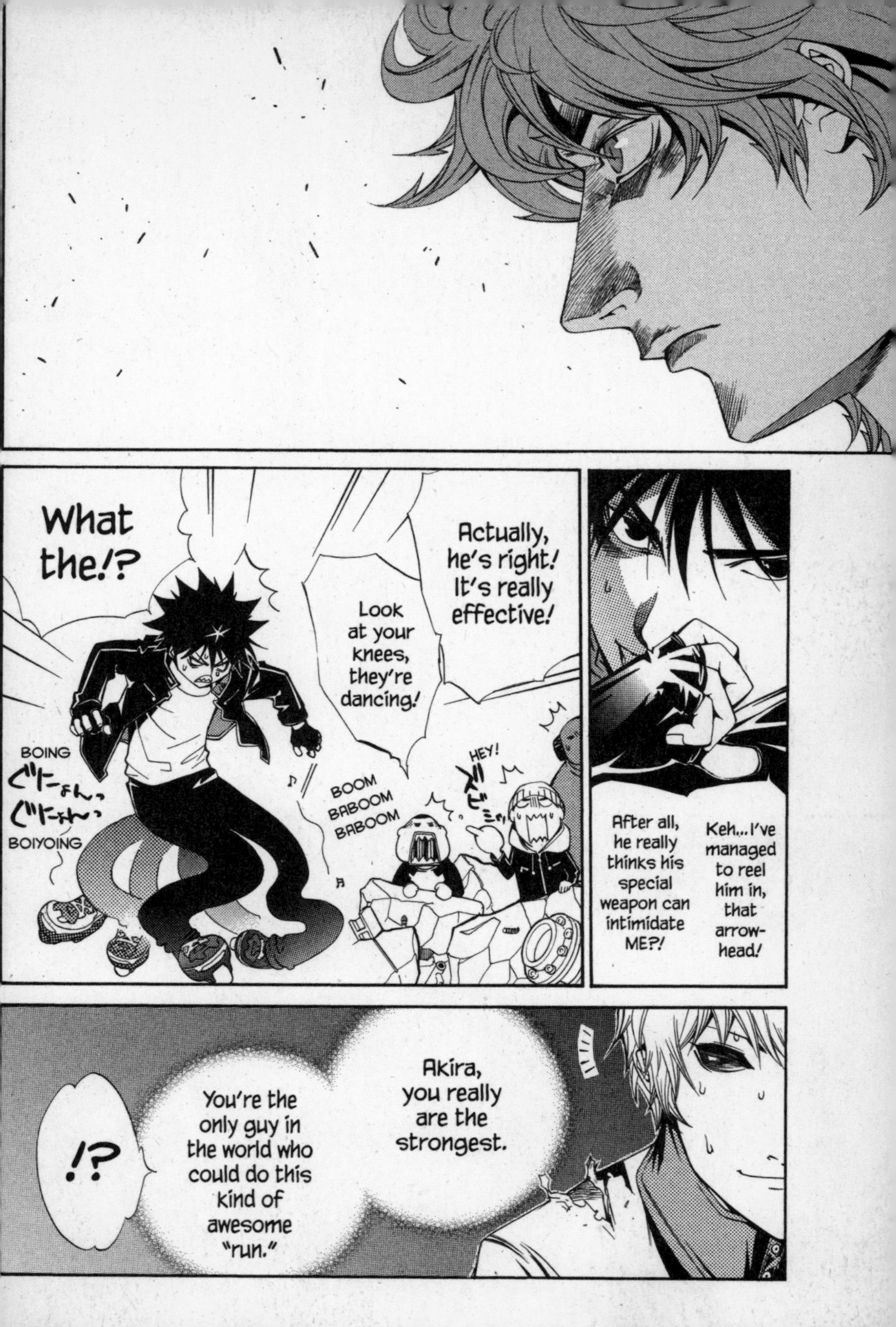
Keh...I've managed to reel him in, that arrowhead!
After all, he really thinks his special weapon can intimidate ME?!
Actually, he's right! It's really effective!
Look at your knees, they're dancing!
HEY!
BOOM BABOOM BABOOM
What the!?
BOING
BOIYOING
Akira, you really are the strongest.
You're the only guy in the world who could do this kind of awesome "run."
!?

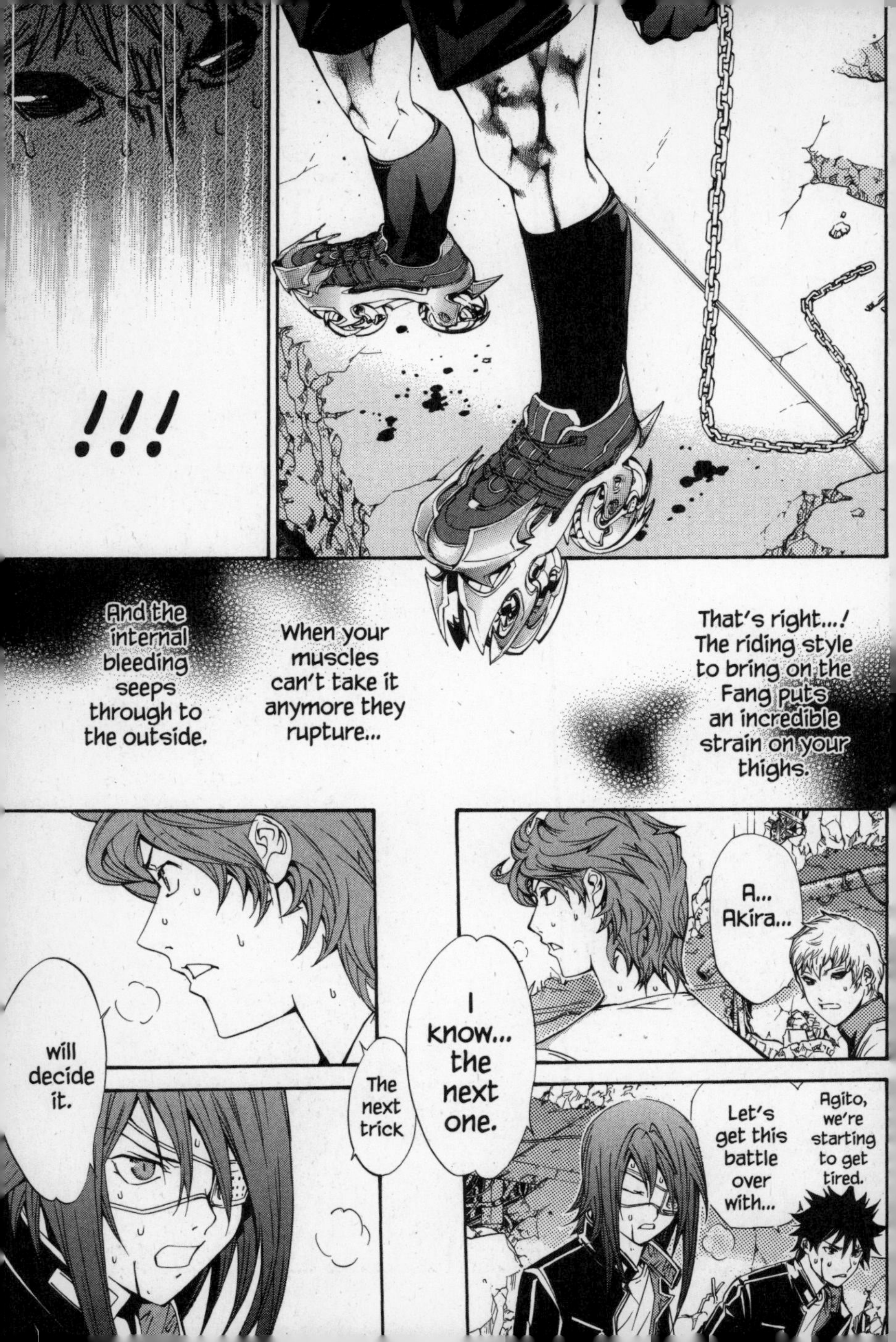
!!!
That's right...! The riding style to bring on the Fang puts an incredible strain on your thighs.
When your muscles can't take it anymore they rupture...
And the internal bleeding seeps through to the outside.
A... Akira...
Agito, we're starting to get tired.
Let's get this battle over with...
I know... the next one.
The next trick
will decide it.

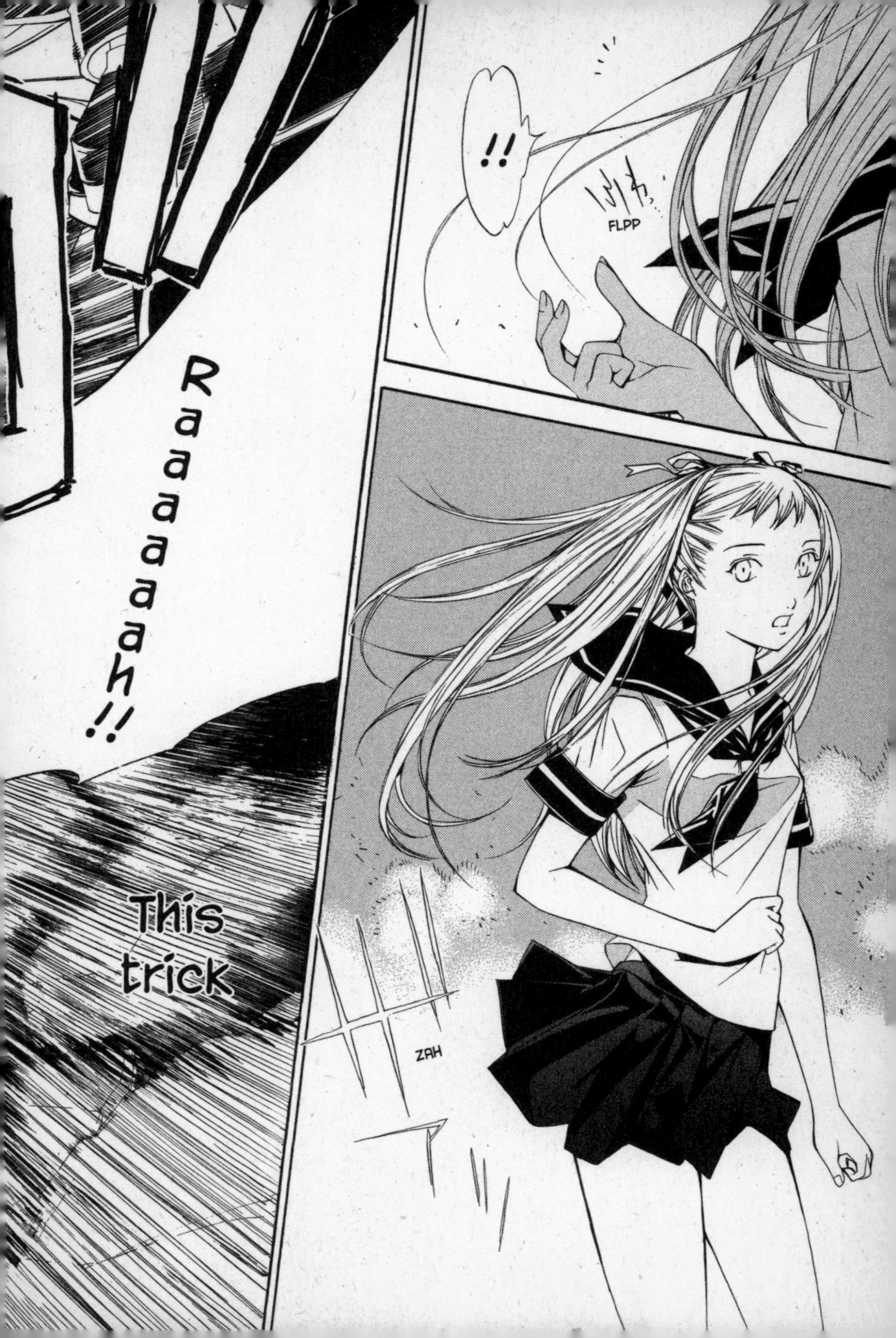
!!
FLPP
ZAH
Raaaaaaah!!
This trick

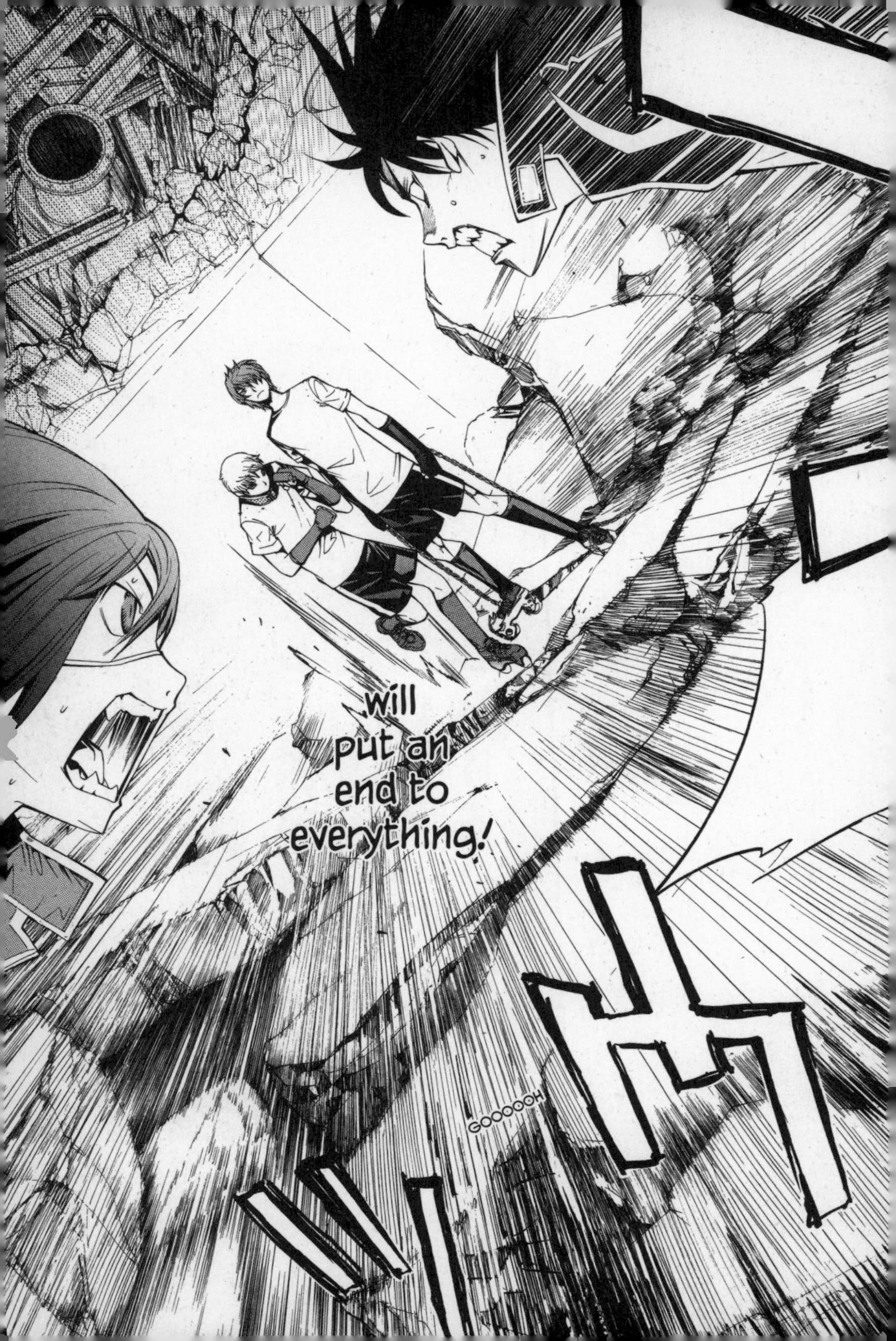
...will put an end to everything!
GOOOOOH

**Event File 1**
**(Toxic Star brand DJ Event)**
**I received a package marked with a bird cage from a fan with a T-shirt in it. I really appreciated it!**

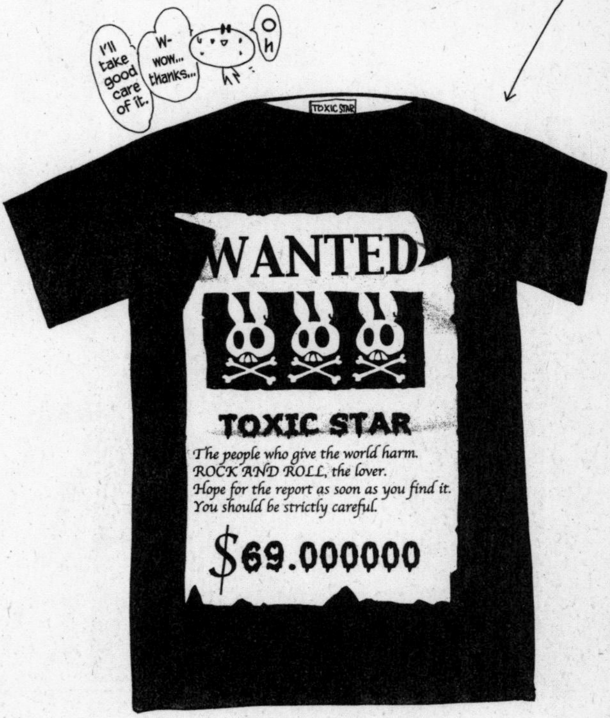
Oh
W- wow... thanks...
I'll take good care of it.
TOXIC STAR
WANTED
TOXIC STAR
The people who give the world harm.
ROCK AND ROLL, the lover.
Hope for the report as soon as you find it.
You should be strictly careful.
$69.000000

I see it in magazines a lot! The pierced ear is cool.

# Trick: 73

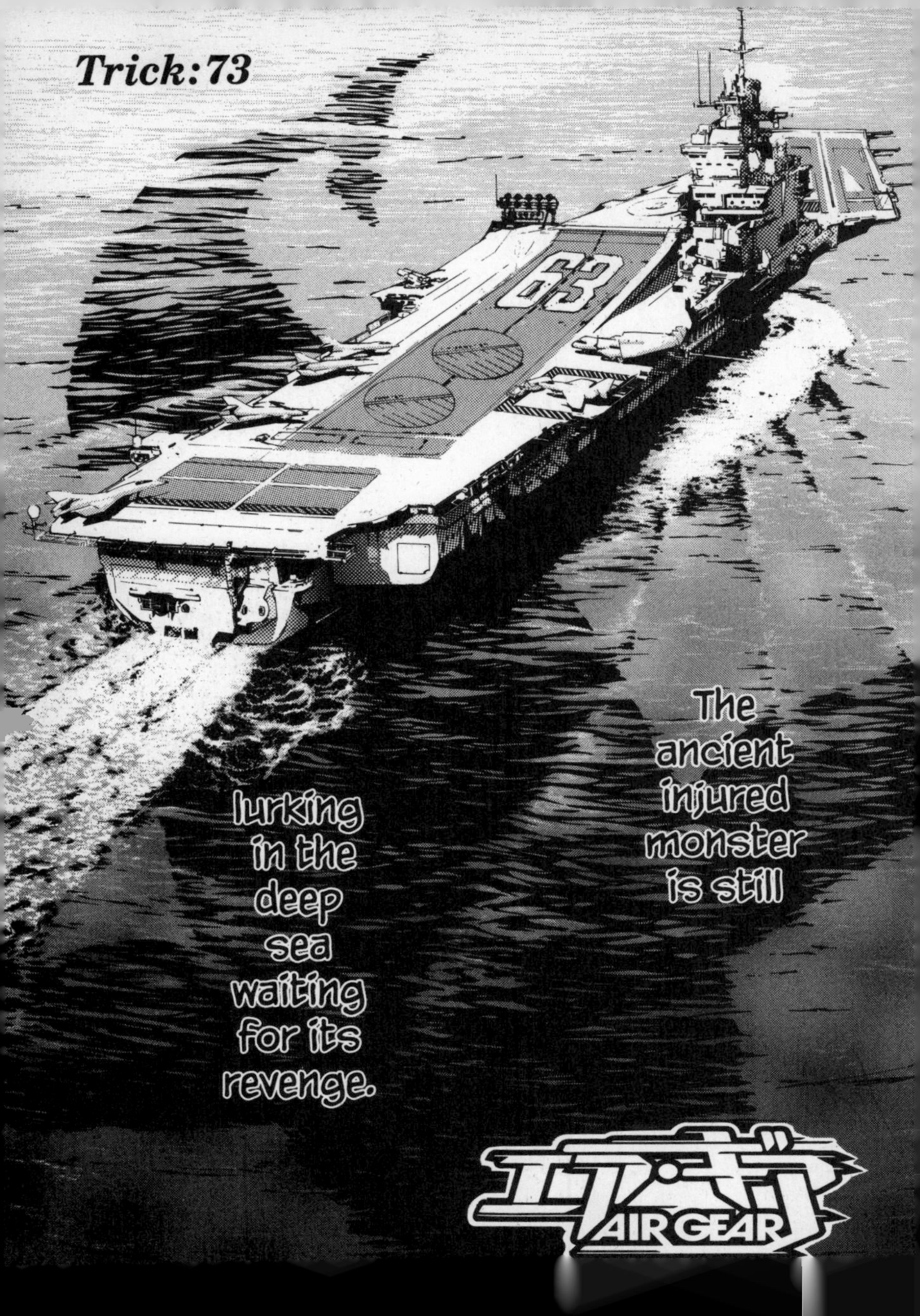
The ancient injured monster is still
lurking in the deep sea waiting for its revenge.
AIR GEAR

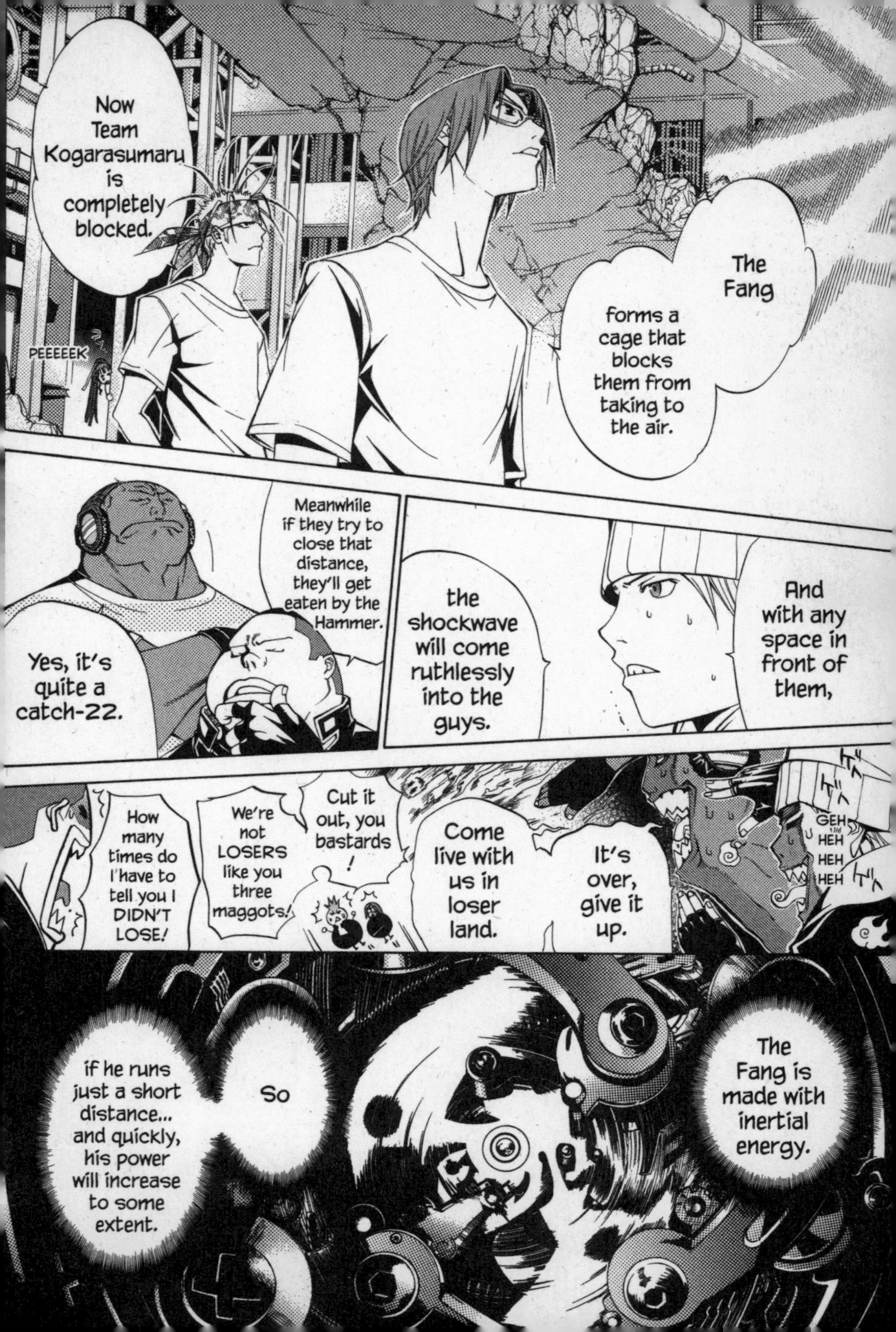

The Fang
forms a cage that blocks them from taking to the air.
Now Team Kogarasumaru is completely blocked.
PEEEEEK
And with any space in front of them,
the shockwave will come ruthlessly into the guys.
Meanwhile if they try to close that distance, they'll get eaten by the Hammer.
Yes, it's quite a catch-22.
GEH HEH HEH HEH
It's over, give it up.
Come live with us in loser land.
Cut it out, you bastards!
We're not LOSERS like you three maggots!
How many times do I have to tell you I DIDN'T LOSE!
The Fang is made with inertial energy.
So
if he runs just a short distance... and quickly, his power will increase to some extent.

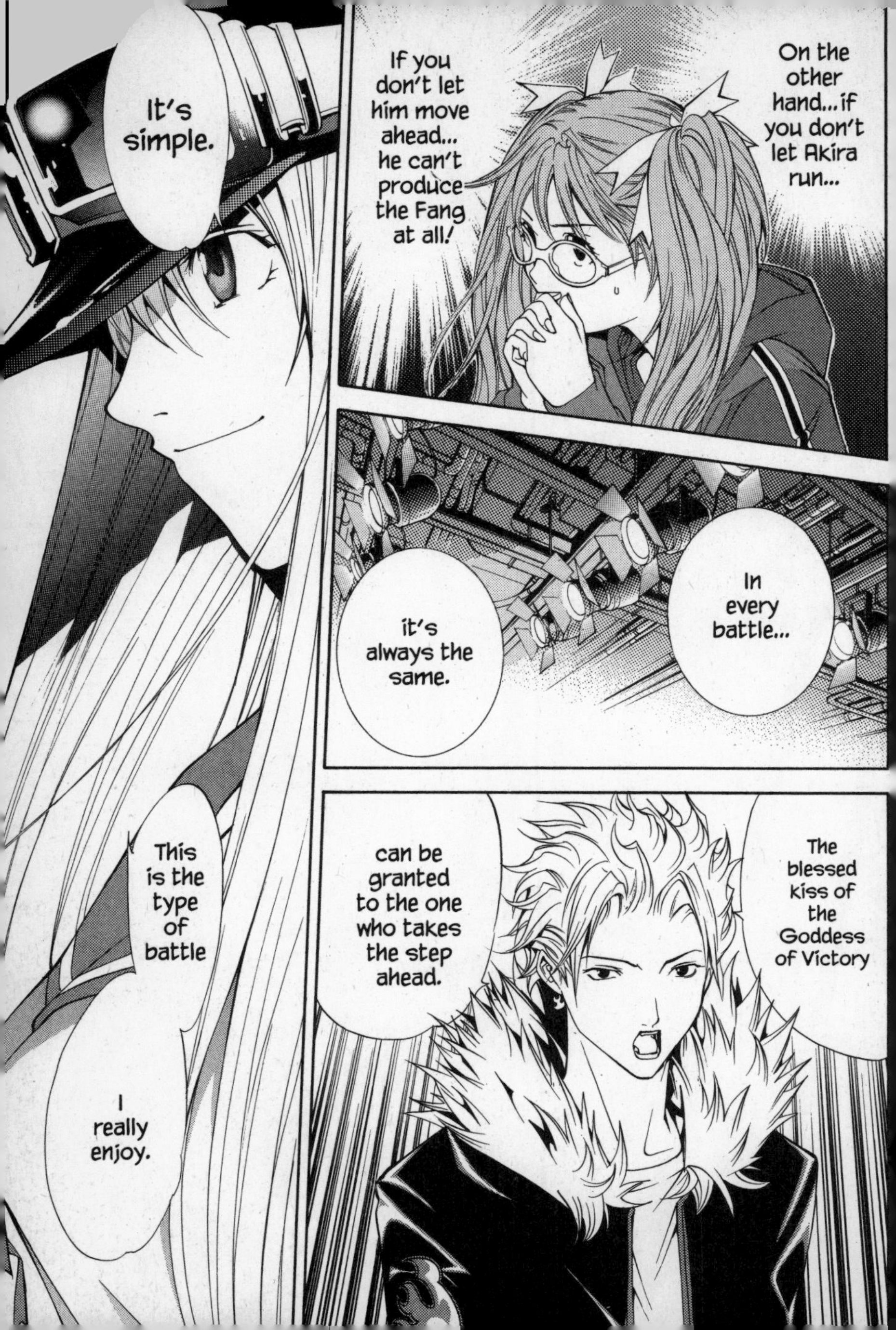
On the other hand...if you don't let Akira run...
If you don't let him move ahead... he can't produce the Fang at all!
In every battle...
it's always the same.
The blessed kiss of the Goddess of Victory
can be granted to the one who takes the step ahead.
It's simple.
This is the type of battle
I really enjoy.

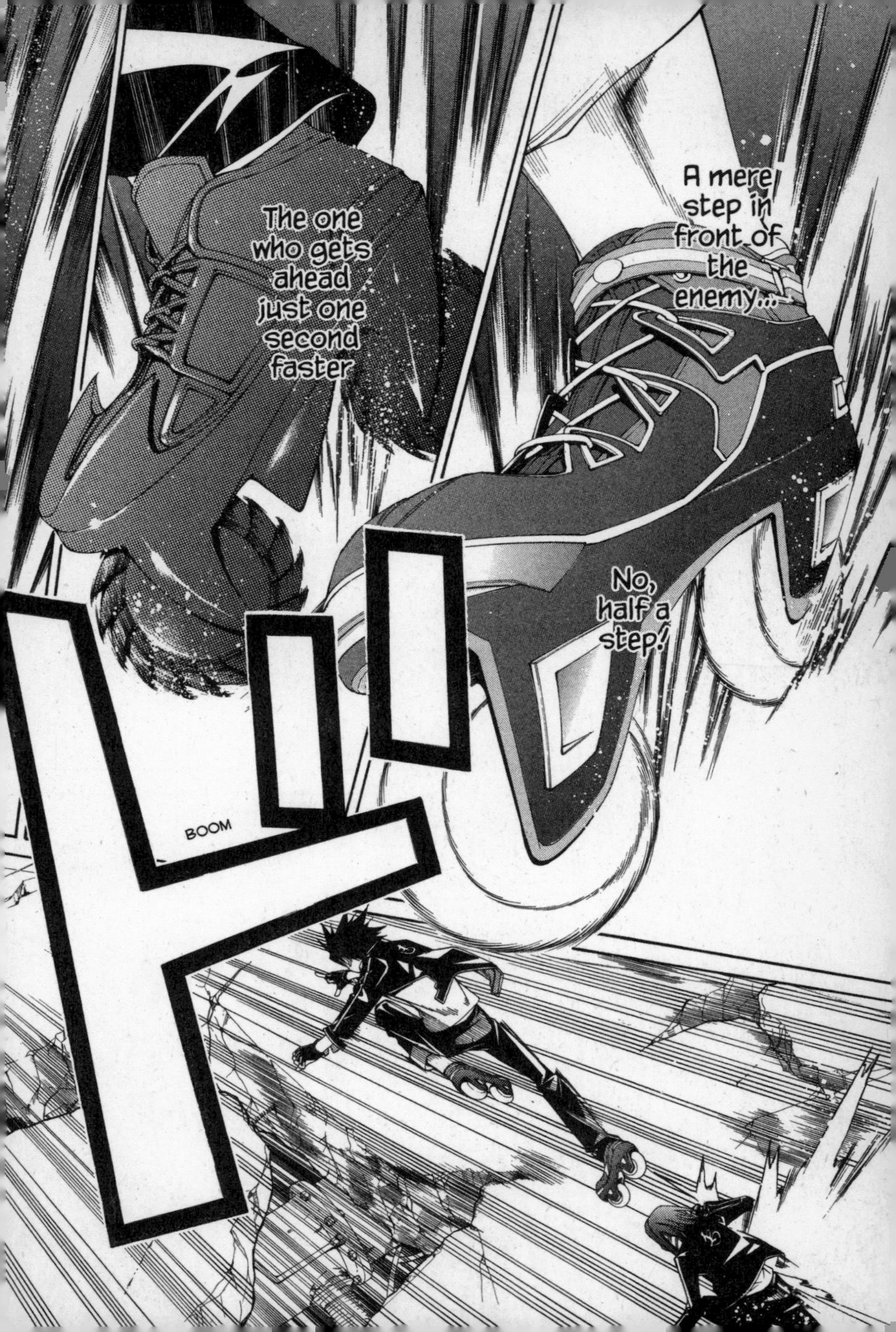
A mere step in front of the enemy...
The one who gets ahead just one second faster
No, half a step!
BOOM

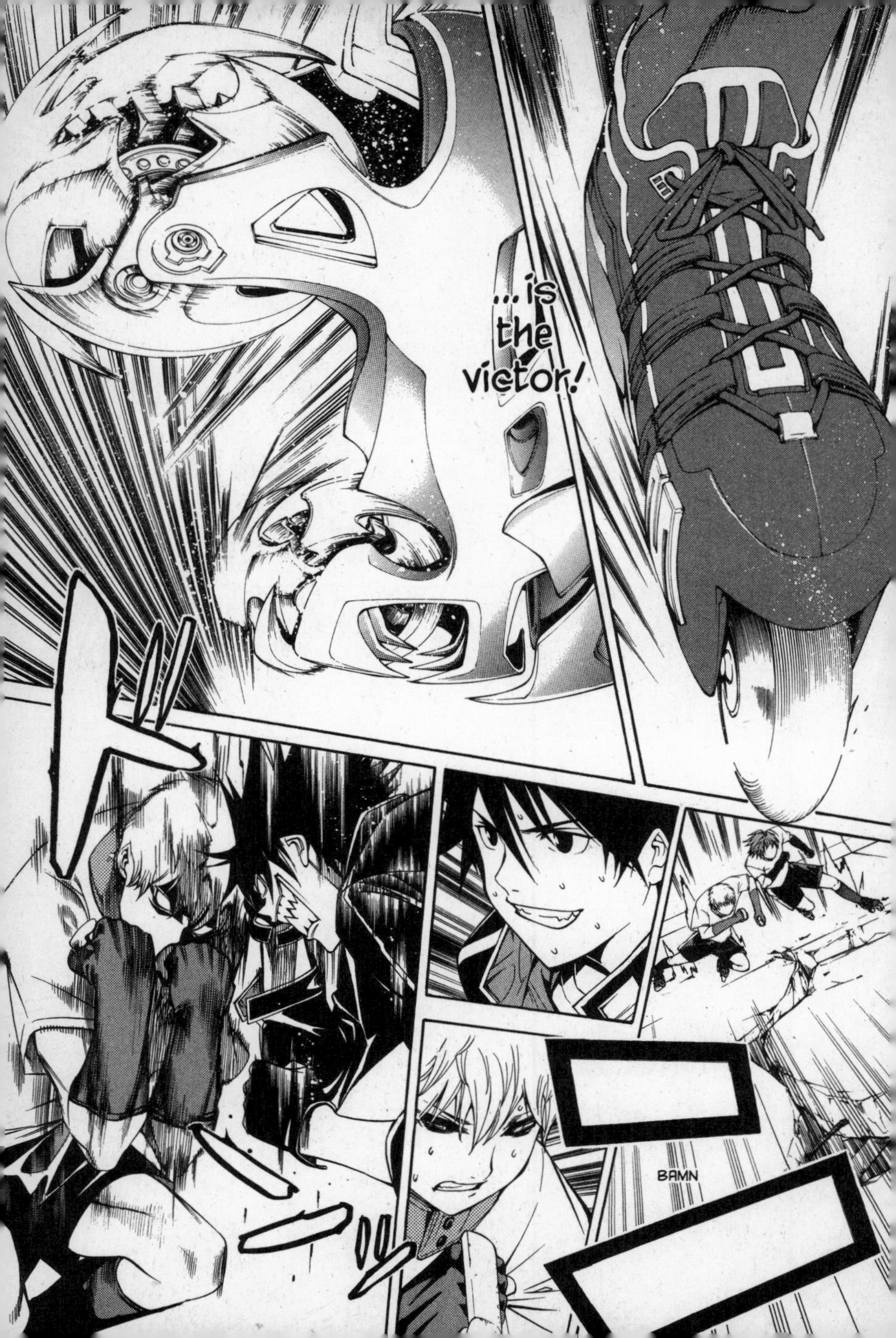
...is the victor!
BAMN

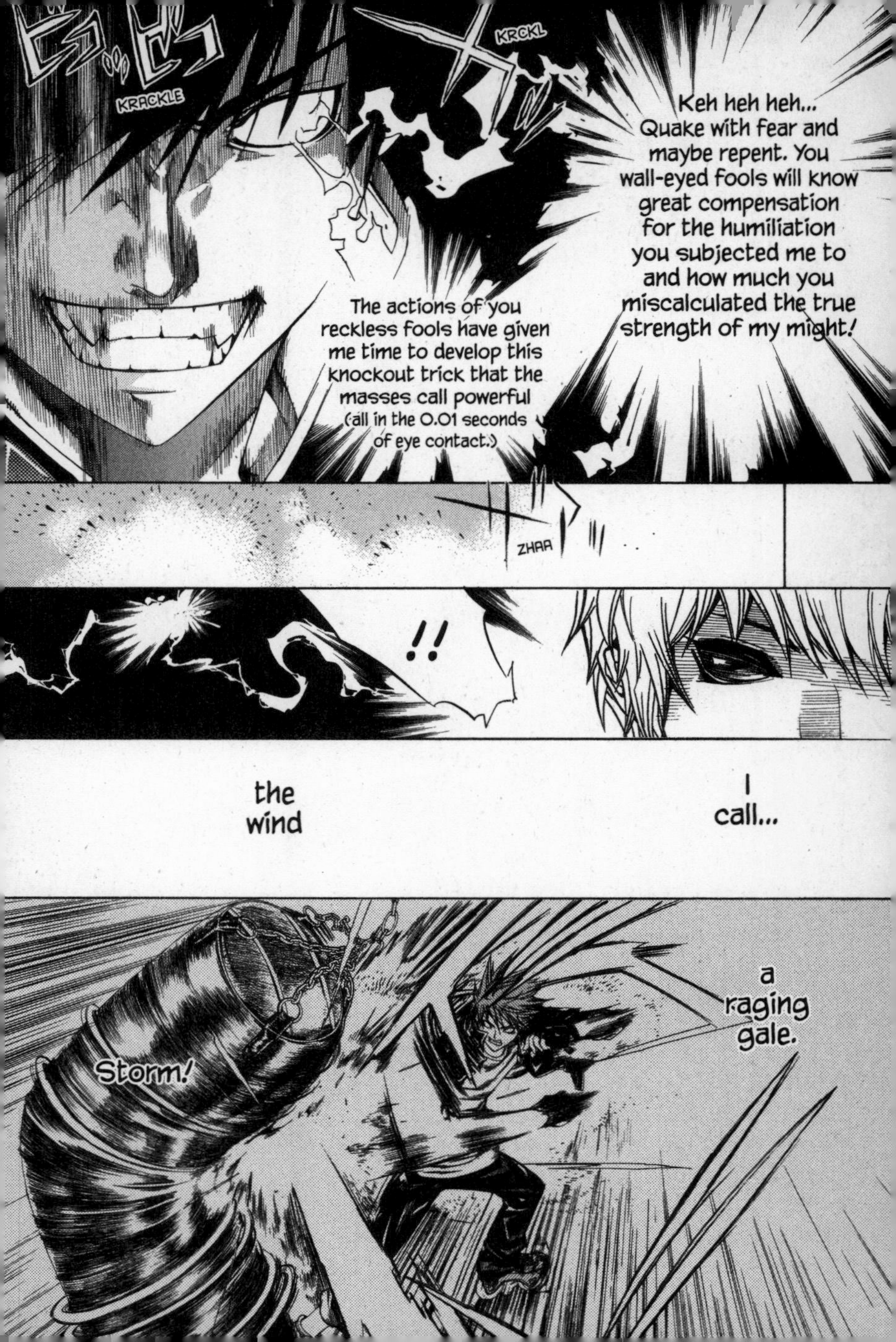
KRCKL
Keh heh heh... Quake with fear and maybe repent. You wall-eyed fools will know great compensation for the humiliation you subjected me to and how much you miscalculated the true strength of my might!
KRACKLE
The actions of you reckless fools have given me time to develop this knockout trick that the masses call powerful (all in the 0.01 seconds of eye contact.)
ZHAA
..
!!
I call...
the wind
a raging gale.
Storm!

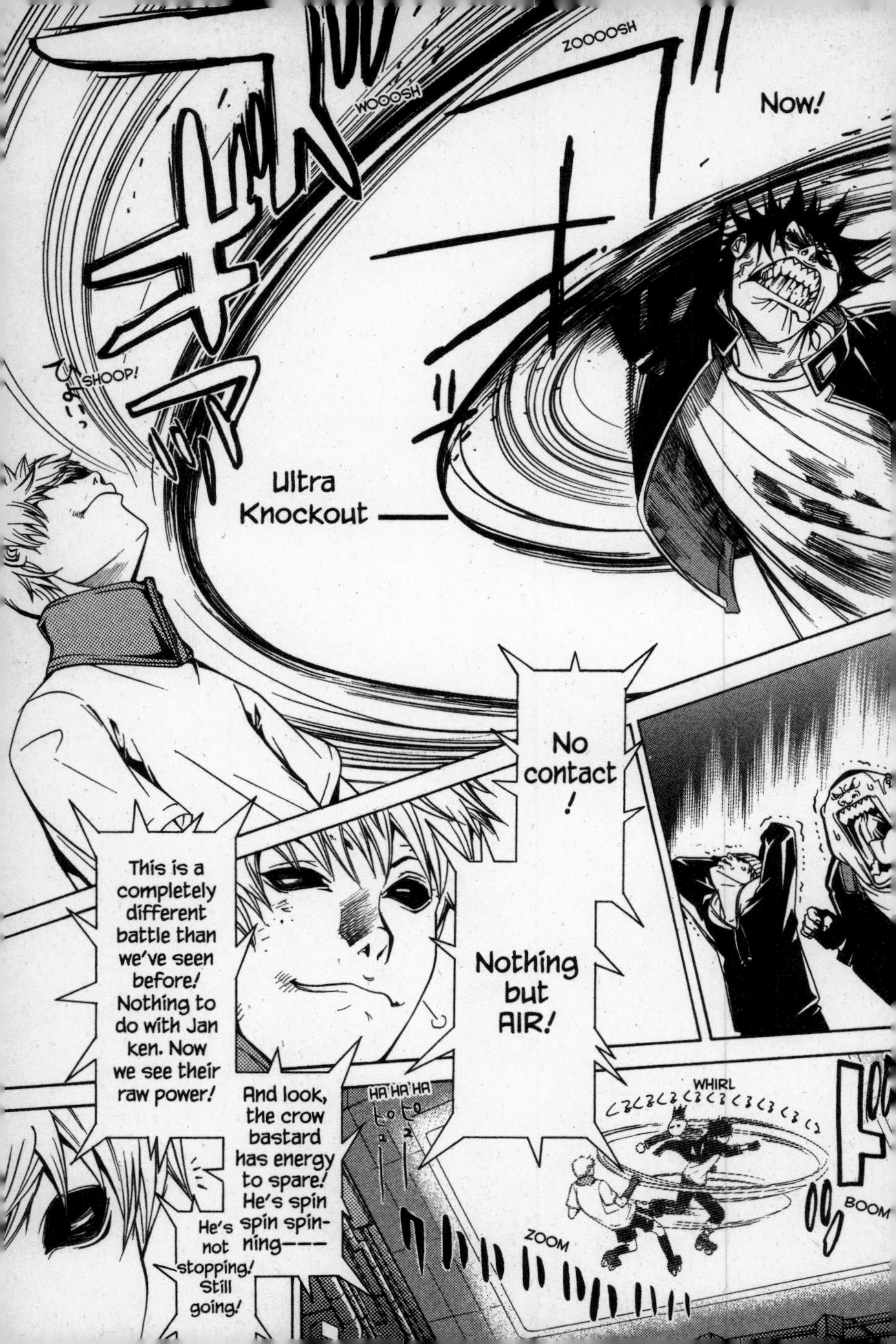
ZOOOOSH
Now!
WOOOSH
SHOOP!
Ultra Knockout ——
No contact!
Nothing but AIR!
This is a completely different battle than we've seen before! Nothing to do with Jan ken. Now we see their raw power!
BOOM
WHIRL
ZOOM
HA HA HA
And look, the crow bastard has energy to spare! He's spin spin spin-ning———
He's not stopping! Still going!

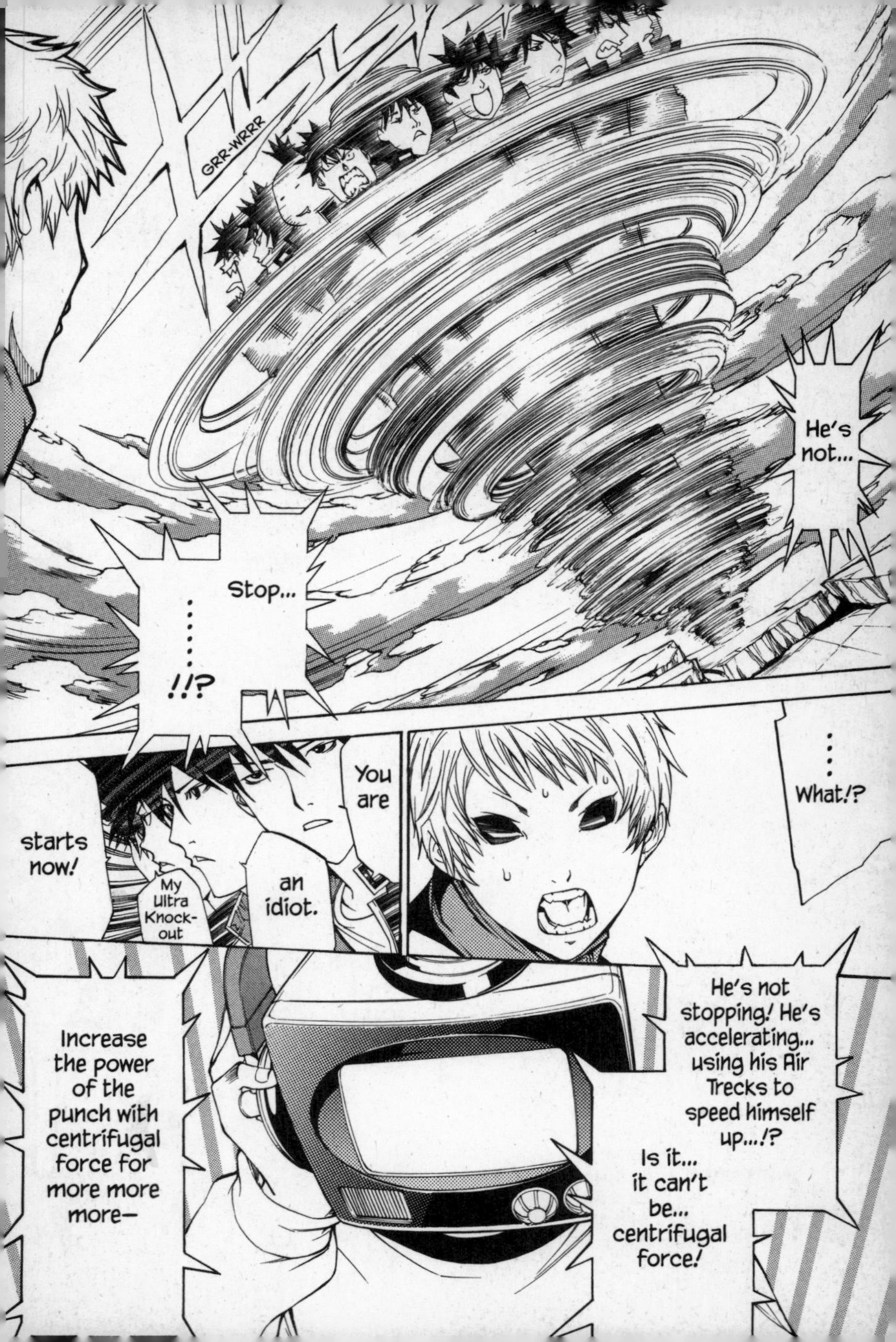
He's not...
GRR-WRRR
Stop... ......!!?
...What!?
You are
an idiot.
My Ultra Knock-out
starts now!
He's not stopping! He's accelerating... using his Air Trecks to speed himself up...!?
Is it... it can't be... centrifugal force!
Increase the power of the punch with centrifugal force for more more more–

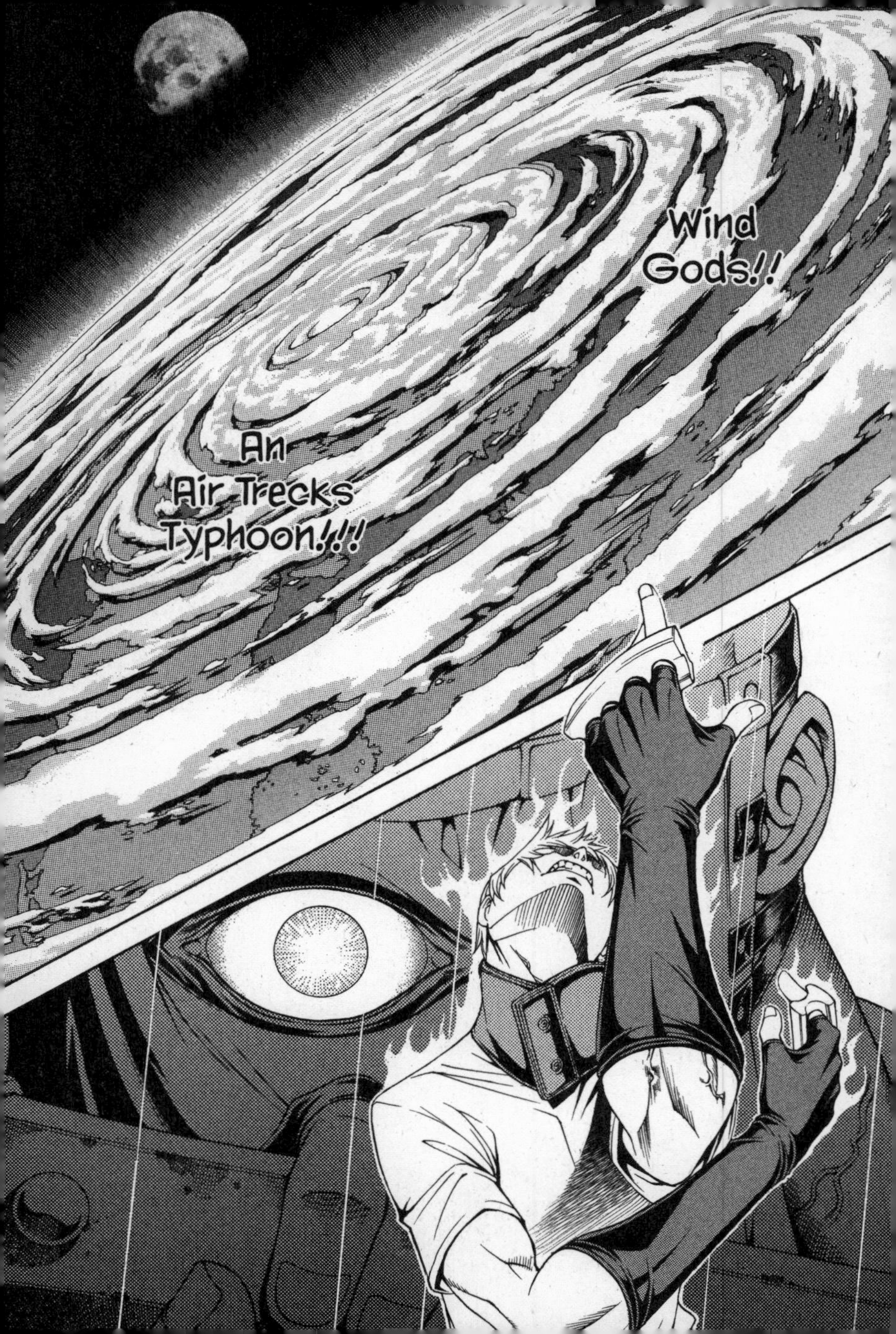
Wind Gods!!
An Air Trecks Typhoon!!!

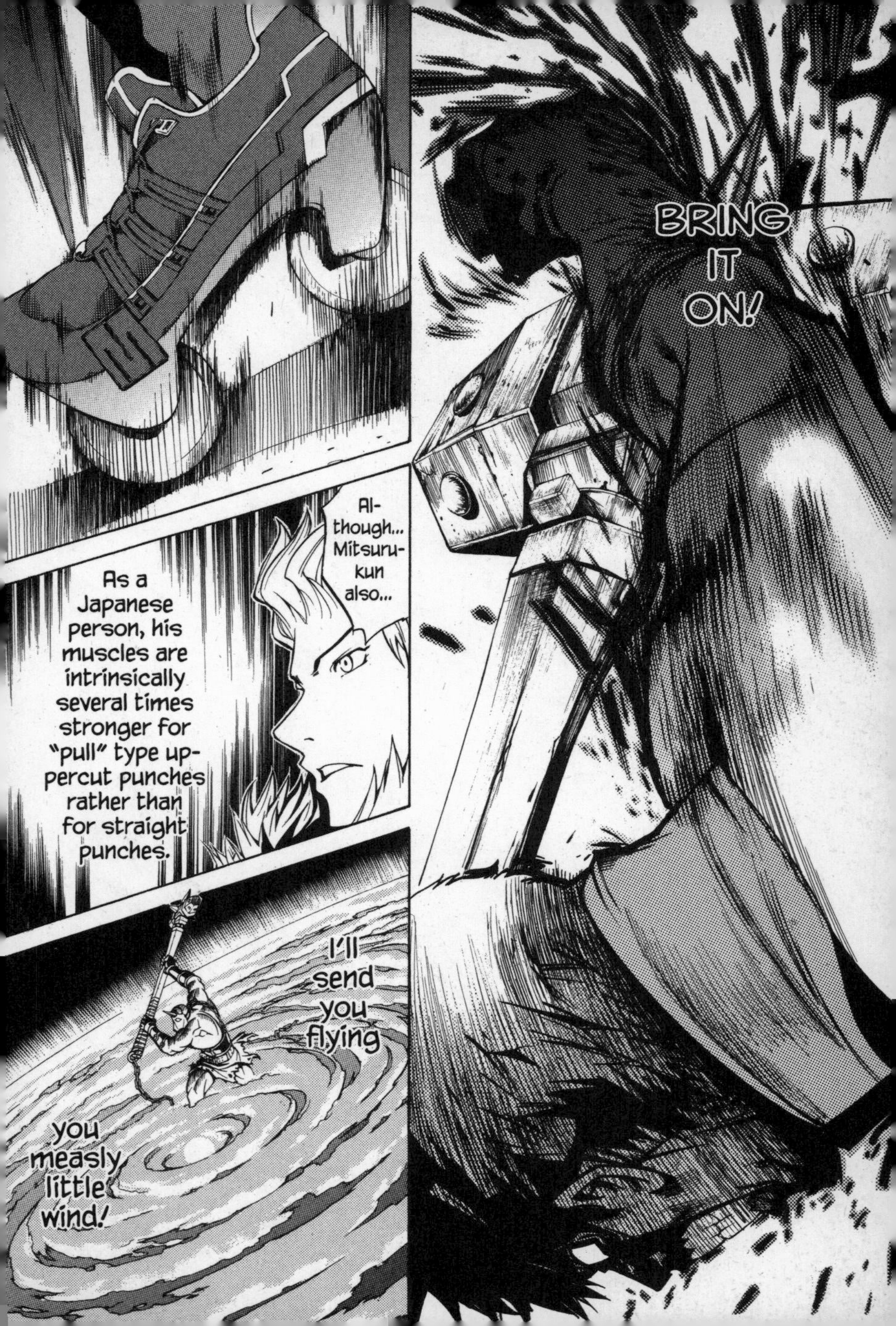
BRING IT ON!
Al-though... Mitsuru-kun also...
As a Japanese person, his muscles are intrinsically several times stronger for "pull" type up-percut punches rather than for straight punches.
I'll send you flying
you measly little wind!

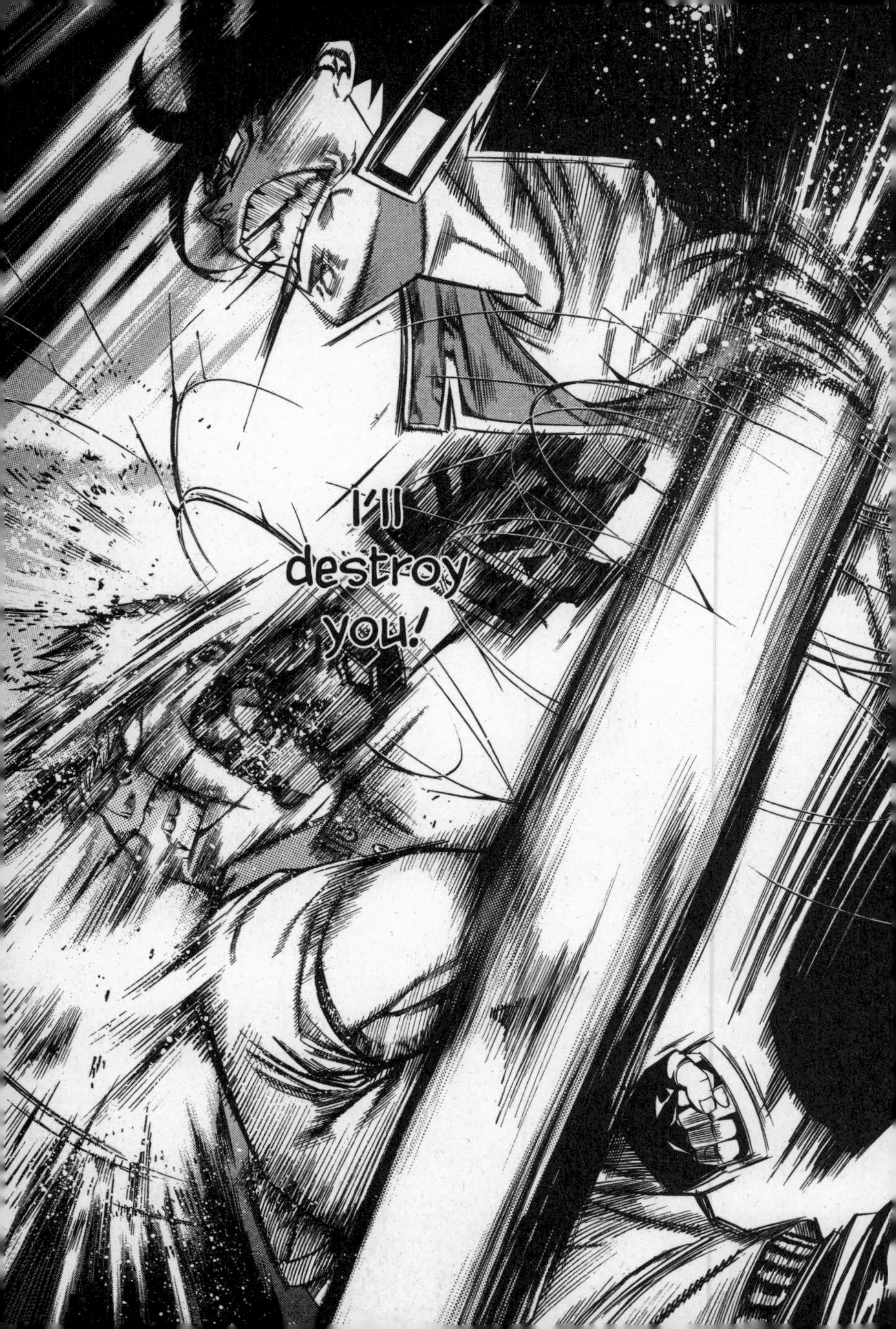
I'll destroy you!

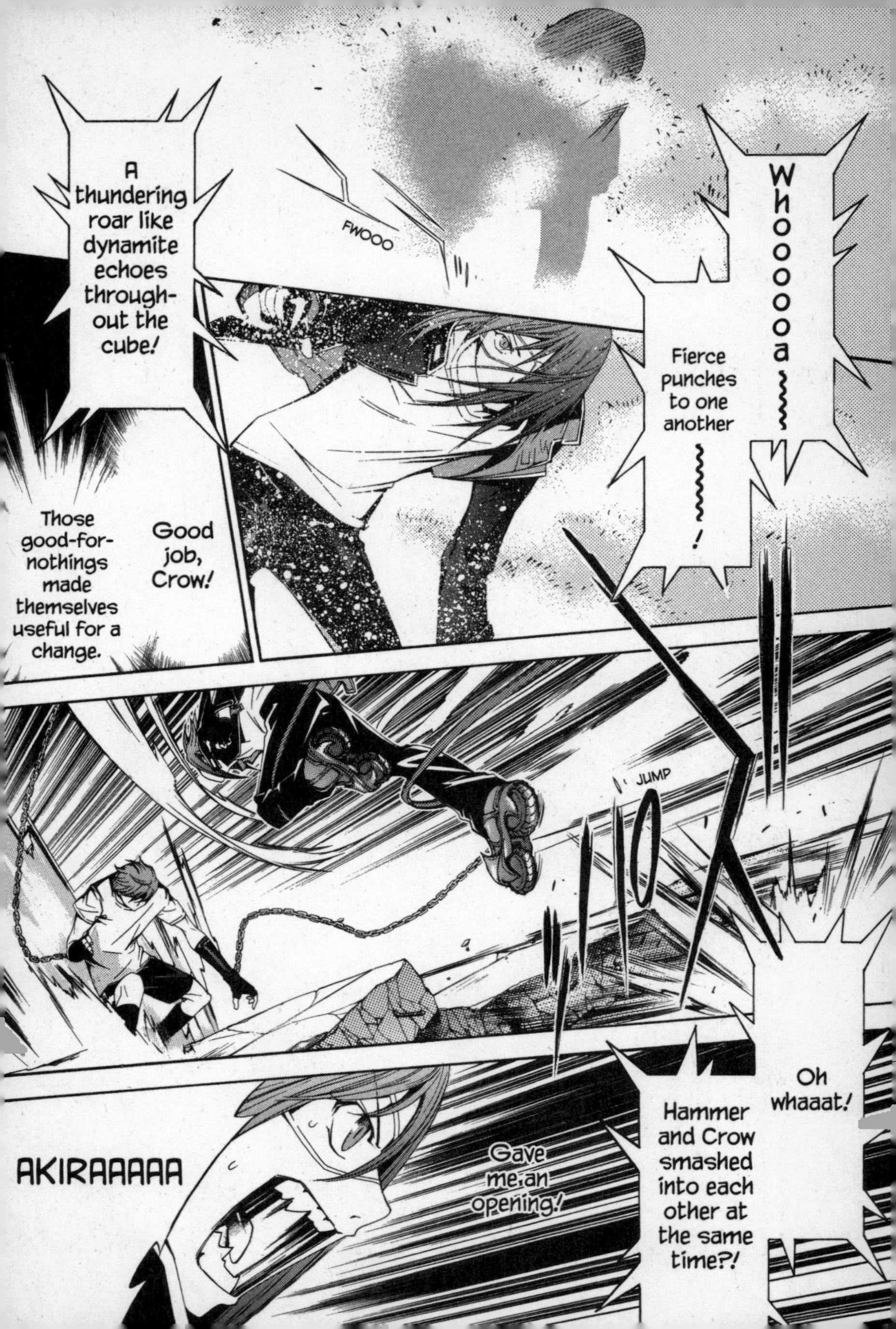

Whoooooa~~~
Fierce punches to one another~~~!
A thundering roar like dynamite echoes throughout the cube!
FWOOO
Good job, Crow!
Those good-for-nothings made themselves useful for a change.
JUMP
Oh whaaat!
Hammer and Crow smashed into each other at the same time?!
Gave me an opening!
AKIRAAAAA

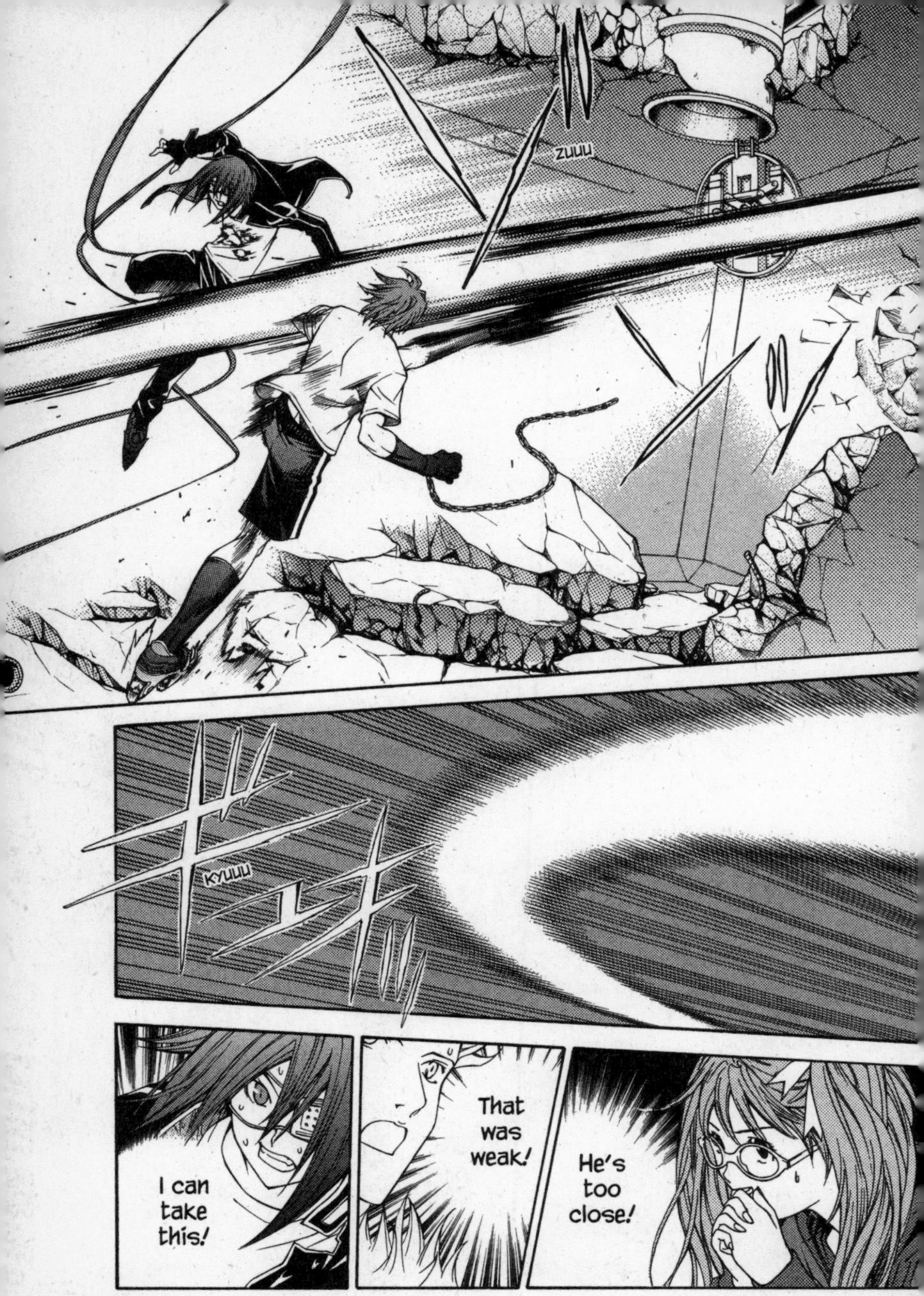
ZUUU
KYUUU
He's too close!
That was weak!
I can take this!

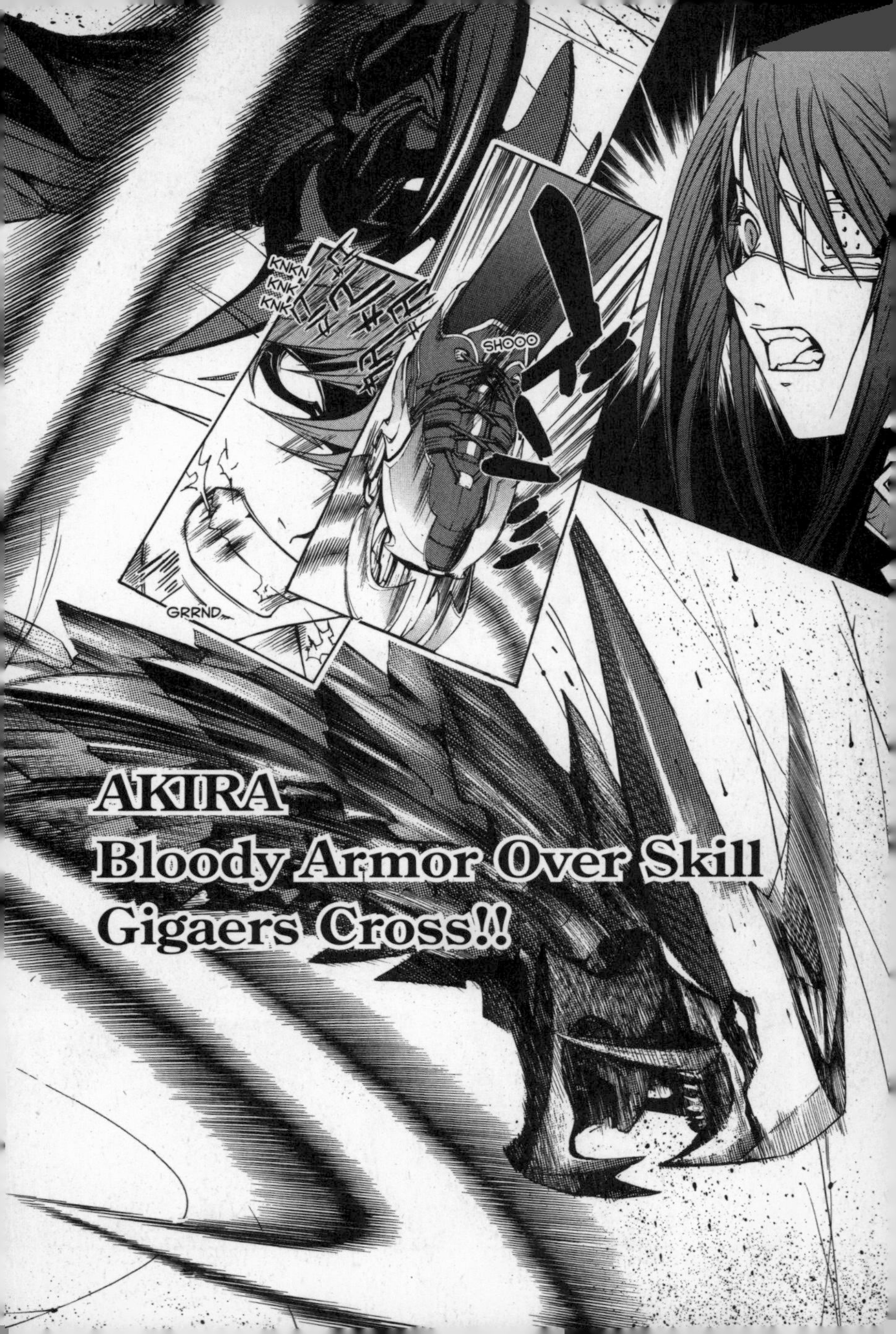
KNKN
KNK
KNK
SHOOO
GRRND
AKIRA
Bloody Armor Over Skill
Gigaers Cross!!

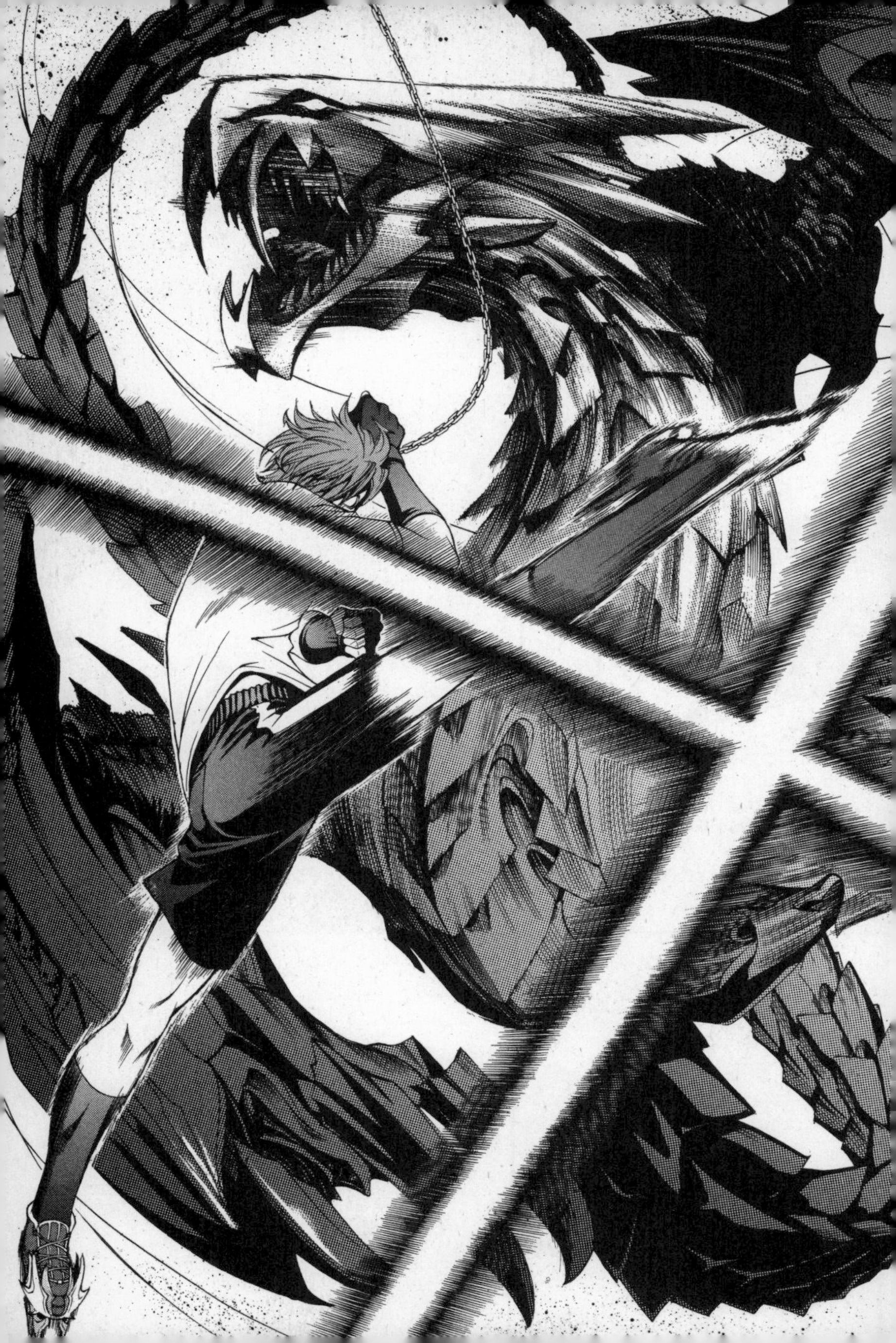

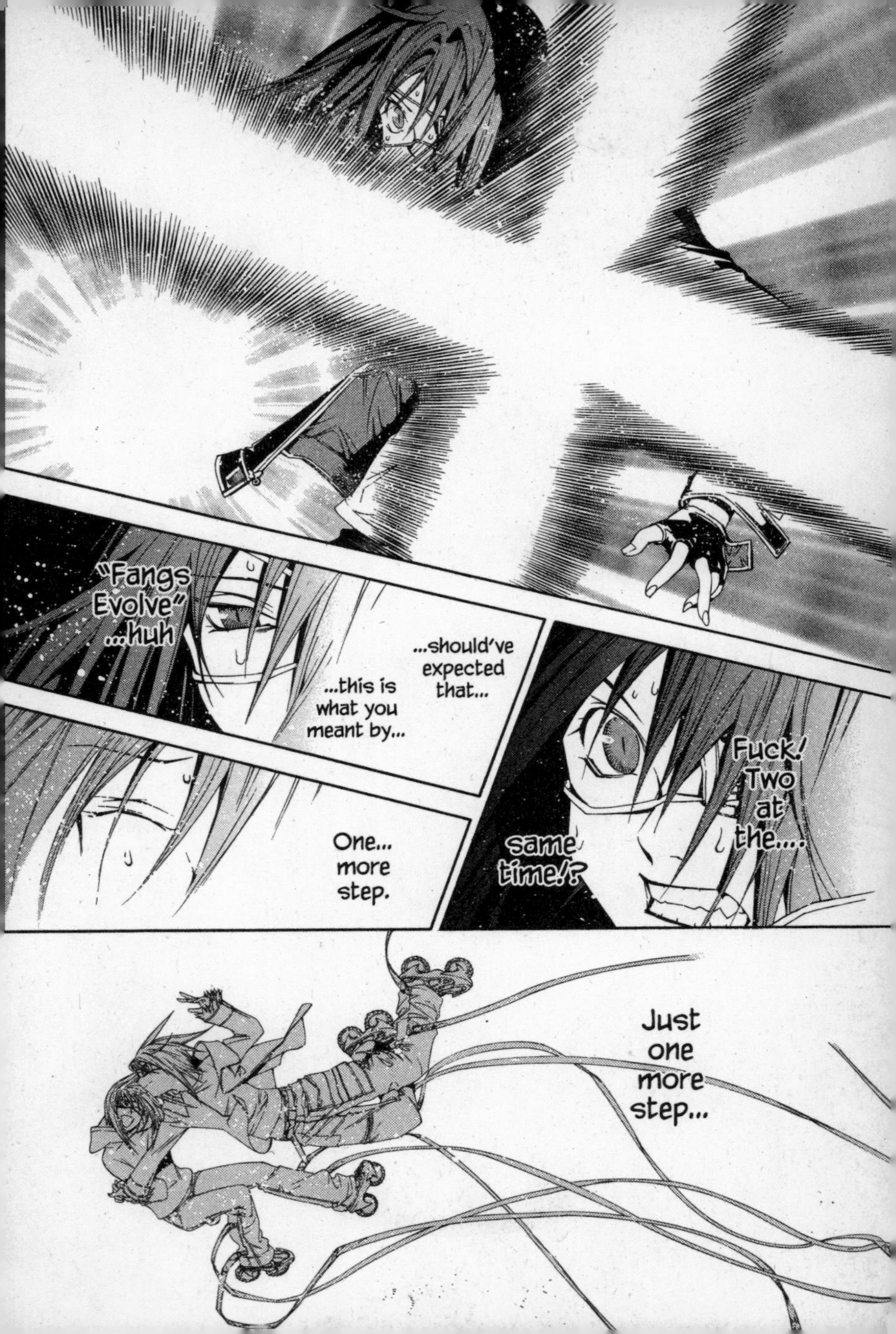
Fuck! Two at the.... same time!?
...should've expected that...
...this is what you meant by...
"Fangs Evolve" ...huh
One... more step.
Just one more step...

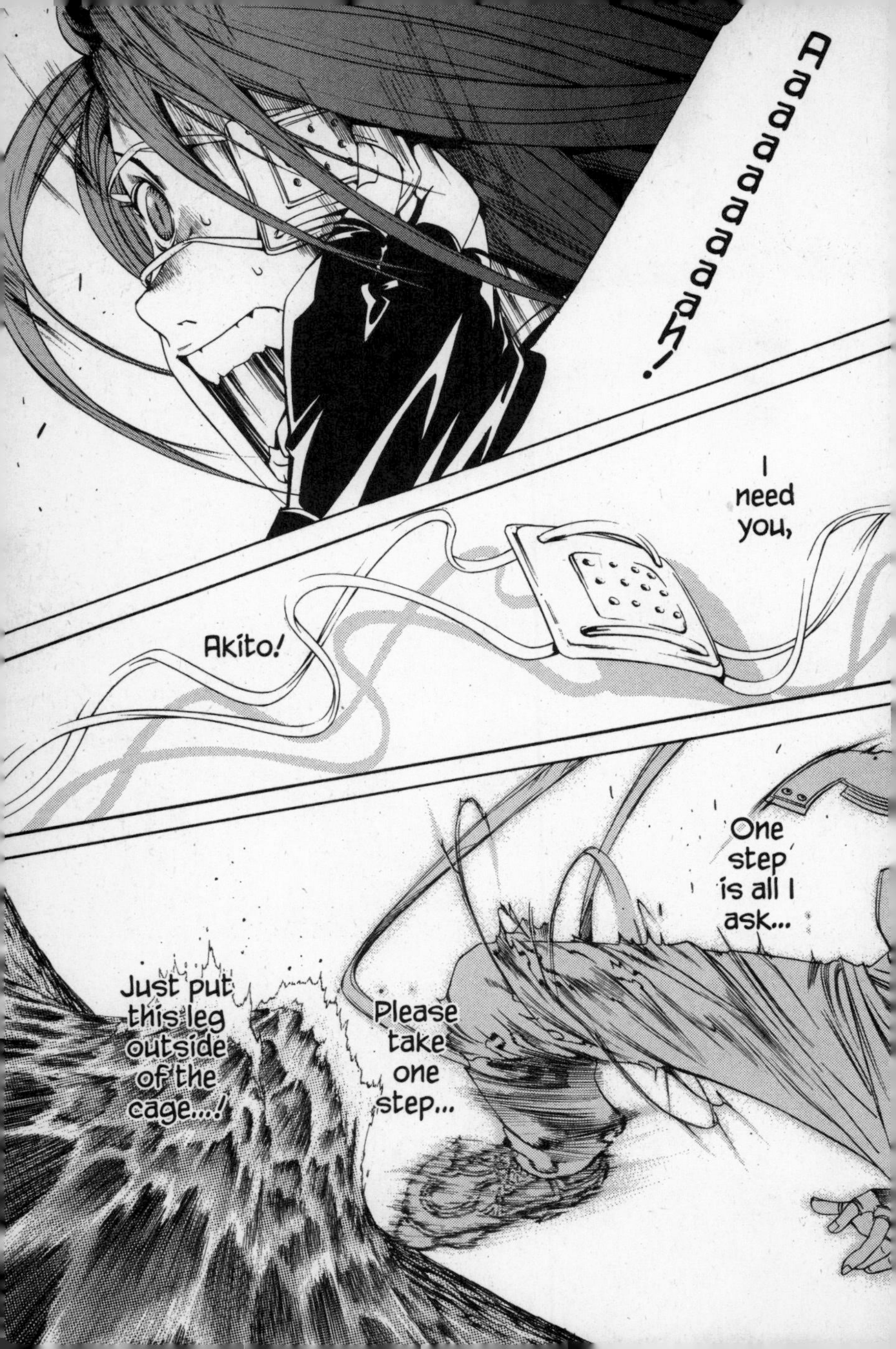
Aaaaaaaaah!
I need you,
Akito!
One step is all I ask...
Please take one step...
Just put this leg outside of the cage...!

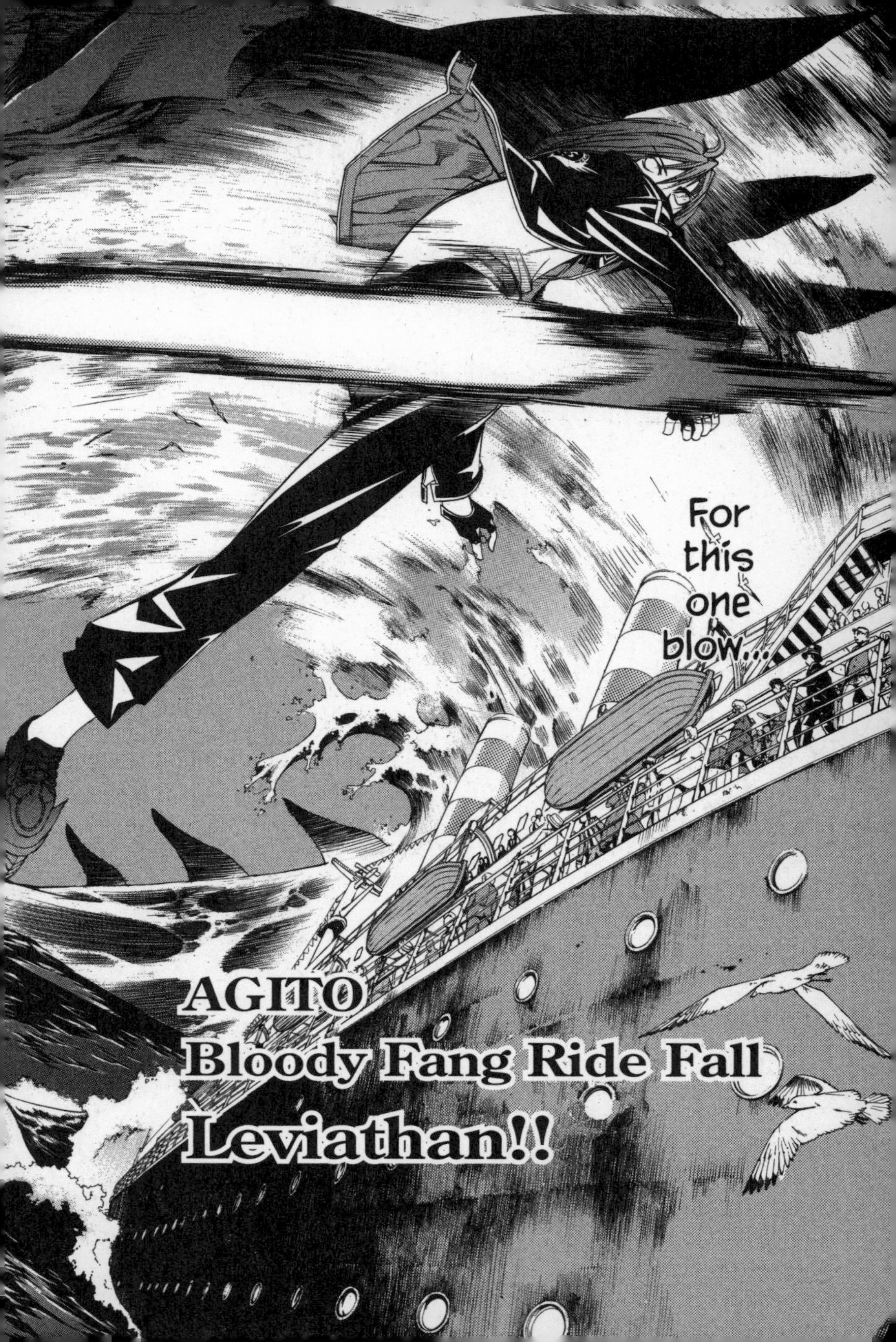
For this one blow...
AGITO
Bloody Fang Ride Fall
Leviathan!!

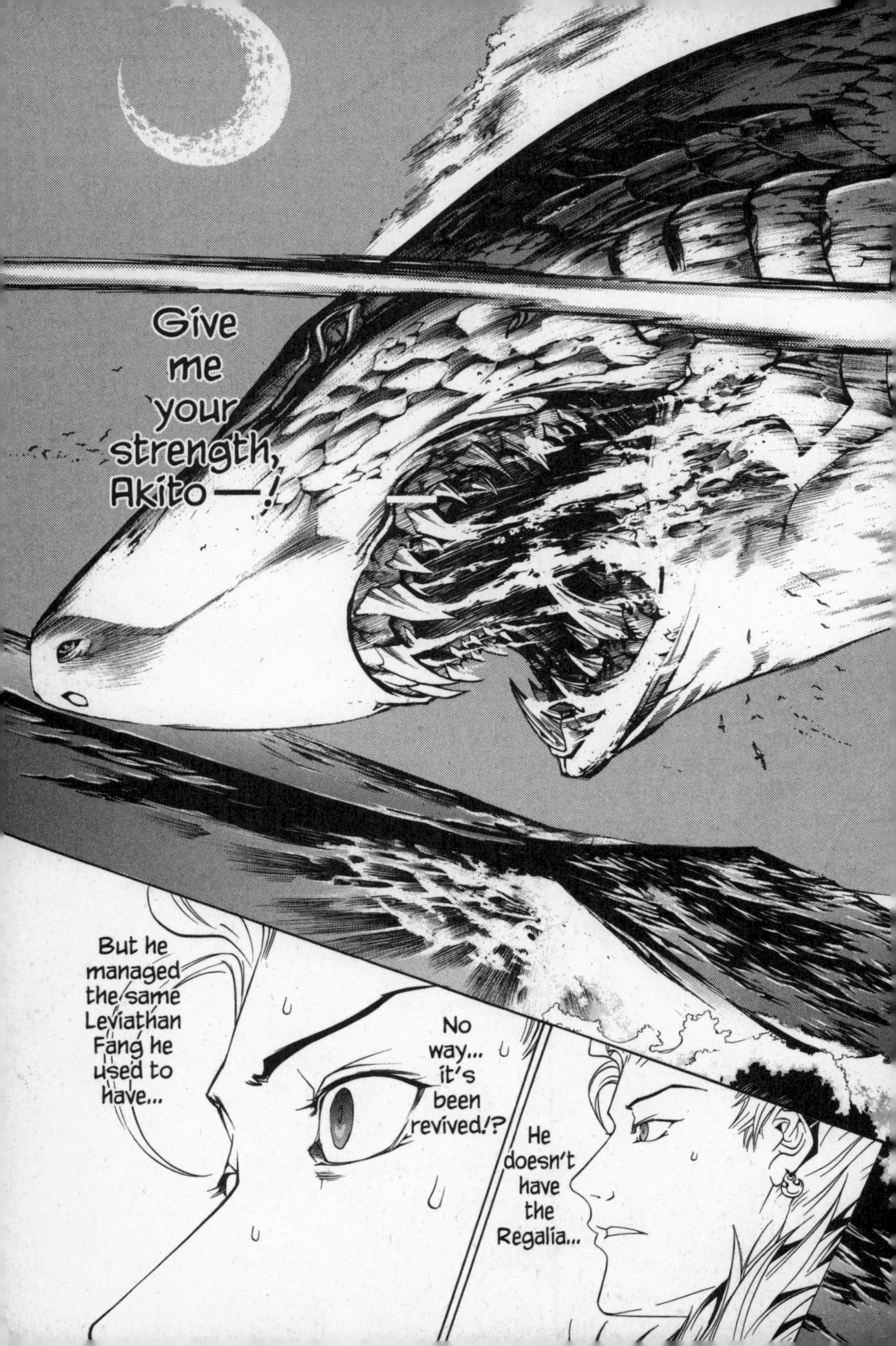
Give me your strength, Akito—!
He doesn't have the Regalia...
No way... it's been revived!?
But he managed the same Leviathan Fang he used to have...

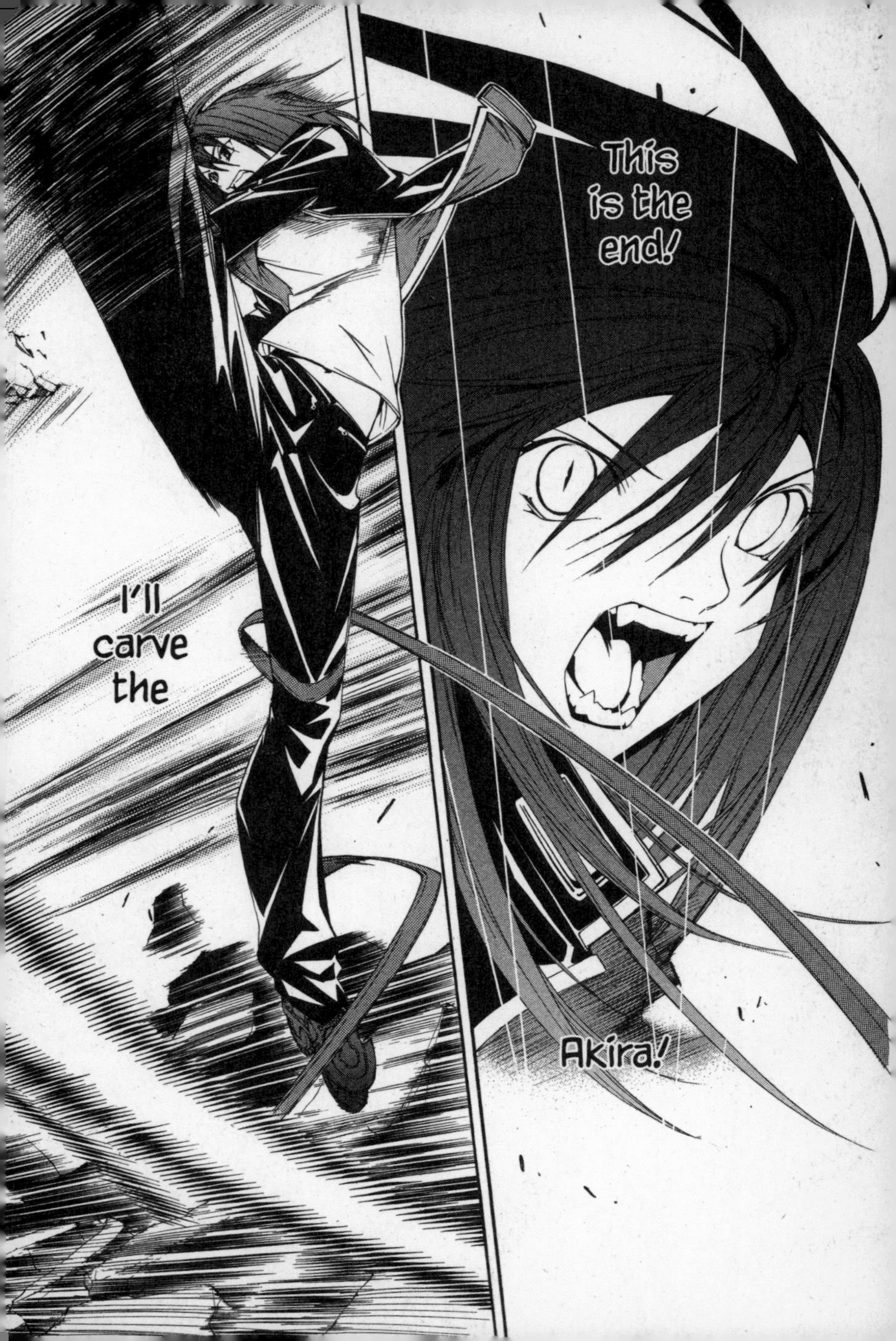
This is the end!
Akira!
I'll carve the

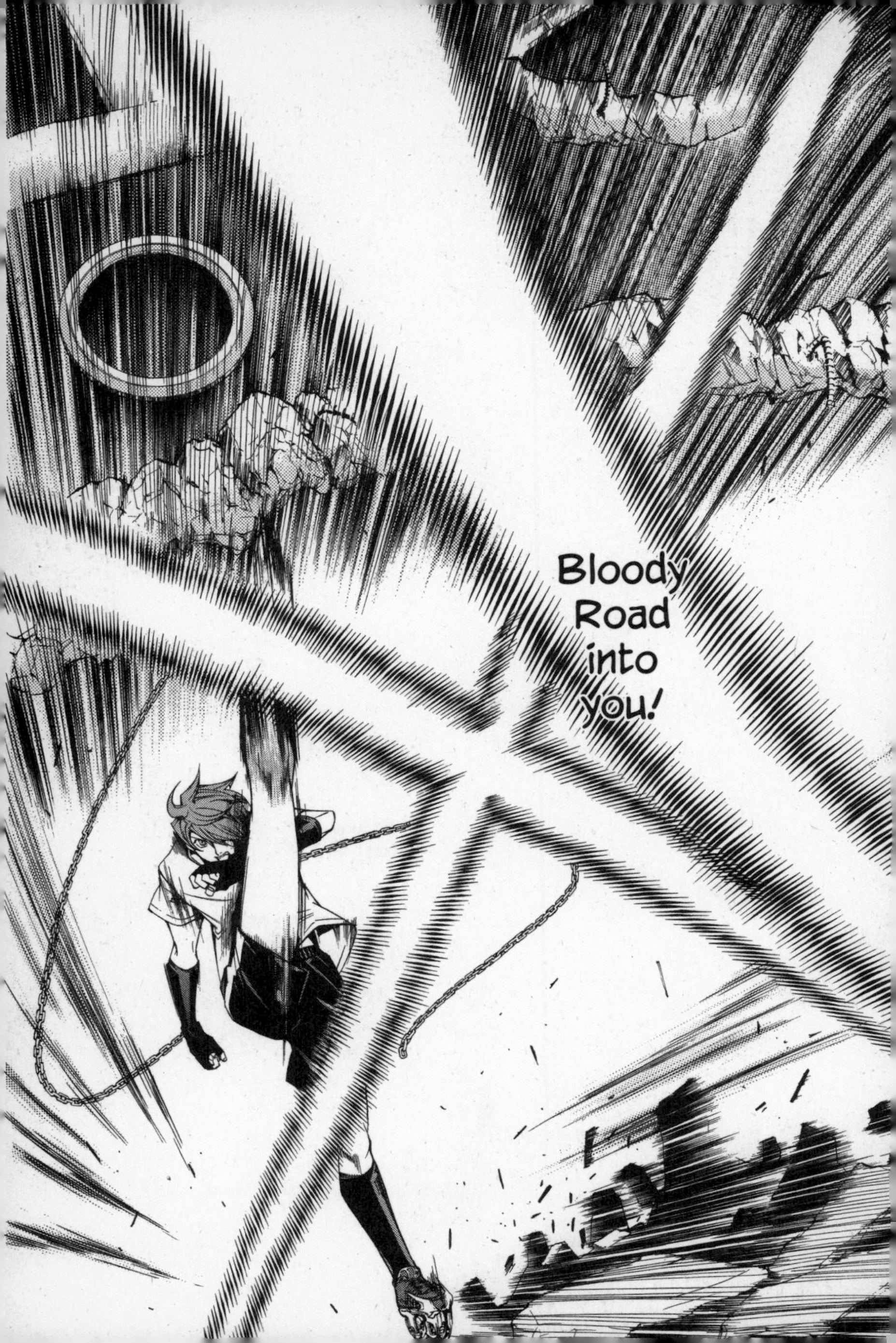
Bloody Road into you!

Air Gear
Event File 2

And I got nothing...

What a cop-out! Oi!

Sometimes there's just nothing to put on this page.

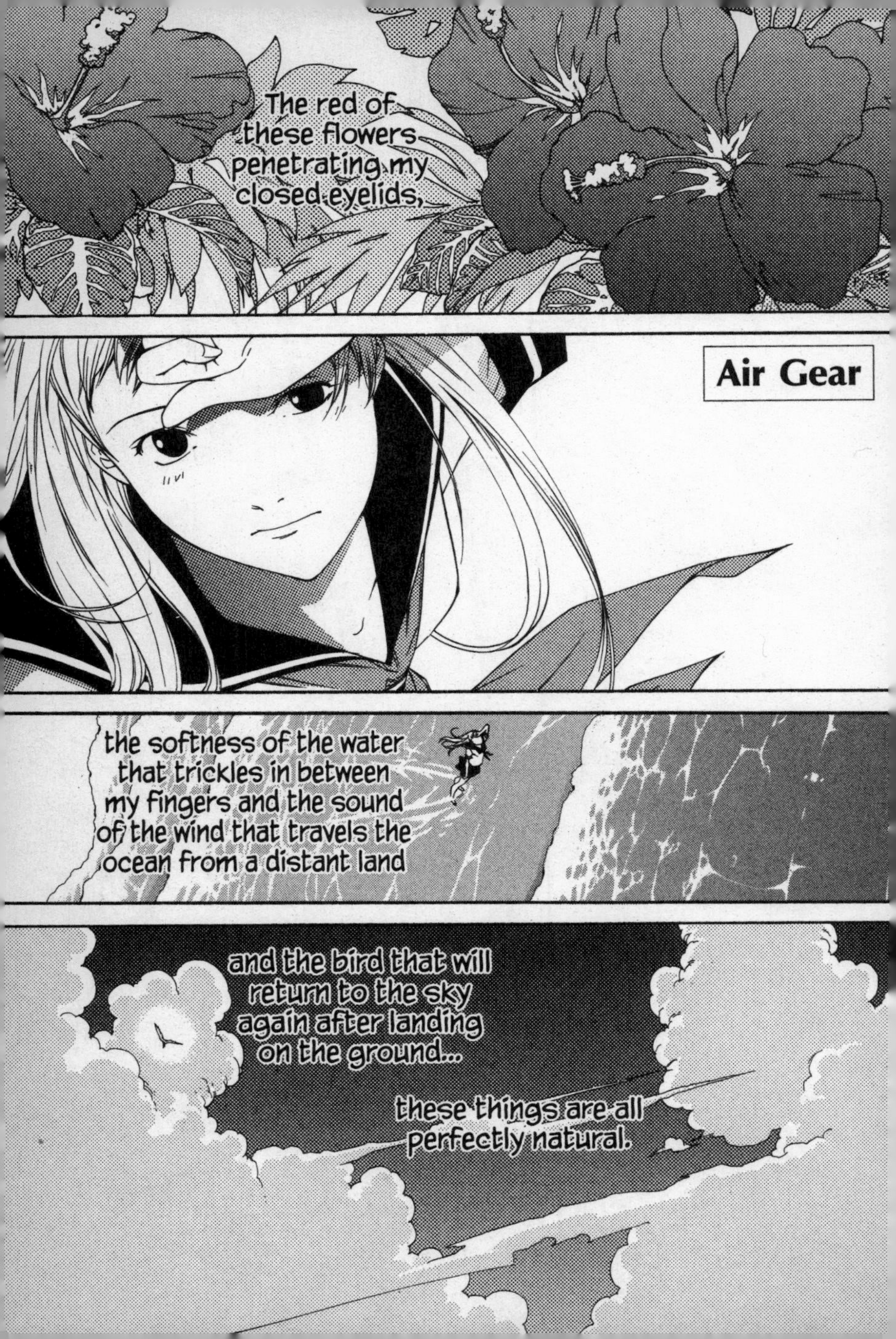
The red of these flowers penetrating my closed eyelids,
Air Gear
the softness of the water that trickles in between my fingers and the sound of the wind that travels the ocean from a distant land
and the bird that will return to the sky again after landing on the ground...
these things are all perfectly natural.

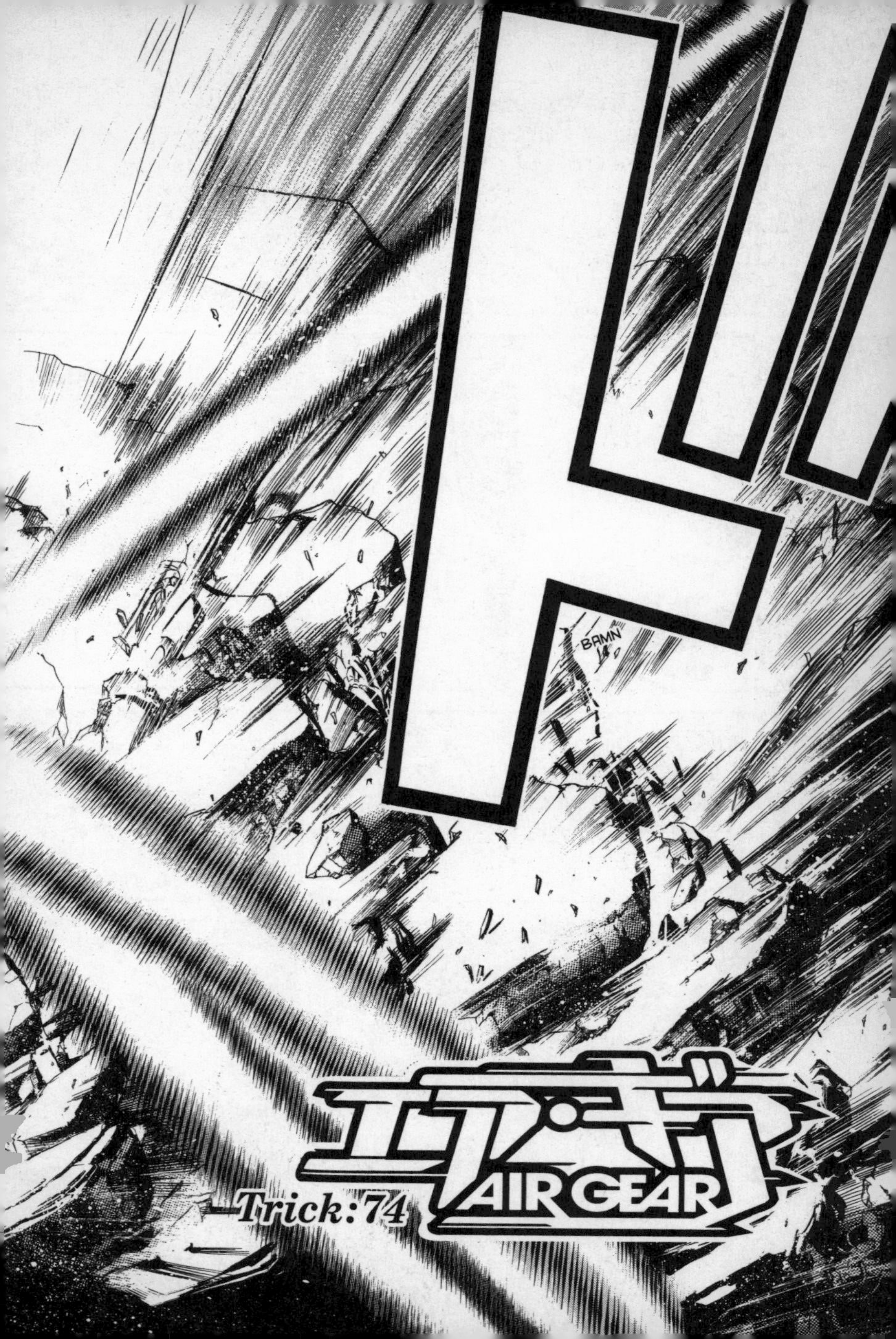
BAMN
エア・ギア
AIR GEAR
Trick:74

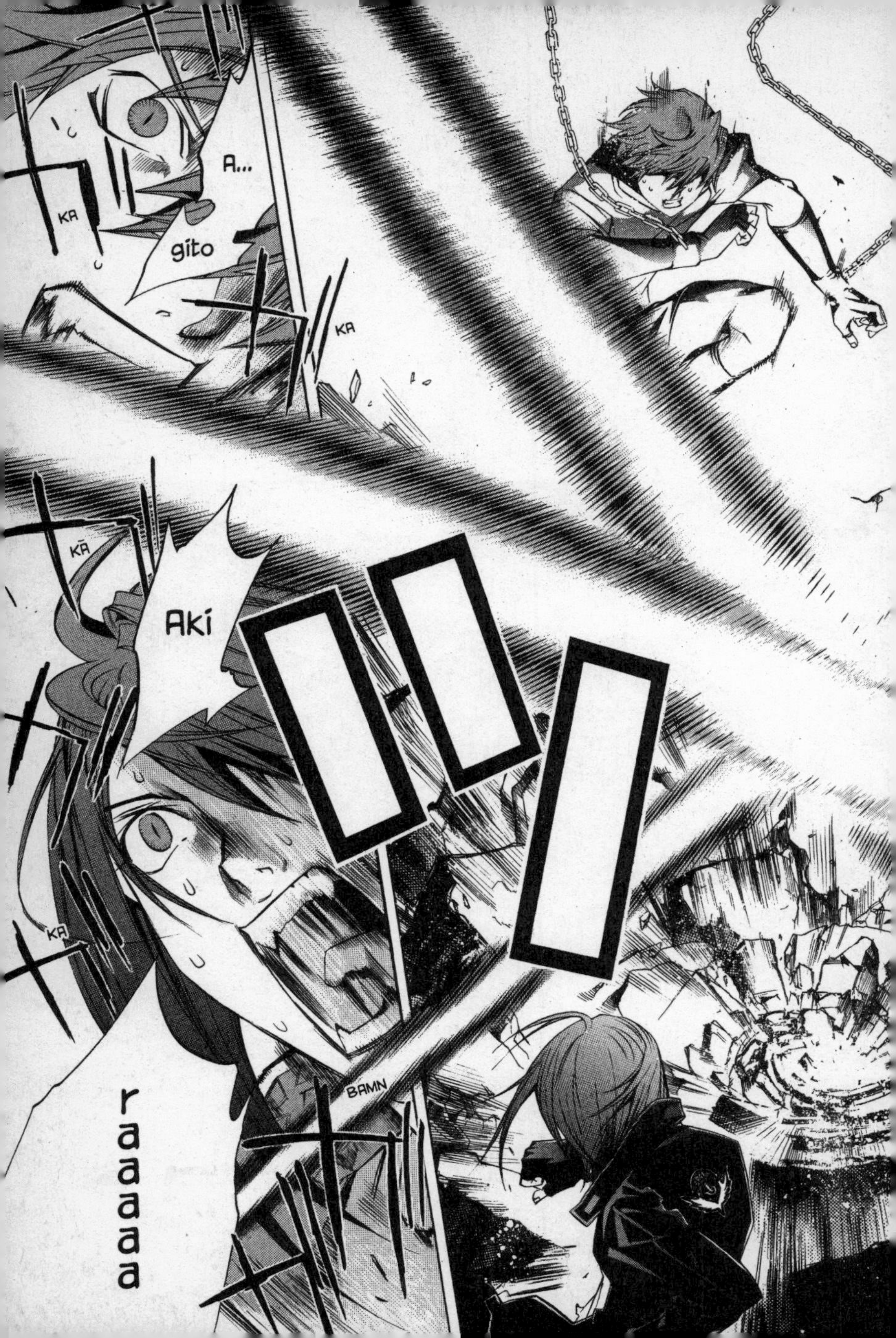
A...
gito
KA
KA
KĀ
Aki
raaaaaa
KA
BAMN

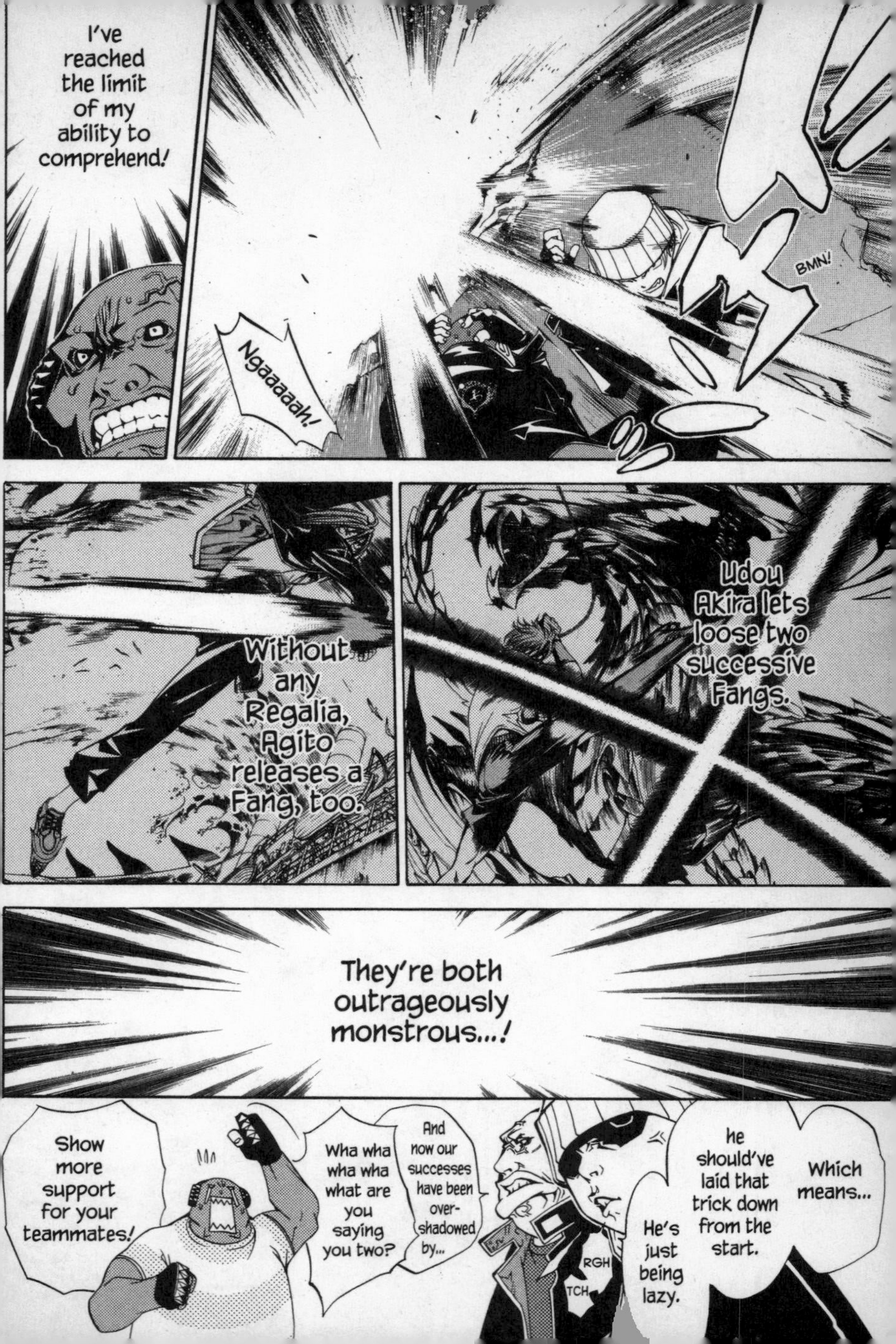
BMN!
Ngaaaaah!
I've reached the limit of my ability to comprehend!
Udou Akira lets loose two successive Fangs.
Without any Regalia, Agito releases a Fang, too.
They're both outrageously monstrous...!
Which means...
he should've laid that trick down from the start.
He's just being lazy.
RGH
TCH
And now our successes have been over-shadowed by...
Wha wha wha wha what are you saying you two?
Show more support for your teammates!

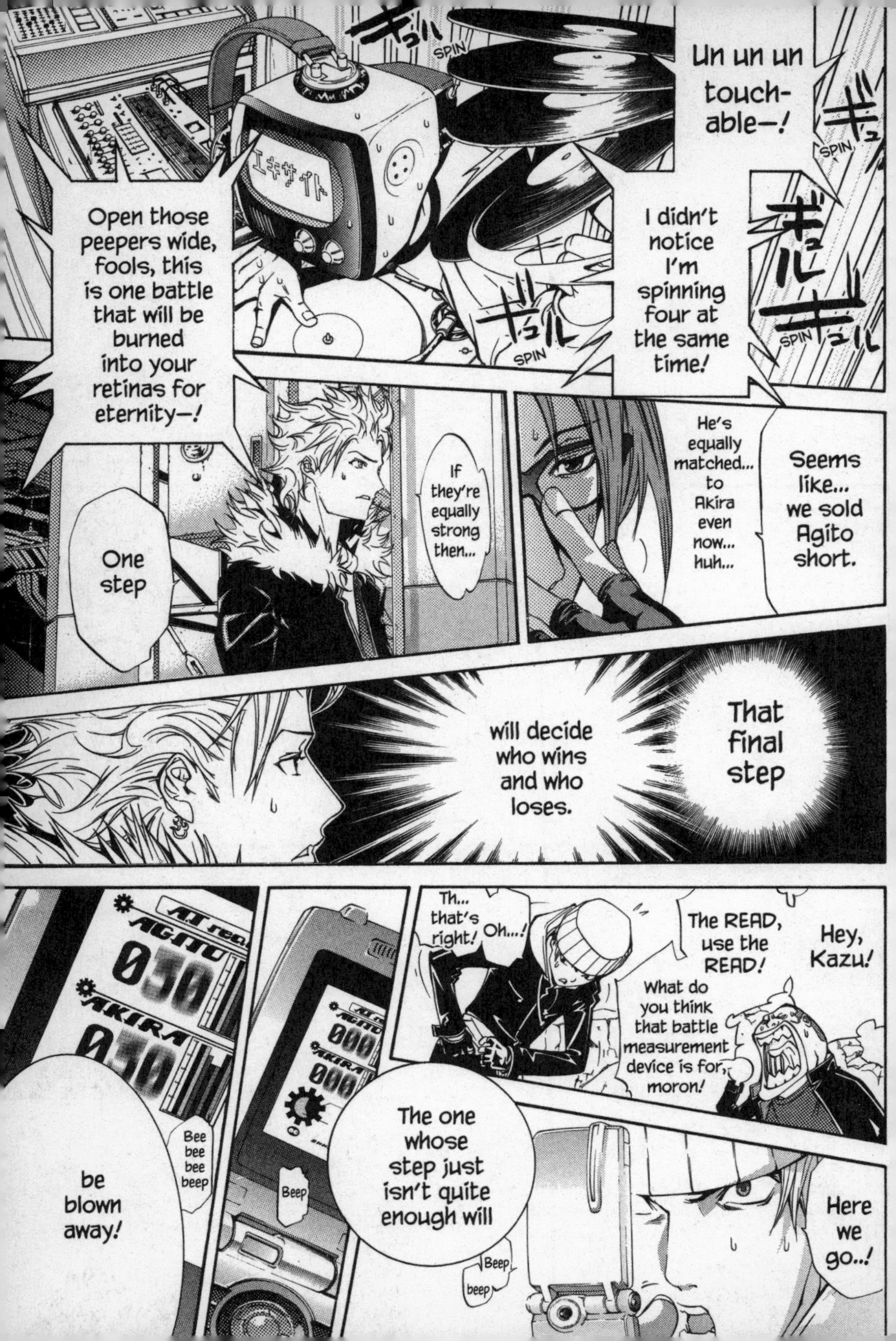

Un un un touch-able—!
SPIN
SPIN
I didn't notice I'm spinning four at the same time!
SPIN
SPIN
Open those peepers wide, fools, this is one battle that will be burned into your retinas for eternity—!
Seems like... we sold Agito short.
He's equally matched... to Akira even now... huh...
If they're equally strong then...
One step
That final step
will decide who wins and who loses.
Hey, Kazu!
The READ, use the READ!
What do you think that battle measurement device is for, moron!
Oh...!
Th... that's right!
Here we go...!
Beep beep
The one whose step just isn't quite enough will
Beep
Bee bee bee beep
be blown away!

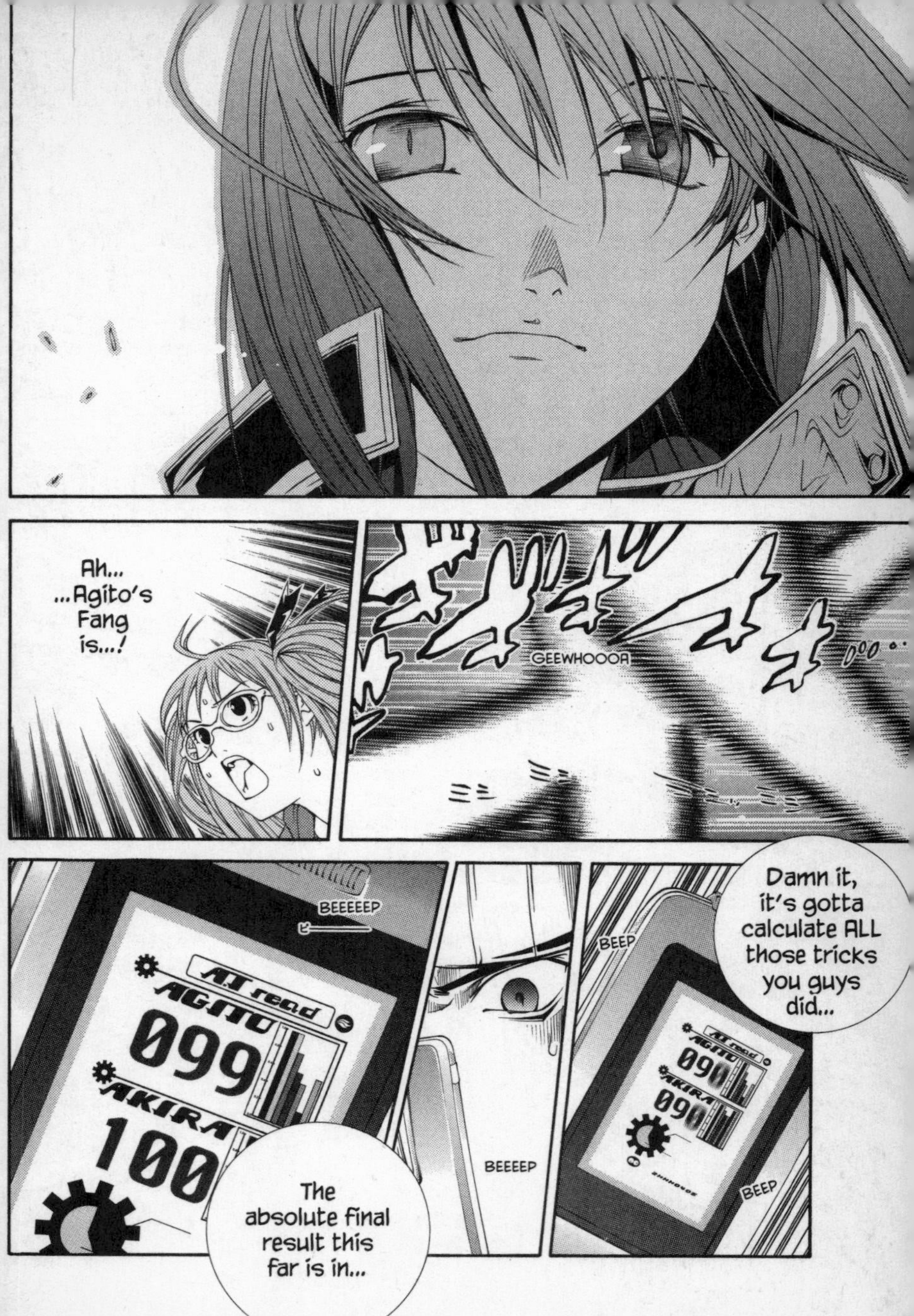
GEEWHOOOA
Ah... ...Agito's Fang is...!
Damn it, it's gotta calculate ALL those tricks you guys did...
BEEP
A.T read AGITO 090 AKIRA 090
BEEP
BEEEEP
BEEEEEP
A.T read AGITO 099 AKIRA 100
The absolute final result this far is in...

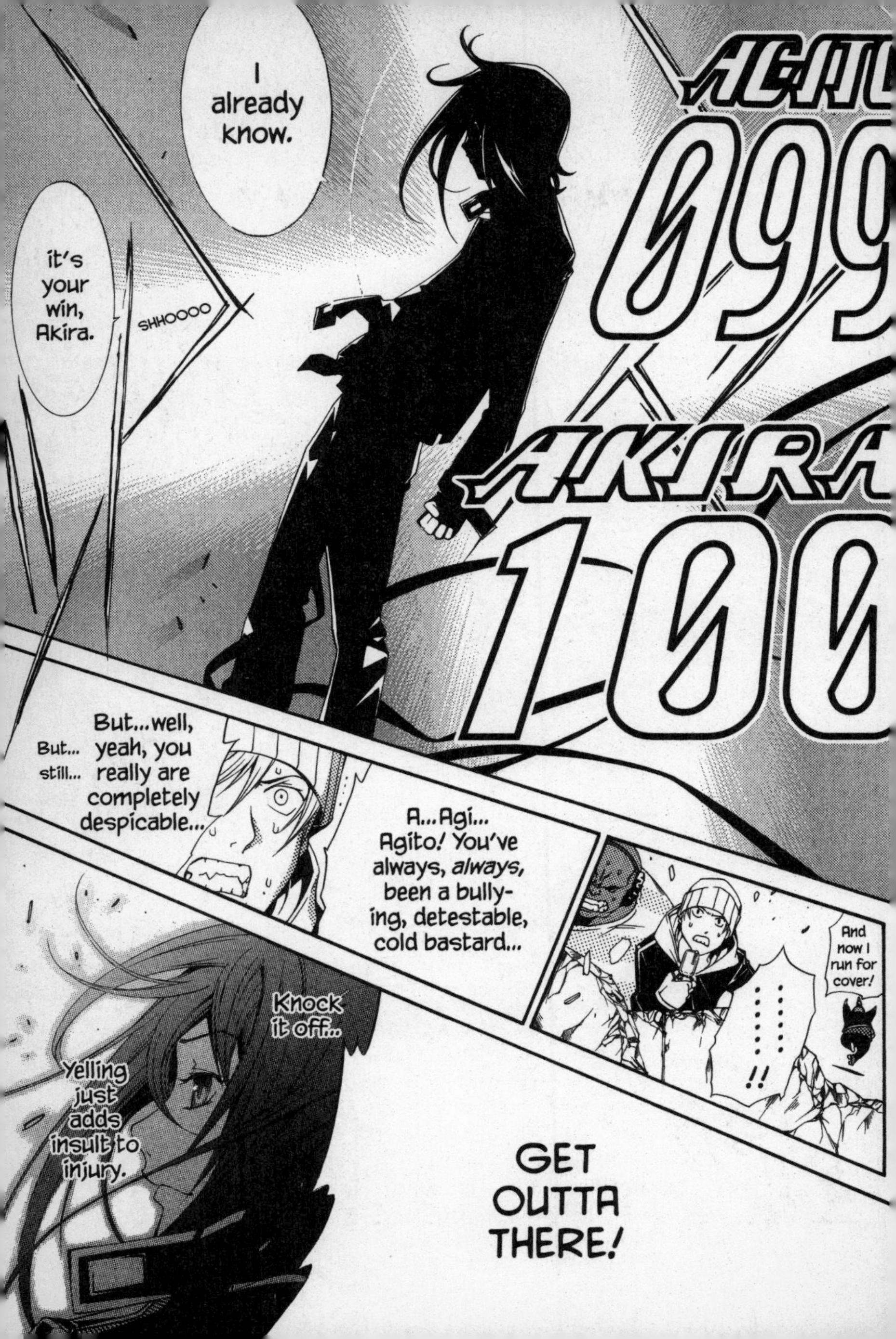
AKIRA
I already know.
it's your win, Akira.
SHHOOOO
And now I run for cover!
......!!
A...Agi... Agito! You've always, *always*, been a bully-ing, detestable, cold bastard...
But...well, yeah, you really are completely despicable...
But... still...
GET OUTTA THERE!
Knock it off...
Yelling just adds insult to injury.

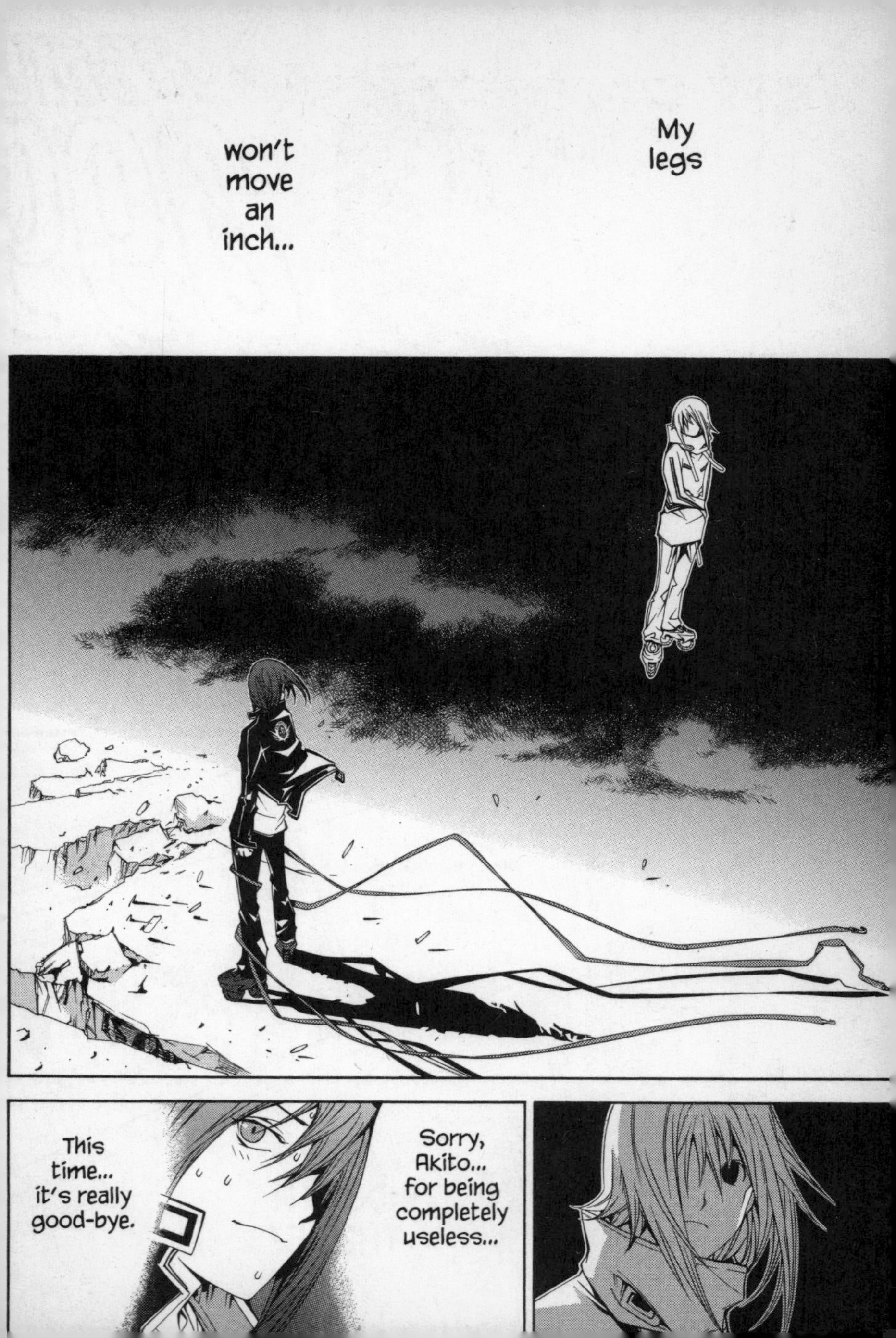
My legs
won't move an inch...
Sorry, Akito... for being completely useless...
This time... it's really good-bye.

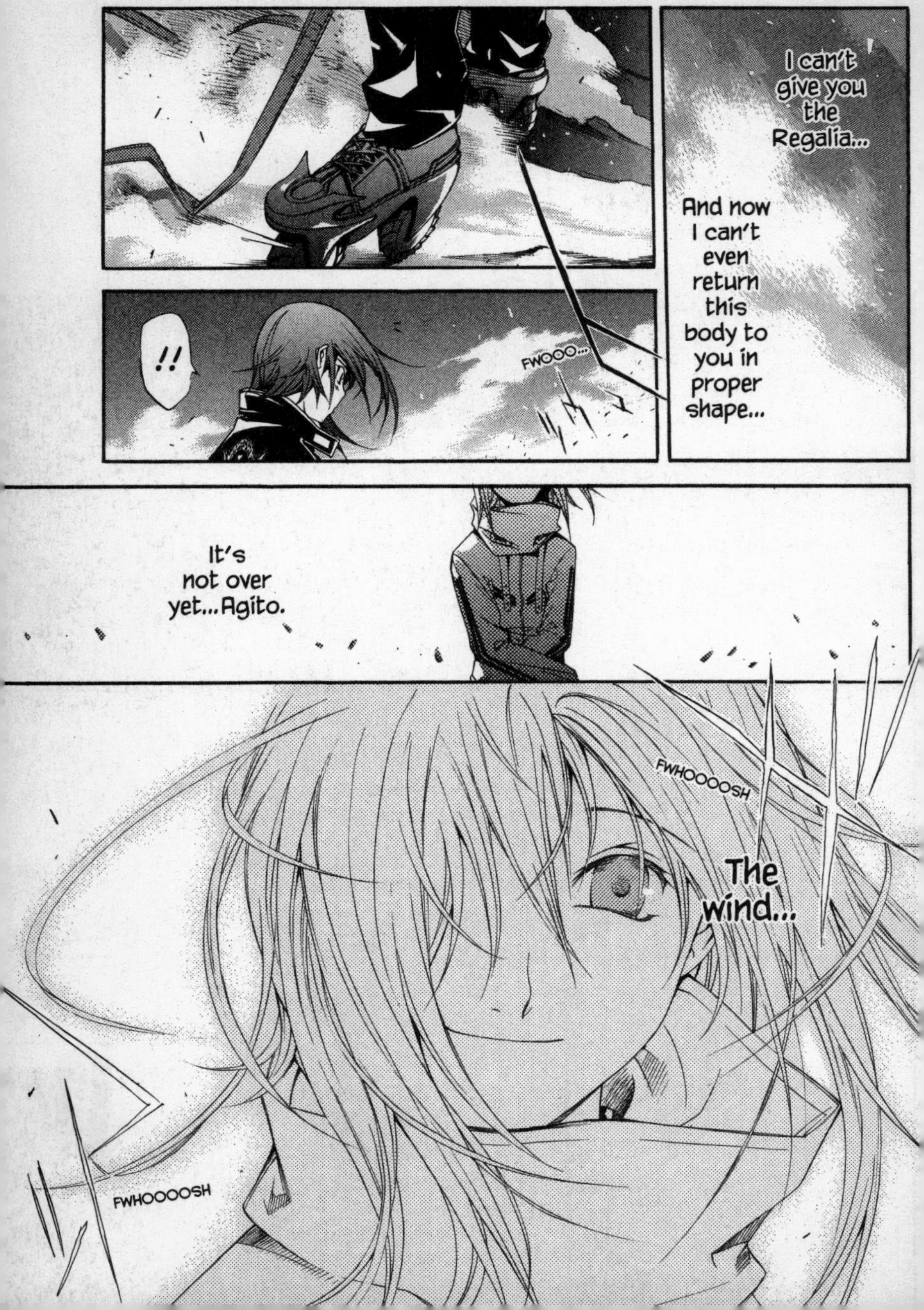
I can't give you the Regalia...
And now I can't even return this body to you in proper shape...
!!
FWOOO...
It's not over yet...Agito.
FWHOOOOSH
The wind...
FWHOOOOSH

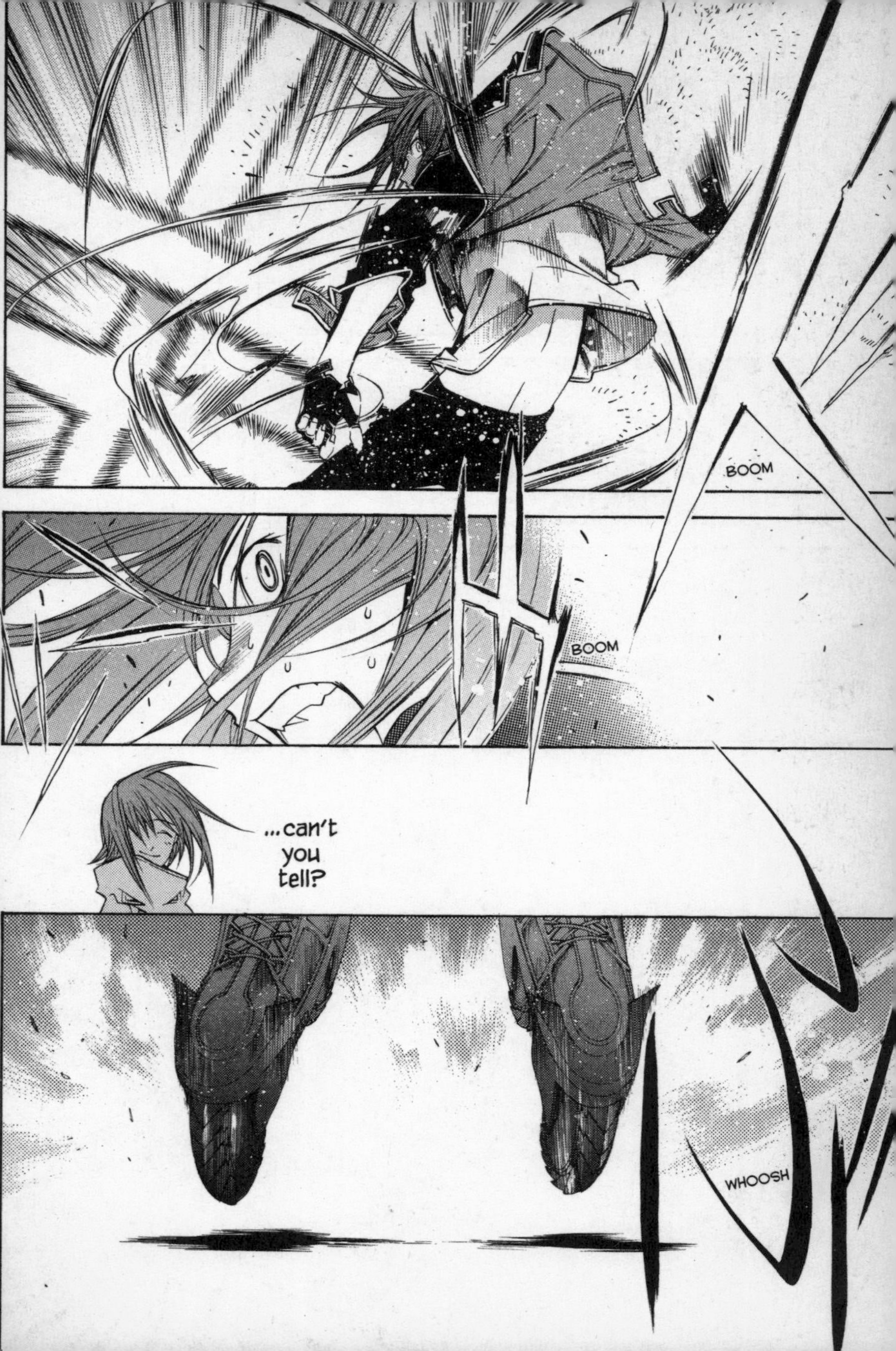
BOOM
BOOM
...can't you tell?
WHOOSH

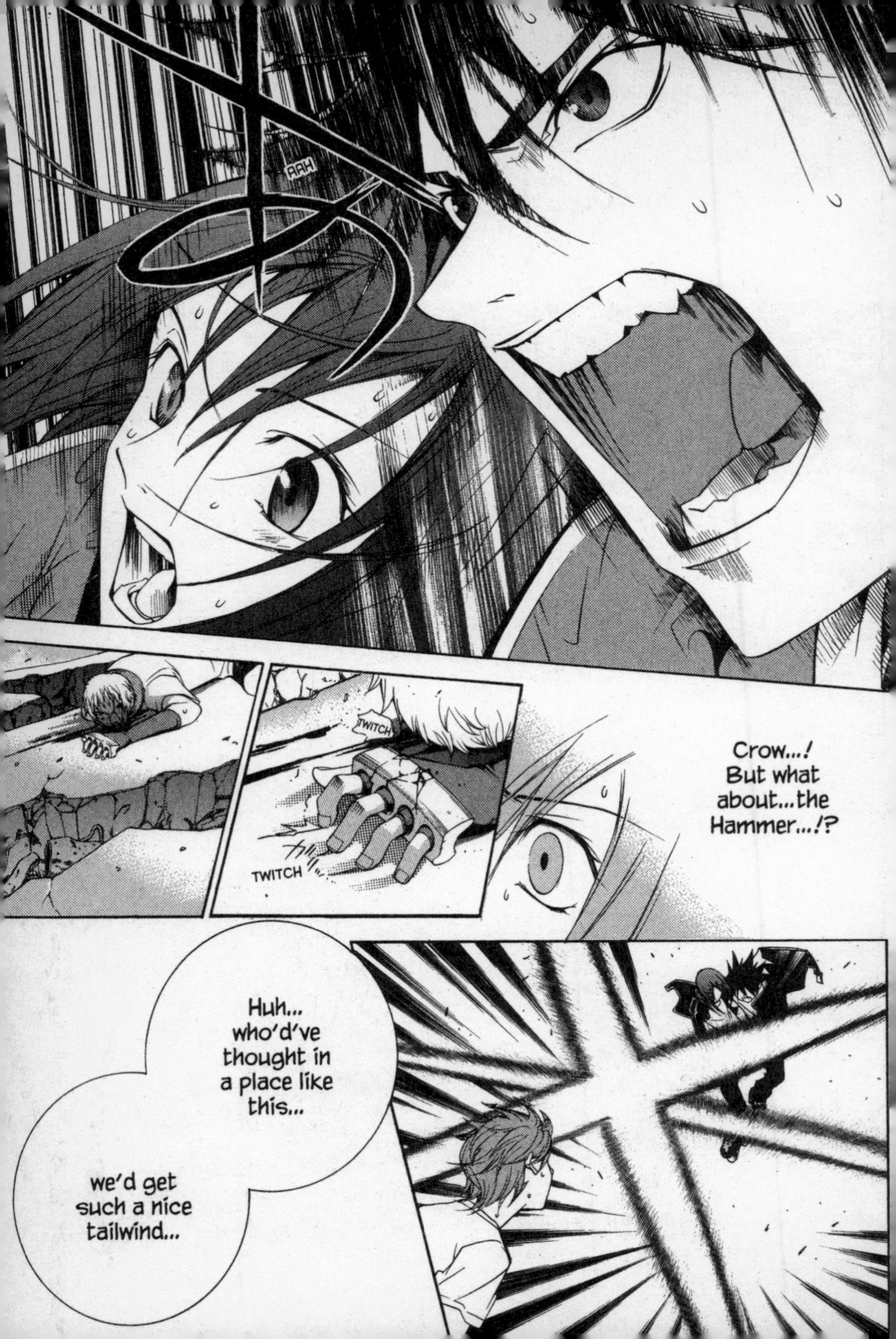
AAH
Crow...! But what about...the Hammer...!?
TWITCH
TWITCH
Huh... who'd've thought in a place like this...
we'd get such a nice tailwind...

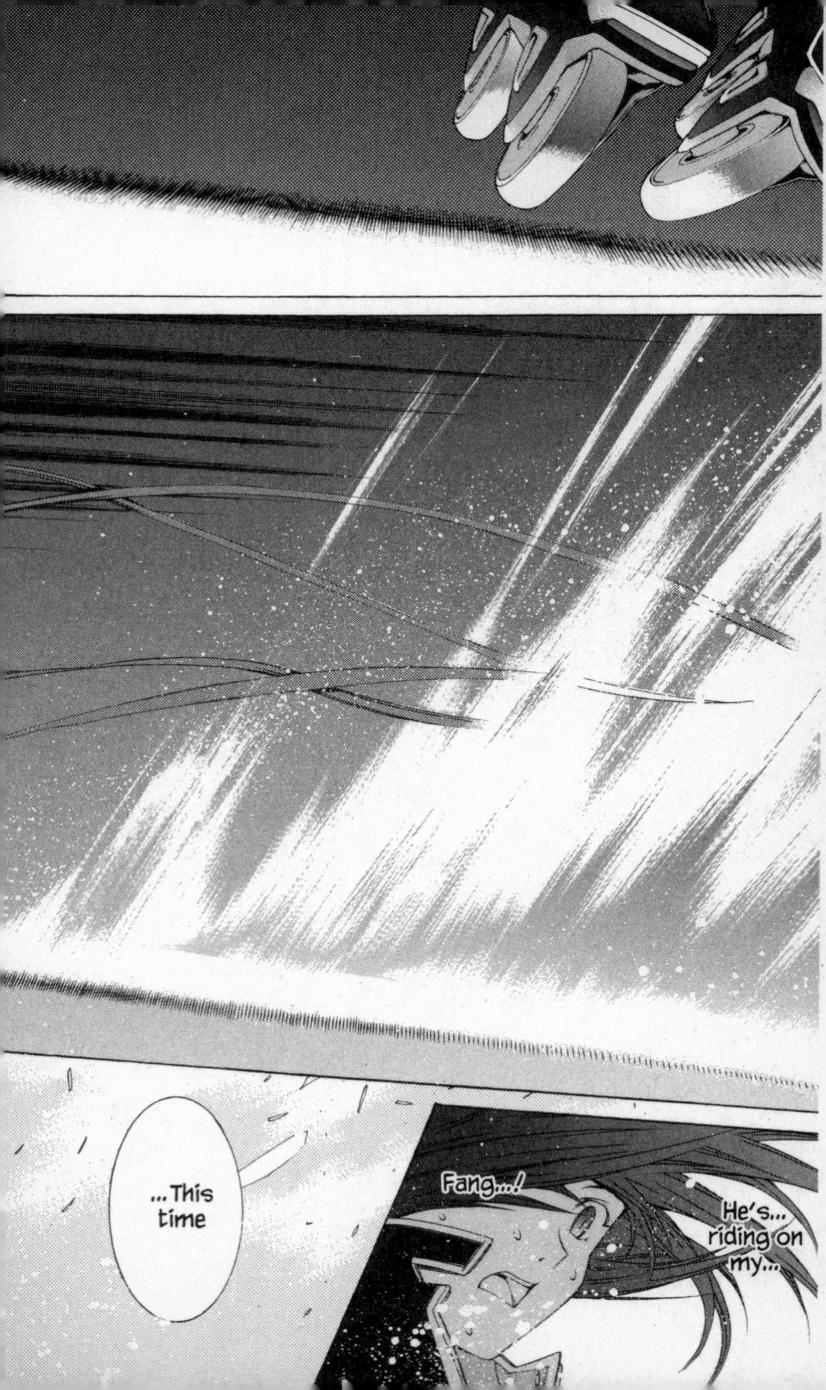
Fang...!
He's... riding on my...
...This time

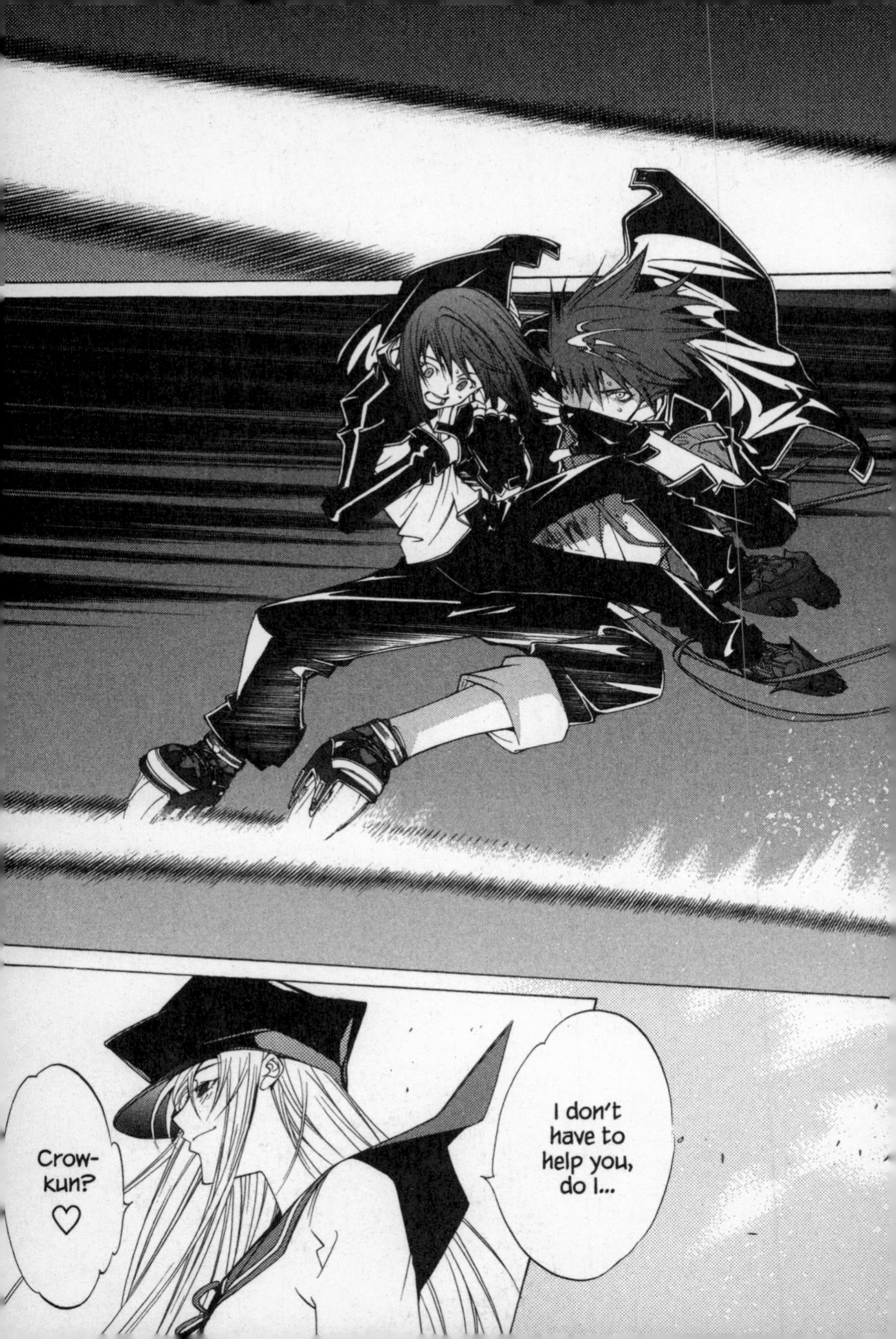
I don't have to help you, do I...
Crow-kun? ♡

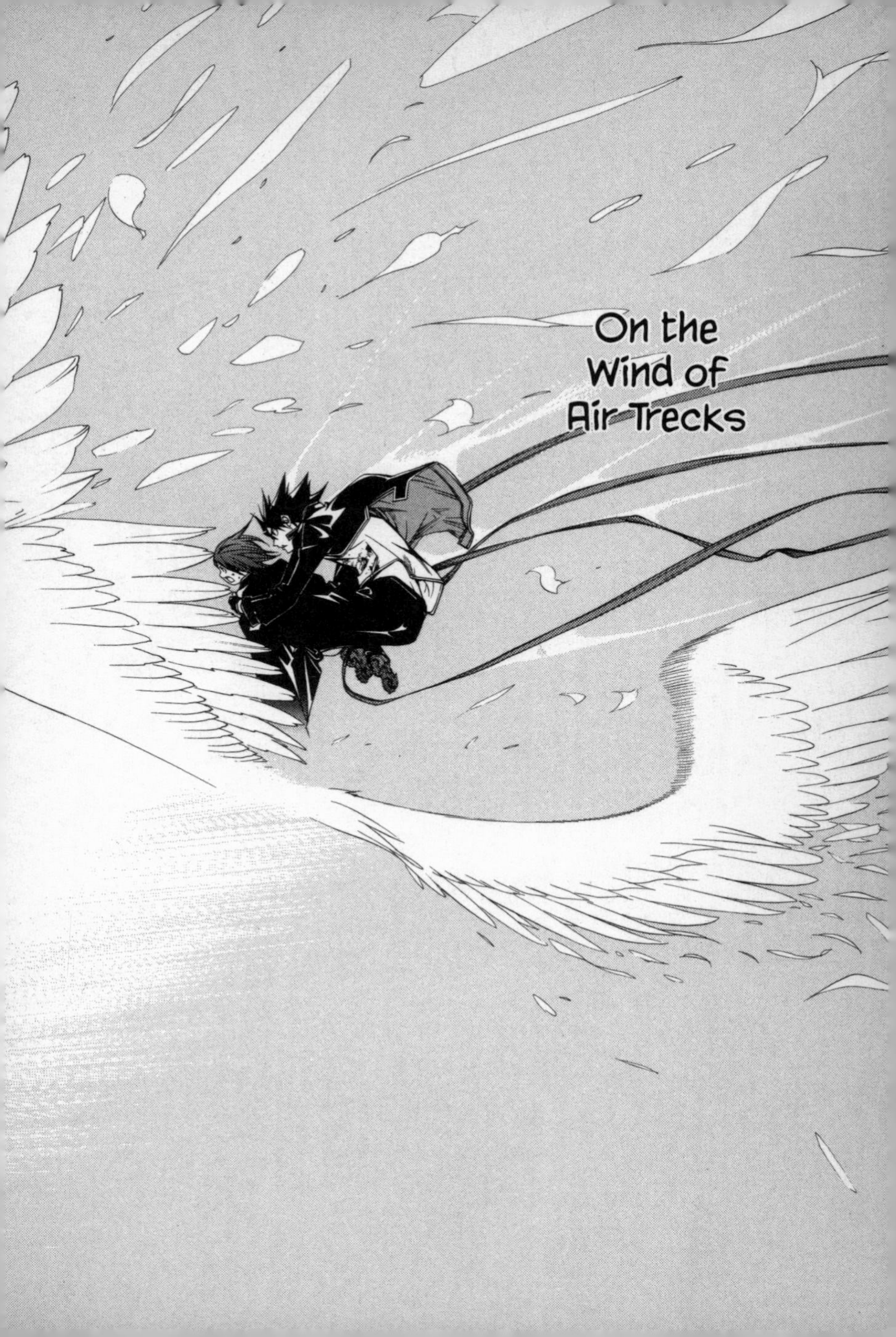
On the Wind of Air Trecks

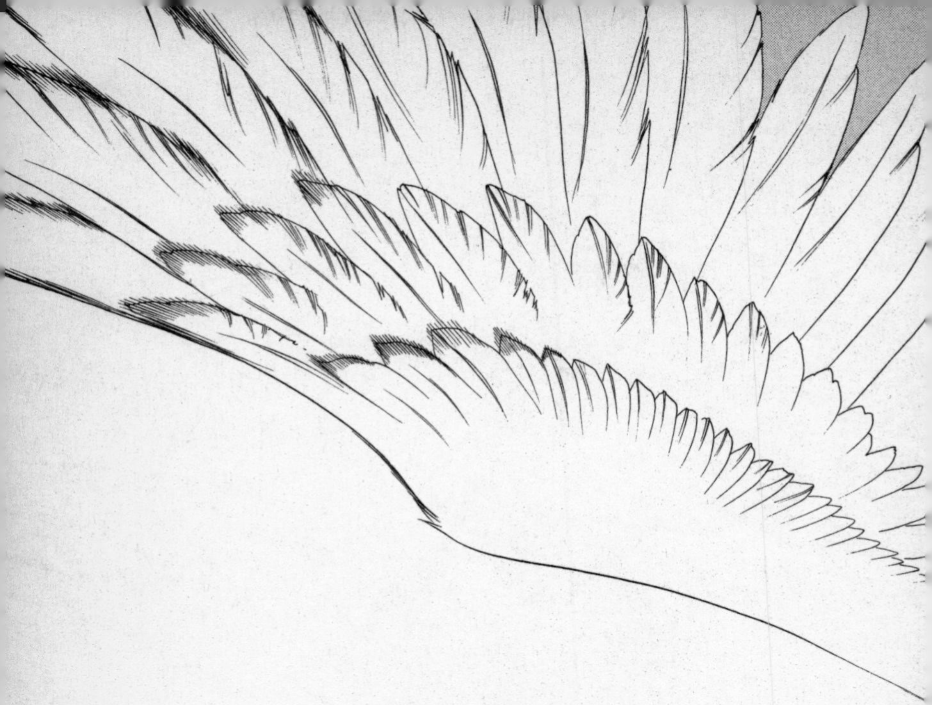

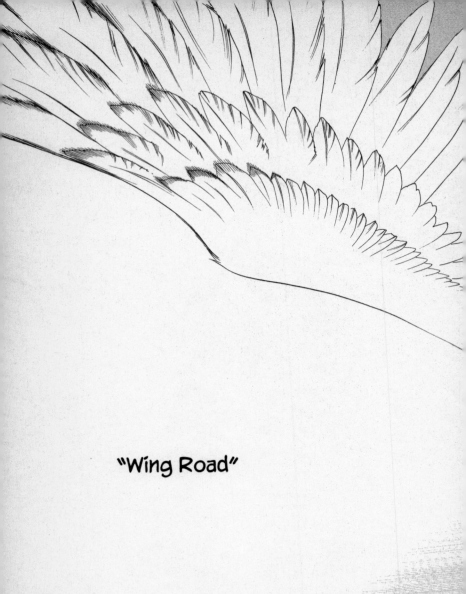

"Wing Road"

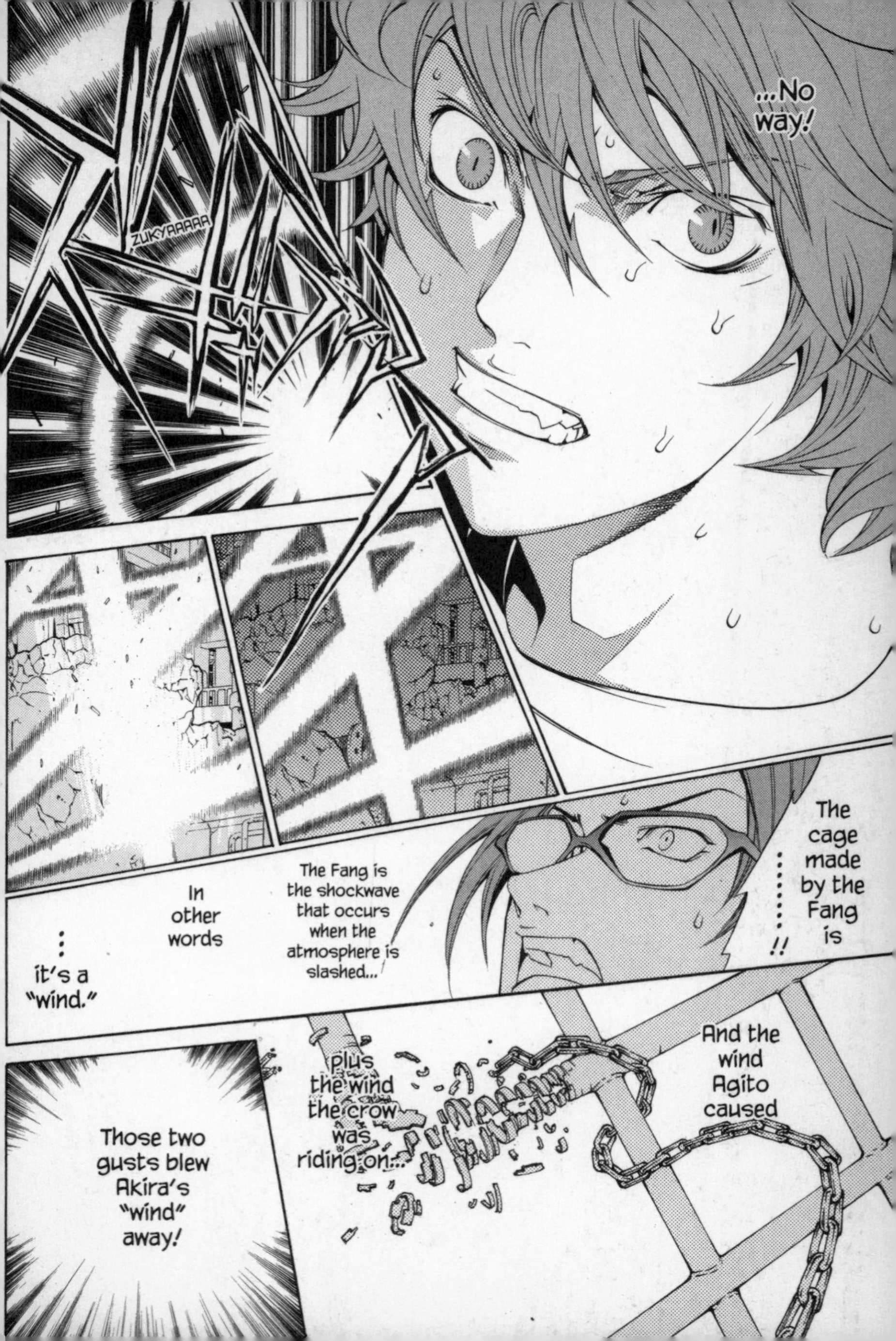
...No way!
ZUKYAAAAA
The cage made by the Fang is
......!!
The Fang is the shockwave that occurs when the atmosphere is slashed...
In other words
...it's a "wind."
And the wind Agito caused
plus the wind the crow was riding on...
Those two gusts blew Akira's "wind" away!

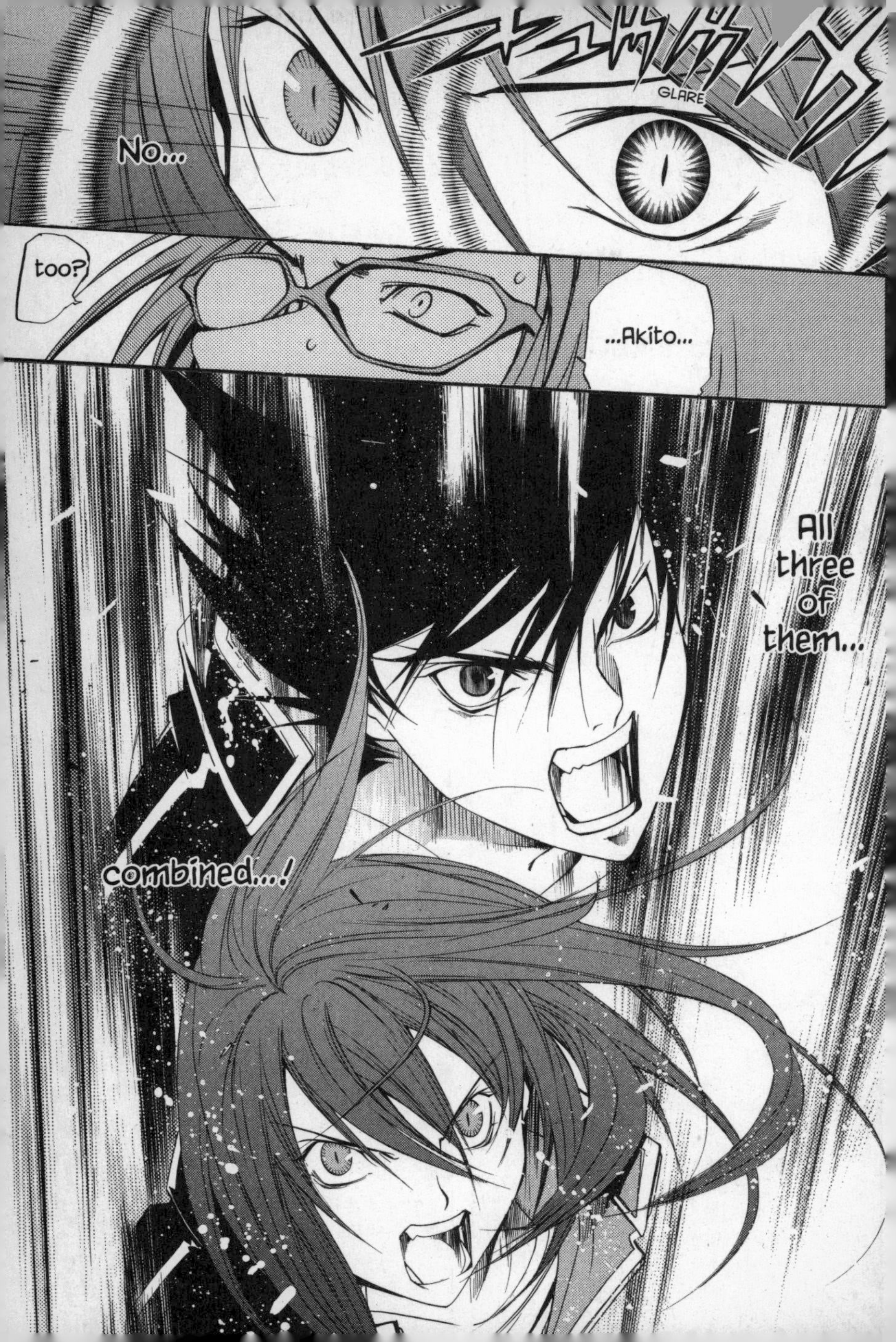
GLARE
No...
...Akito...
too?
All three of them...
combined...!

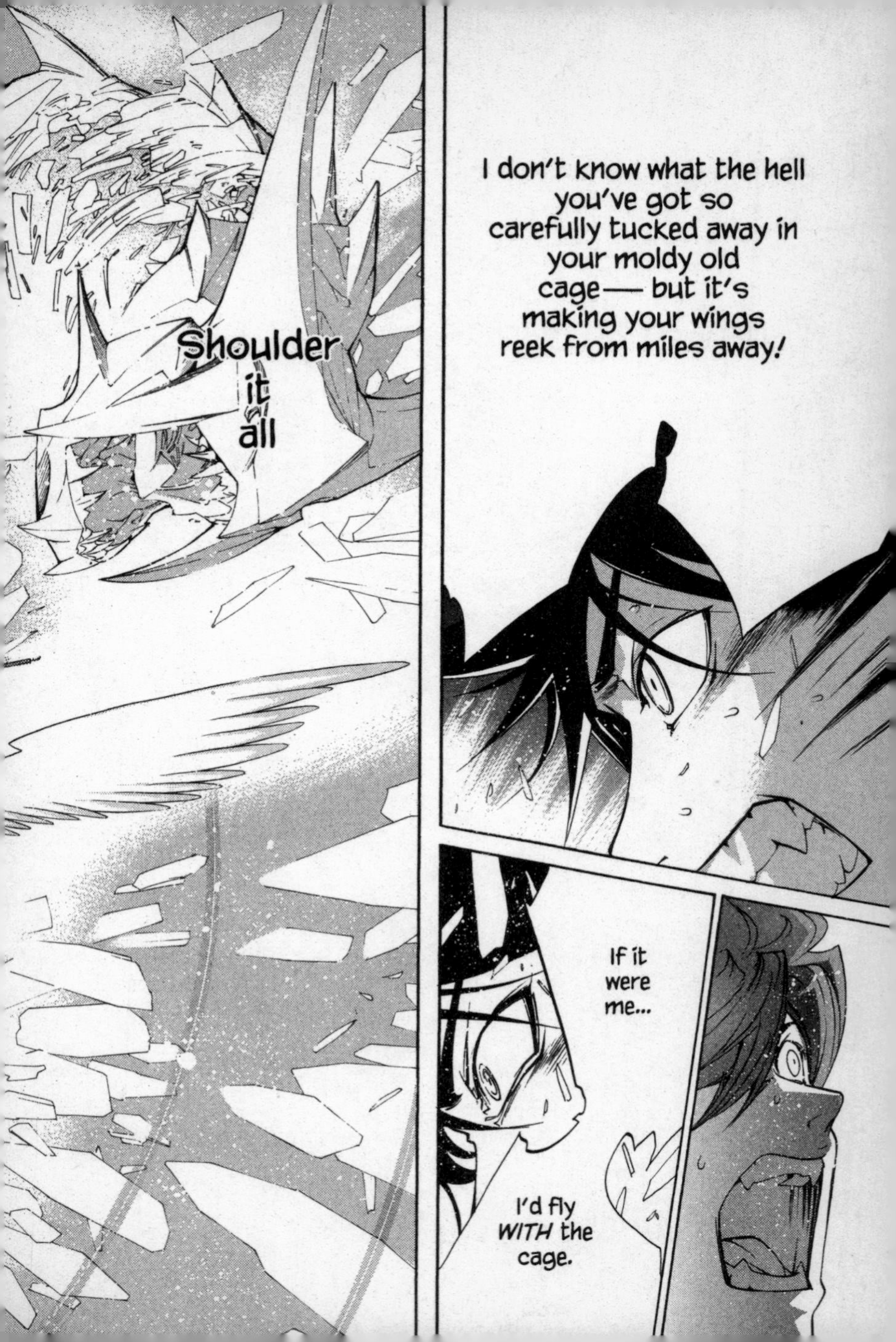

I don't know what the hell you've got so carefully tucked away in your moldy old cage— but it's making your wings reek from miles away!
If it were me...
I'd fly *WITH* the cage.
Shoulder it all

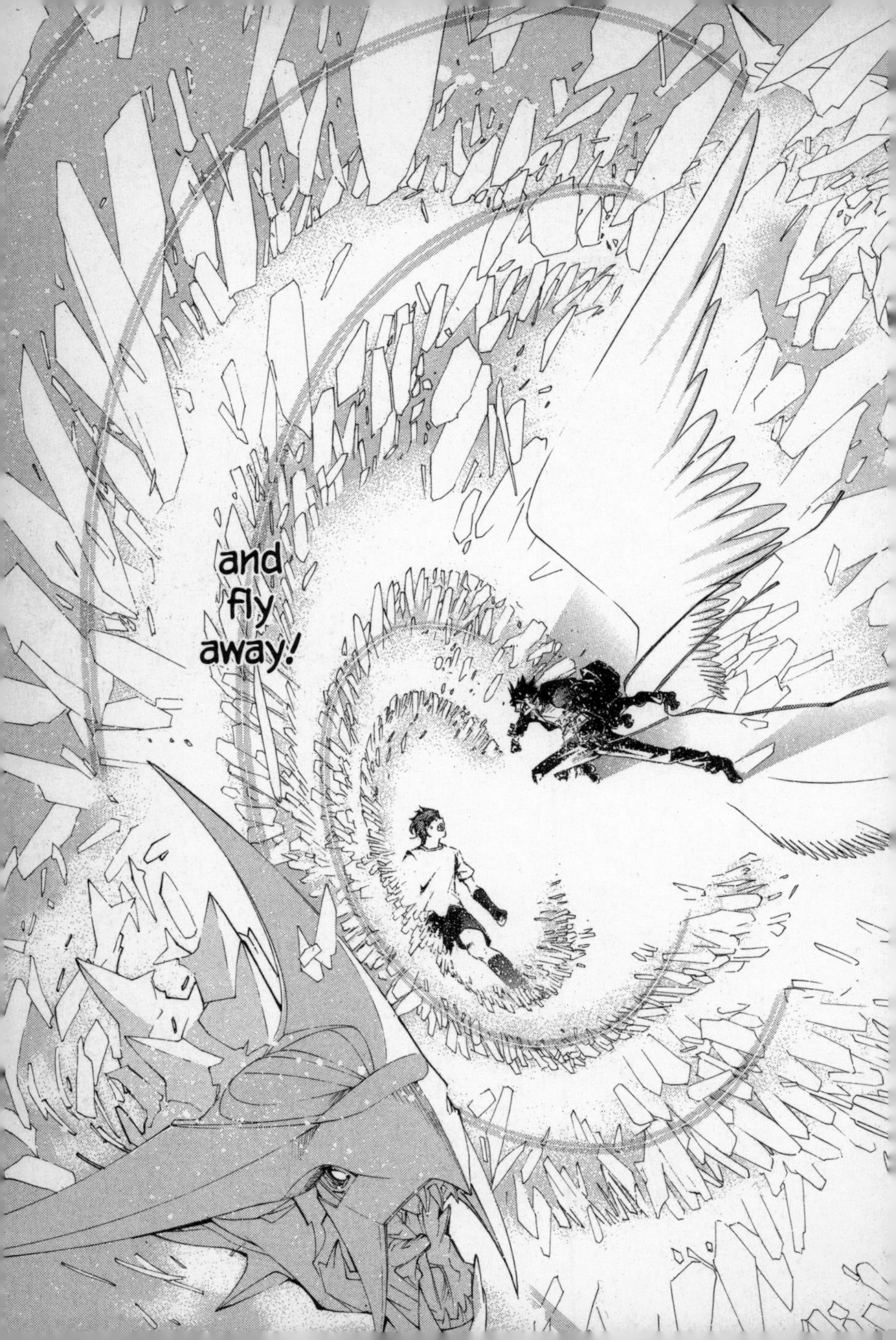
and fly away!

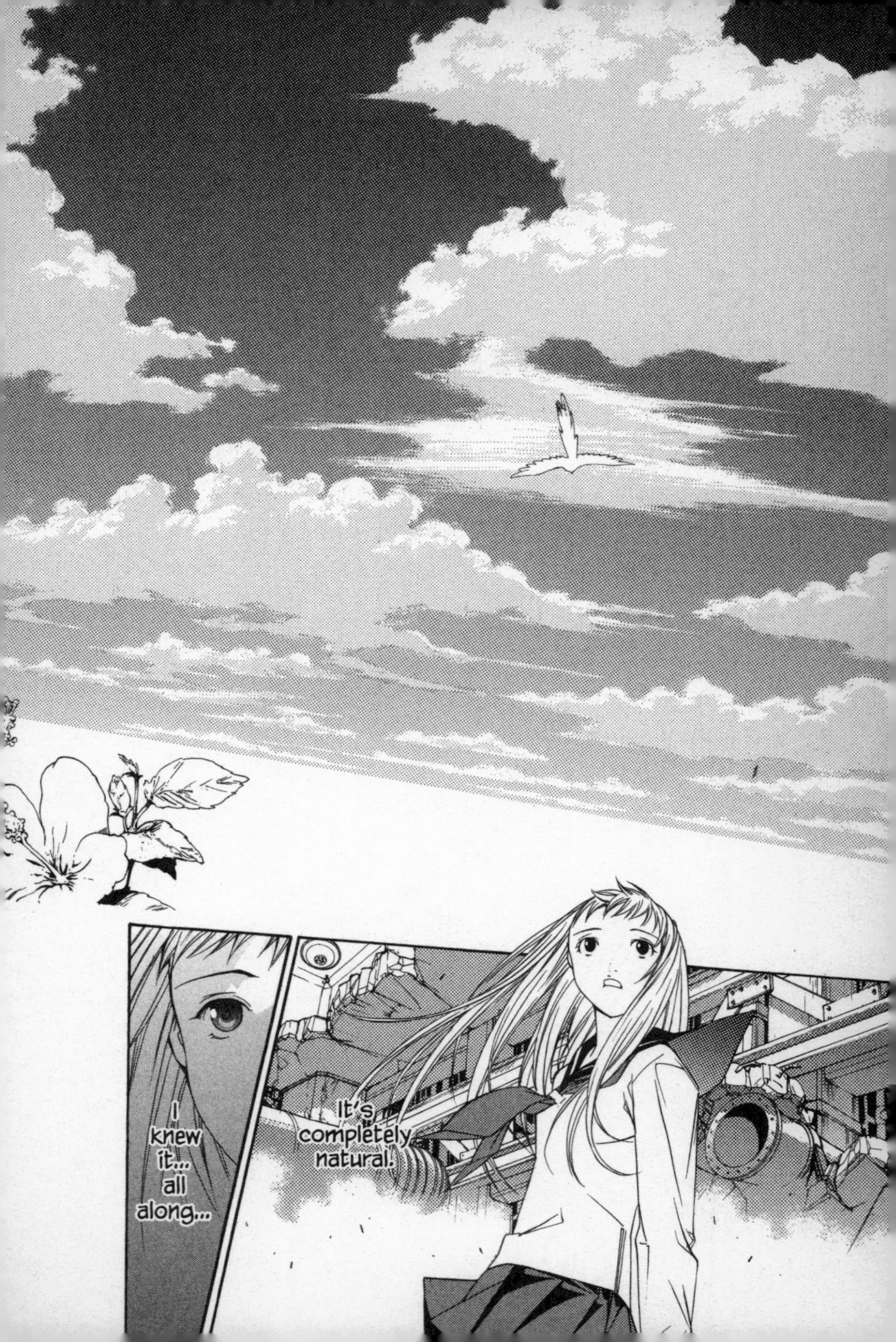
It's completely natural.
I knew it... all along...

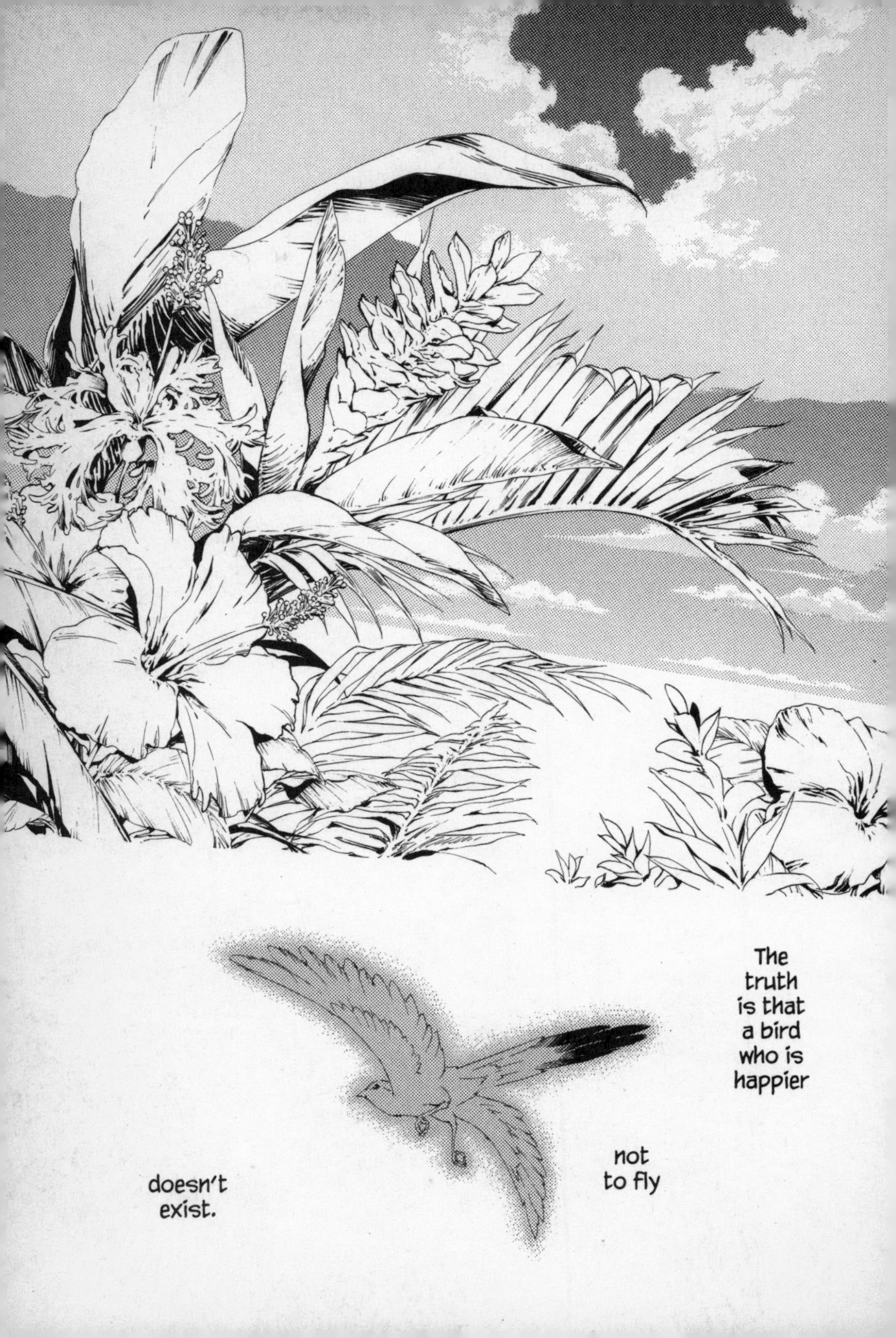
The truth is that a bird who is happier
not to fly
doesn't exist.

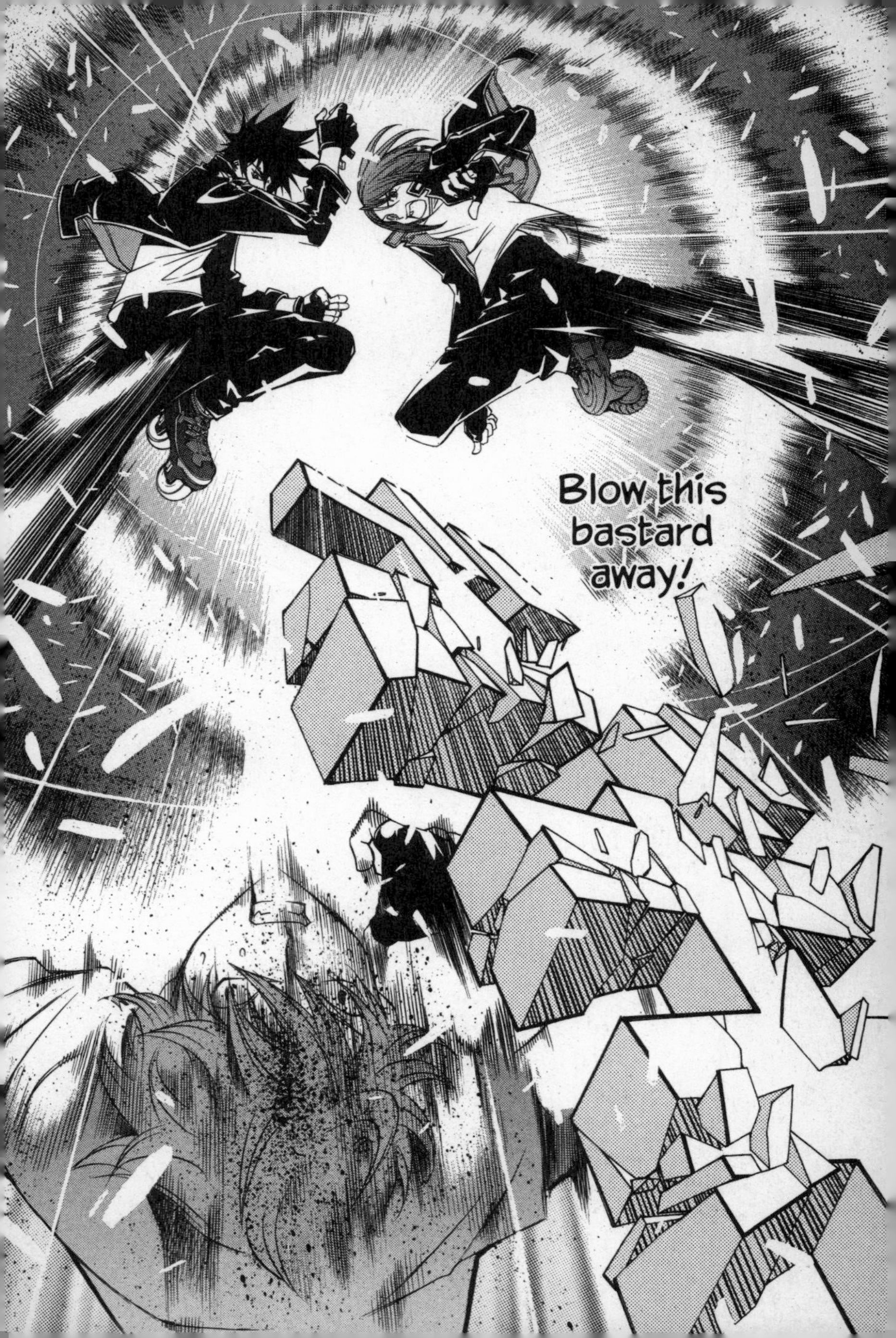
Blow this bastard away!

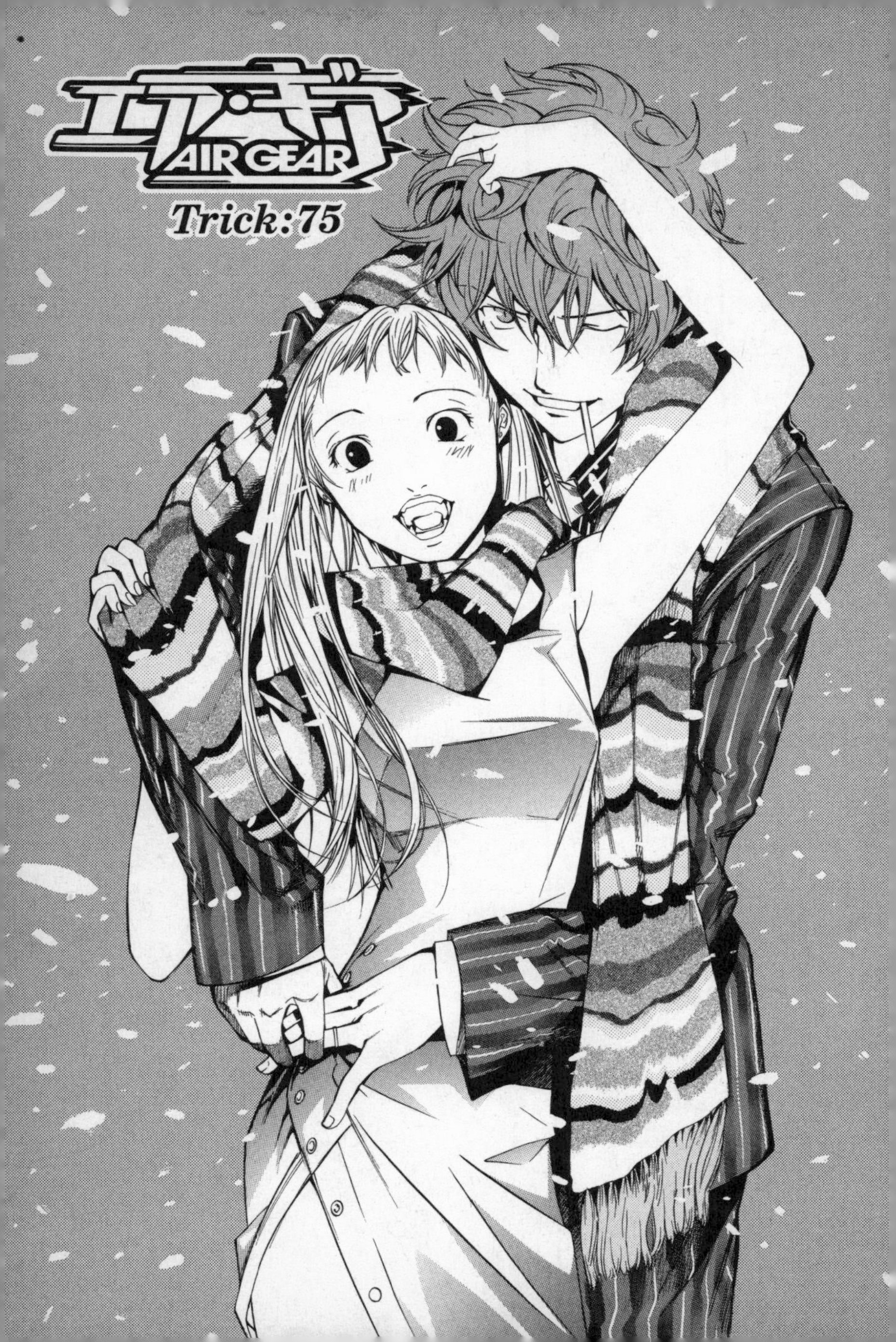
エア・ギア
AIR GEAR
Trick:75

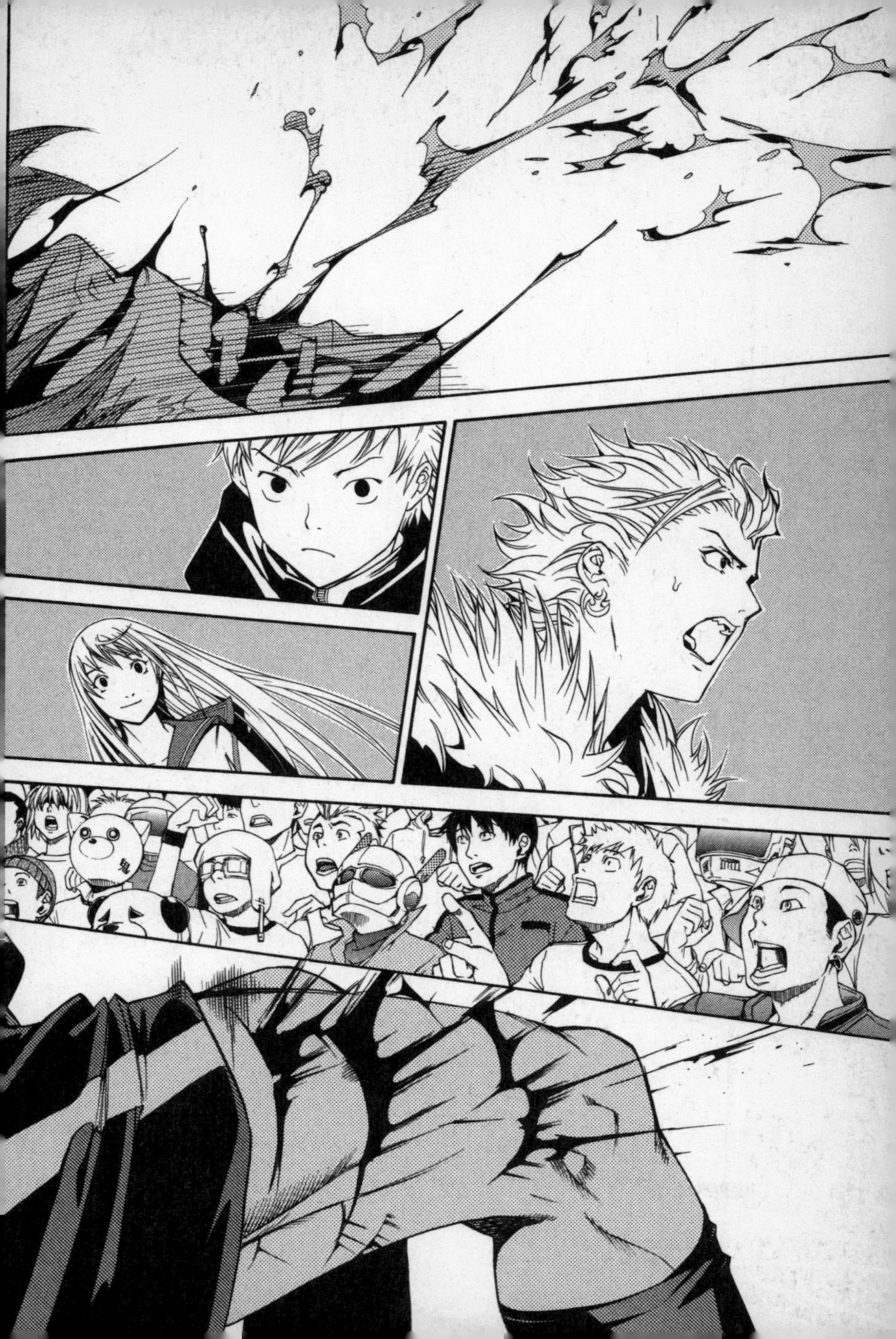

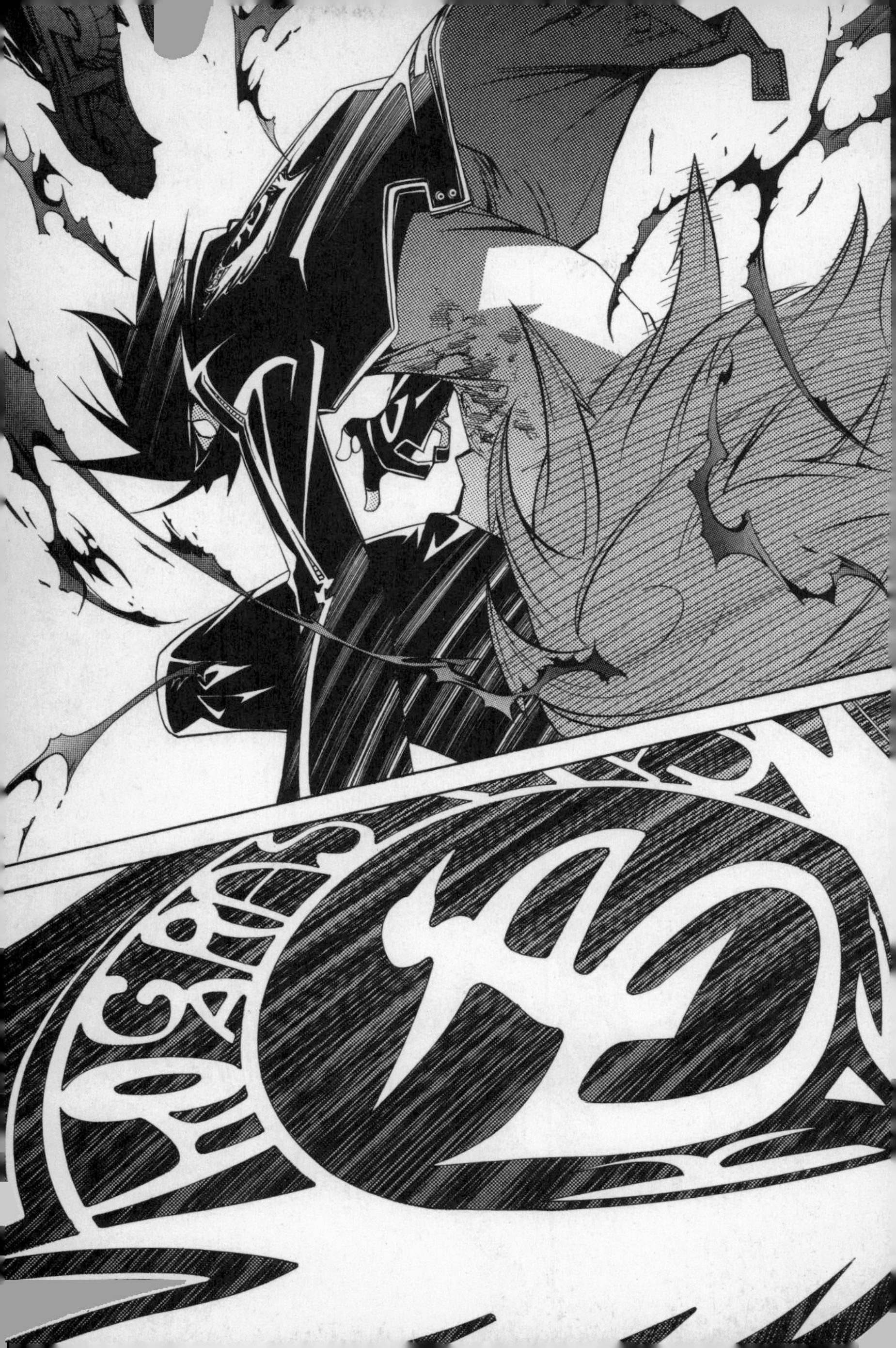

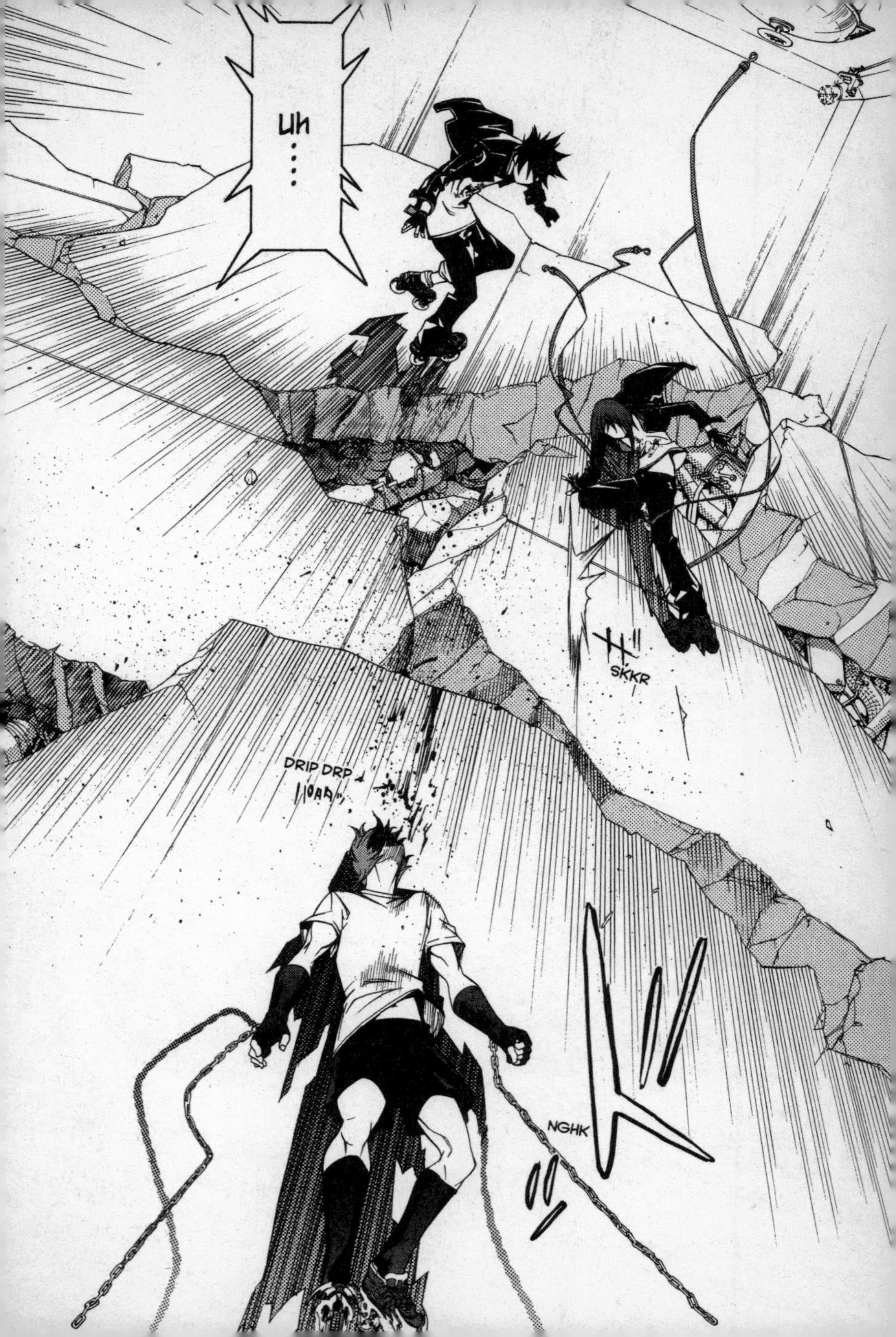
uh ....
SKKR
DRIP DRP
NGHK

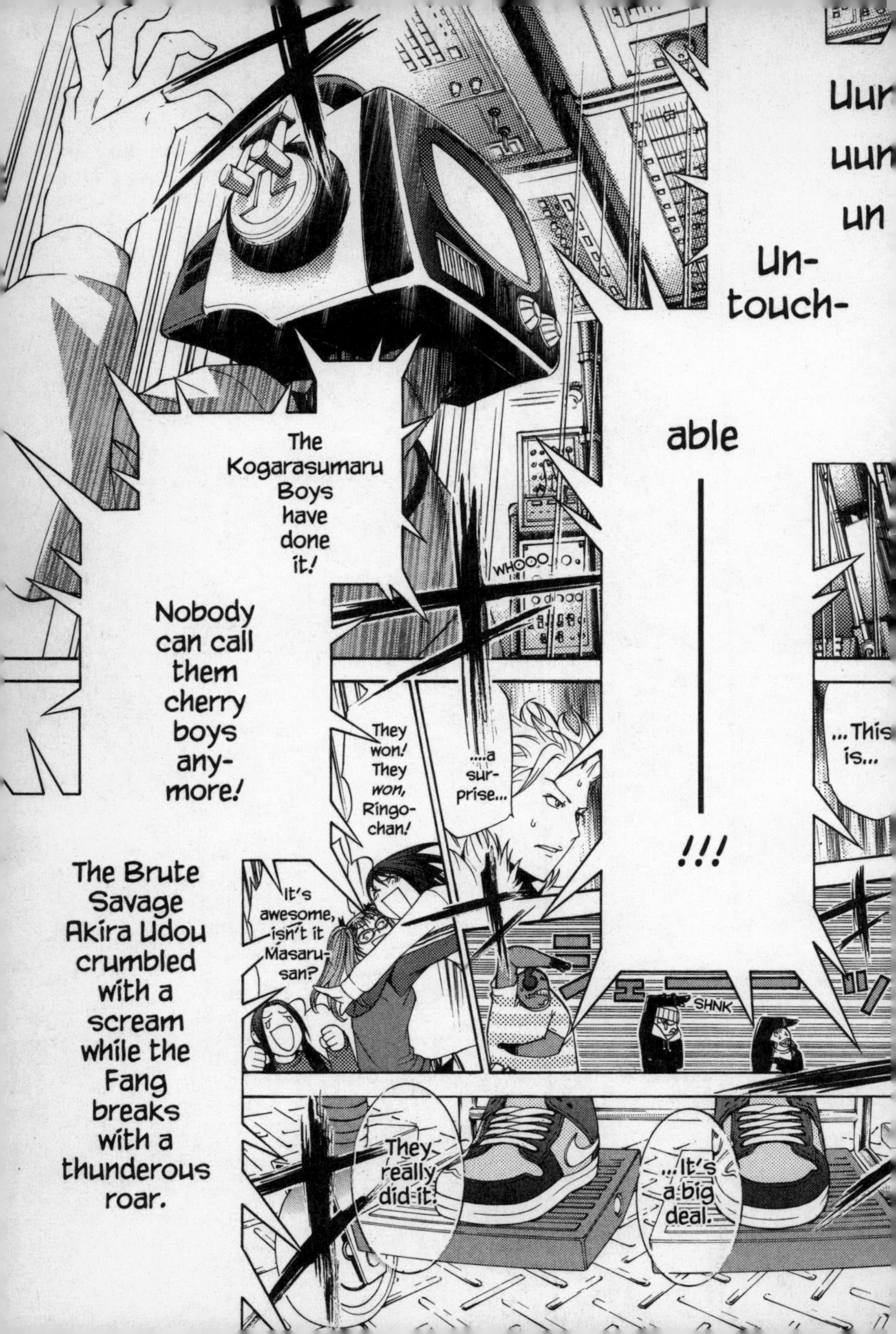
Uur uun un Un- touch- able
!!!
The Kogarasumaru Boys have done it!
WHOOO
Nobody can call them cherry boys anymore!
The Brute Savage Akira Udou crumbled with a scream while the Fang breaks with a thunderous roar.
...This is...
....a surprise...
They won! They won, Ringo-chan!
It's awesome, isn't it Masaru-san?
SHNK
...It's a big deal.
They really did it.

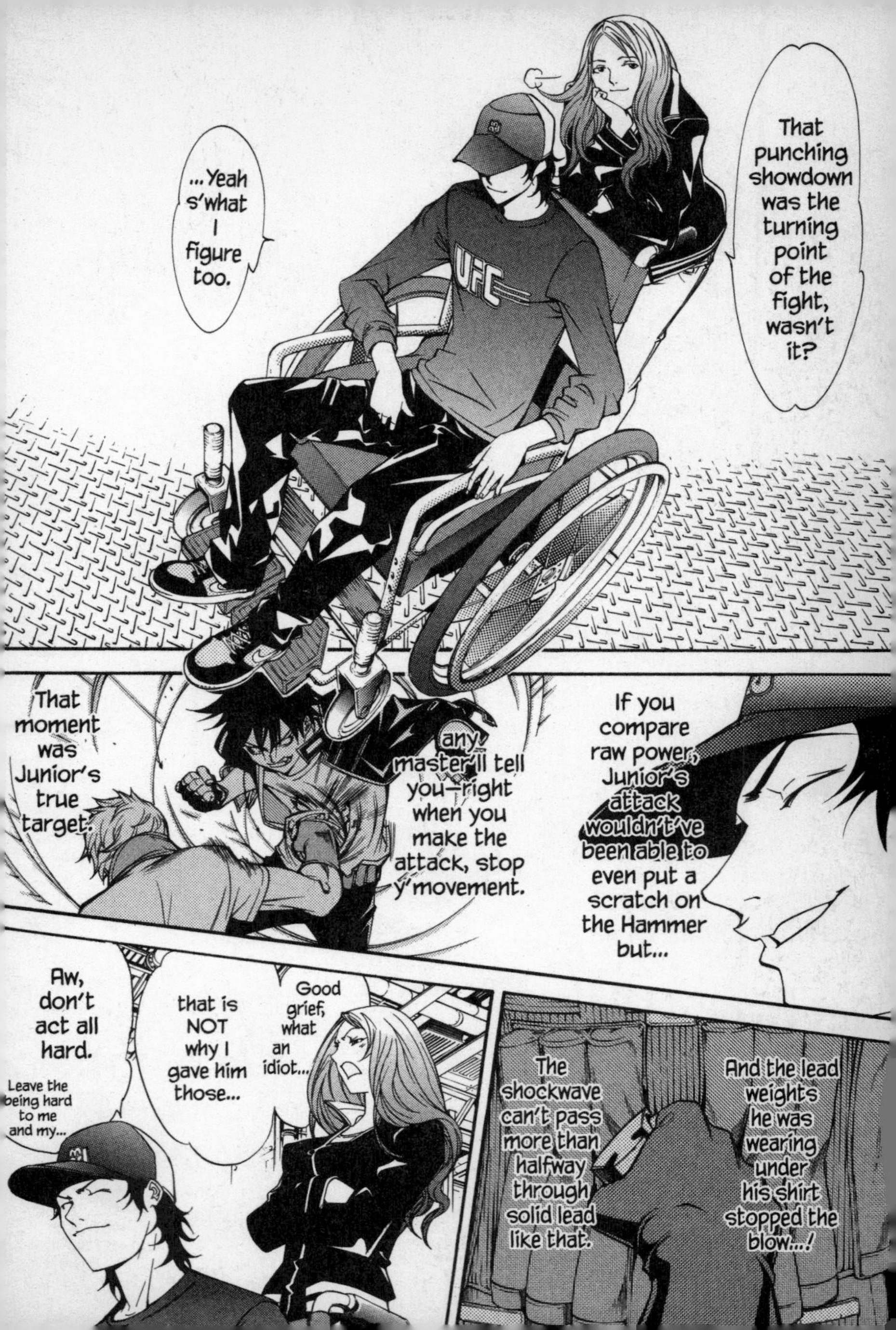
That punching showdown was the turning point of the fight, wasn't it?
...Yeah s'what I figure too.
If you compare raw power, Junior's attack wouldn't've been able to even put a scratch on the Hammer but...
any master'll tell you—right when you make the attack, stop y'movement.
That moment was Junior's true target.
And the lead weights he was wearing under his shirt stopped the blow...!
The shockwave can't pass more than halfway through solid lead like that.
Good grief, what an idiot...
that is NOT why I gave him those...
Aw, don't act all hard.
Leave the being hard to me and my...

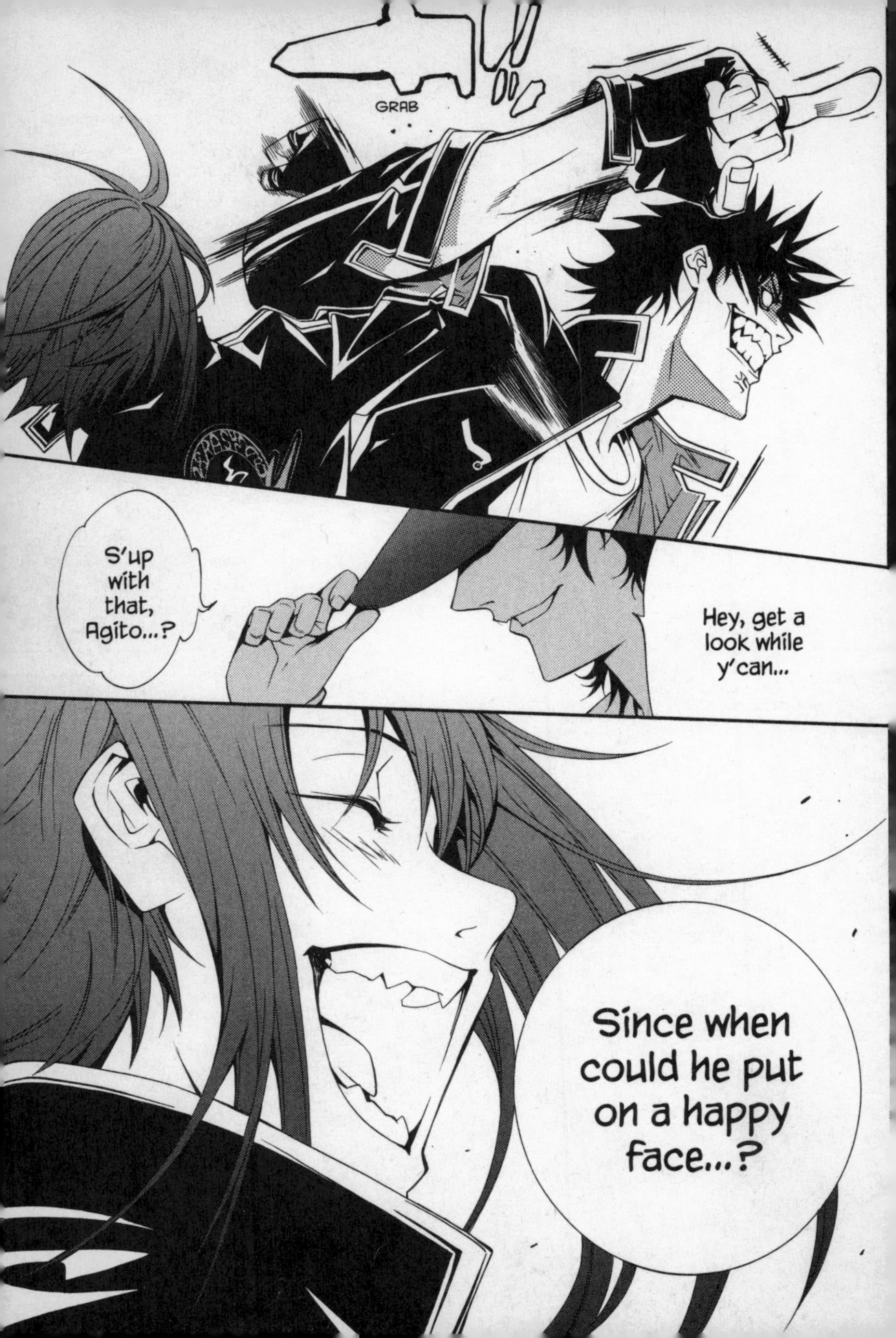
GRAB
Hey, get a look while y'can...
S'up with that, Agito...?
Since when could he put on a happy face...?

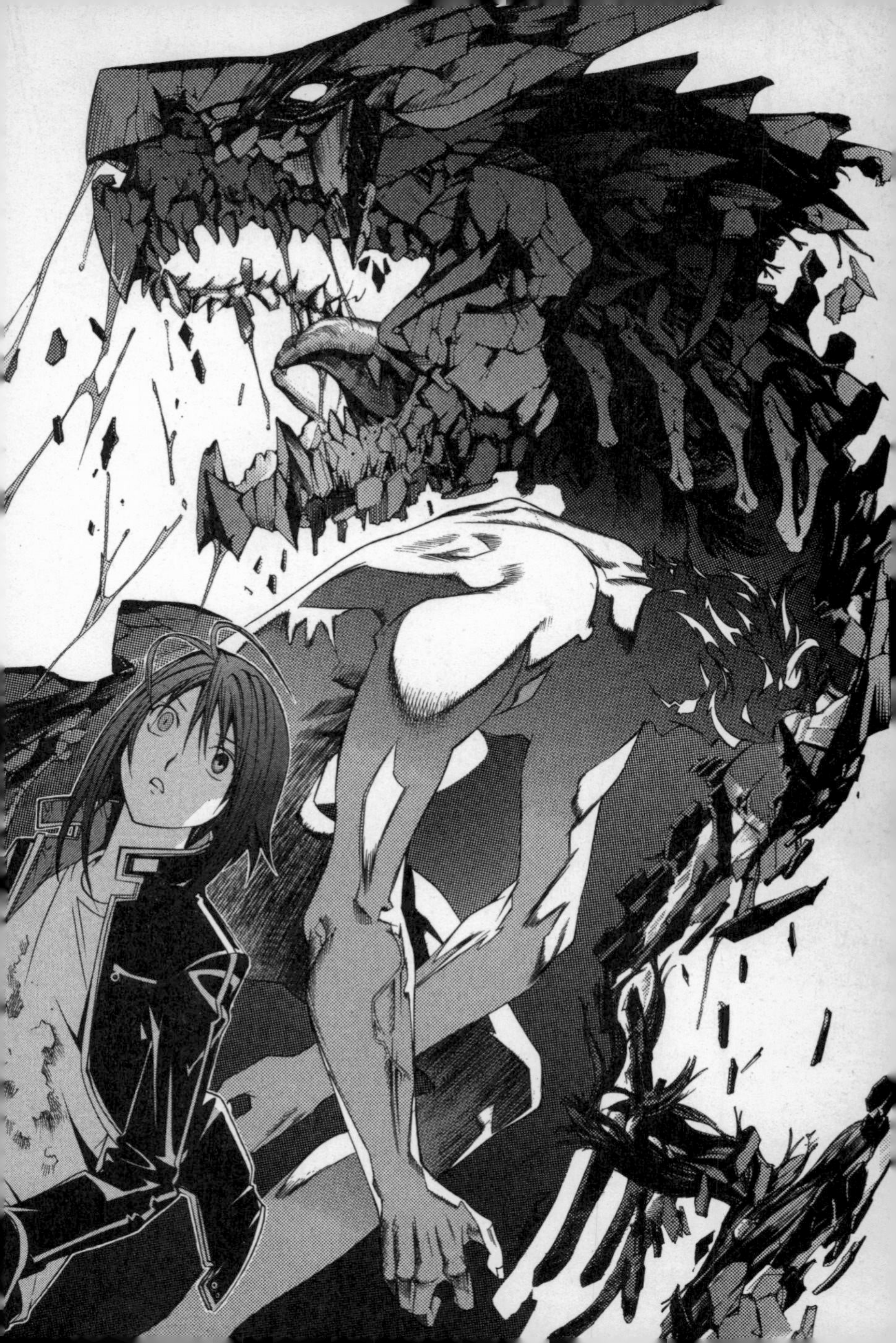

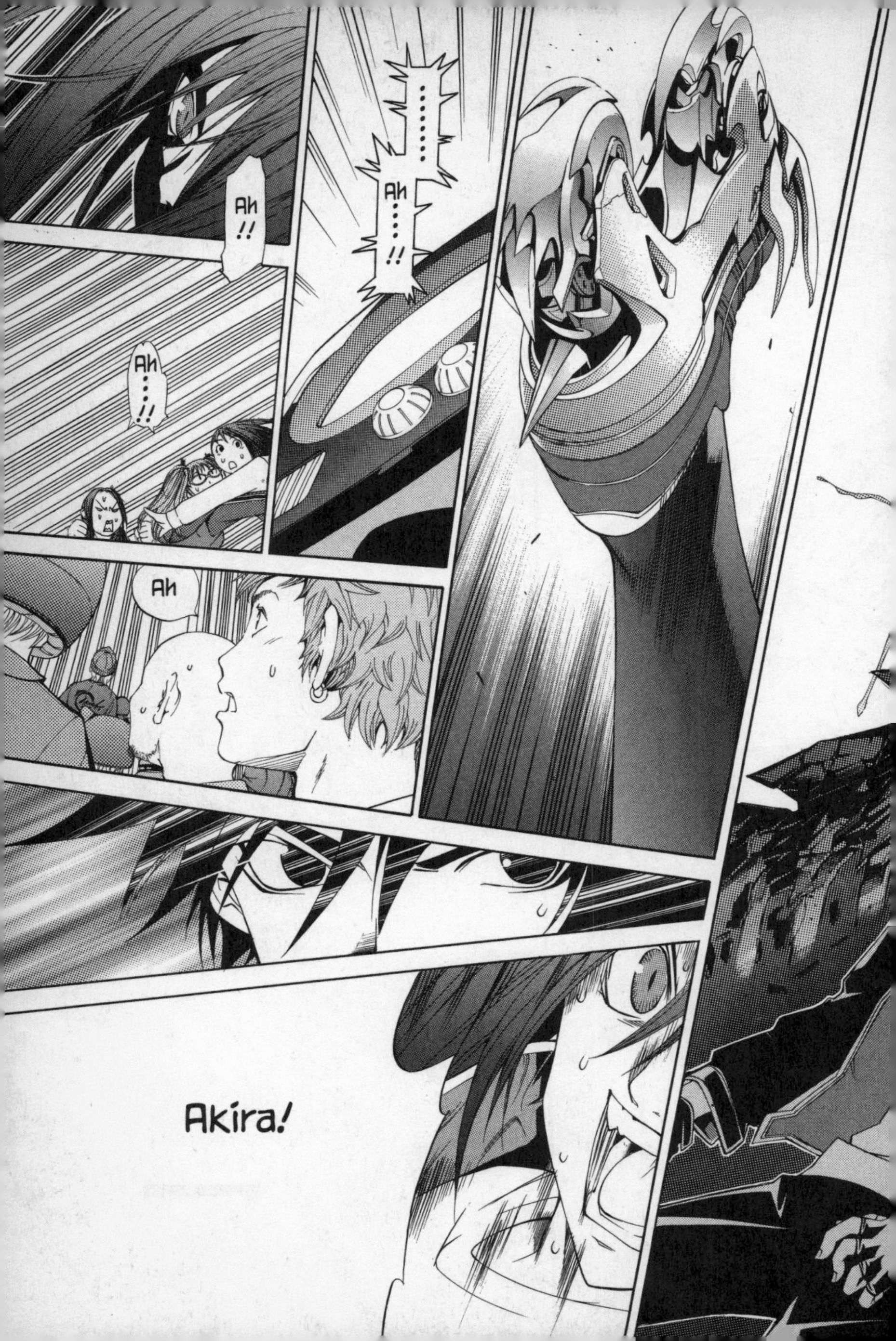

......
Ah......!!
Ah!!
Ah......!!
Ah
Akira!

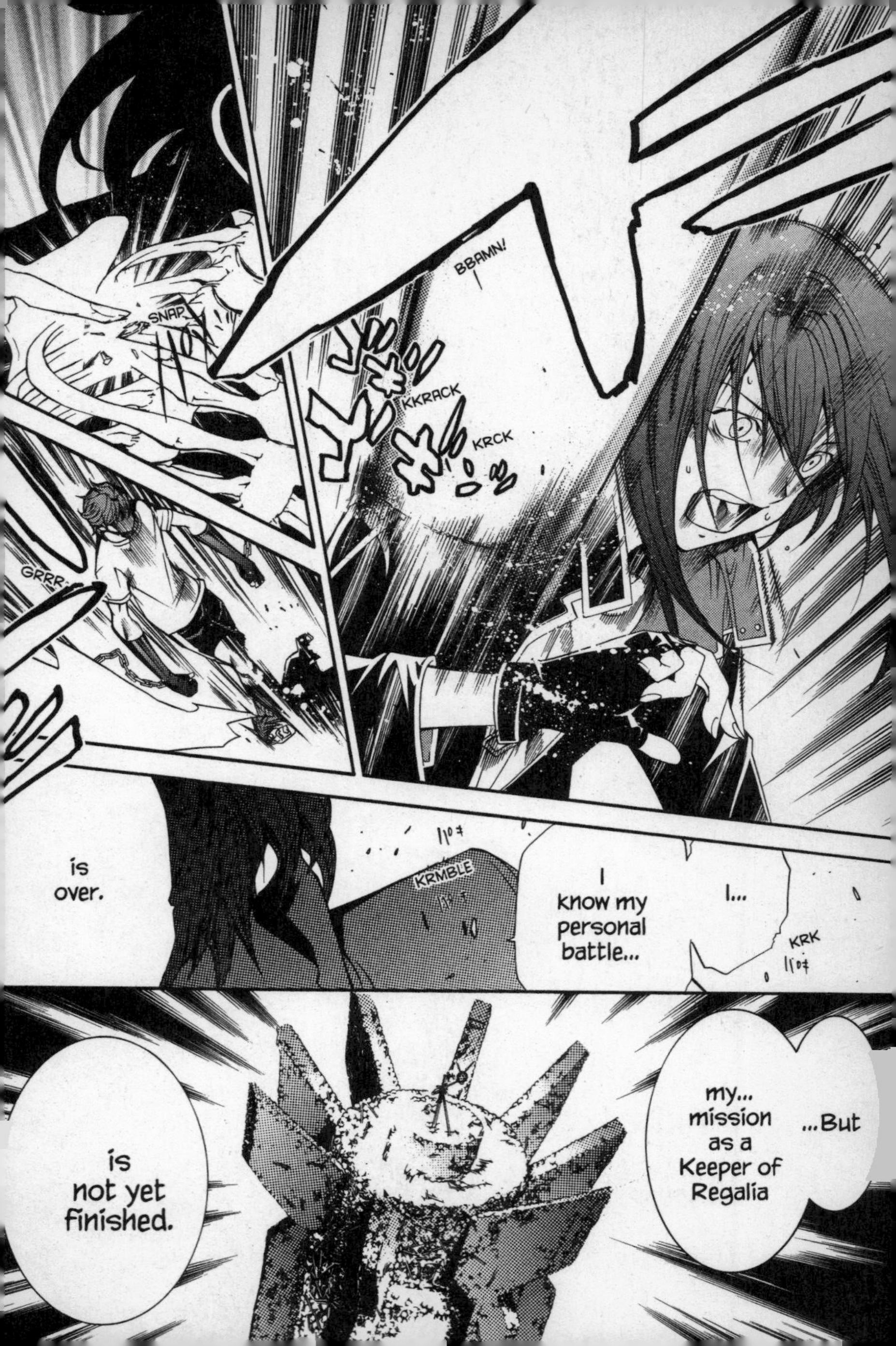
BBAMN!
KKRACK
KRCK
SNAP
GRRR
I...
KRK
I know my personal battle...
KRMBLE
is over.
...But
my... mission as a Keeper of Regalia
is not yet finished.

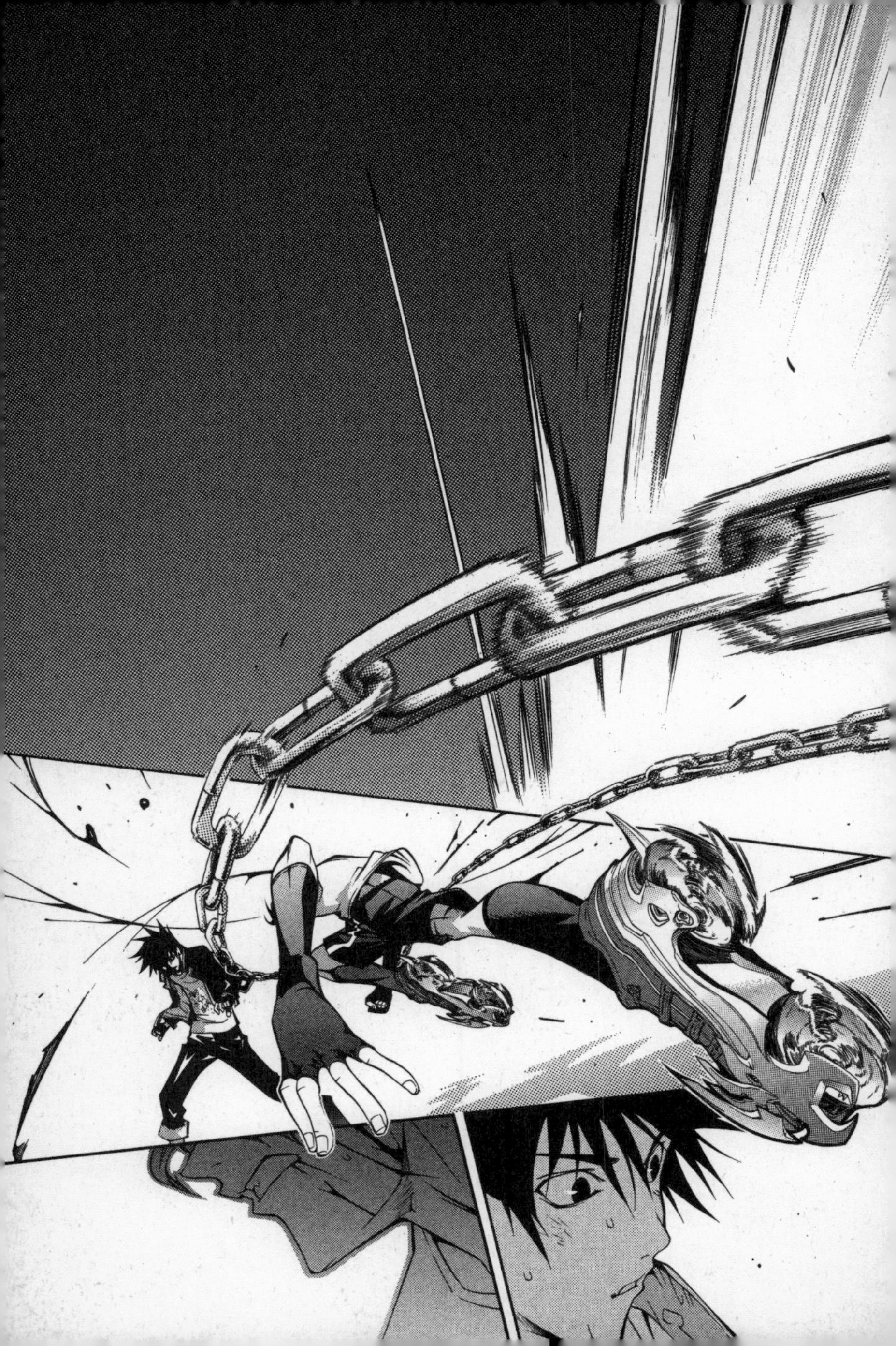

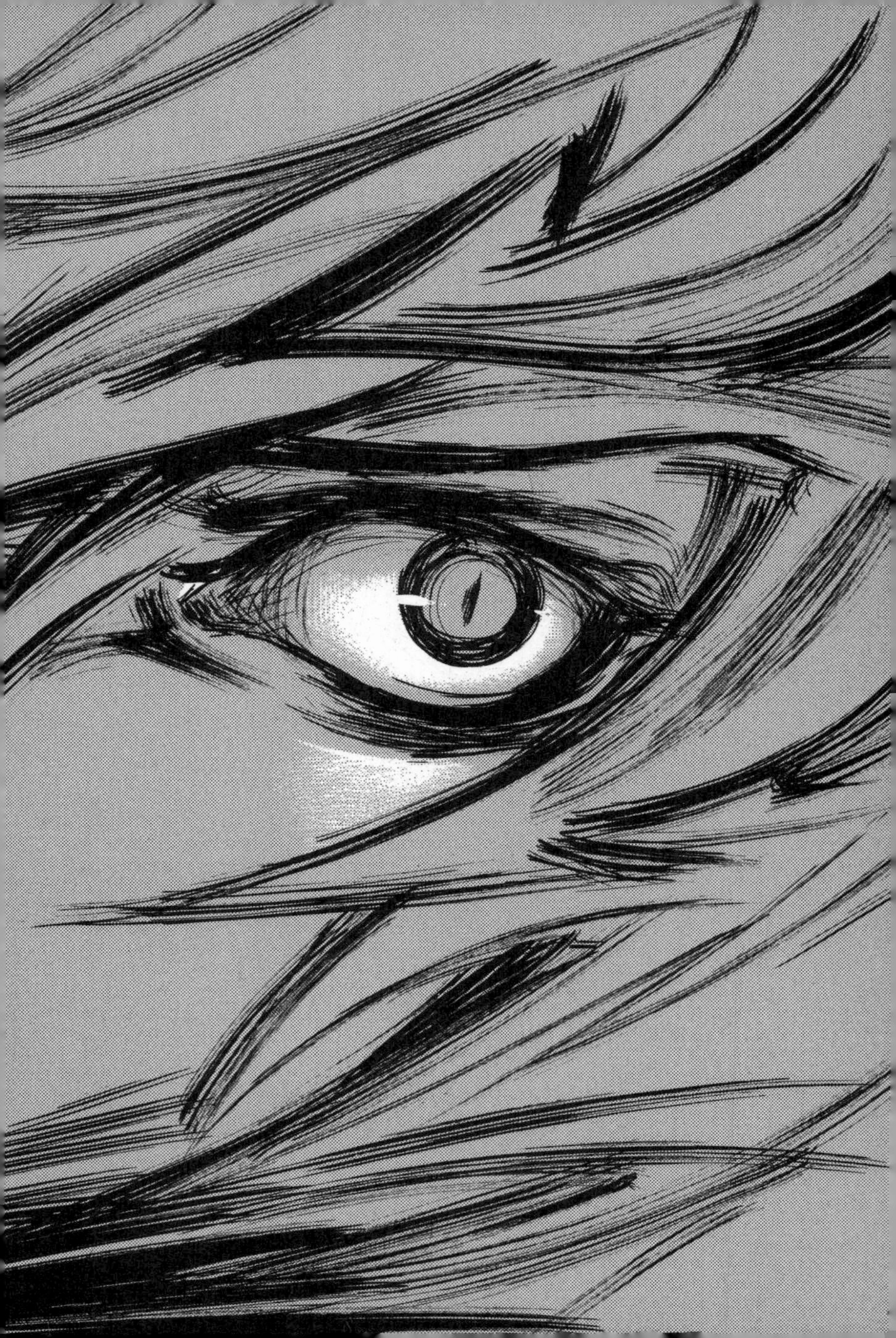

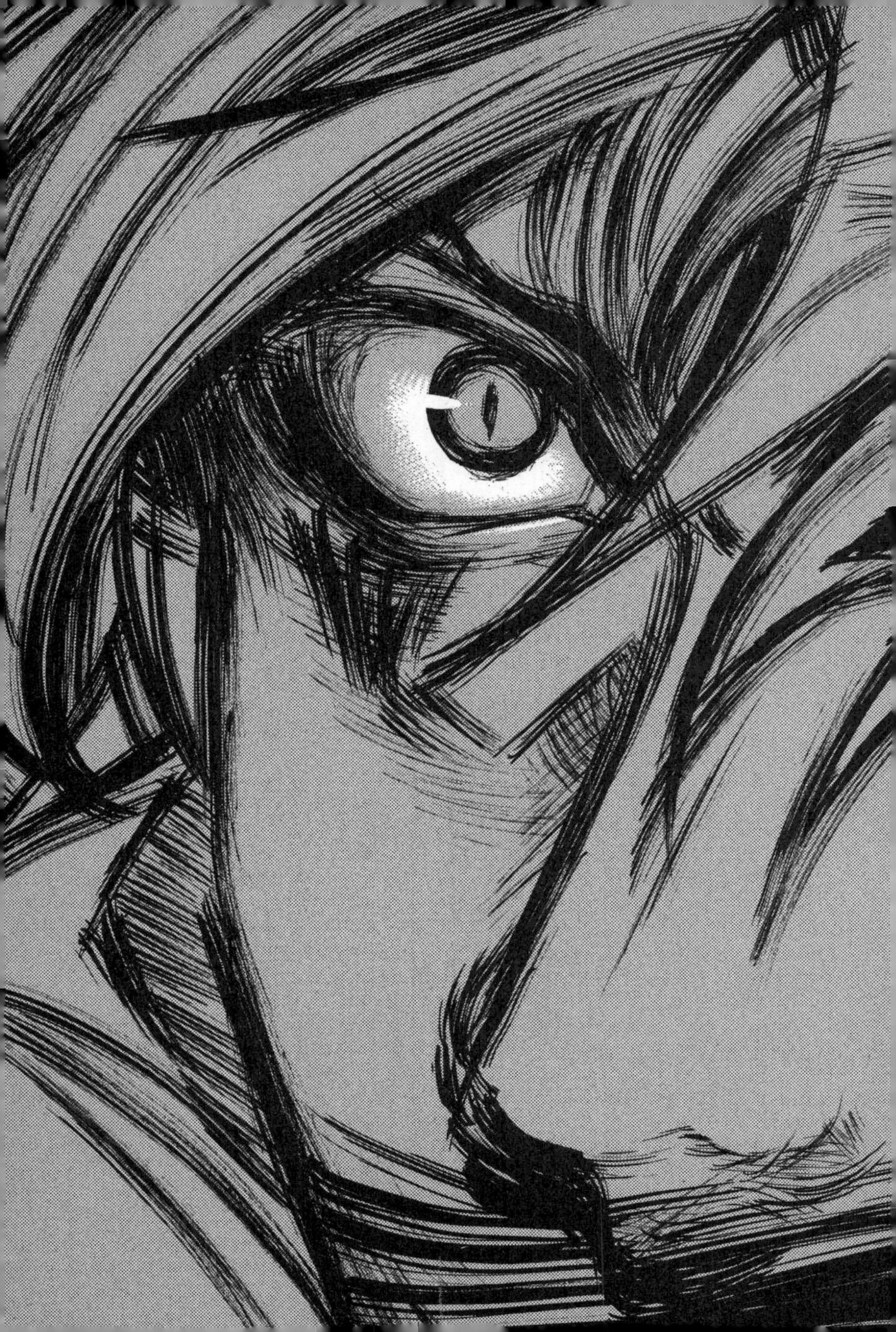

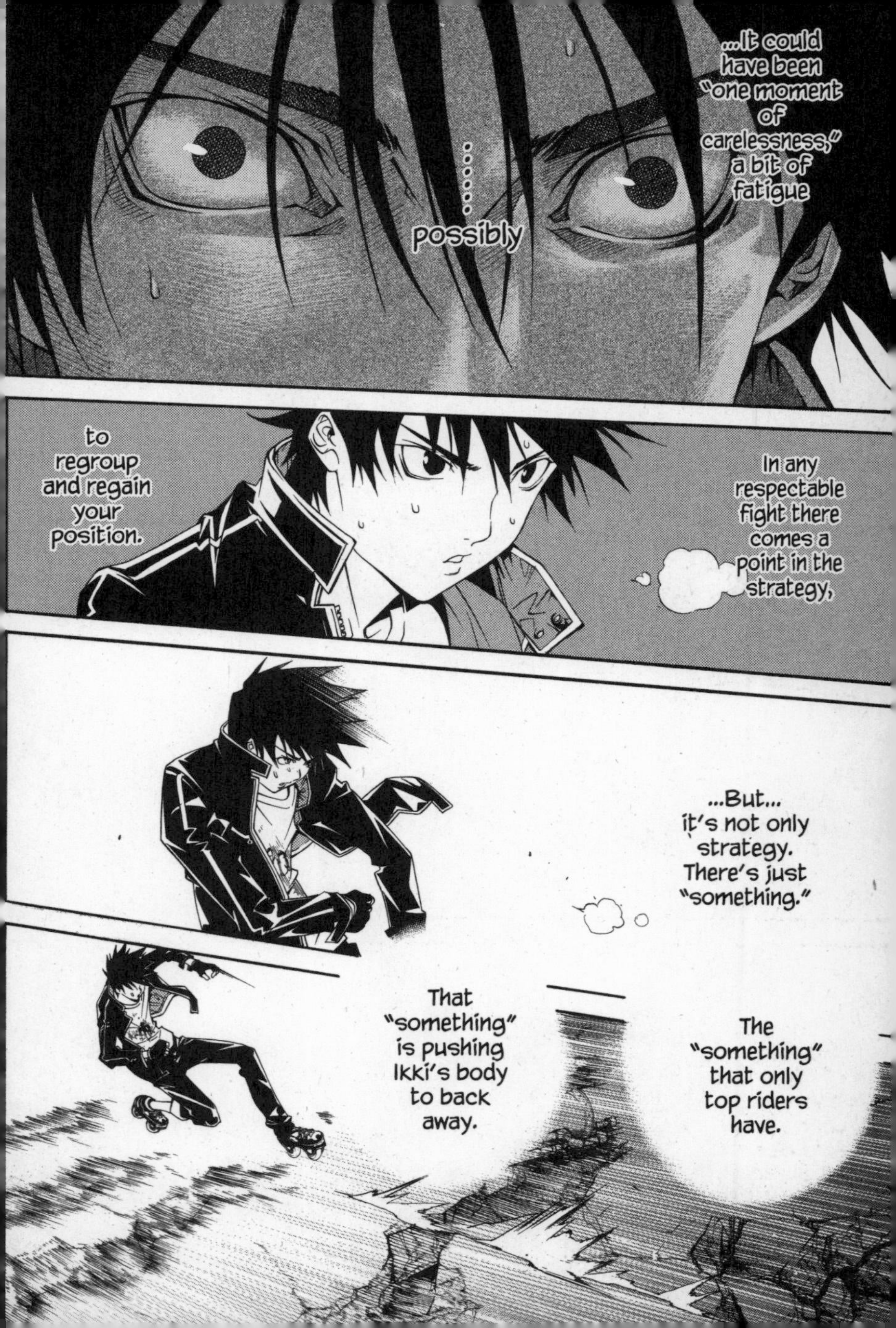
...It could have been "one moment of carelessness," a bit of fatigue
...... possibly
In any respectable fight there comes a point in the strategy,
to regroup and regain your position.
...But... it's not only strategy. There's just "something."
The "something" that only top riders have.
That "something" is pushing Ikki's body to back away.

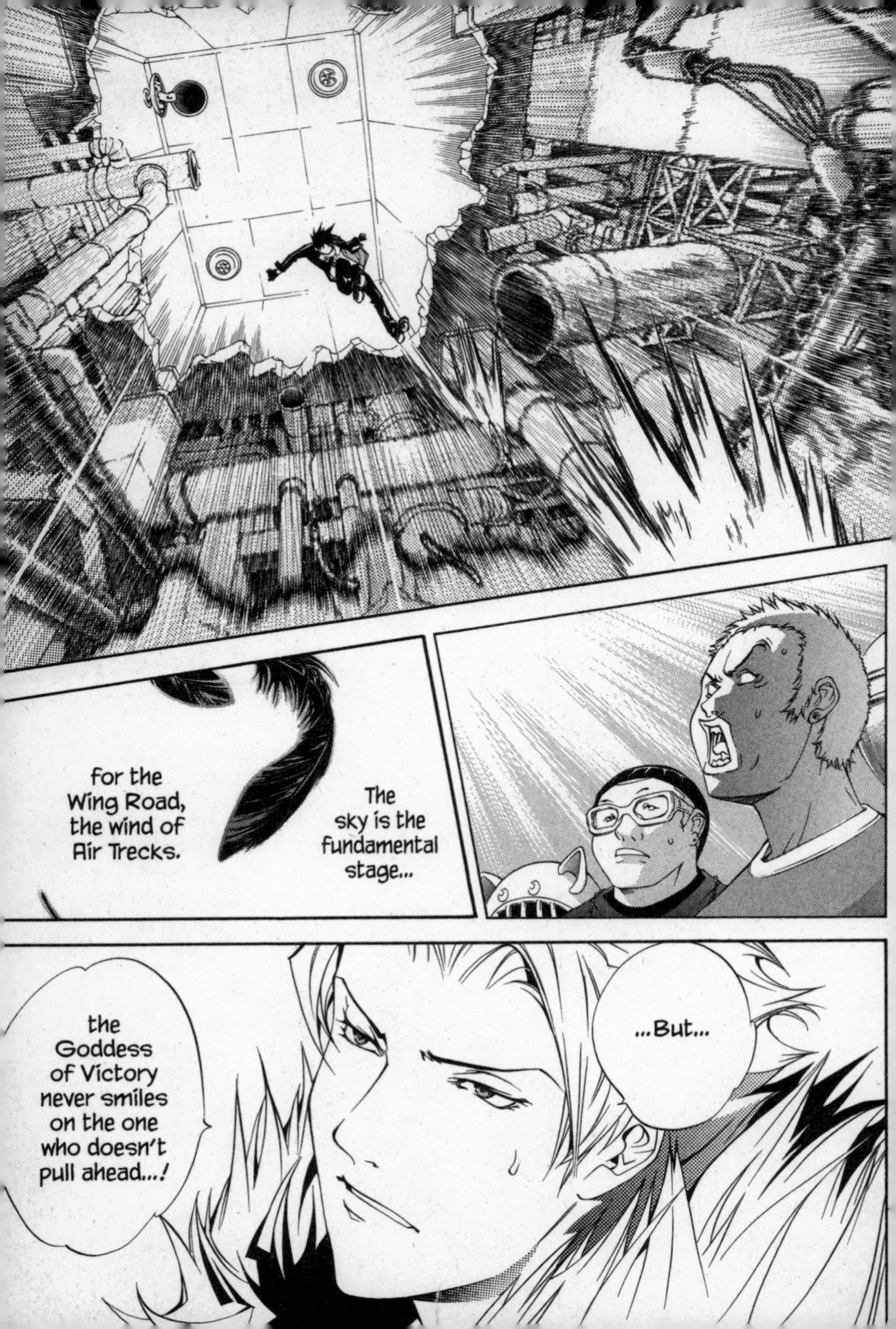
The sky is the fundamental stage...
for the Wing Road, the wind of Air Trecks.
...But...
the Goddess of Victory never smiles on the one who doesn't pull ahead...!

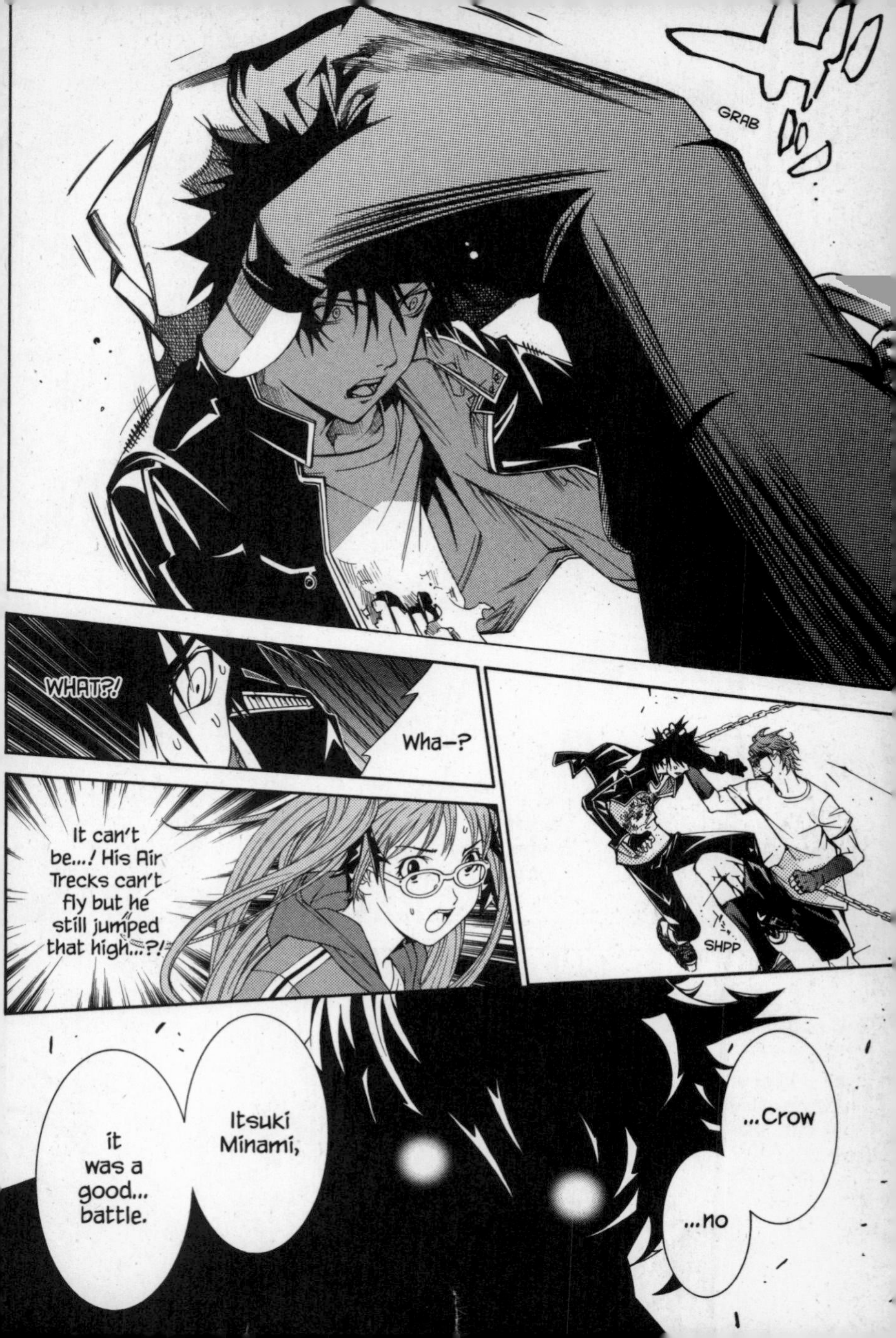
GRAB
SHPP
WHAT?!
Wha–?
It can't be...! His Air Trecks can't fly but he still jumped that high...?!
...Crow
...no
Itsuki Minami,
it was a good... battle.

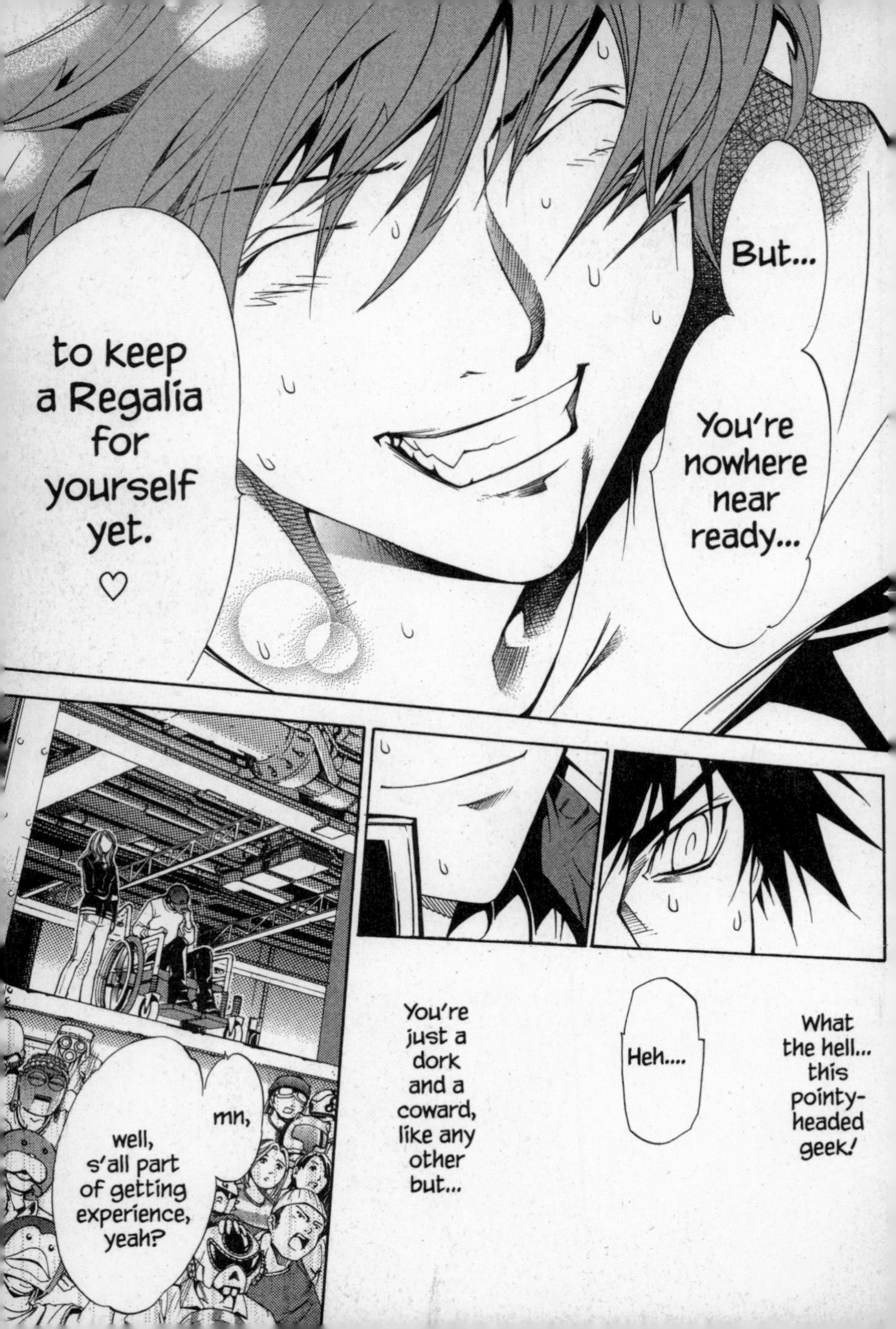
But...
You're nowhere near ready...
to keep a Regalia for yourself yet. ♡
What the hell... this pointy-headed geek!
Heh....
You're just a dork and a coward, like any other but...
mn,
well, s'all part of getting experience, yeah?

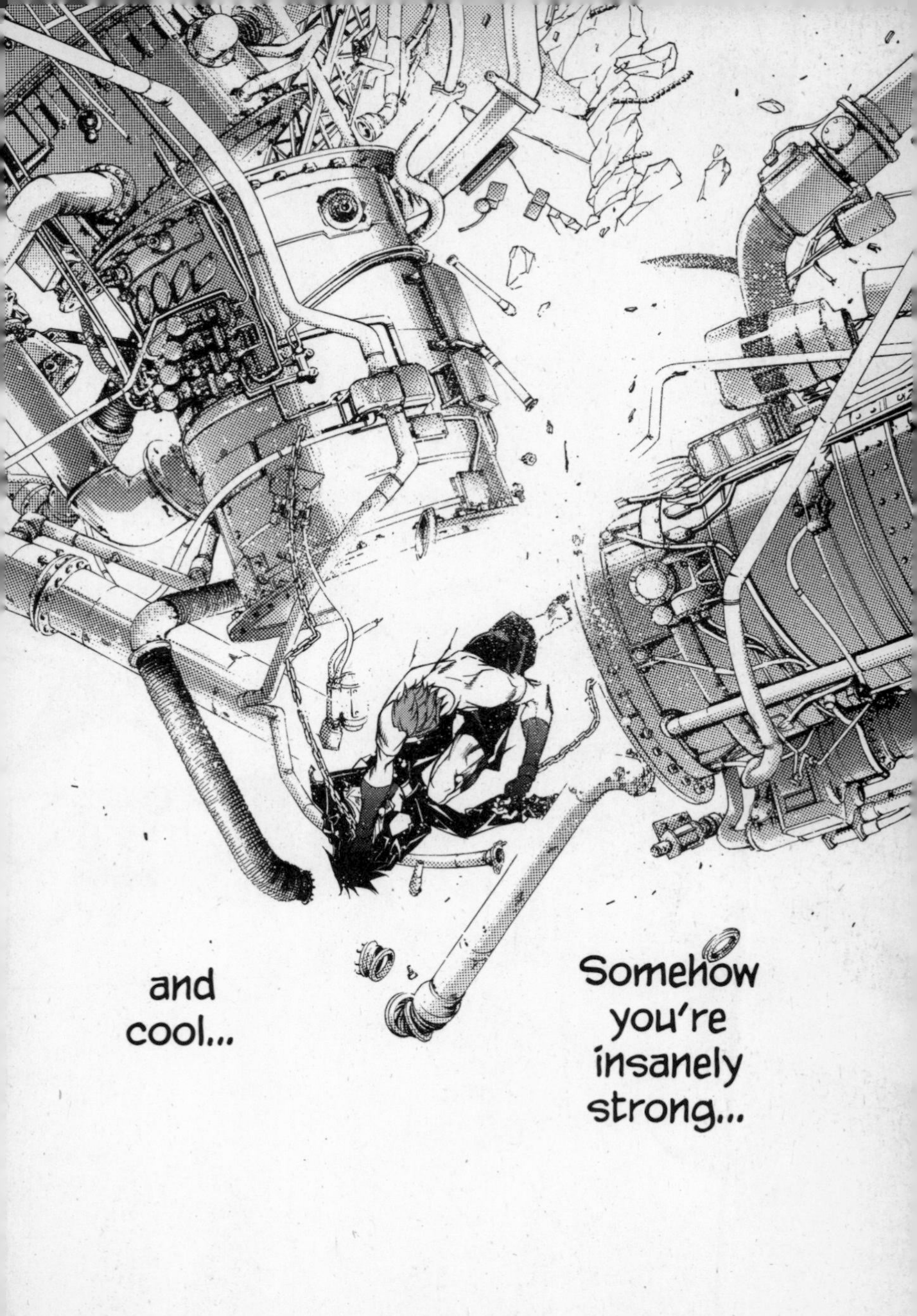
Somehow you're insanely strong...
and cool...

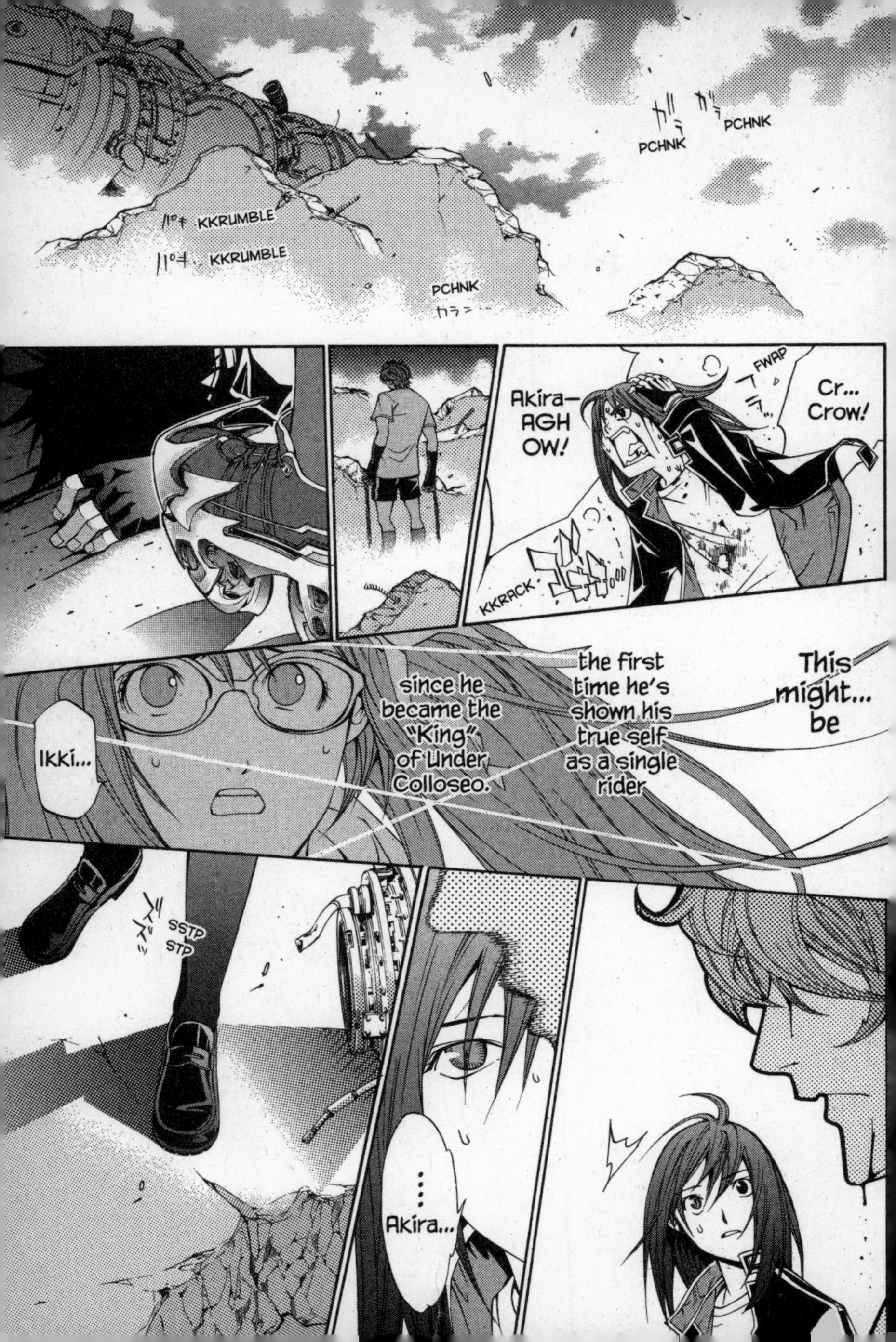
PCHNK
PCHNK
KKRUMBLE
KKRUMBLE
PCHNK
Cr... Crow!
FWAP
Akira—AGH OW!
KKRACK
This might... be
the first time he's shown his true self as a single rider
since he became the "King" of Under Colloseo.
Ikki...
...Akira...
SSTP STP

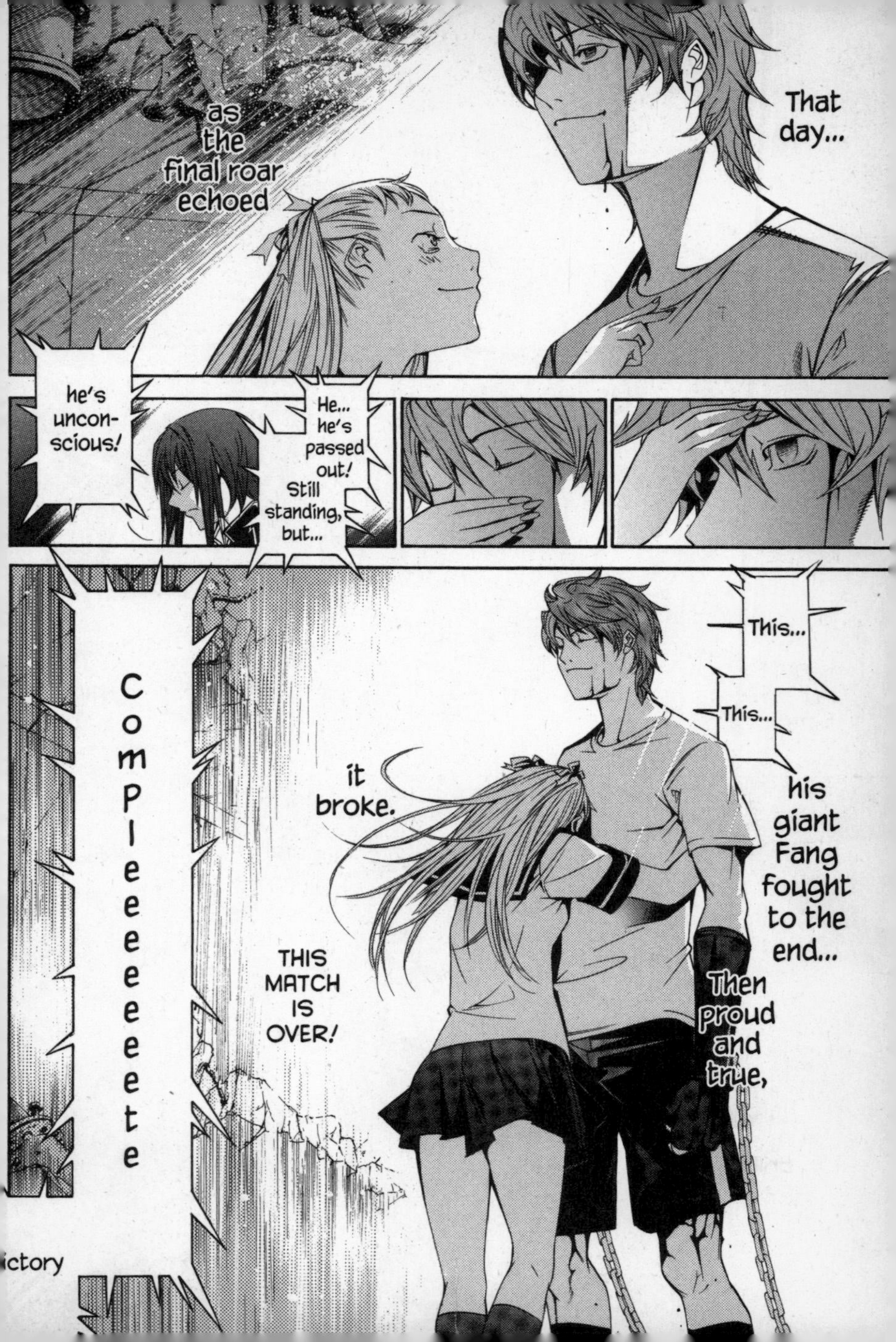
That day...
as the final roar echoed
He... he's passed out!
Still standing, but...
he's uncon-scious!
This...
This...
his giant Fang fought to the end...
Then proud and true,
it broke.
THIS MATCH IS OVER!
Compleeeeeeete
ictory

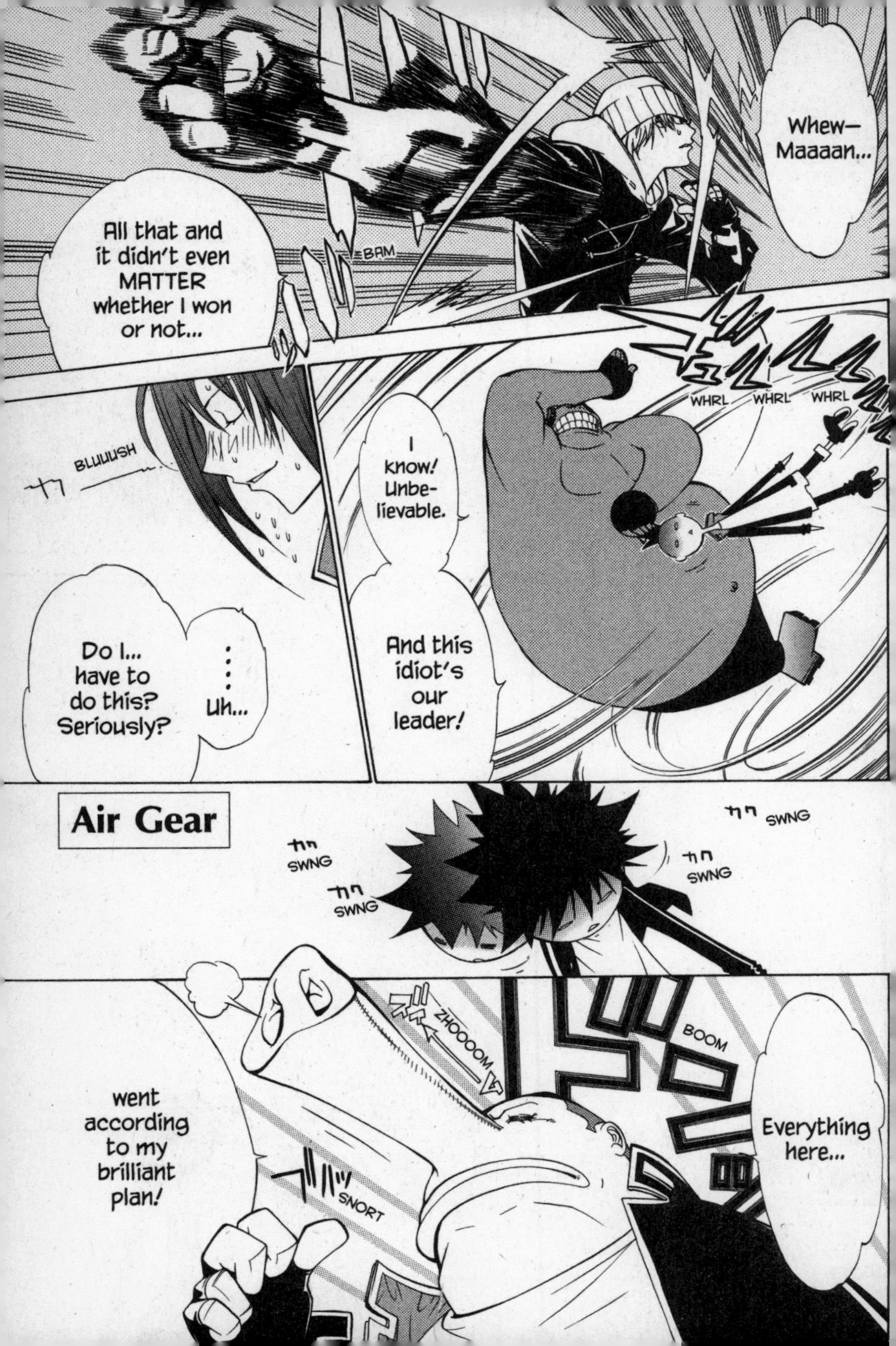
Whew—
Maaaan...
BAM
All that and it didn't even MATTER whether I won or not...
WHRL WHRL WHRL
I know! Unbe-lievable.
And this idiot's our leader!
BLUUUSH
... Uh...
Do I... have to do this? Seriously?
SWNG
SWNG
SWNG
SWNG
BOOM
Everything here...
ZHOOOOM
went according to my brilliant plan!
SNORT

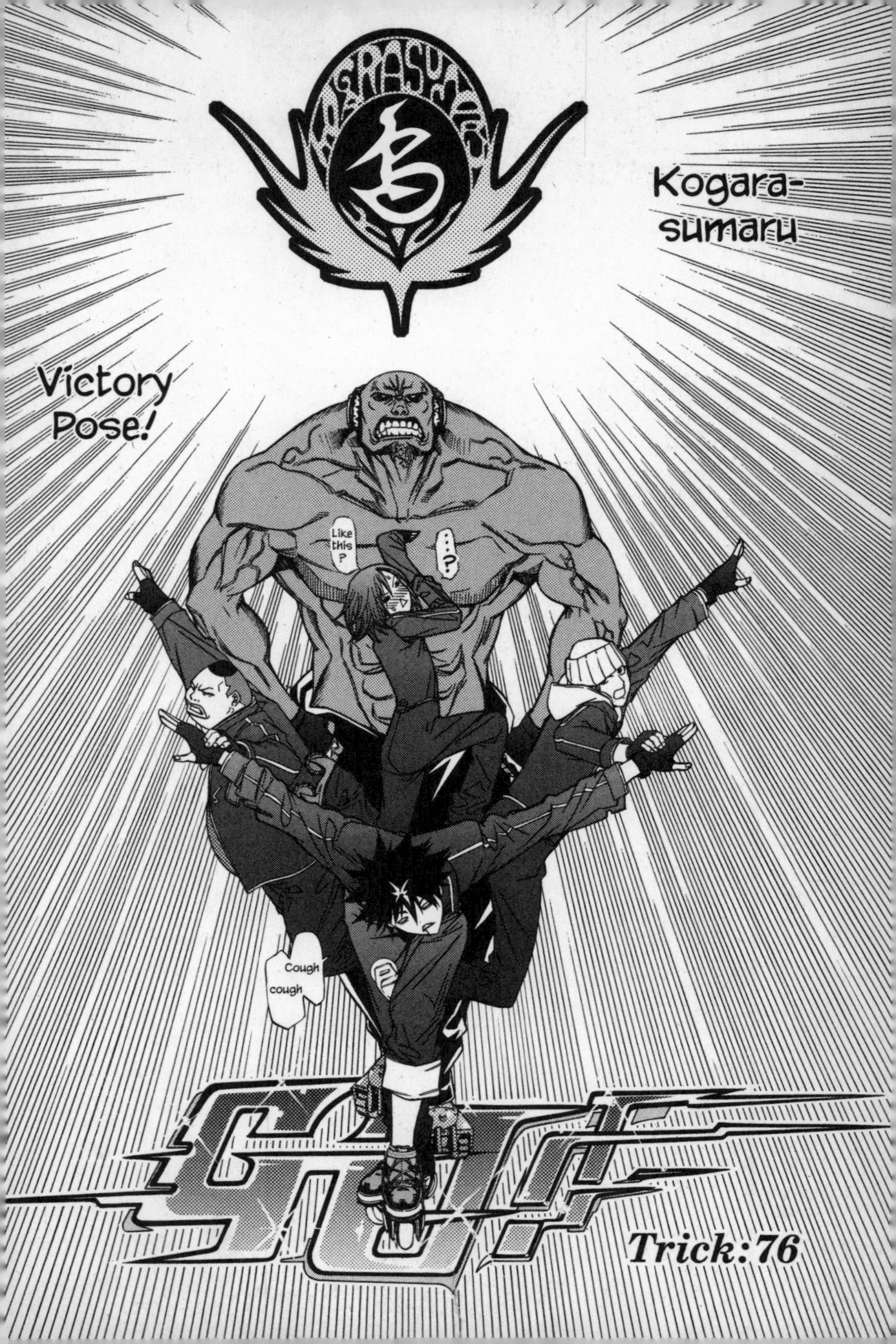
Kogara-
sumaru
Victory
Pose!
...?
Like this?
Cough
cough
Trick: 76

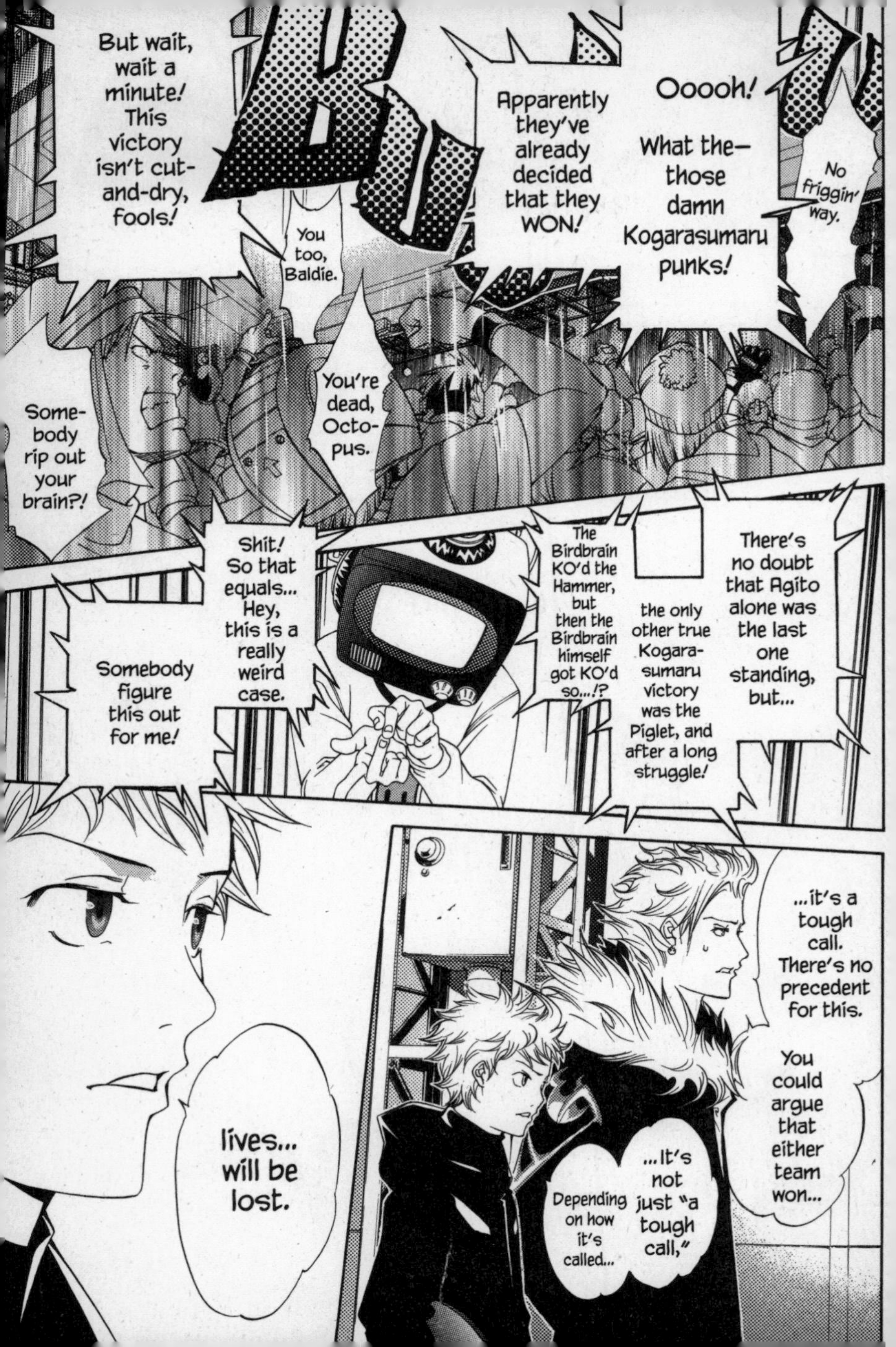
No friggin' way.
Ooooh! What the— those damn Kogarasumaru punks!
Apparently they've already decided that they WON!
You too, Baldie.
But wait, wait a minute! This victory isn't cut-and-dry, fools!
You're dead, Octopus.
Somebody rip out your brain?!
There's no doubt that Agito alone was the last one standing, but...
the only other true Kogarasumaru victory was the Piglet, and after a long struggle!
The Birdbrain KO'd the Hammer, but then the Birdbrain himself got KO'd so...!?
Shit! So that equals... Hey, this is a really weird case.
Somebody figure this out for me!
...it's a tough call. There's no precedent for this.
You could argue that either team won...
...It's not just "a tough call,"
Depending on how it's called...
lives... will be lost.

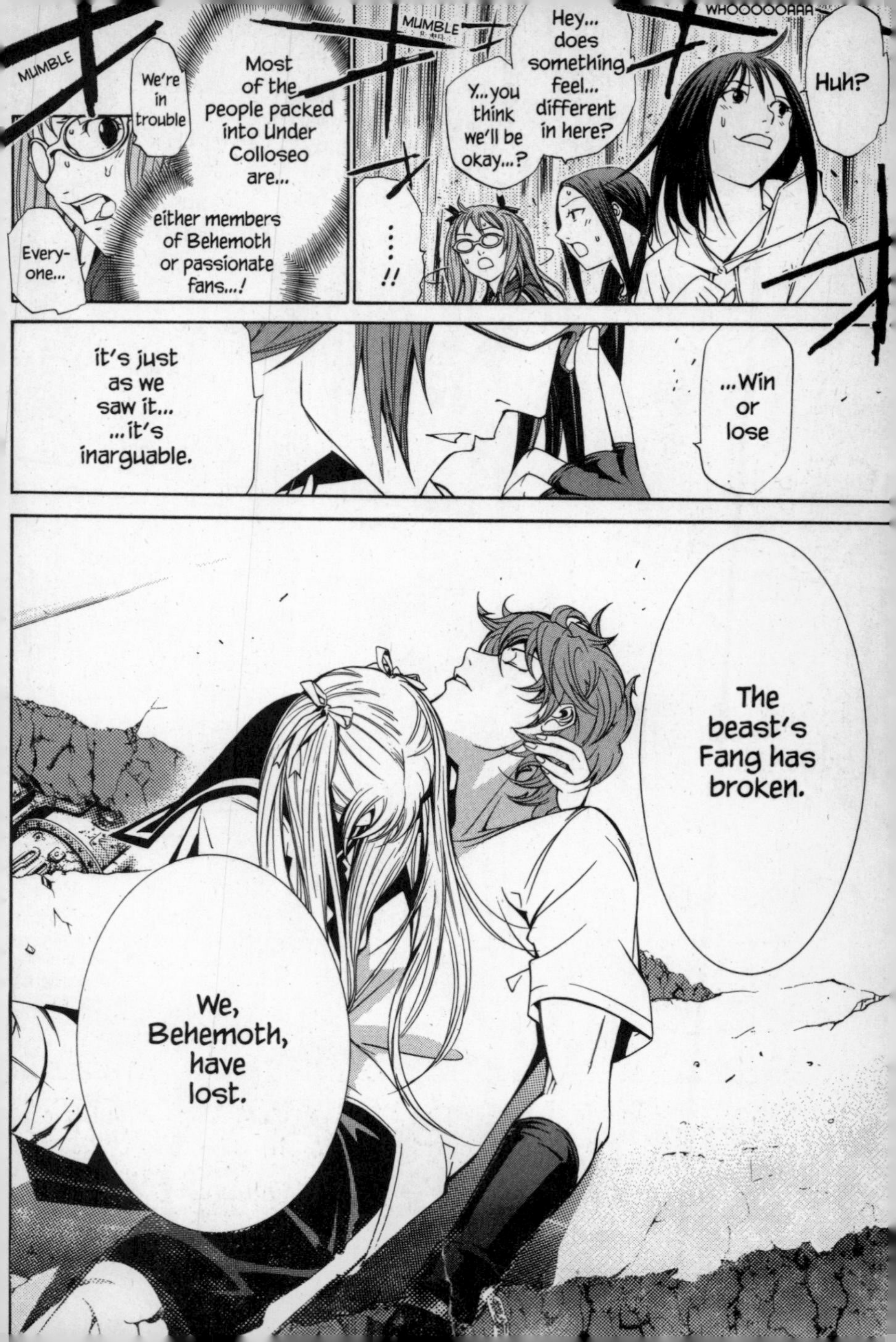
WHOOOOOOAAA
Huh?
Hey... does something feel... different in here?
Y...you think we'll be okay...?
MUMBLE
...!!
Most of the people packed into Under Colloseo are...
We're in trouble
MUMBLE
either members of Behemoth or passionate fans...!
Every-one...
...Win or lose
it's just as we saw it... ...it's inarguable.
The beast's Fang has broken.
We, Behemoth, have lost.

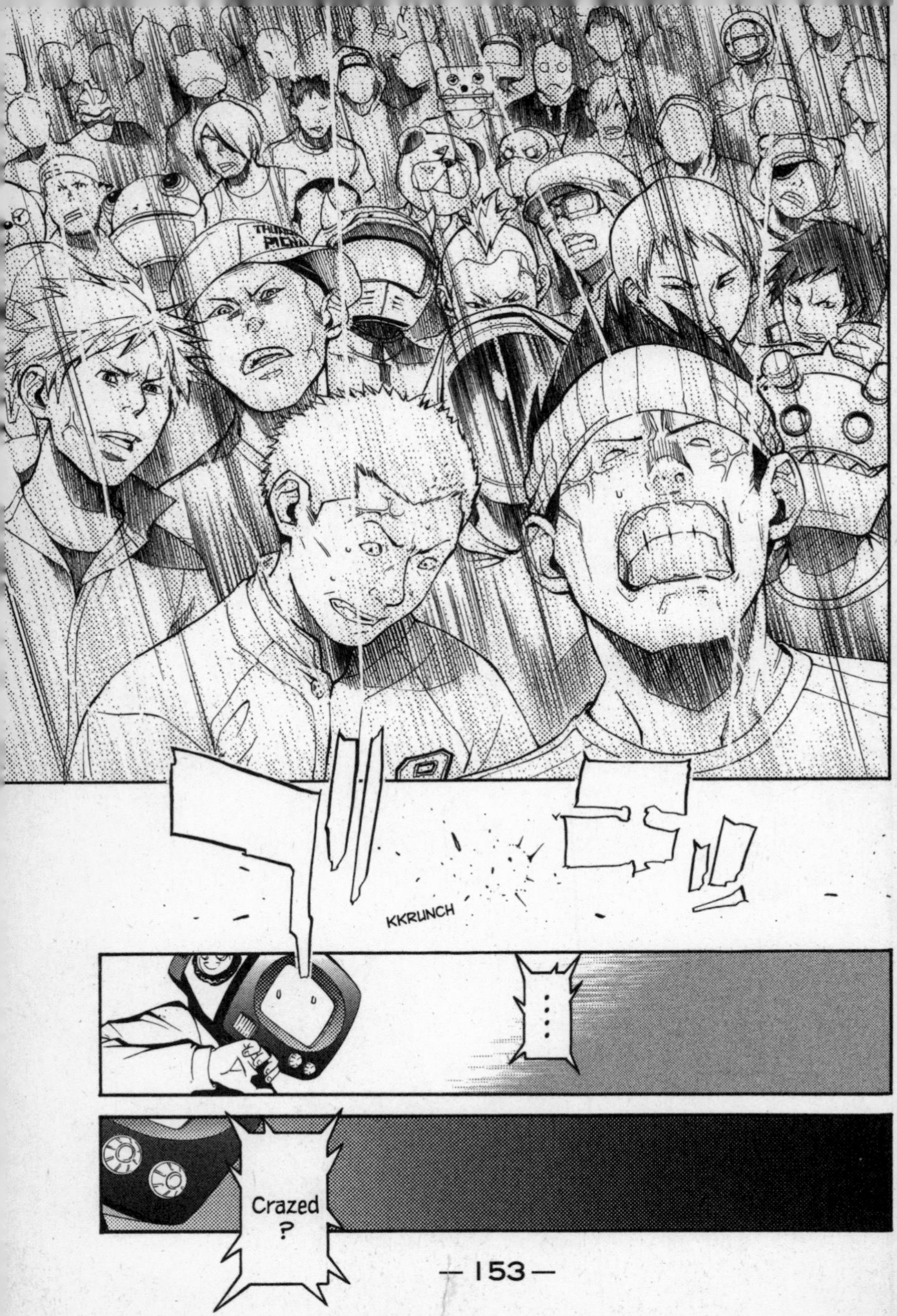
KKRUNCH
...
Crazed
?

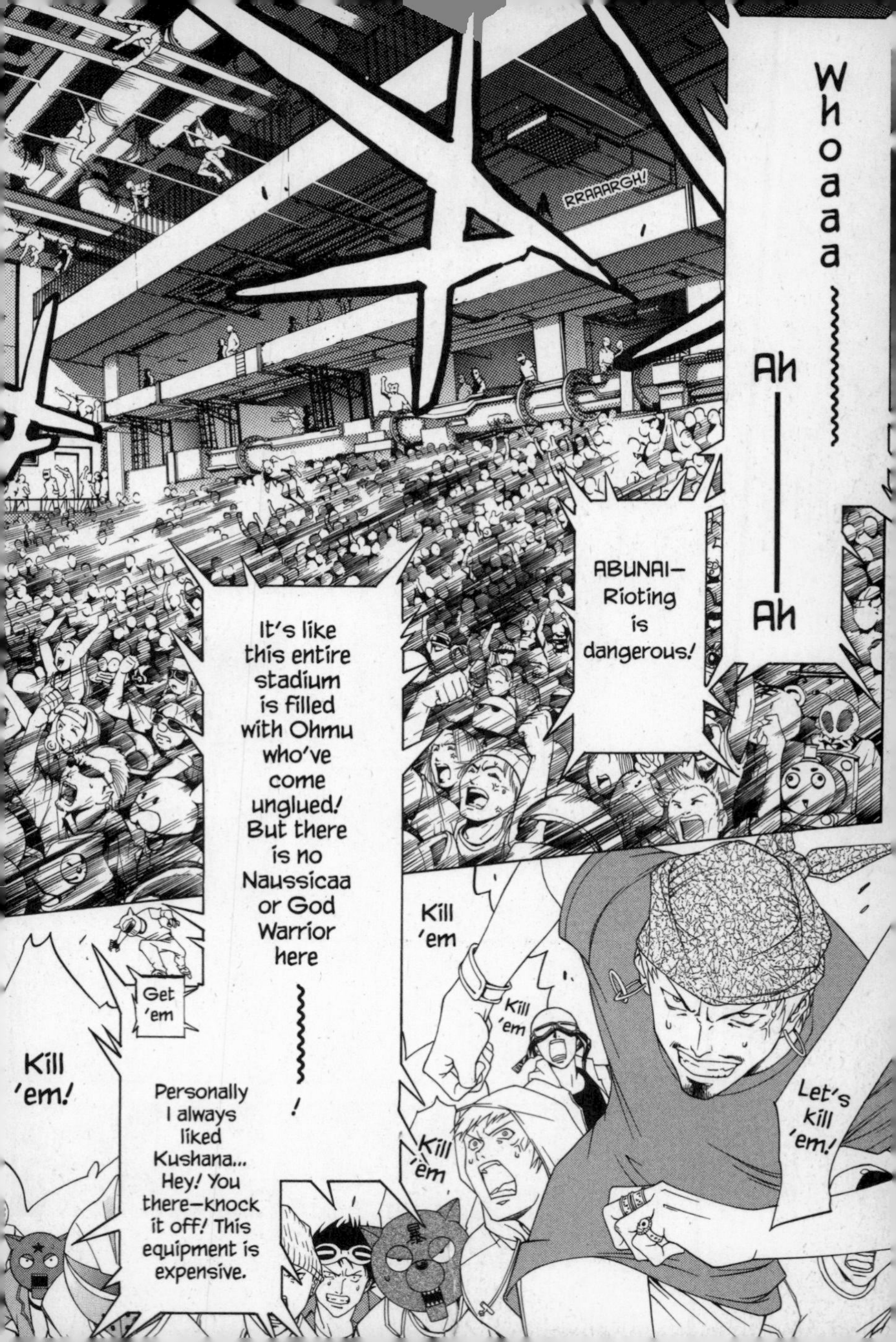
Whoaaa~~~~
Ah—Ah
RRAAARGH!
ABUNAI—Rioting is dangerous!
It's like this entire stadium is filled with Ohmu who've come unglued! But there is no Naussicaa or God Warrior here~~~~!
Let's kill 'em!
Kill 'em
Kill 'em
Kill 'em
Get 'em
Kill 'em!
Personally I always liked Kushana... Hey! You there—knock it off! This equipment is expensive.

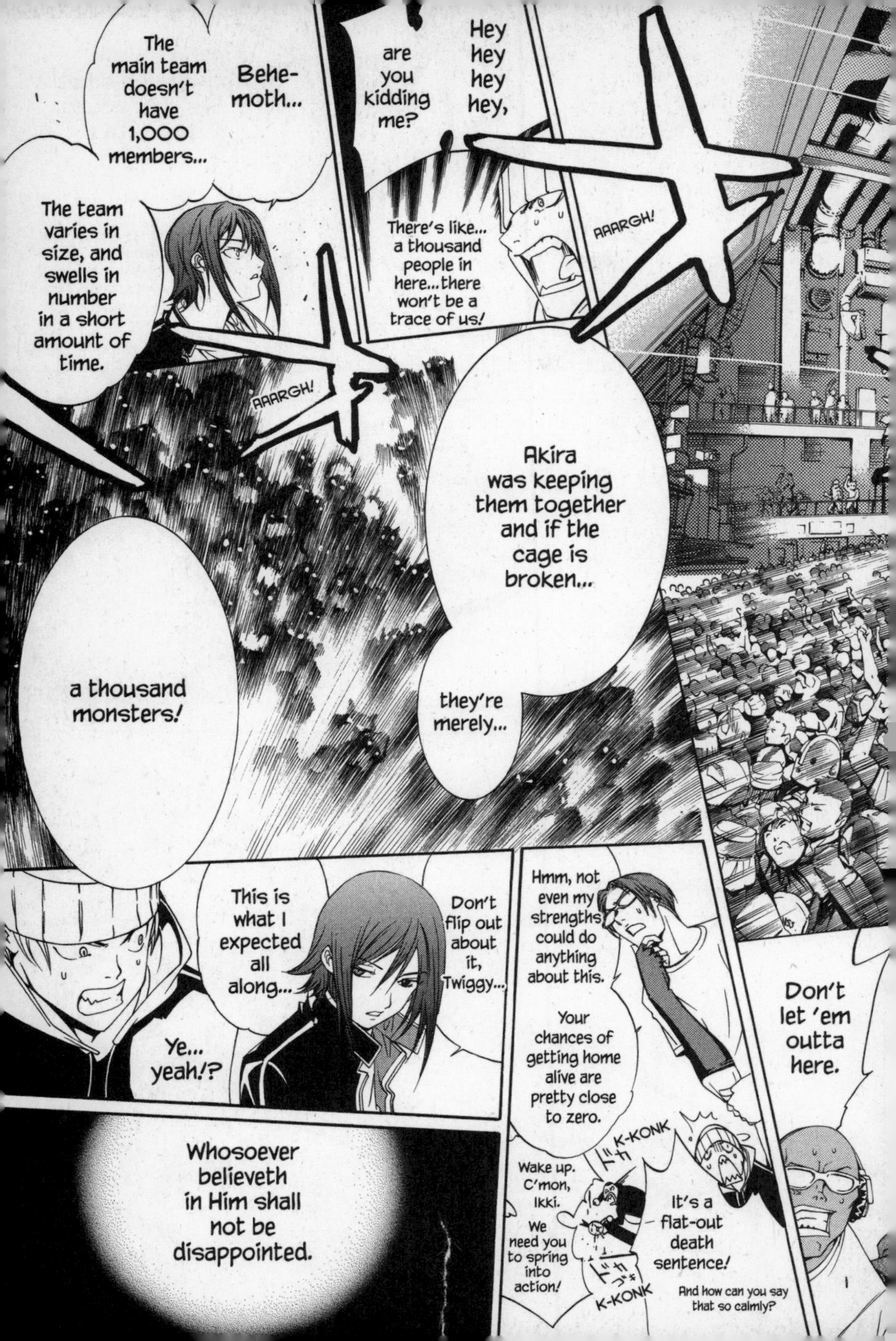

Hey hey hey hey,
are you kidding me?
There's like... a thousand people in here...there won't be a trace of us!
AAARGH!
Behe-moth...
The main team doesn't have 1,000 members...
The team varies in size, and swells in number in a short amount of time.
AAARGH!
Akira was keeping them together and if the cage is broken...
they're merely...
a thousand monsters!
Hmm, not even my strengths could do anything about this.
Your chances of getting home alive are pretty close to zero.
Don't flip out about it, Twiggy...
This is what I expected all along...
Ye... yeah!?
Don't let 'em outta here.
It's a flat-out death sentence!
K-KONK
Wake up. C'mon, Ikki.
We need you to spring into action!
K-KONK
And how can you say that so calmly?
Whosoever believeth in Him shall not be disappointed.

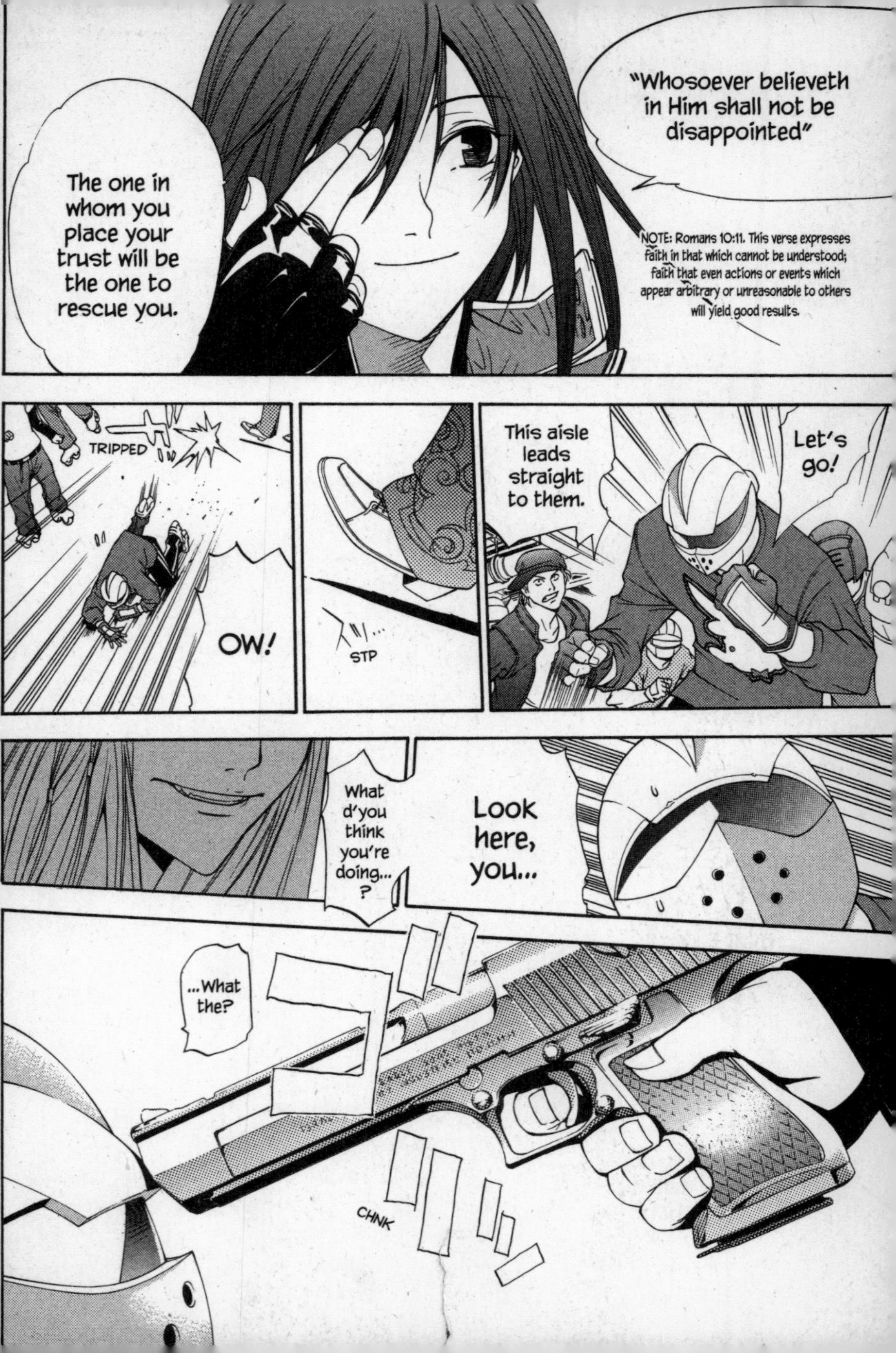
"Whosoever believeth in Him shall not be disappointed"
NOTE: Romans 10:11. This verse expresses faith in that which cannot be understood; faith that even actions or events which appear arbitrary or unreasonable to others will yield good results.
The one in whom you place your trust will be the one to rescue you.
Let's go!
This aisle leads straight to them.
STP
TRIPPED
OW!
Look here, you...
What d'you think you're doing...?
...What the?
CHNK

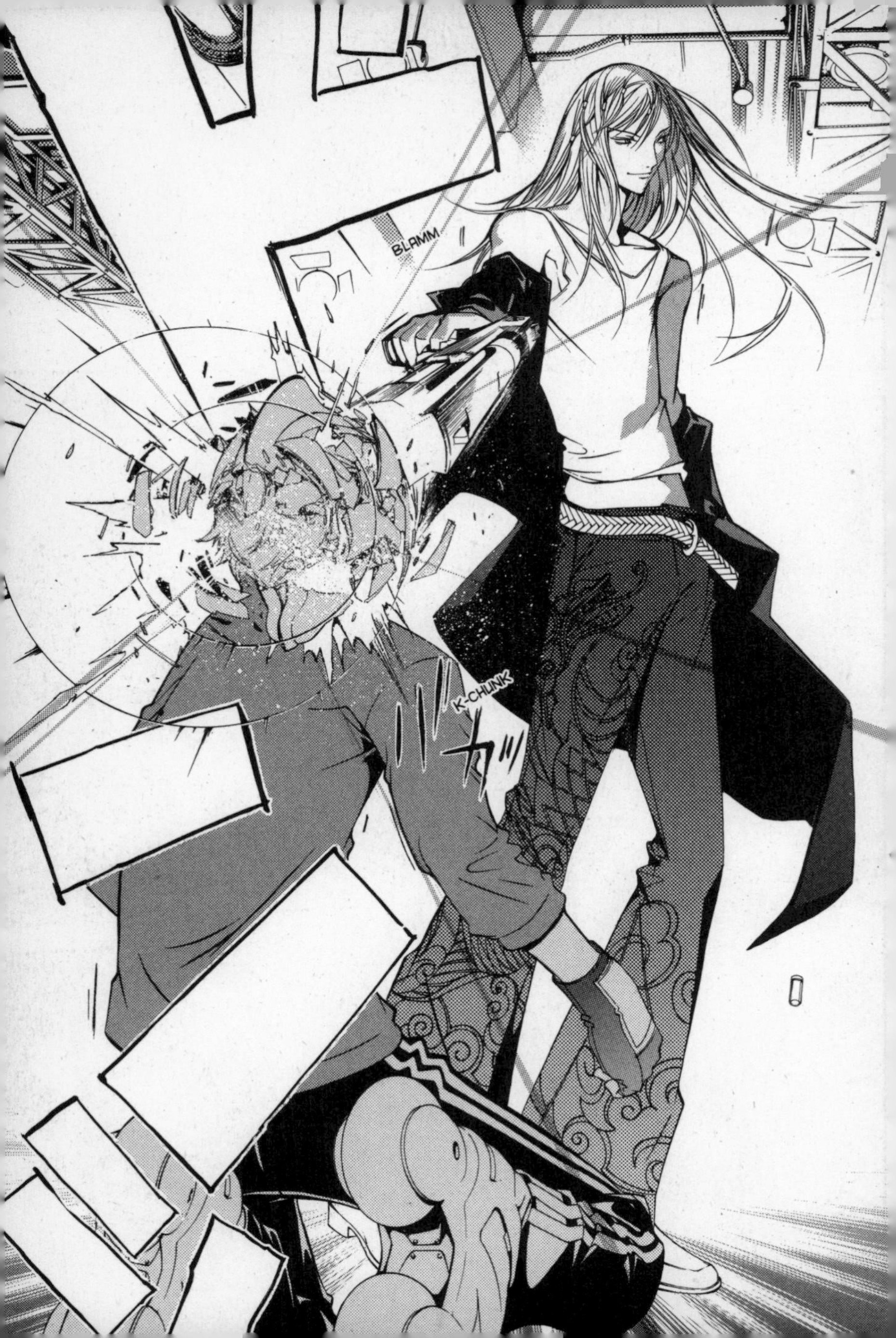
BLAMM
K-CHUNK

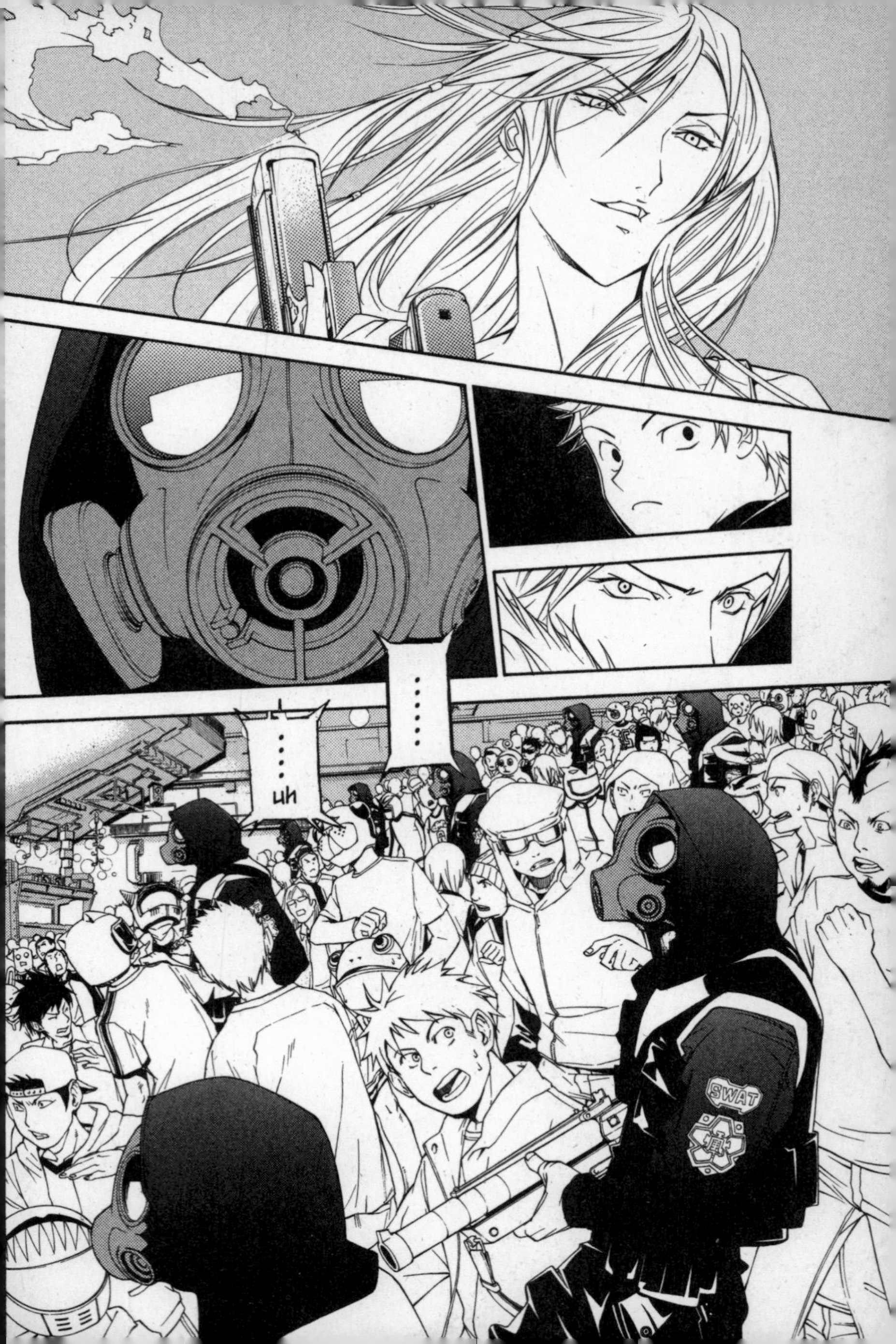
......
....uh

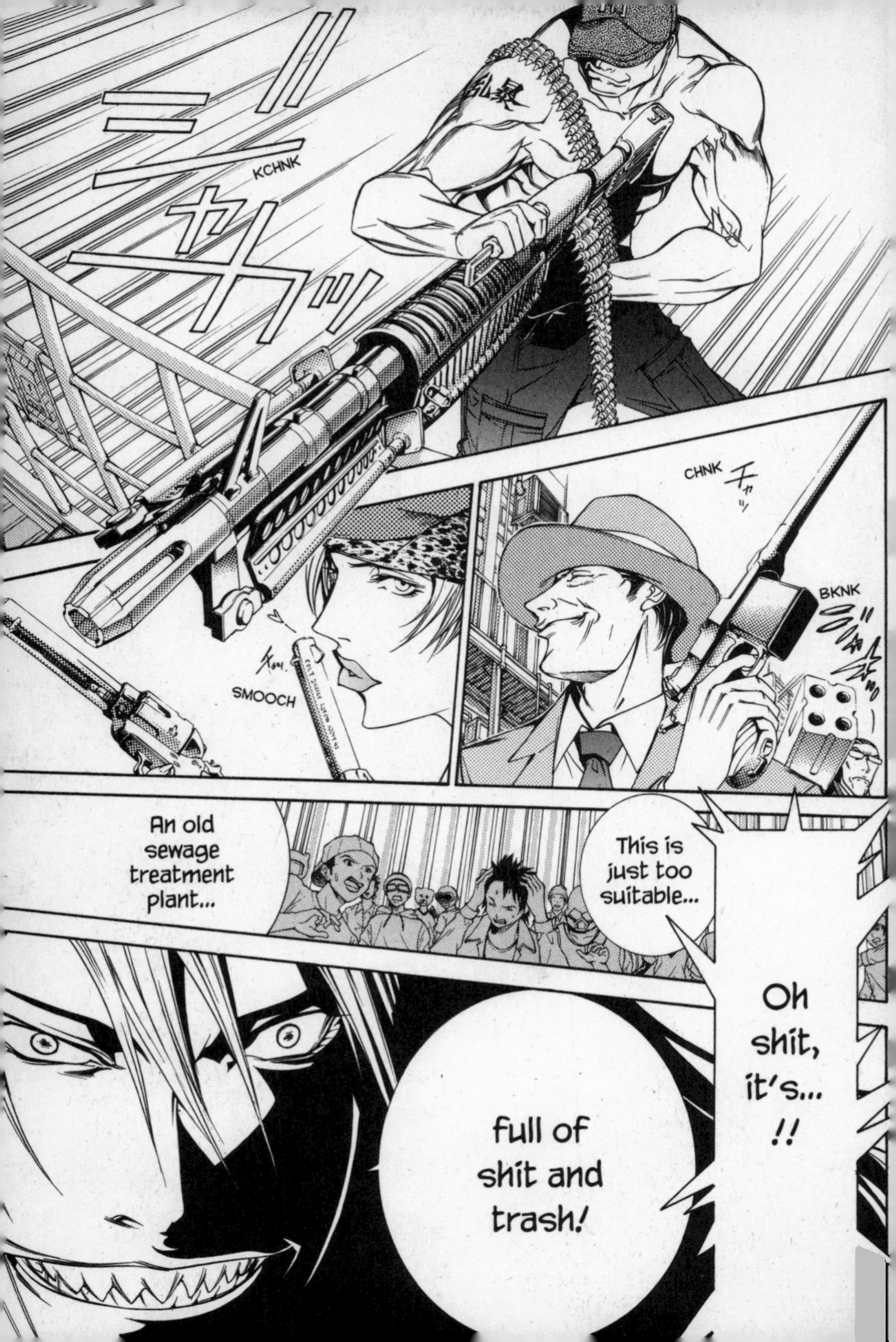
KCHNK
CHNK
BKNK
SMOOCH
This is just too suitable...
An old sewage treatment plant...
Oh shit, it's... !!
full of shit and trash!

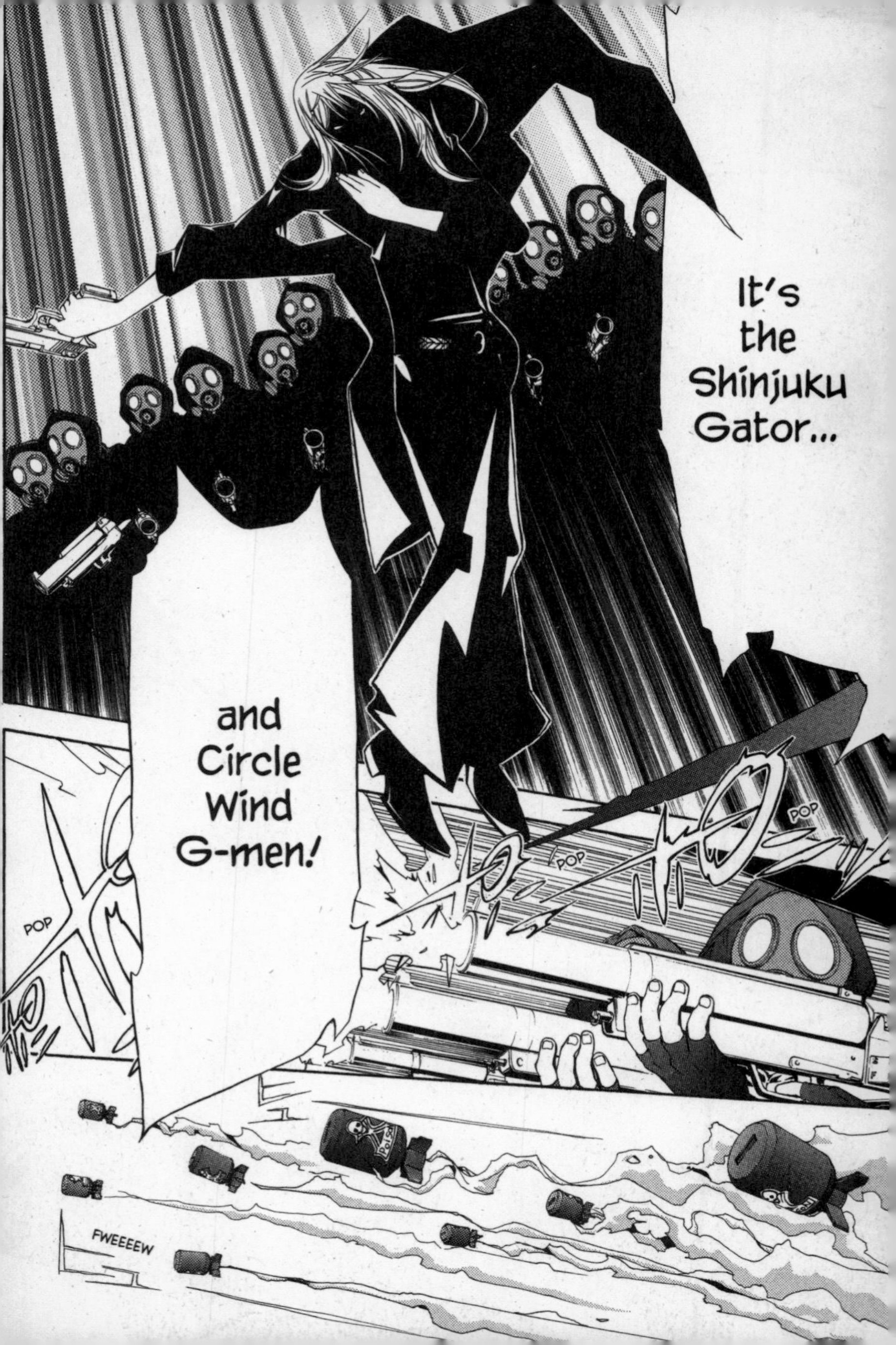
It's the Shinjuku Gator...
and Circle Wind G-men!
POP
POP
POP
FWEEEEW

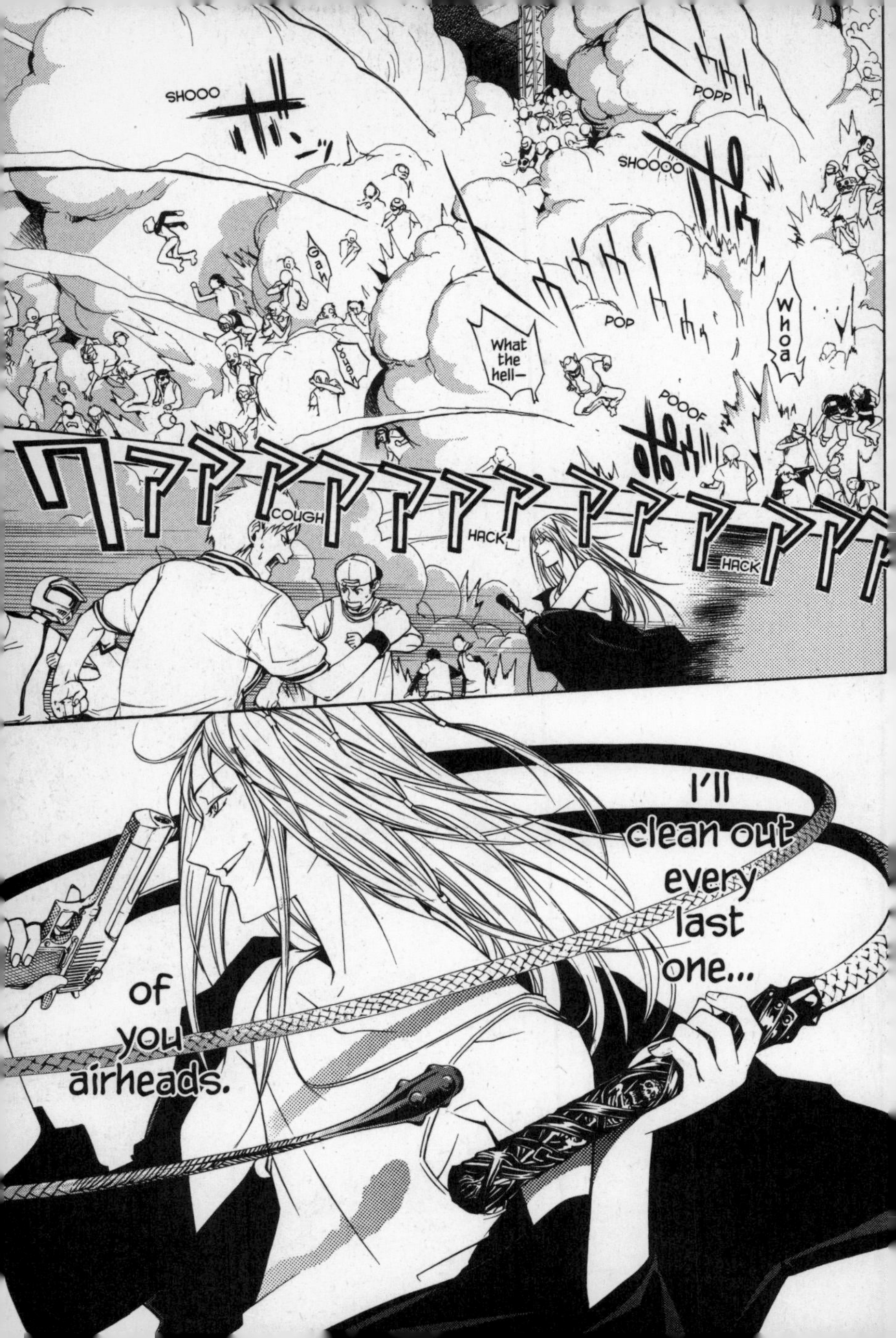
POPP
SHOOOO
Whoa
POP
What the hell—
POOOF
SHOOO
Gah
Cough
HACK
HACK
COUGH
I'll clean out every last one...
of you airheads.

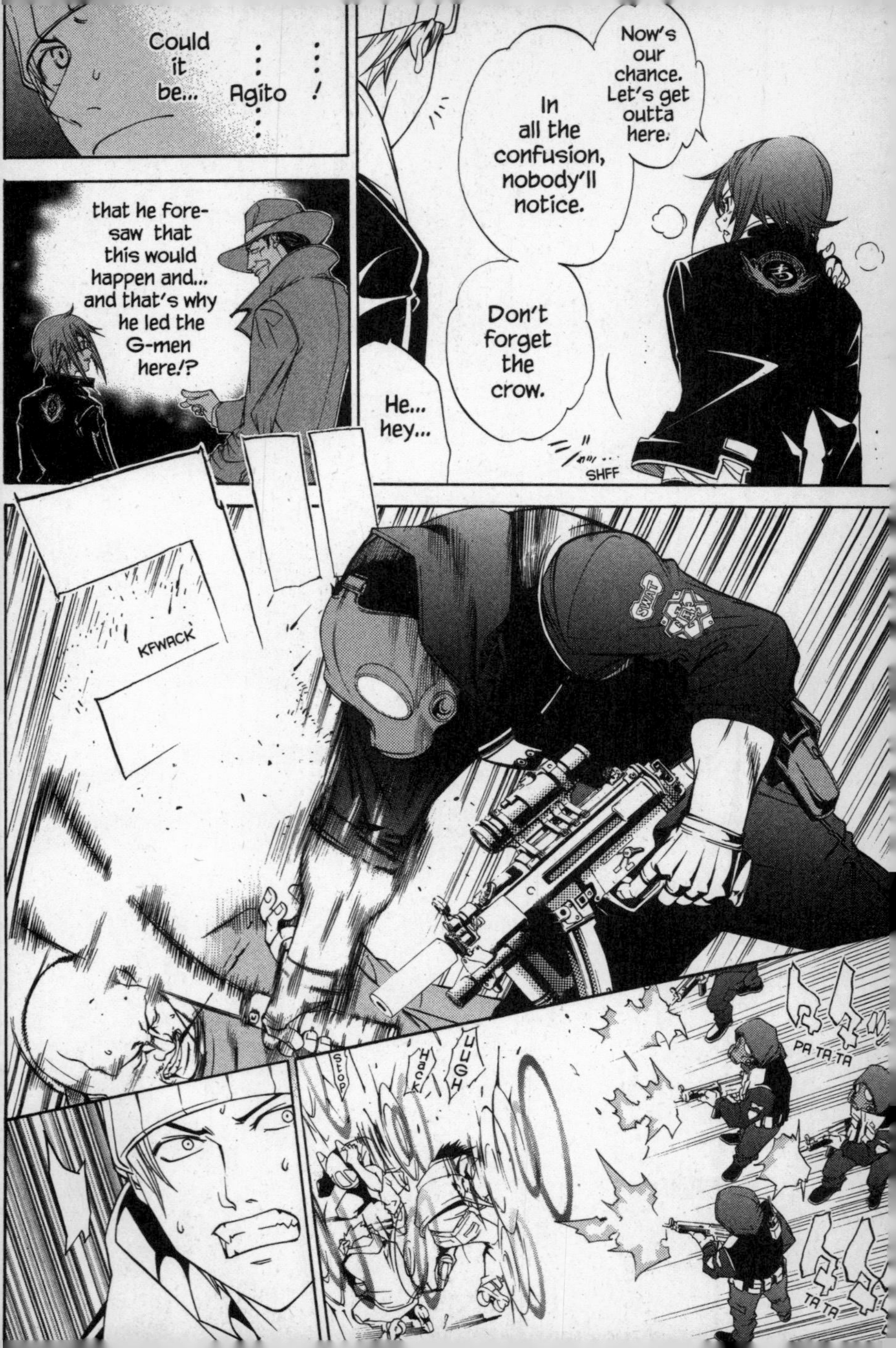
Now's our chance. Let's get outta here.
In all the confusion, nobody'll notice.
Don't forget the crow.
He... hey...
SHFF
Could it be...
...Agito...
...!
that he fore-saw that this would happen and... and that's why he led the G-men here!?
KFWACK
PA TA TA
TA TA
UGH
Hack
Stop

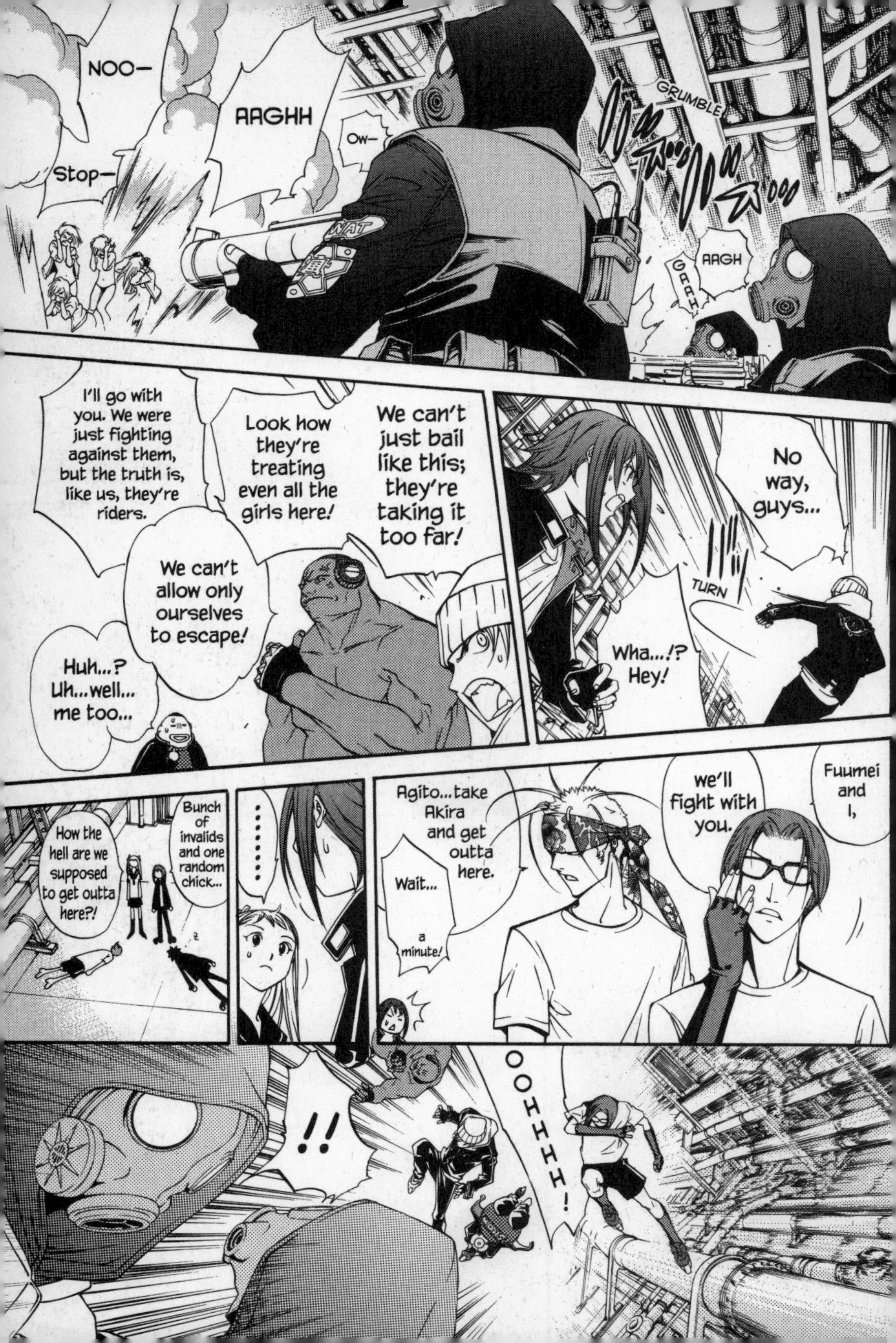
GRUMBLE
AARGH
GAAAH
Ow—
AAGHH
NOO—
Stop—
No way, guys...
TURN
Wha...!? Hey!
We can't just bail like this; they're taking it too far!
Look how they're treating even all the girls here!
I'll go with you. We were just fighting against them, but the truth is, like us, they're riders.
We can't allow only ourselves to escape!
Huh...? Uh...well... me too...
Fuumei and I,
we'll fight with you.
Agito...take Akira and get outta here.
Wait...
a minute!
.......
Bunch of invalids and one random chick...
How the hell are we supposed to get outta here?!
OOHHHH!
!!

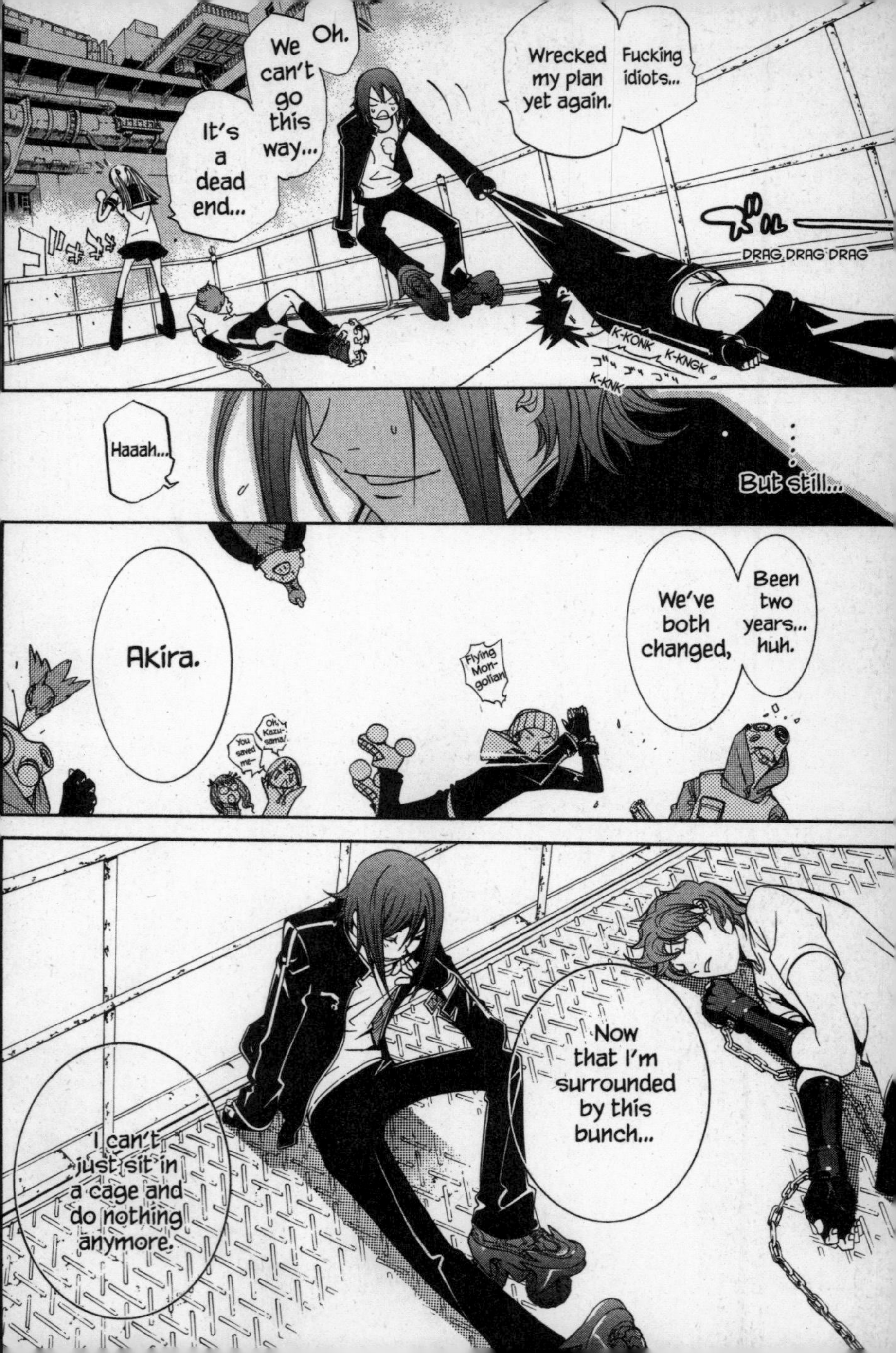
Fucking idiots...
Wrecked my plan yet again.
Oh. We can't go this way...
It's a dead end...
DRAG DRAG DRAG
K-KONK K-KNGK K-KNK
...
But still...
Haaah...
Been two years... huh.
We've both changed,
Flying Mongolian
Oh, Kazu-sama!
You saved me—
Akira.
Now that I'm surrounded by this bunch...
I can't just sit in a cage and do nothing anymore.

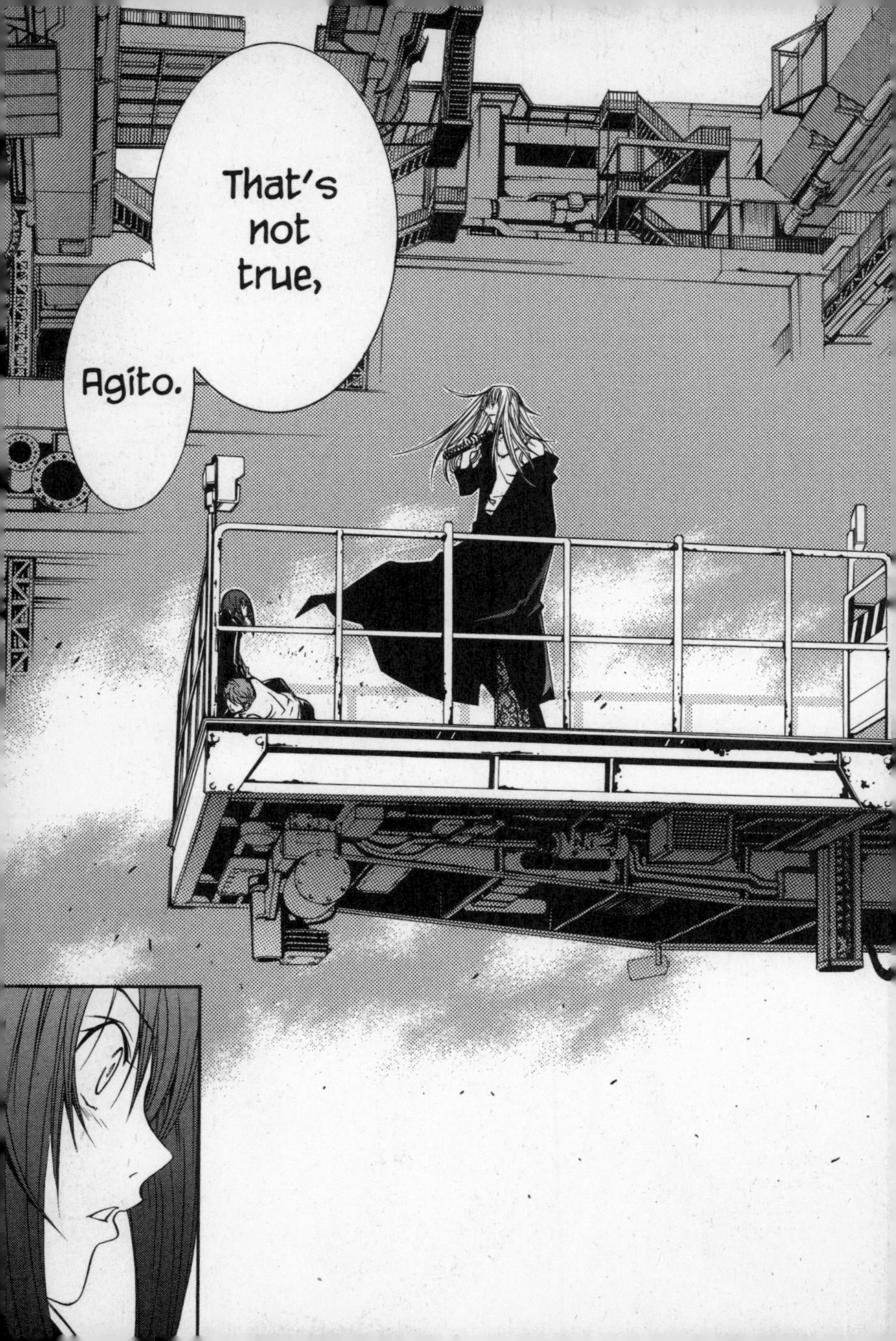
That's not true,
Agito.

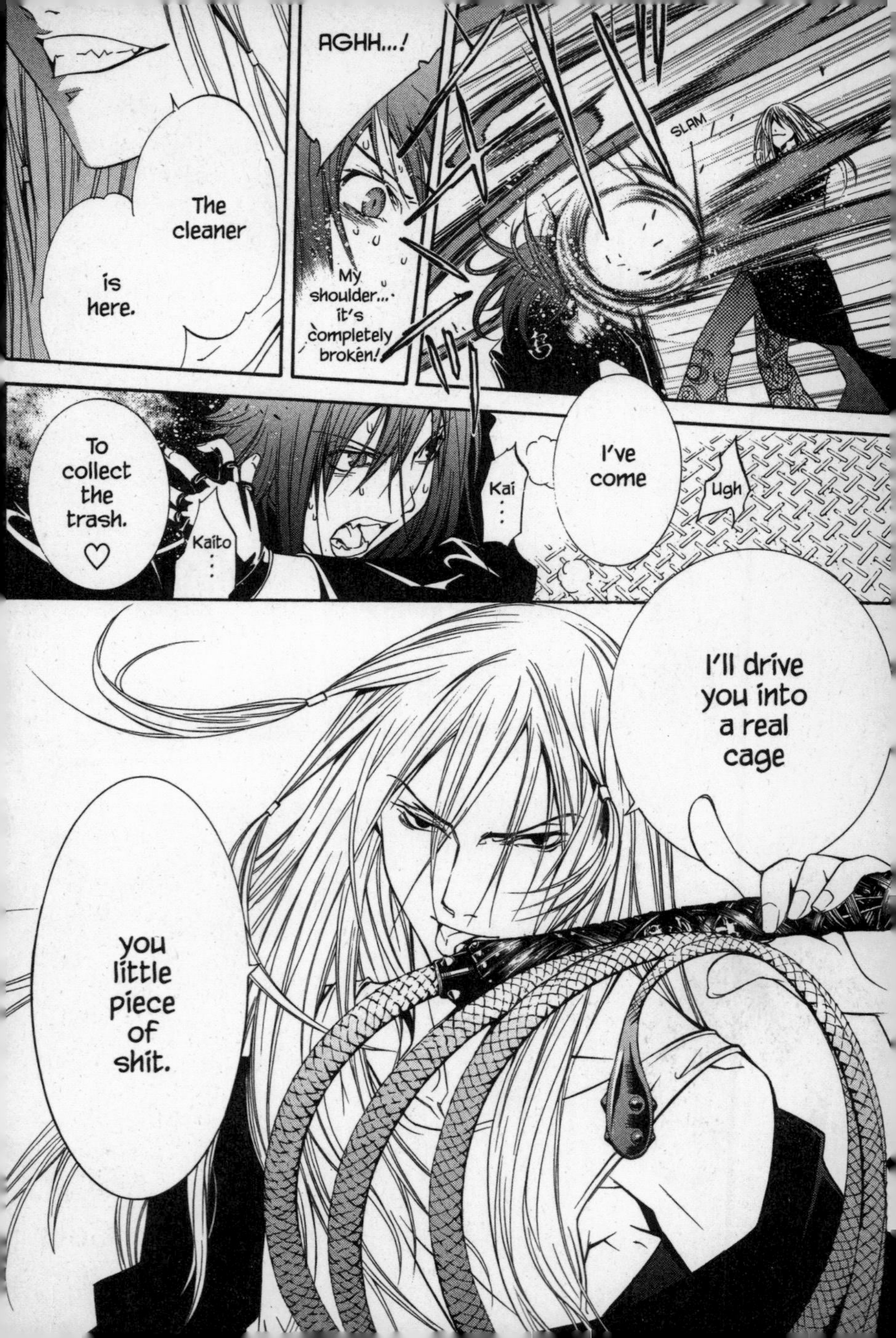
AGHH...!
SLAM
My shoulder... it's completely broken!
The cleaner
is here.
Ugh
I've come
Kai...
Kaito...
To collect the trash. ♡
I'll drive you into a real cage
you little piece of shit.

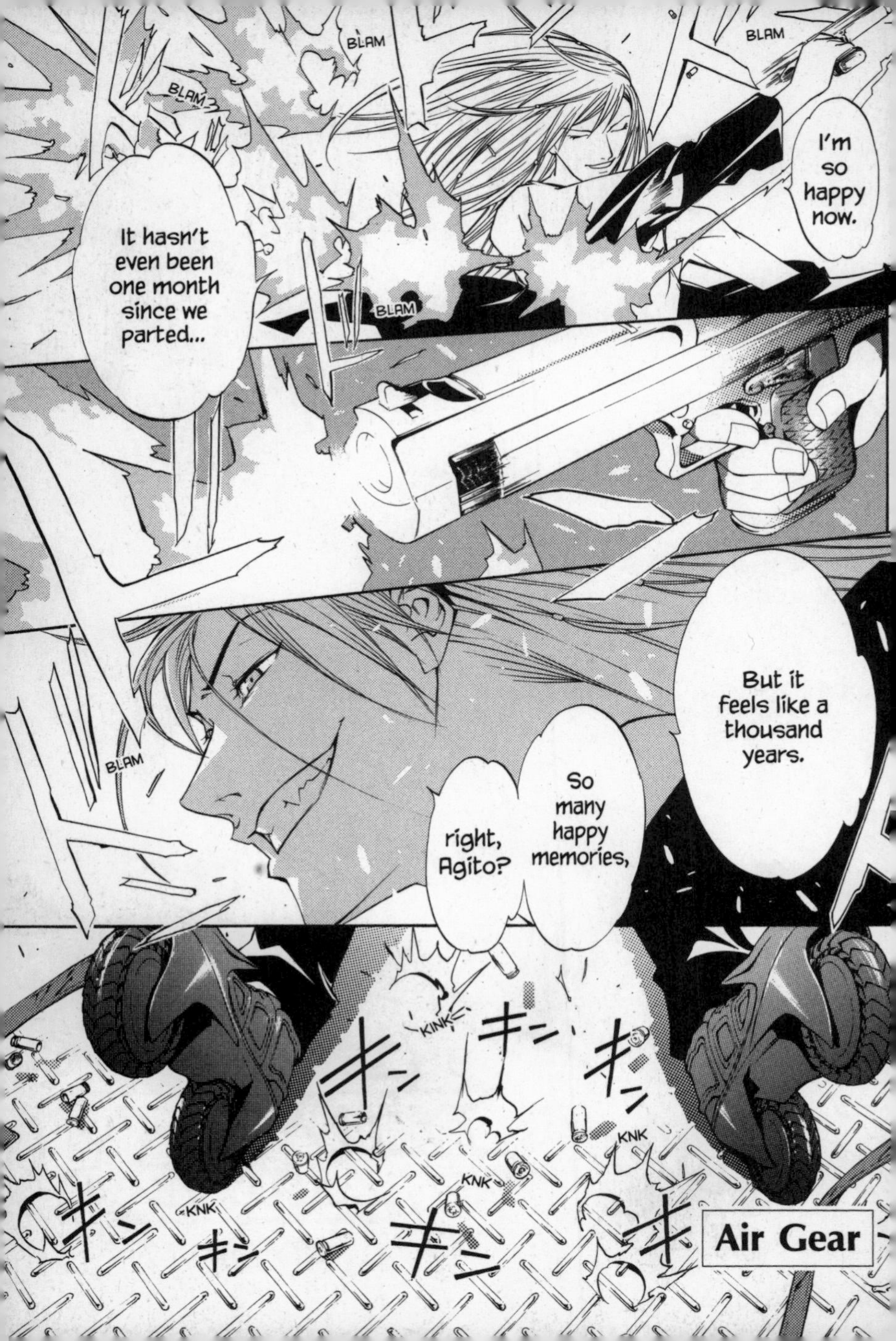
BLAM
BLAM
BLAM
I'm so happy now.
It hasn't even been one month since we parted...
BLAM
But it feels like a thousand years.
So many happy memories,
right, Agito?
BLAM
KINK
KNK
KNK
KNK
Air Gear

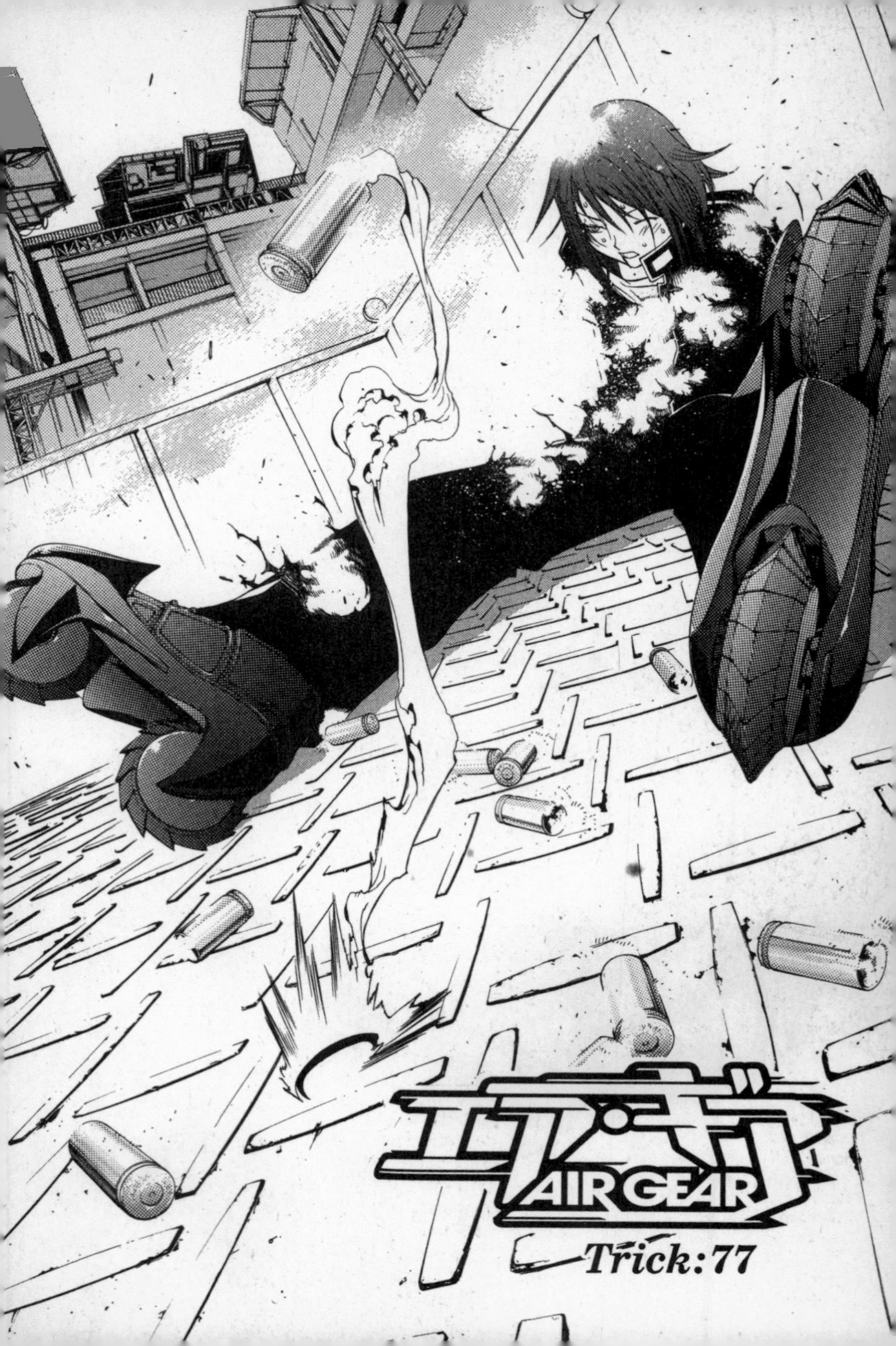

エア・ギア
AIR GEAR
Trick:77

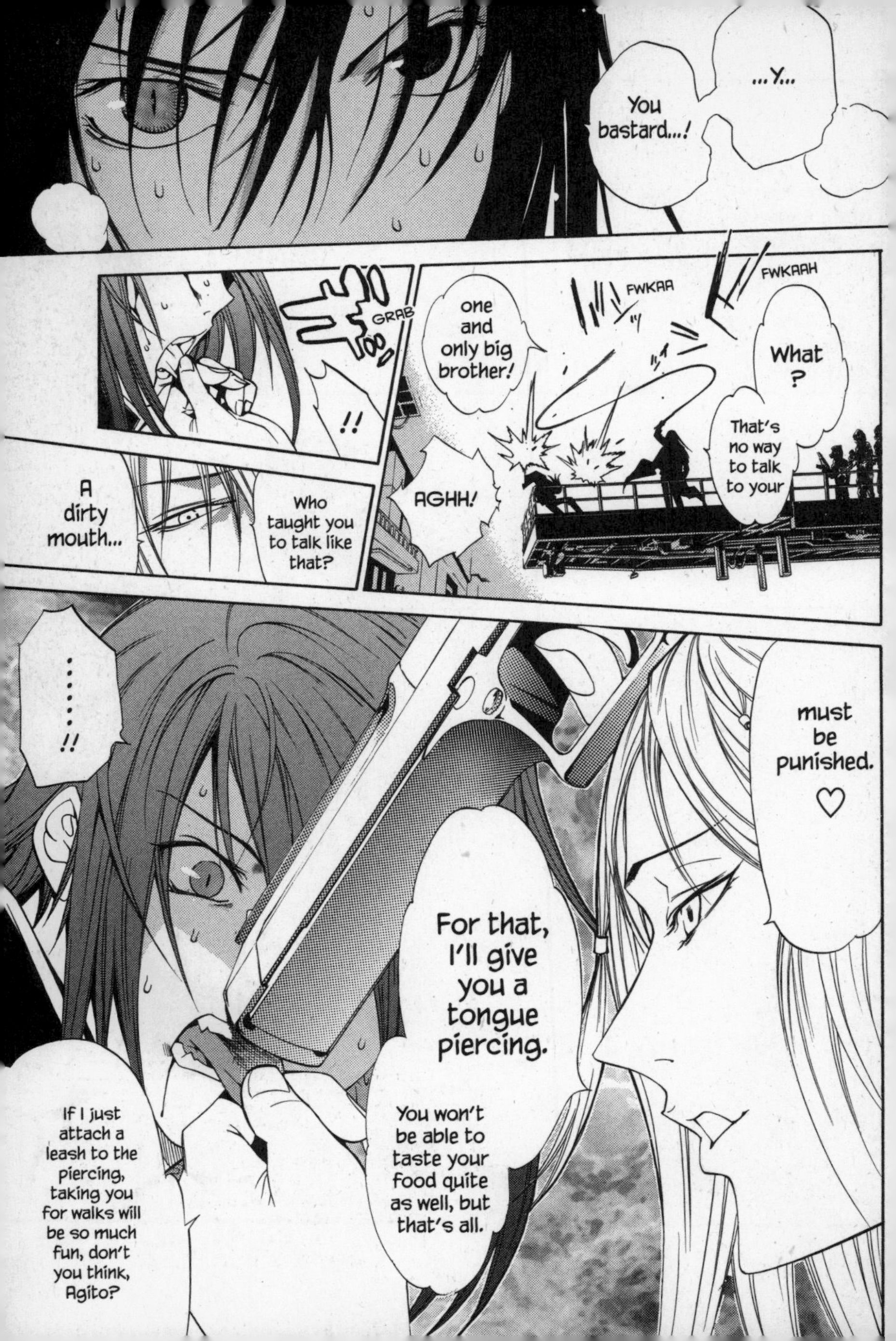

...Y...
You bastard...!
FWKAAH
What?
That's no way to talk to your
FWKAA
AGHH!
one and only big brother!
GRAB
!!
Who taught you to talk like that?
A dirty mouth...
must be punished. ♡
For that, I'll give you a tongue piercing.
You won't be able to taste your food quite as well, but that's all.
If I just attach a leash to the piercing, taking you for walks will be so much fun, don't you think, Agito?
......!!

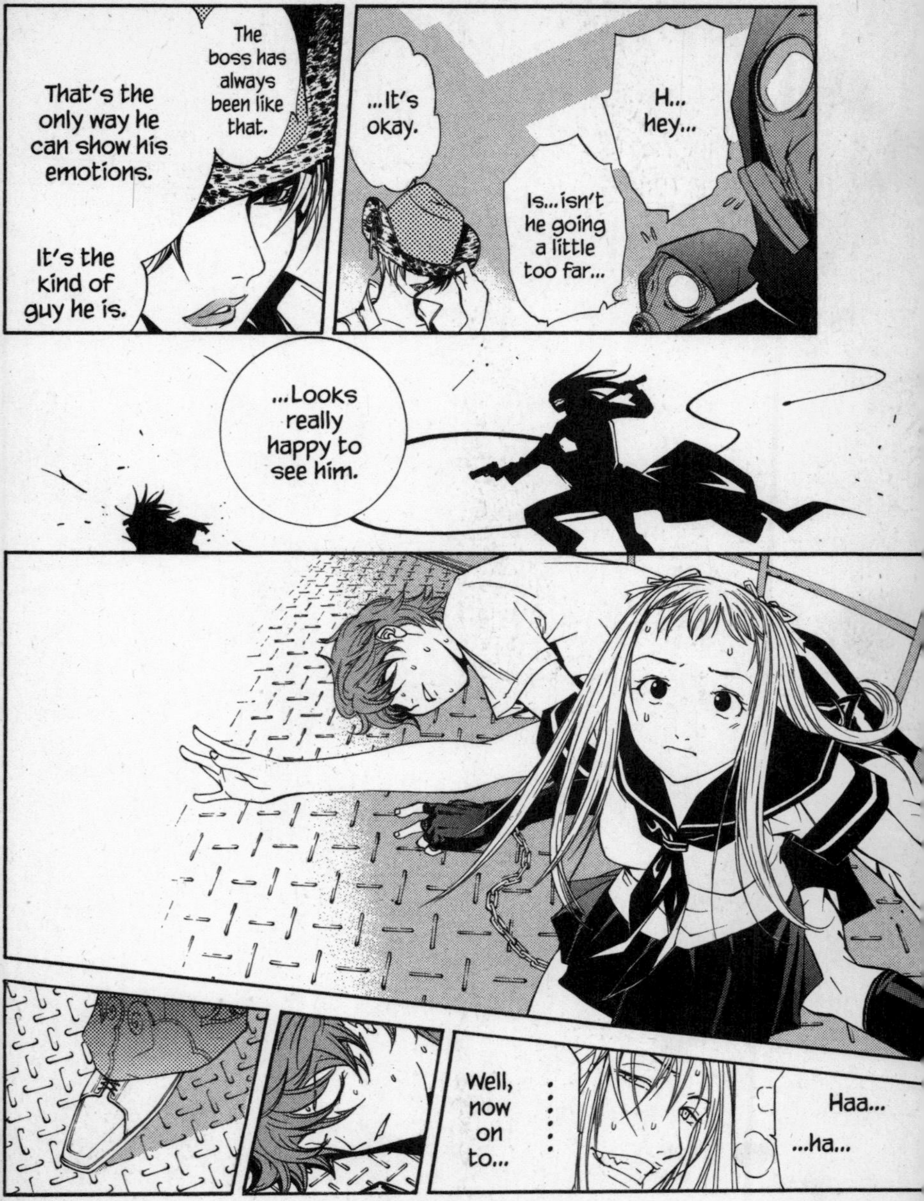
H... hey...
Is...isn't he going a little too far...
...It's okay.
The boss has always been like that.
That's the only way he can show his emotions.
It's the kind of guy he is.
...Looks really happy to see him.
Haa...
...ha...
.....
Well, now on to...

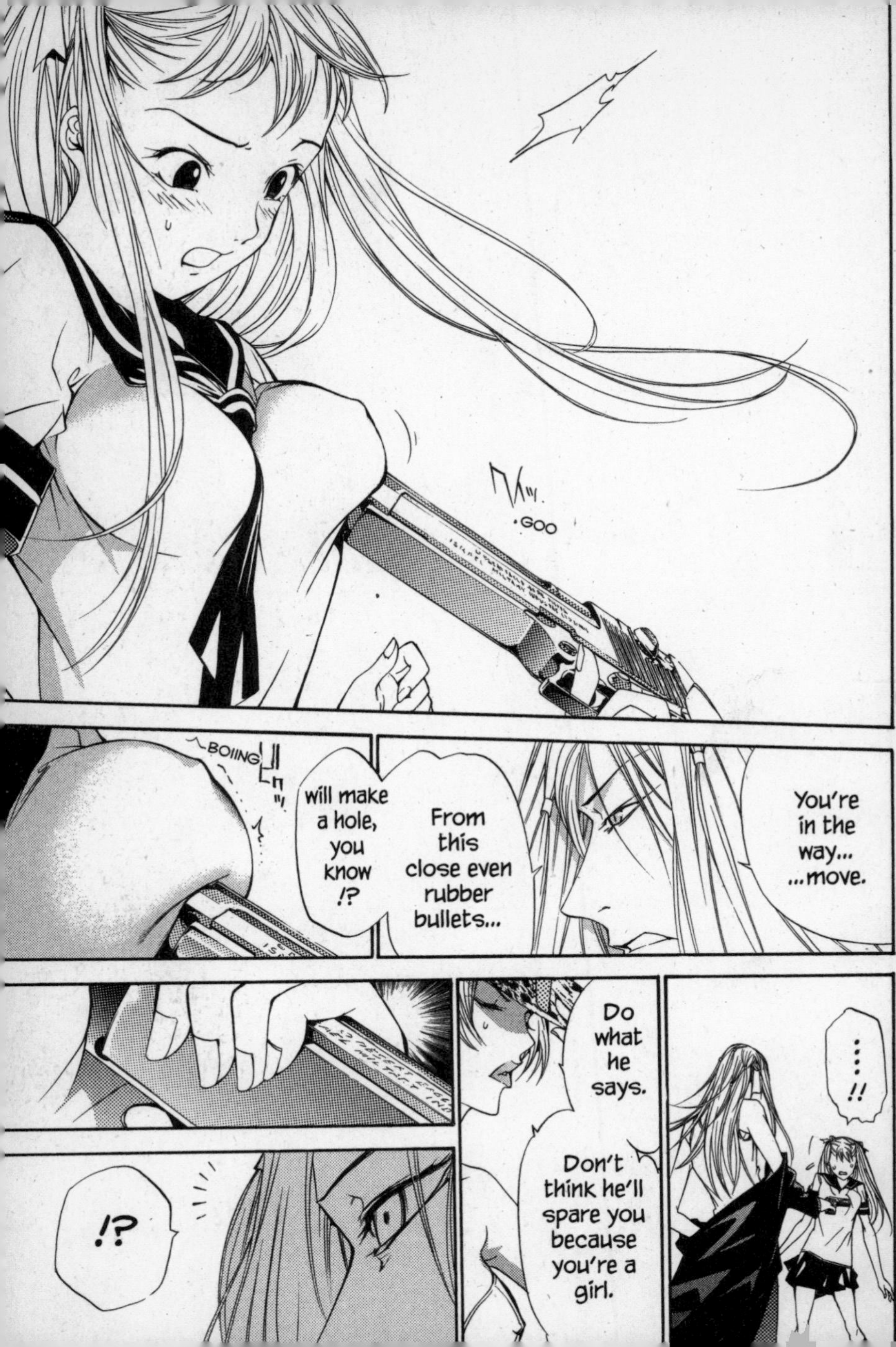
GOO
You're in the way... ...move.
From this close even rubber bullets...
will make a hole, you know !?
BOIING
......!!
Do what he says.
Don't think he'll spare you because you're a girl.
!?

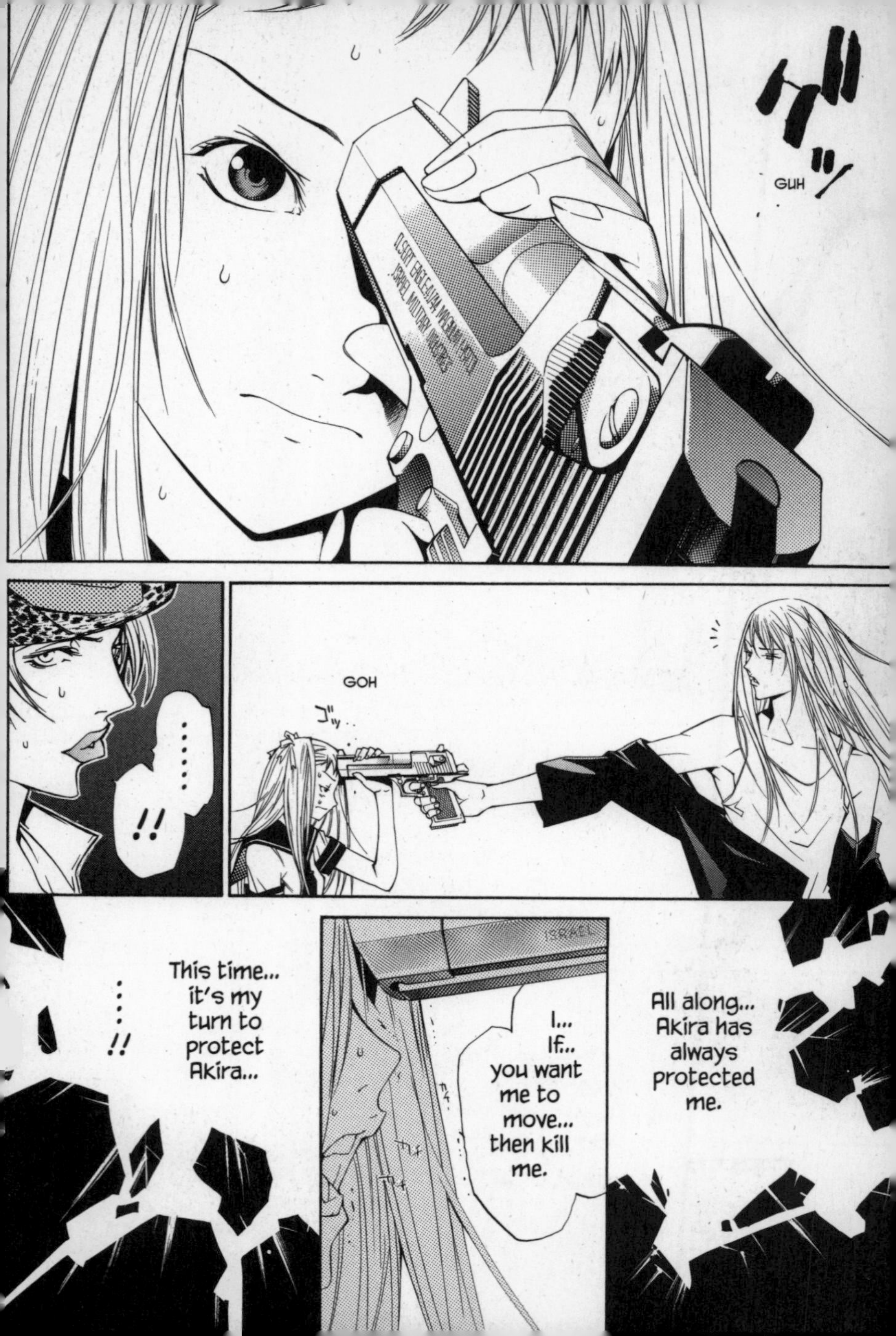
GUH
GOH
. . . . . !!
All along... Akira has always protected me.
ISRAEL
I... If... you want me to move... then kill me.
This time... it's my turn to protect Akira...
. . . !!

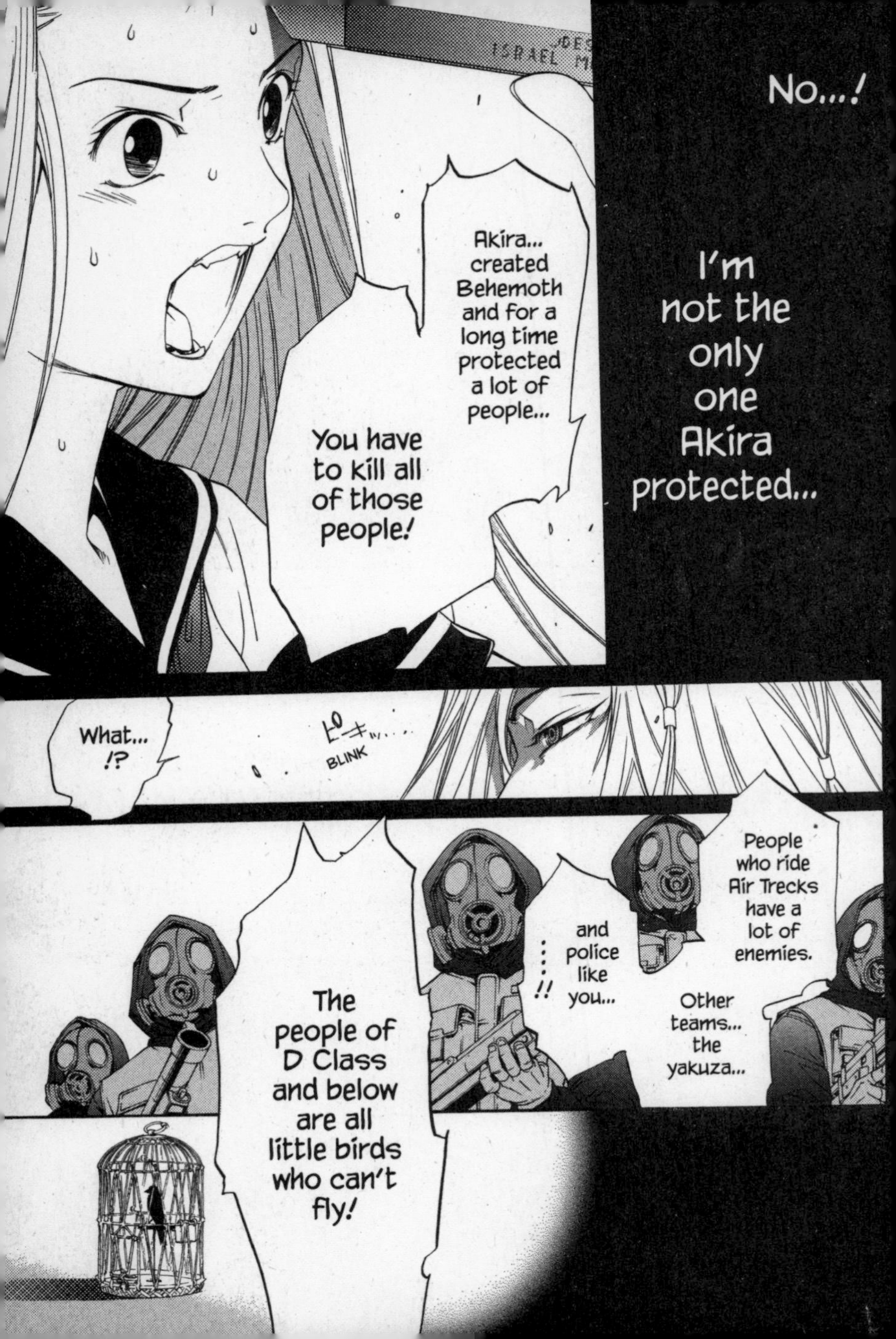

No...!
I'm not the only one Akira protected...
Akira... created Behemoth and for a long time protected a lot of people...
You have to kill all of those people!
BLINK
What...!?
People who ride Air Trecks have a lot of enemies.
Other teams... the yakuza...
and police like you...
......!!
The people of D Class and below are all little birds who can't fly!

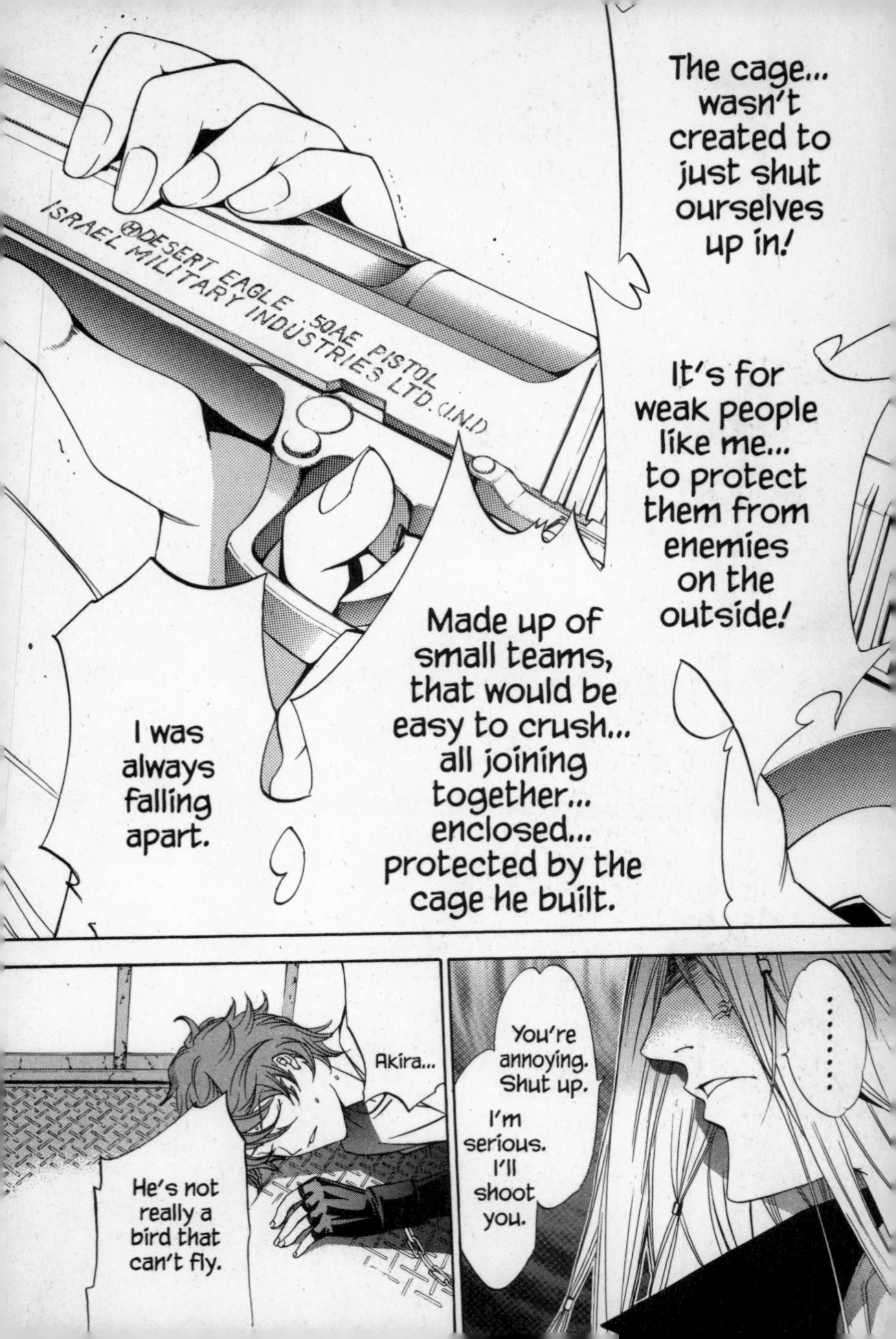
The cage... wasn't created to just shut ourselves up in!
It's for weak people like me... to protect them from enemies on the outside!
DESERT EAGLE 50AE PISTOL
ISRAEL MILITARY INDUSTRIES LTD.
Made up of small teams, that would be easy to crush... all joining together... enclosed... protected by the cage he built.
I was always falling apart.
......
You're annoying. Shut up.
I'm serious. I'll shoot you.
Akira...
He's not really a bird that can't fly.

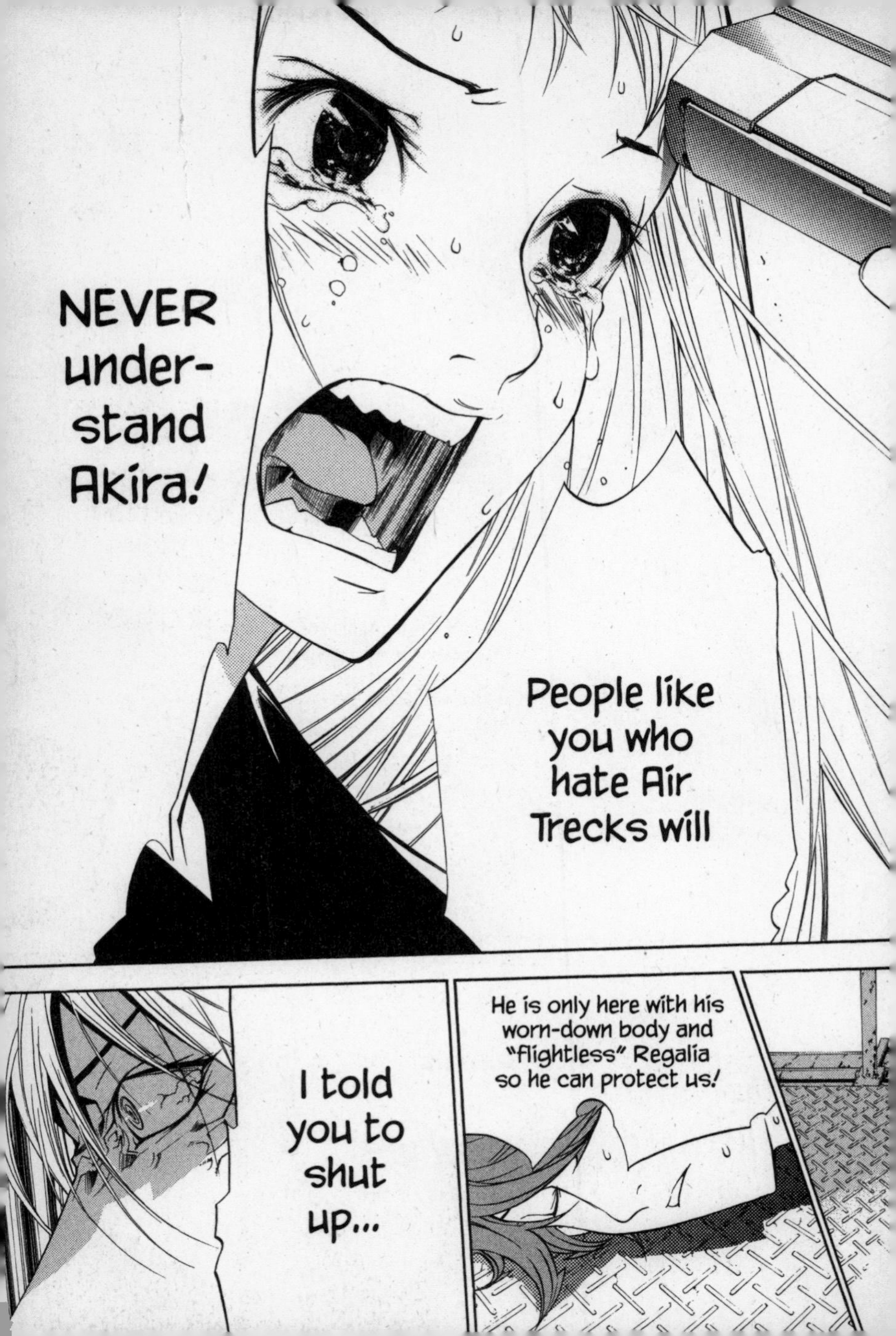
People like you who hate Air Trecks will
NEVER under-stand Akira!
He is only here with his worn-down body and "flightless" Regalia so he can protect us!
I told you to shut up...

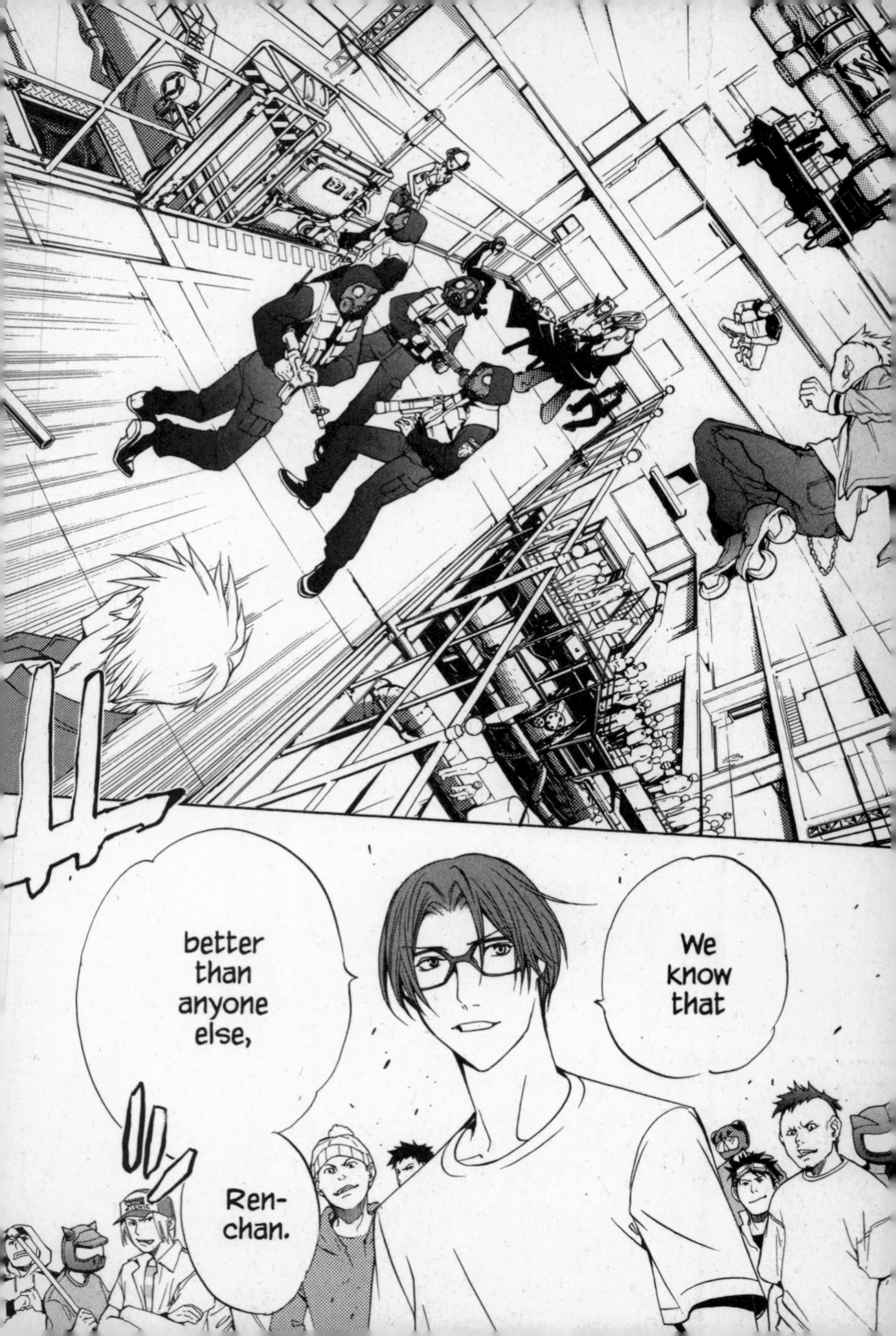
We know that
better than anyone else,
Ren-chan.

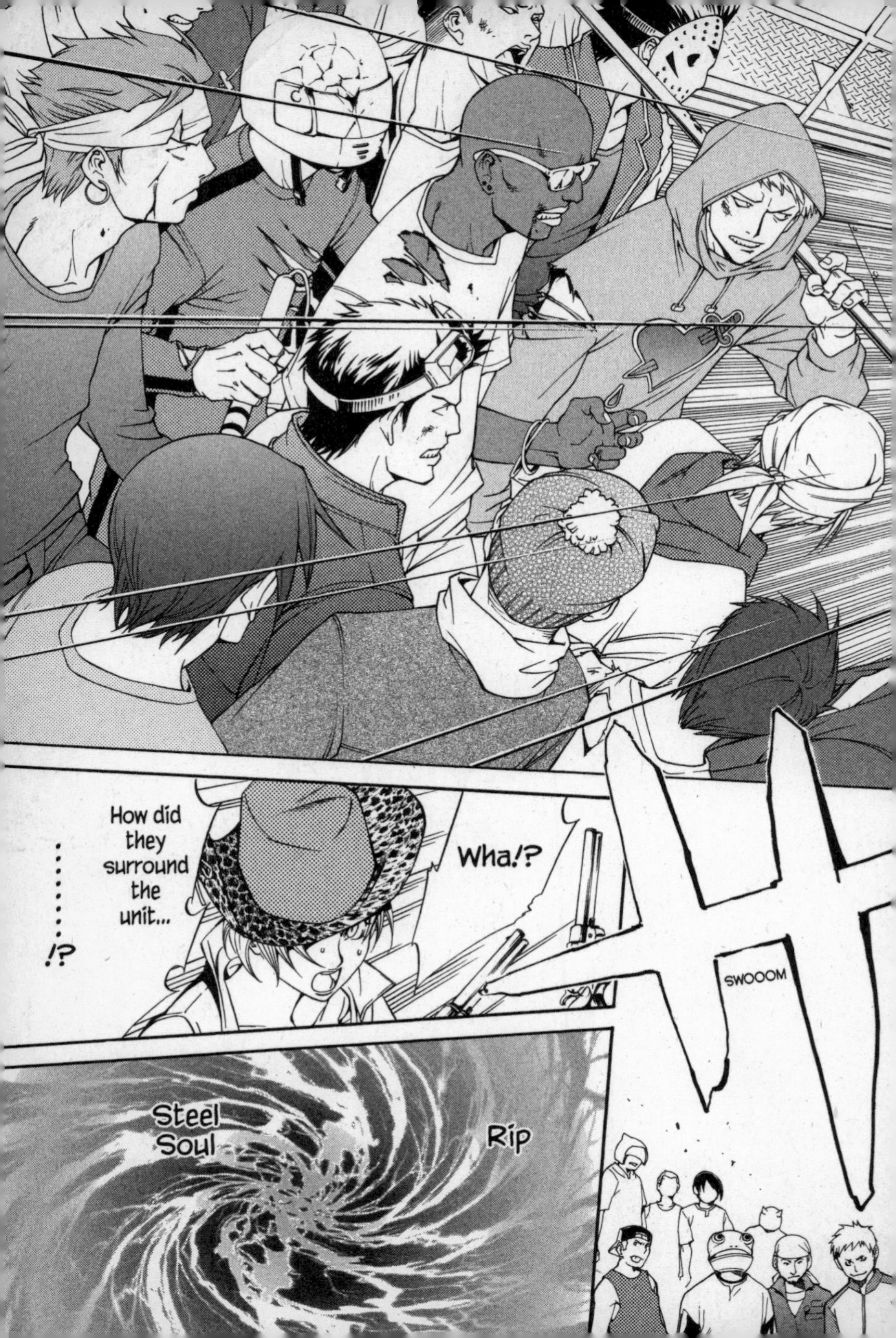
SWOOOM
Wha!?
How did they surround the unit...
......!?
Rip
Steel Soul

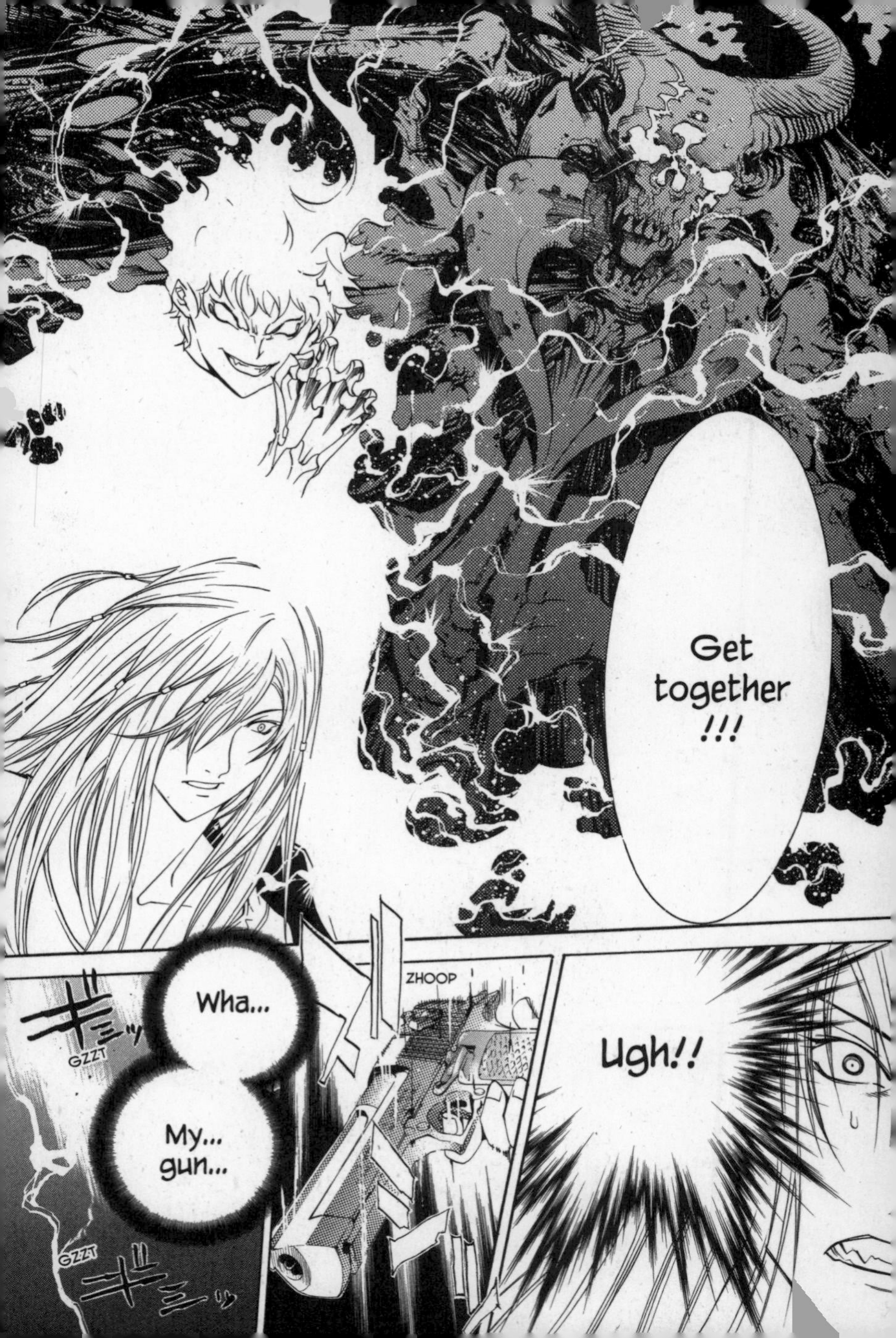
Get together !!!
Ugh!!
ZHOOP
Wha...
My... gun...
GZZT
GZZT

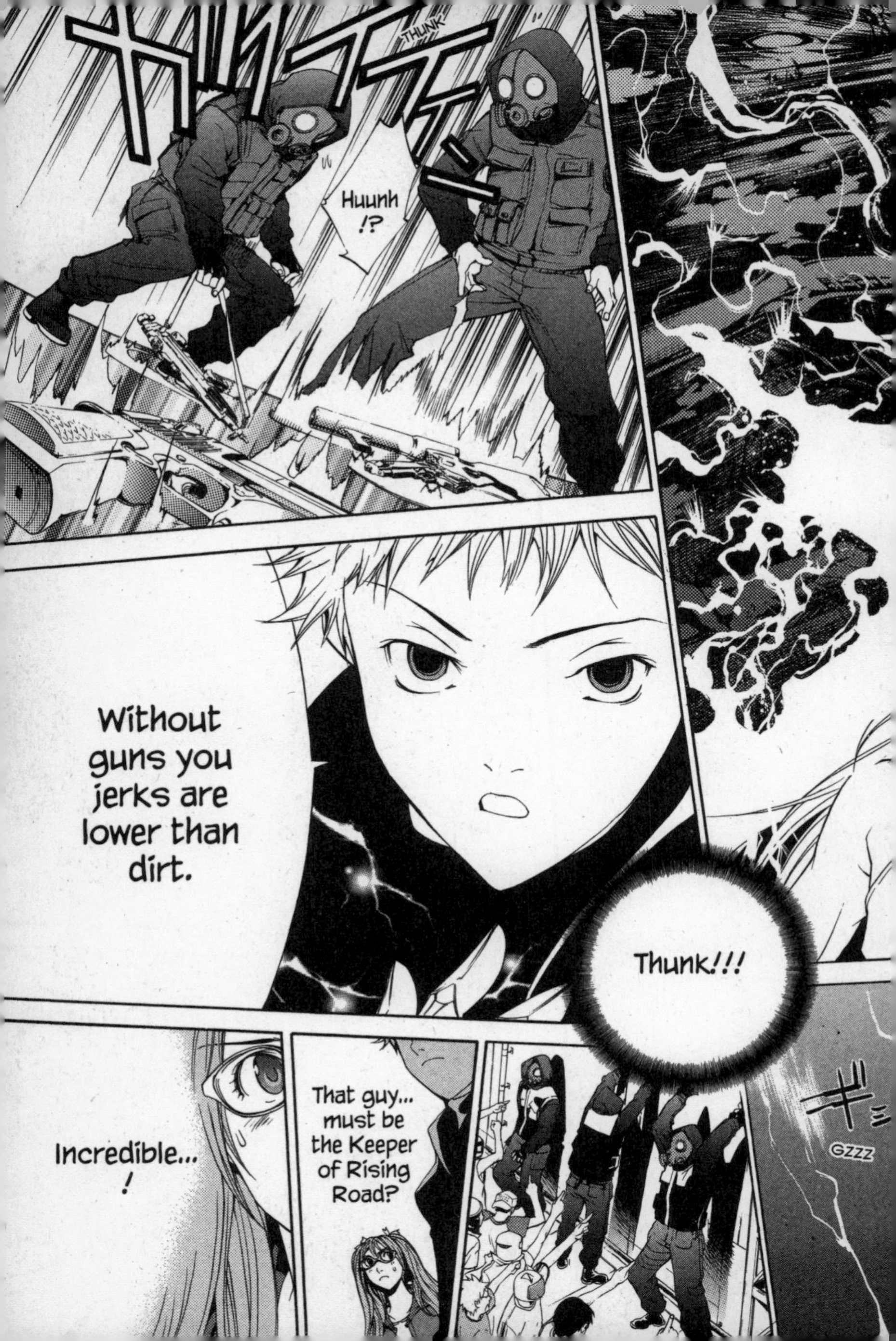
THUNK
Huunh !?
Without guns you jerks are lower than dirt.
Thunk!!!
GZZZ
That guy... must be the Keeper of Rising Road?
Incredible... !

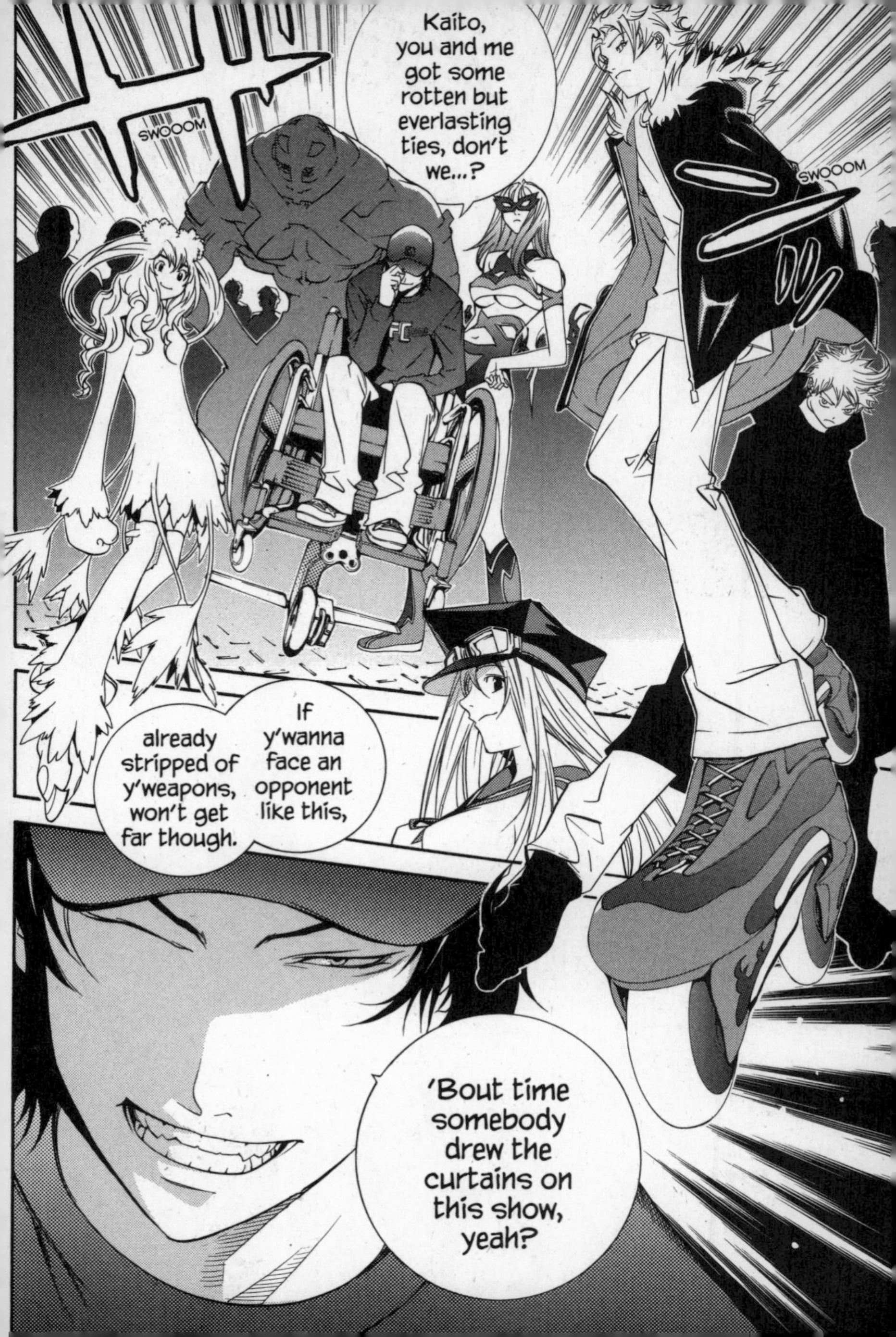
SWOOOM
Kaito, you and me got some rotten but everlasting ties, don't we...?
SWOOOM
If y'wanna face an opponent like this,
already stripped of y'weapons, won't get far though.
'Bout time somebody drew the curtains on this show, yeah?

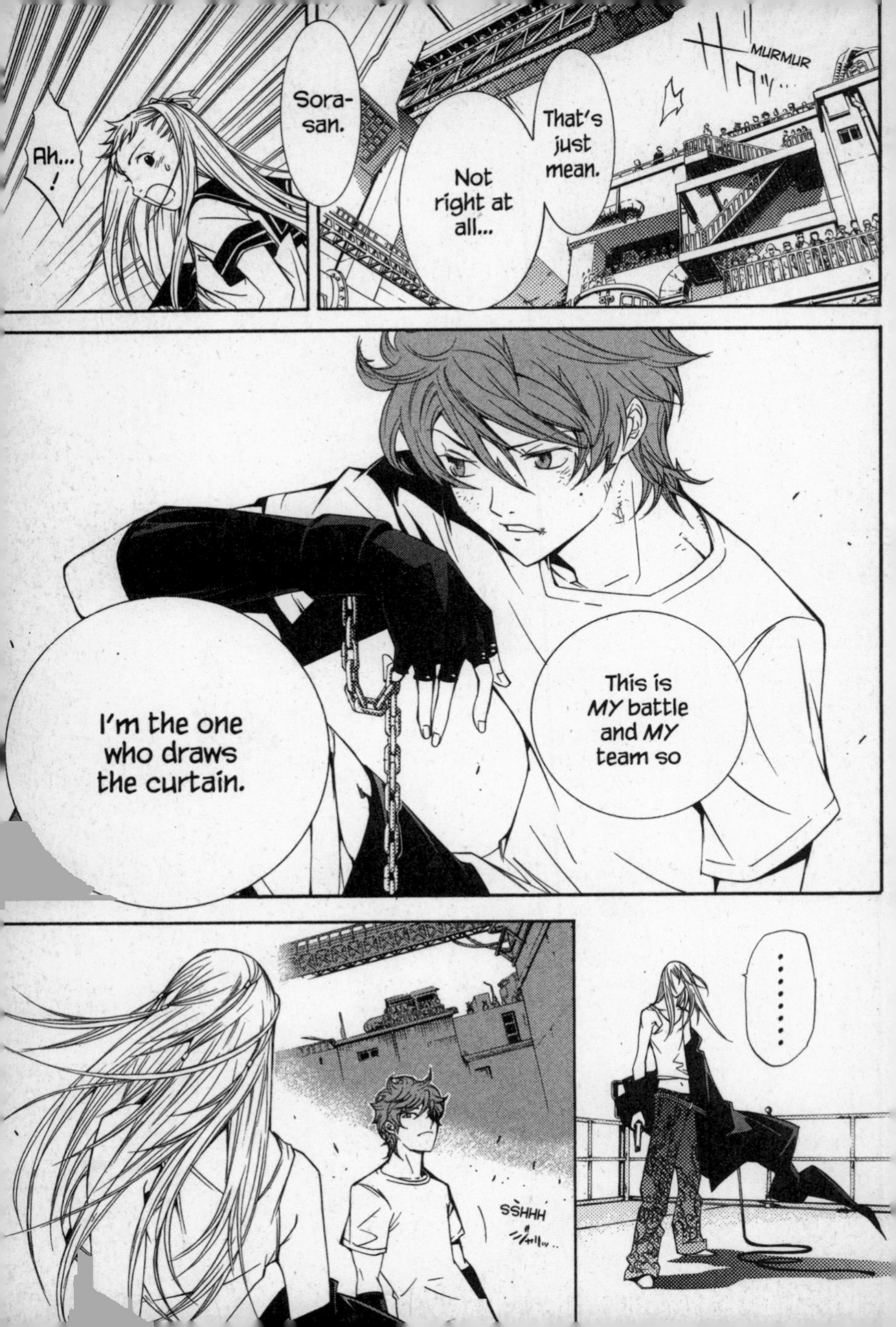
MURMUR
That's just mean.
Not right at all...
Sora-san.
Ah...!
This is MY battle and MY team so
I'm the one who draws the curtain.
........
SSHHH

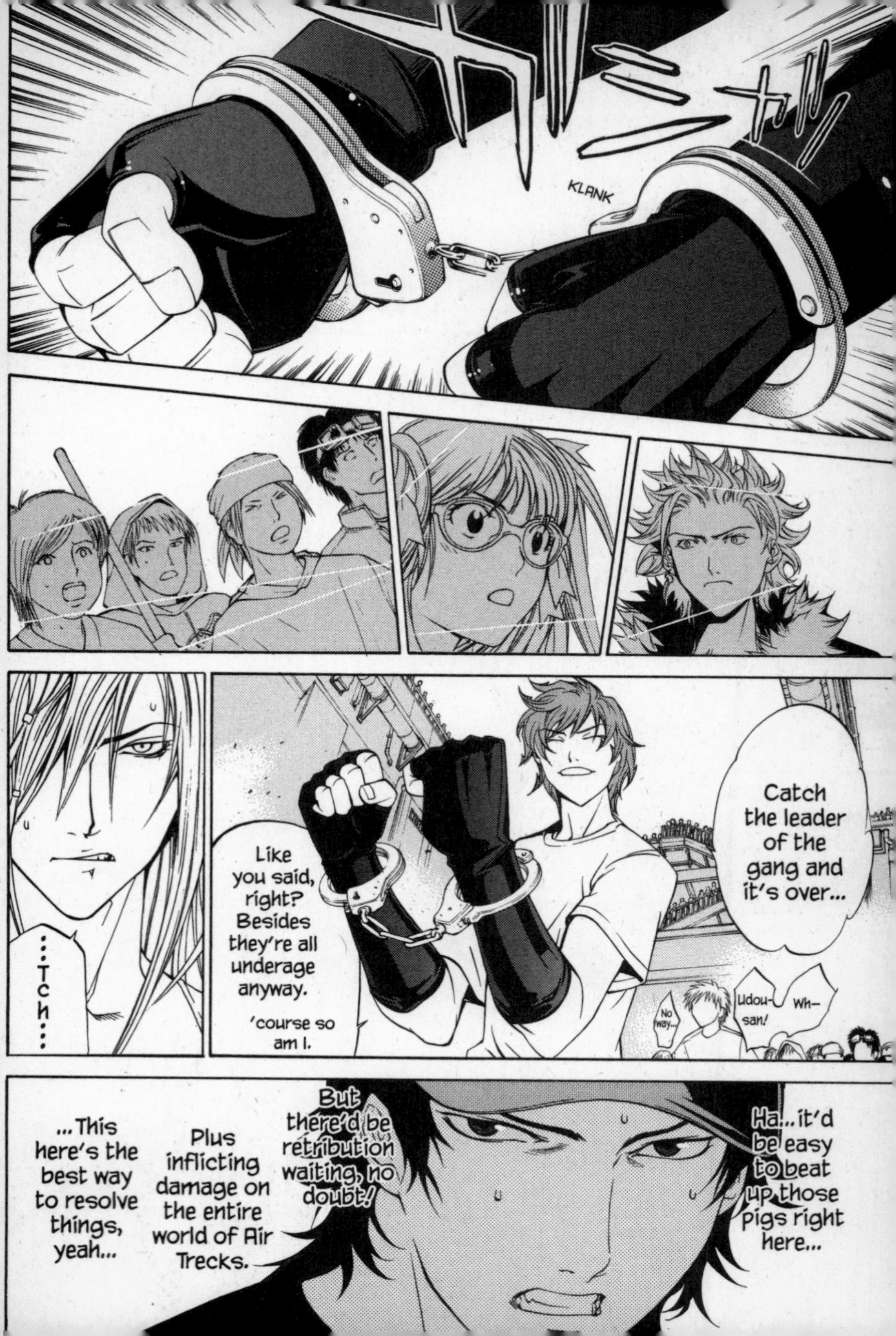
KLANK
Catch the leader of the gang and it's over...
Wh—
Udou-san!
No way...
Like you said, right? Besides they're all underage anyway.
'course so am I.
...Tch...
Ha...it'd be easy to beat up those pigs right here...
But there'd be retribution waiting, no doubt!
Plus inflicting damage on the entire world of Air Trecks.
...This here's the best way to resolve things, yeah...

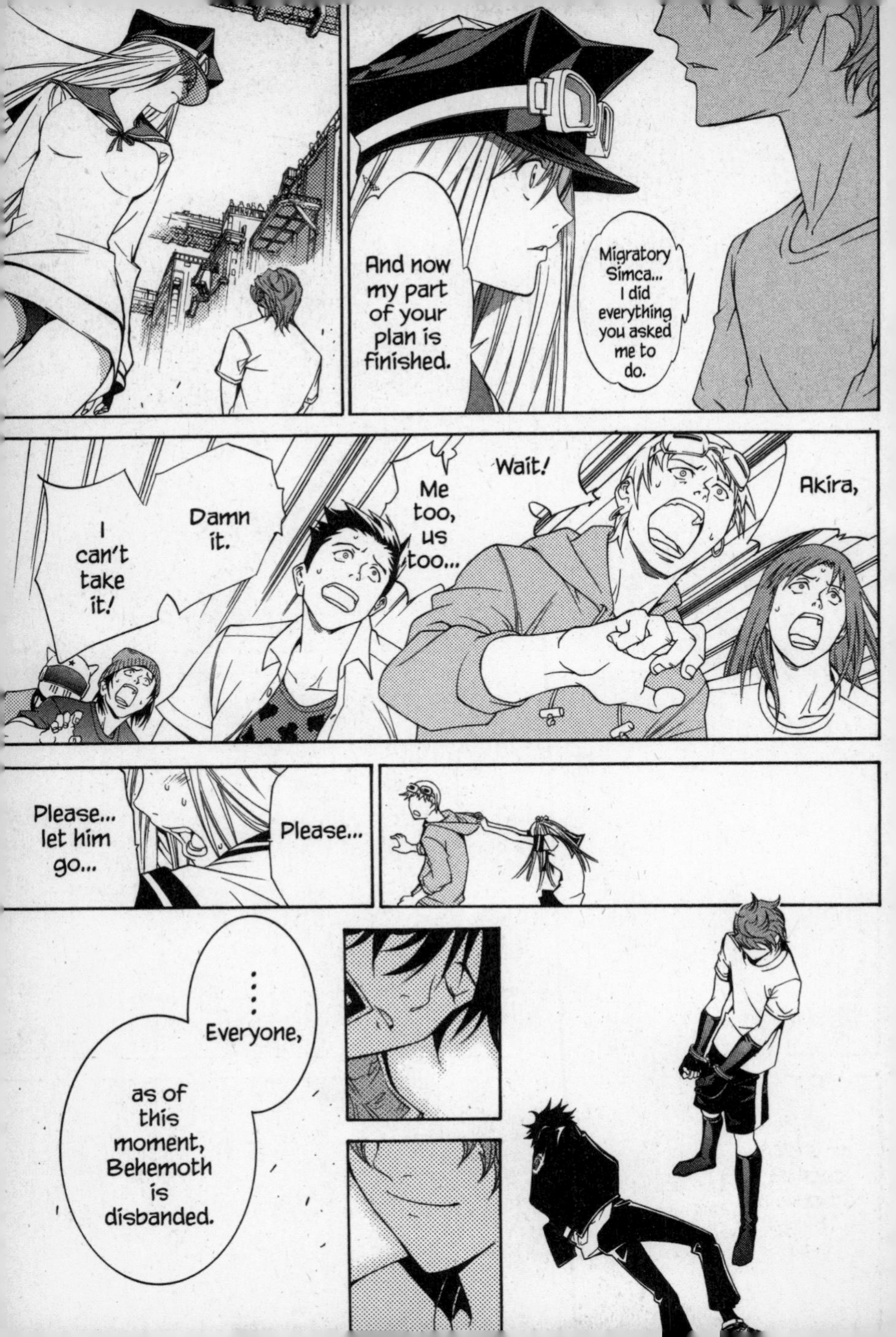
Migratory Simca... I did everything you asked me to do.
And now my part of your plan is finished.
Akira,
Wait!
Me too, us too...
Damn it.
I can't take it!
Please...
Please... let him go...
... Everyone,
as of this moment, Behemoth is disbanded.

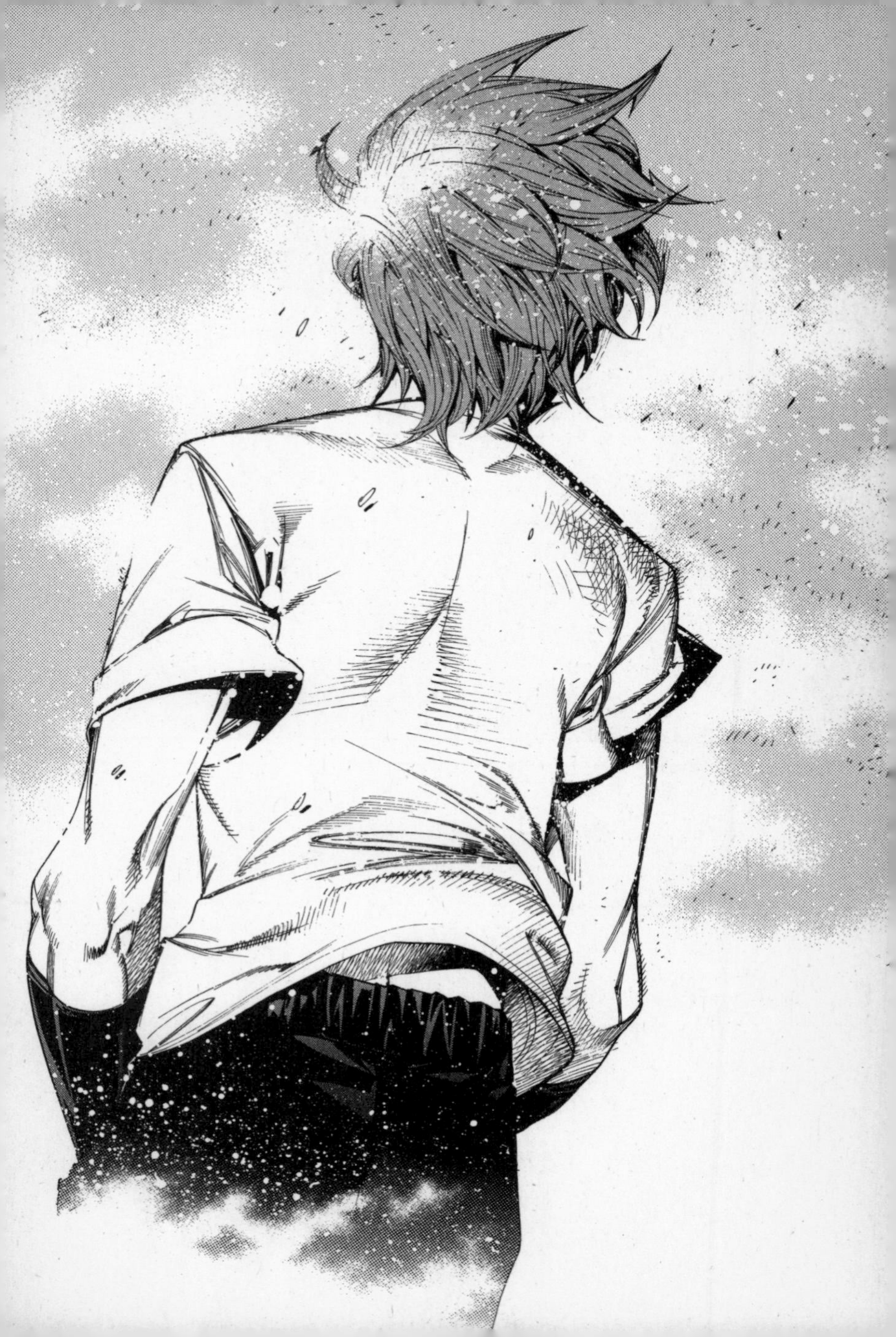

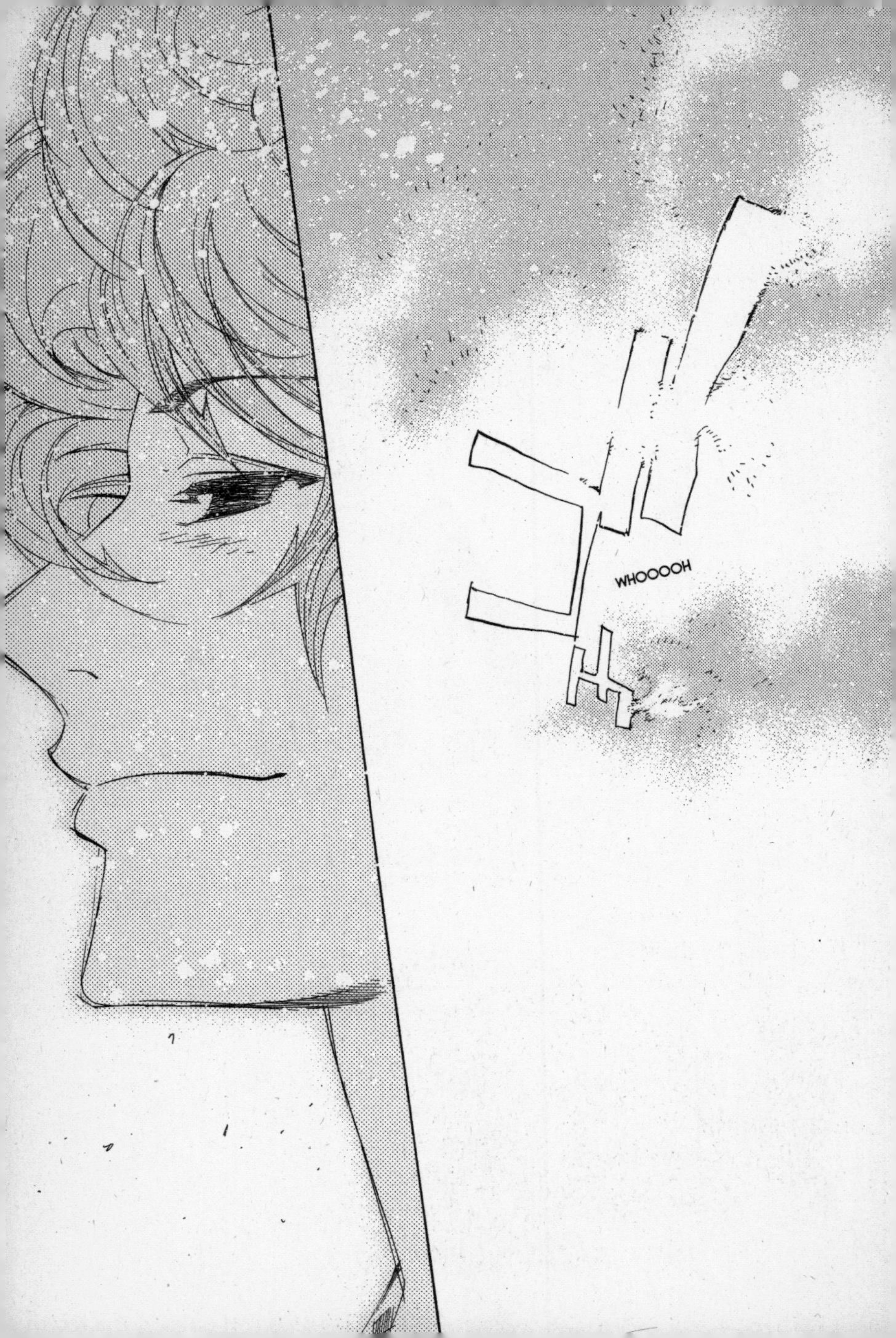
WHOOOOH

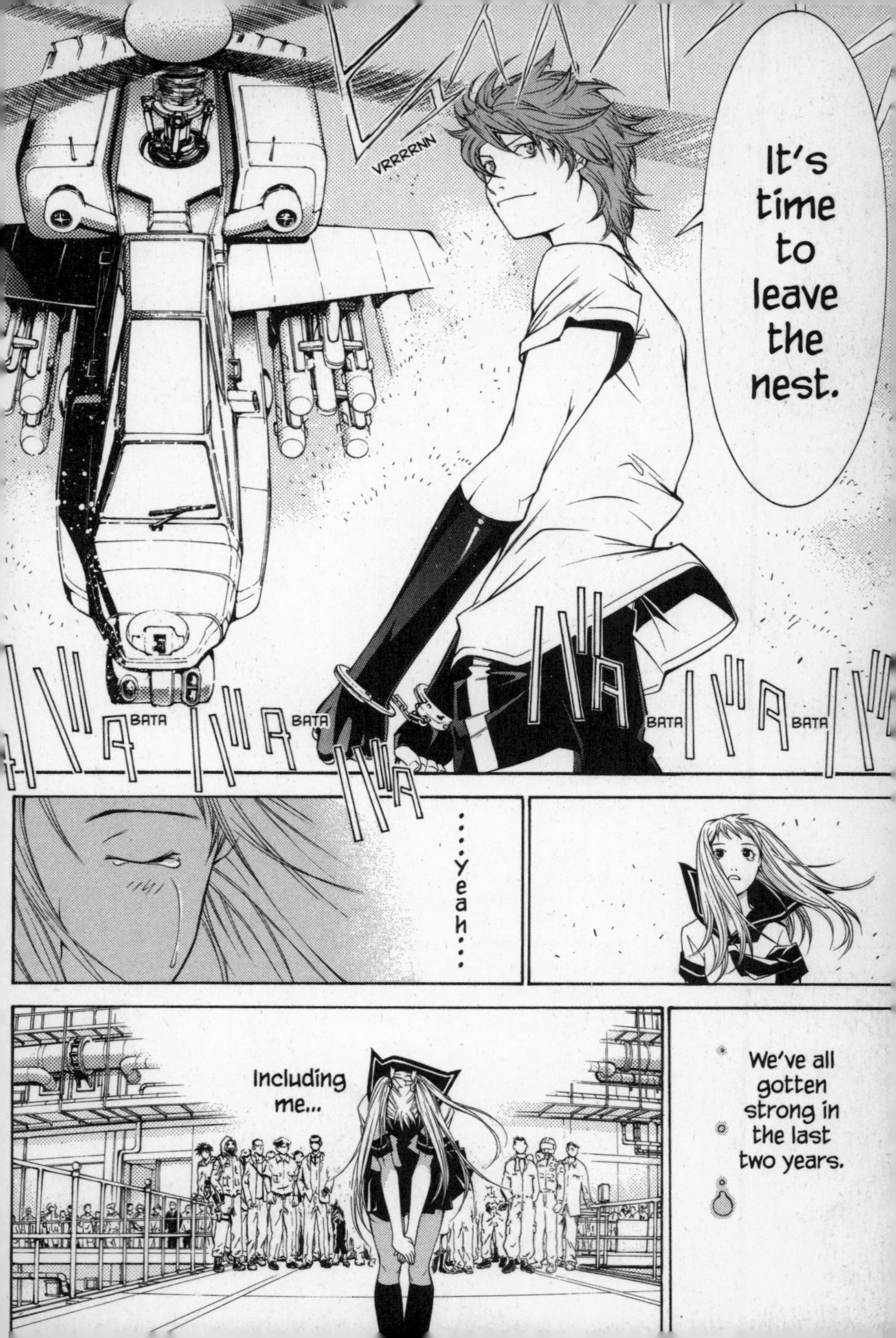
It's time to leave the nest.
VRRRRNN
BATA
BATA
BATA
BATA
...Yeah...
We've all gotten strong in the last two years.
Including me...

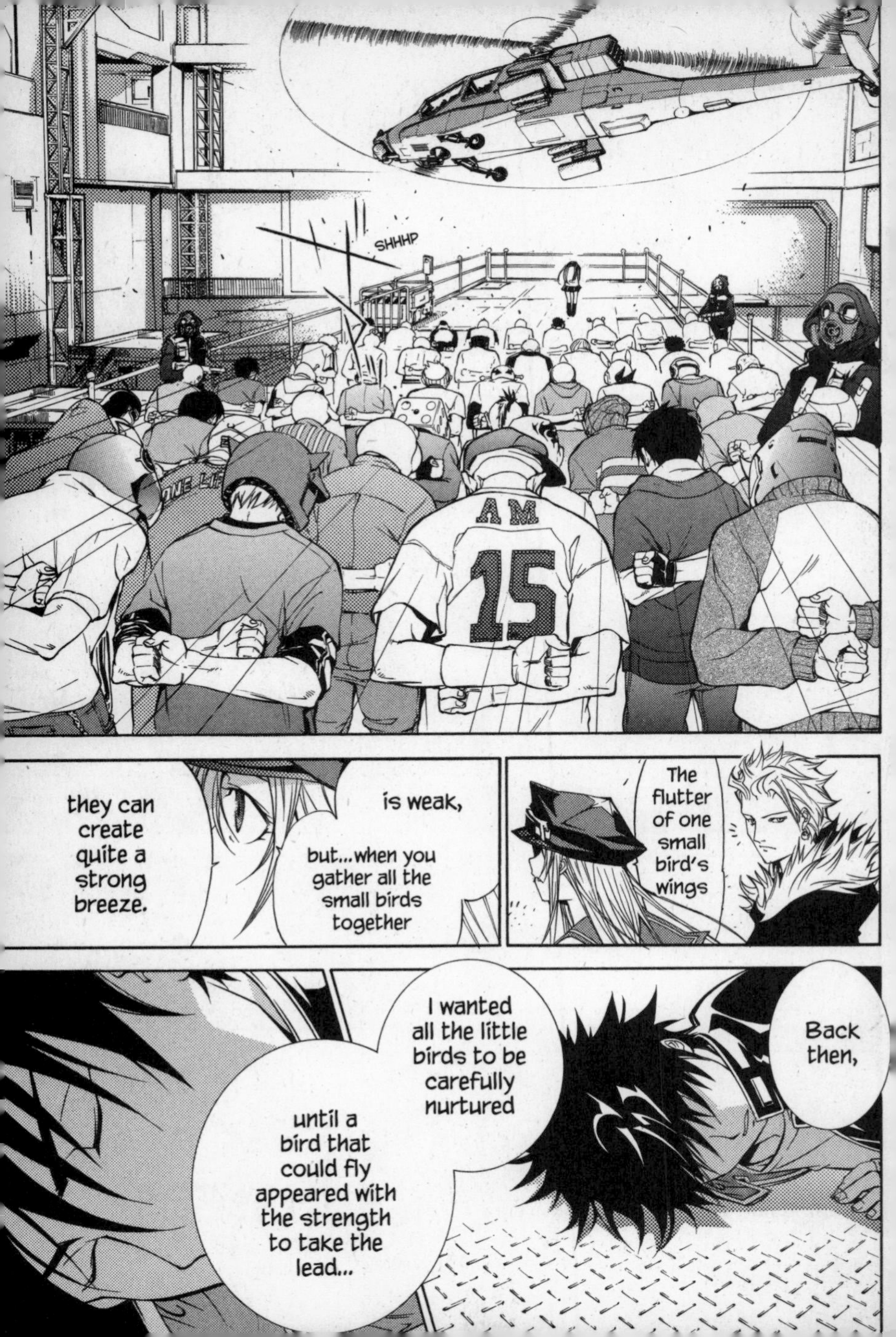
SHHHP
The flutter of one small bird's wings
is weak,
but...when you gather all the small birds together
they can create quite a strong breeze.
Back then,
I wanted all the little birds to be carefully nurtured
until a bird that could fly appeared with the strength to take the lead...

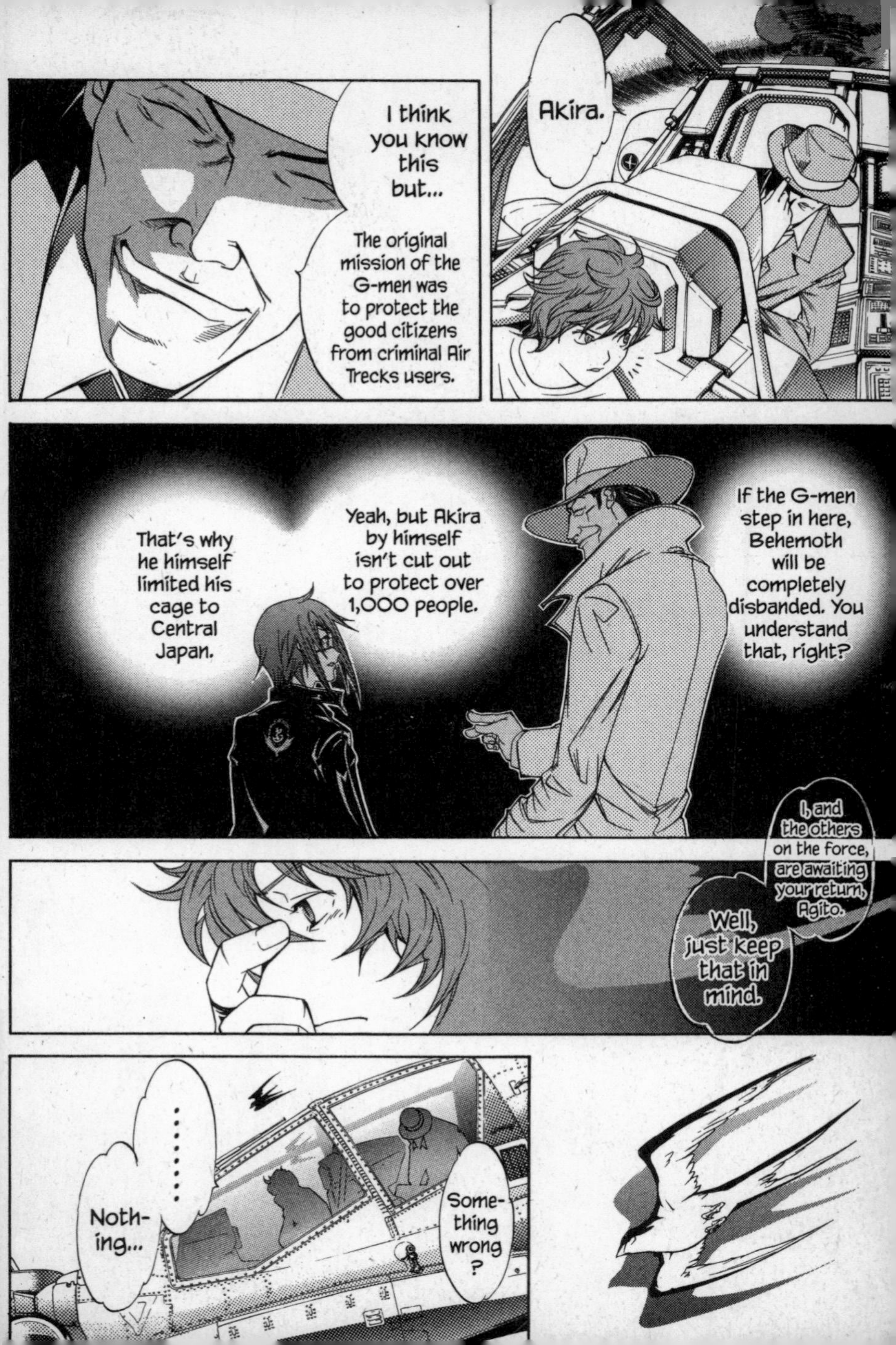
Akira.
I think you know this but...
The original mission of the G-men was to protect the good citizens from criminal Air Trecks users.
If the G-men step in here, Behemoth will be completely disbanded. You understand that, right?
Yeah, but Akira by himself isn't cut out to protect over 1,000 people.
That's why he himself limited his cage to Central Japan.
I, and the others on the force, are awaiting your return, Agito.
Well, just keep that in mind.
Something wrong?
......
Nothing...

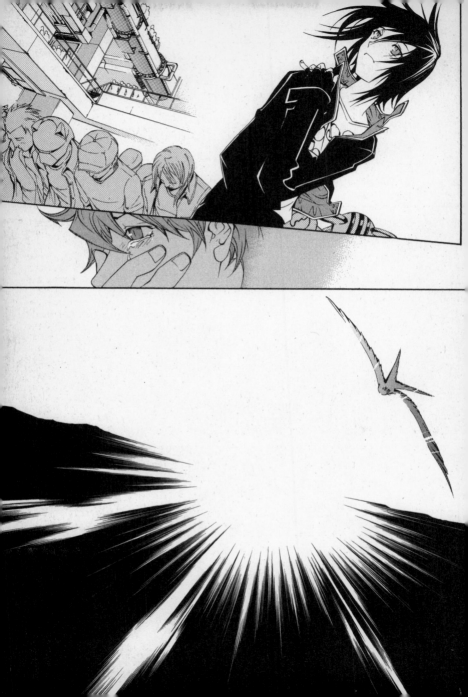

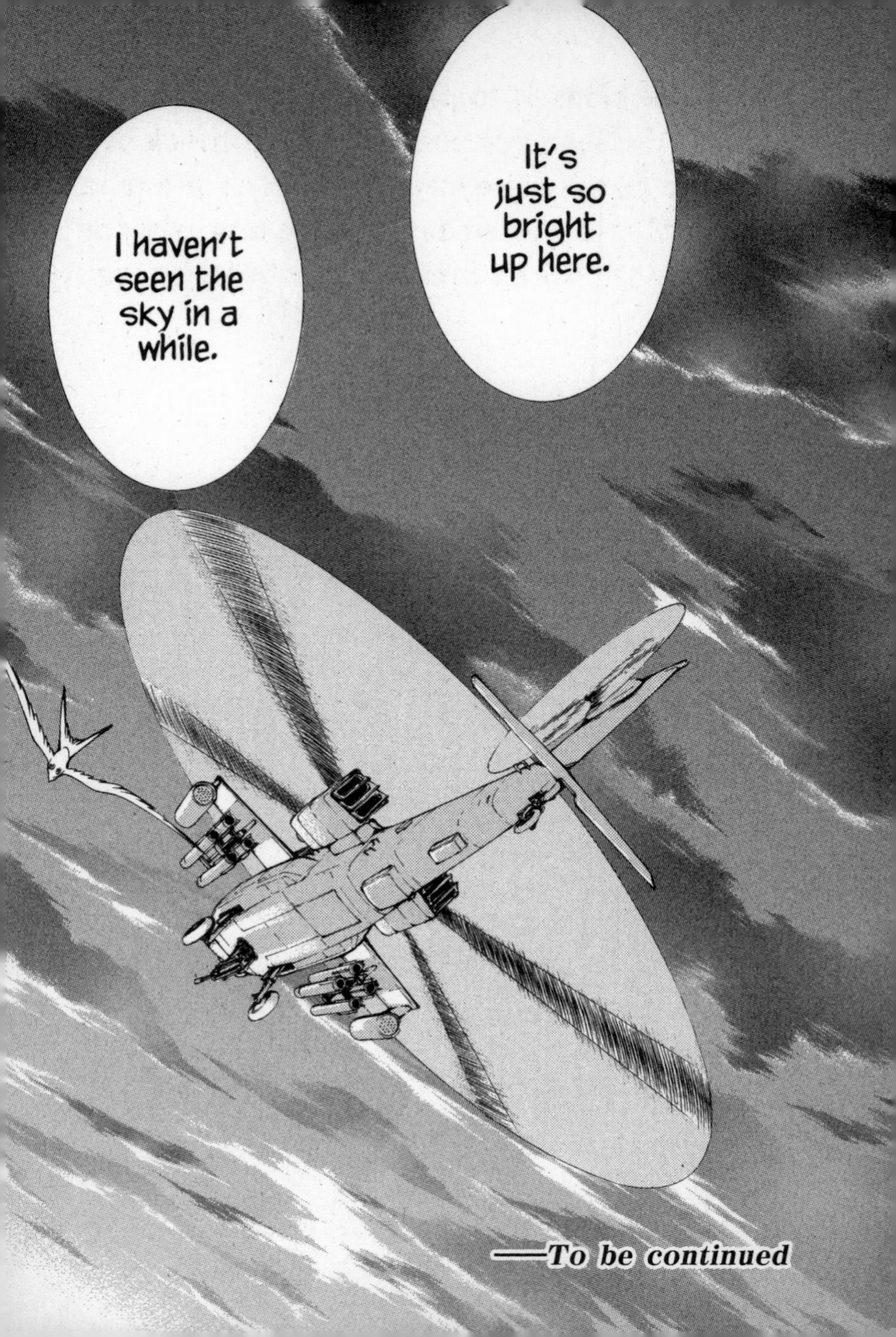
It's just so bright up here.
I haven't seen the sky in a while.
—To be continued

We're pleased to present you a preview from Air Gear, volume 10. Please check our website (www.delreymanga.com) to see when this volume will be available in English. For now you'll have to make do with Japanese!

少し<ruby>少<rt>すこ</rt></ruby>だけ

後悔<ruby>後悔<rt>こうかい</rt></ruby>していた

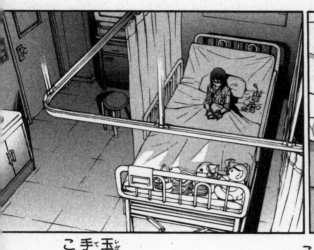

超獣<ruby>超獣<rt>アキラ</rt></ruby>と戦った<ruby>戦<rt>たたか</rt></ruby>ったことも

玉璽<ruby>玉璽<rt>レガリア</rt></ruby>を手<ruby>手<rt>て</rt></ruby>に入れたことも

アイツと…

出逢<ruby>出逢<rt>であ</rt></ruby>っちまったことも……

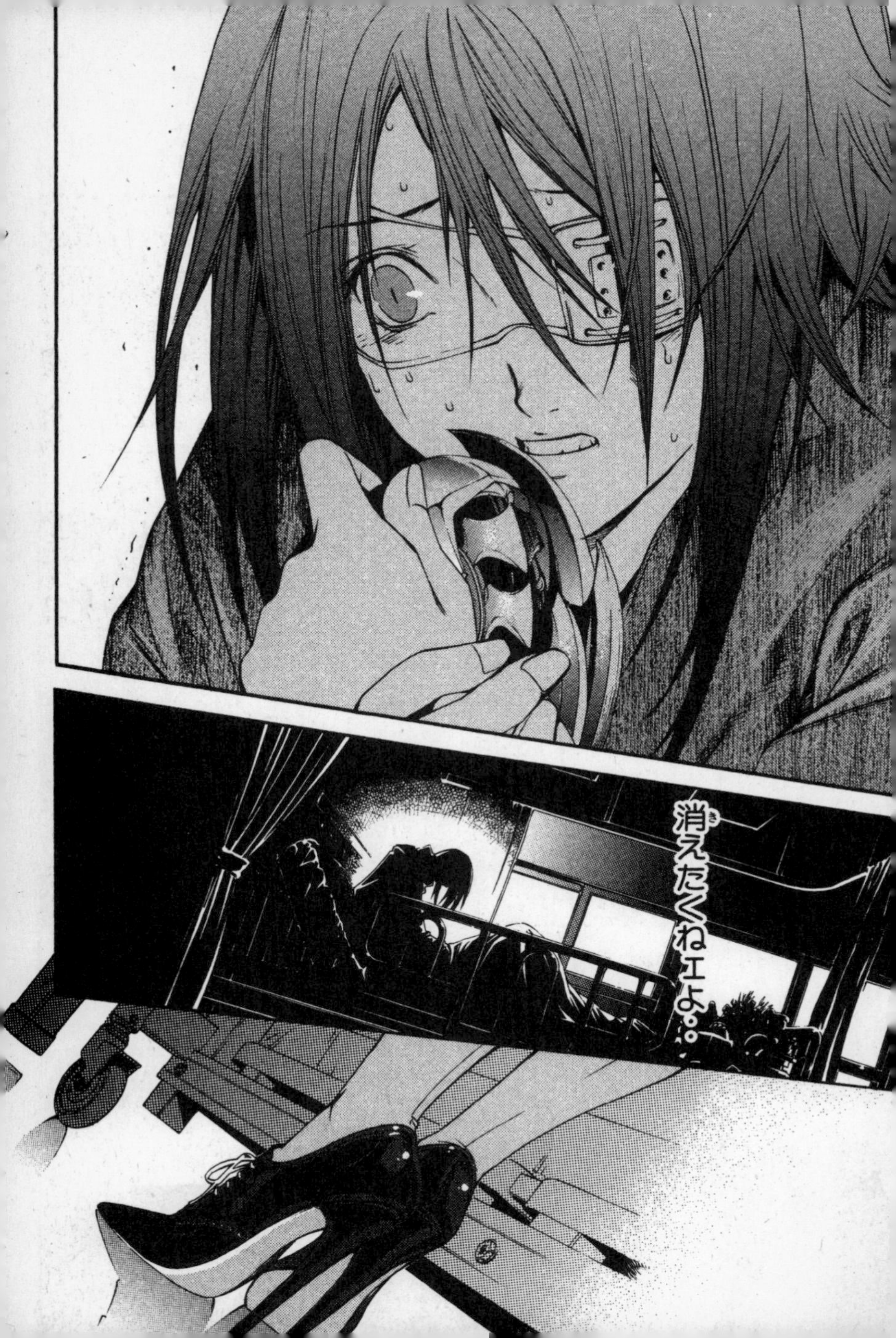
消えたくねェよ…

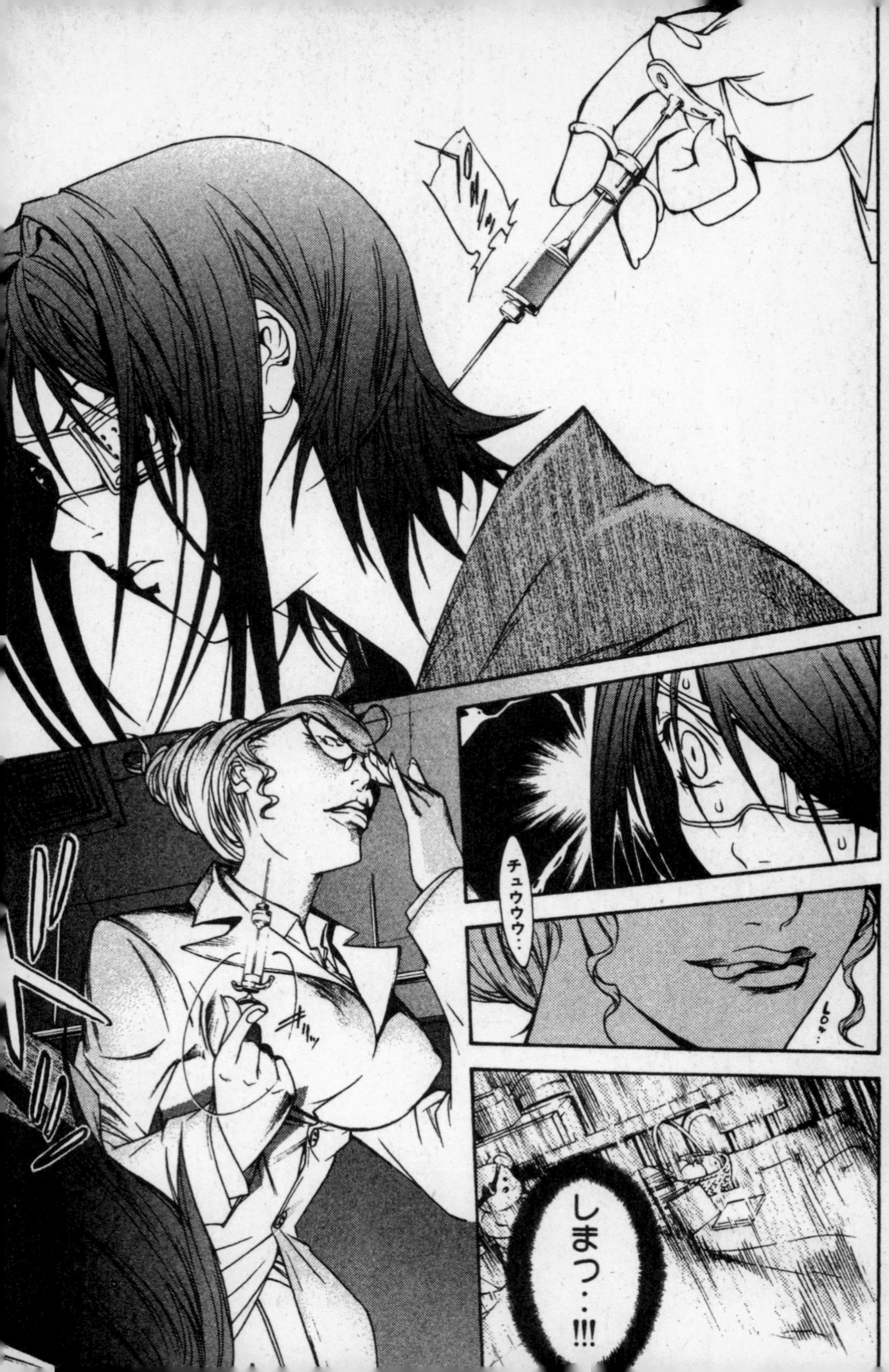
チュウウウ‥
レロッ‥
しまっ‥!!!

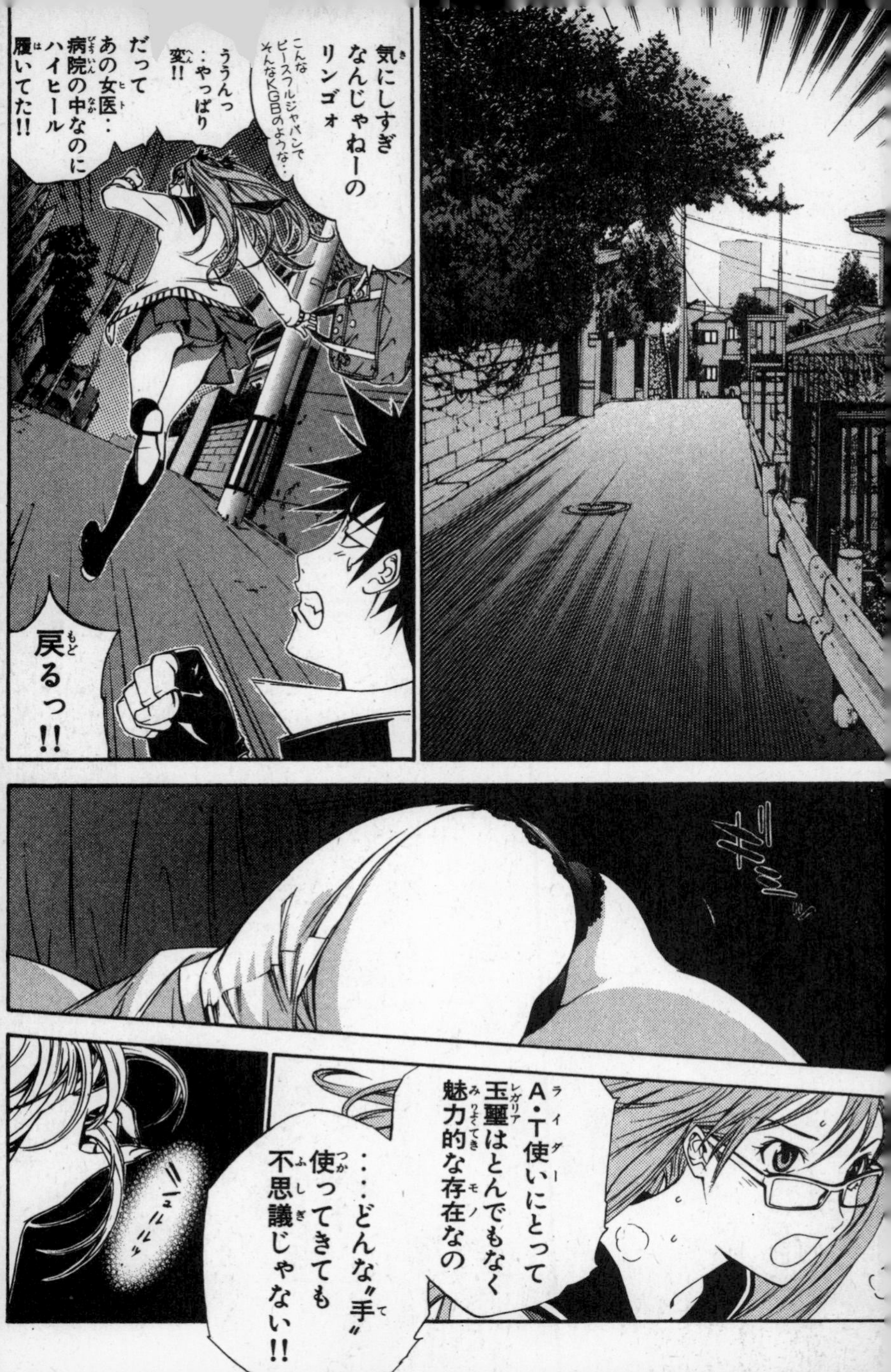

気にしすぎなんじゃねーのリンゴォ
こんなピースフルジャパンでそんなKGBのような‥
ううんっ‥やっぱり変!!
だってあの女医‥病院の中なのにハイヒール履いてた!!
戻るっ!!
A・T使いにとって玉璽はとんでもなく魅力的な存在なの
‥‥どんな〝手〟使ってきても不思議じゃない!!

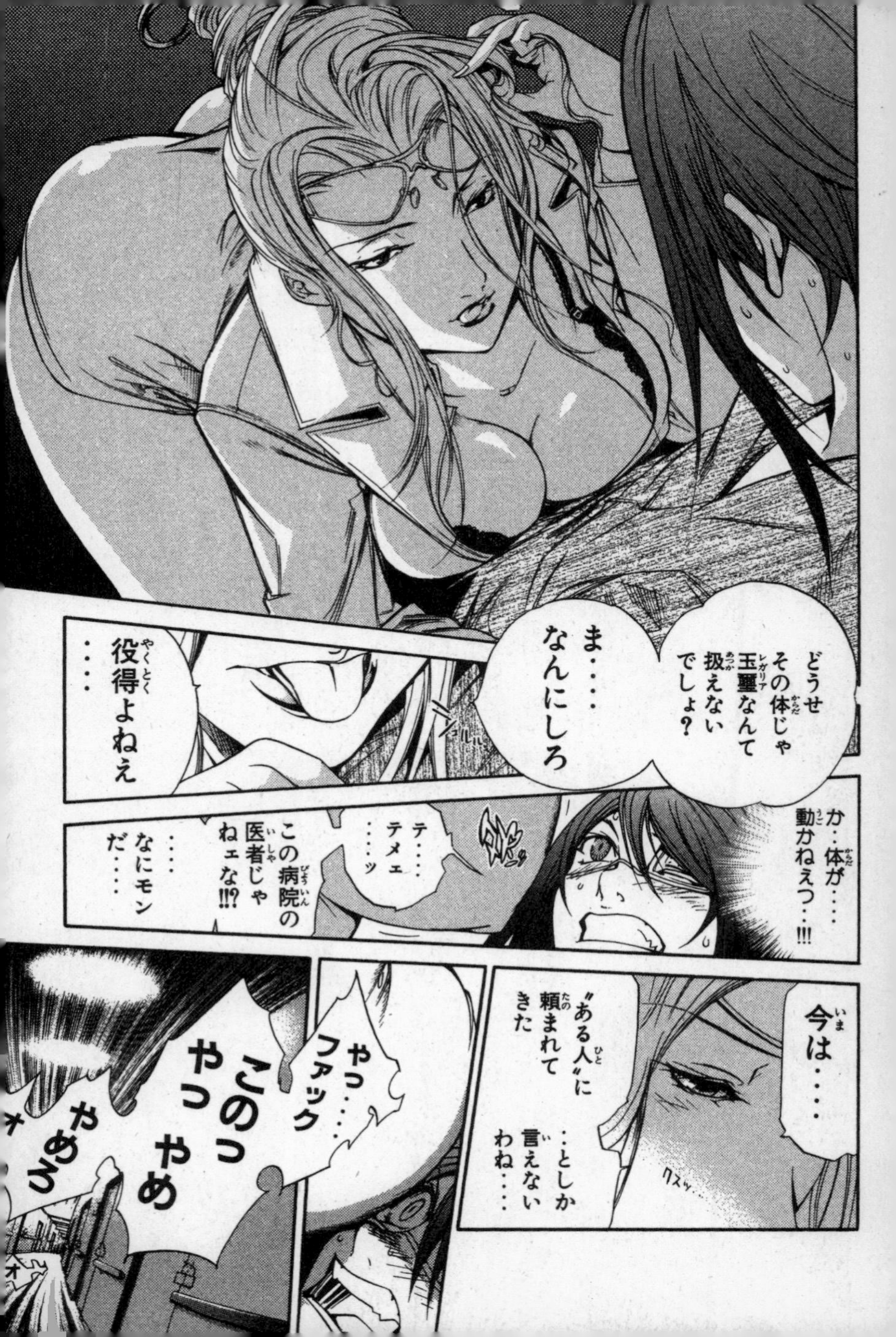
どうせその体じゃ玉璽なんて扱えないでしょ?
ま‥‥なんにしろ
シュル
役得よねぇ‥‥
か‥体が‥‥動かねえっ‥!!!
テ‥‥テメェ‥‥ッ
この病院の医者じゃねェな!!?
‥‥なにモンだ‥‥
今は‥‥
“ある人”に頼まれてきた
‥としか言えないわね‥‥
クスッ‥‥
やっ‥‥ファック
このっやっ やめ
やめろォオ

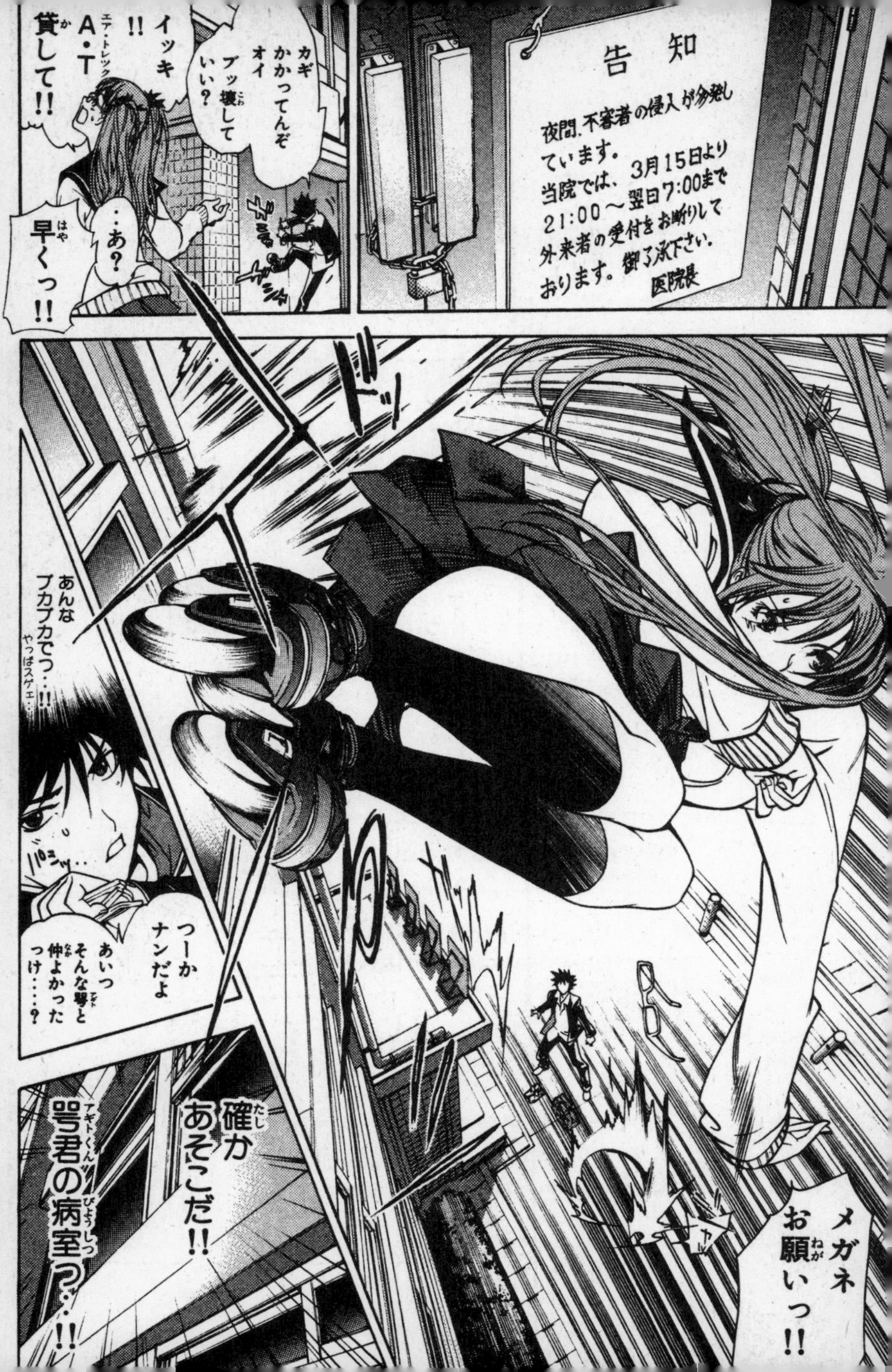
告知
夜間、不審者の侵入が多発しています。
当院では、3月15日より
21:00〜翌日7:00まで
外来者の受付をお断りしております。御了承下さい。
医院長
カギかかってんぞ
オイ ブッ壊していい？
イッキ!!
A・T貸して!!
…あ？
早くっ!!
ドッ
メガネお願いっ!!
確かあそこだ!!
号君の病室っ…!!
あんなブカブカでっ…!!
やっぱスゲェ…
つーかナンだよ
あいつそんな琴と仲よかったっけ…？

# Le Chevalier d'Eon

## STORY BY TOU UBUKATA
## MANGA BY KIRIKO YUMEJI

### DARKNESS FALLS ON PARIS

**A** mysterious cult is sacrificing beautiful young women to a demonic force that threatens the entire country. Only one man can save Paris from chaos and terror, the king's top secret agent: The Chevalier d'Eon.

• Available on DVD from ADV Films.

*Special extras in each volume! Read them all!*

# SHIKI TSUKAI

## STORY BY TO-RU ZEKUU
## ART BY YUNA TAKANAGI

### DEFENDING THE NATURAL ORDER OF THE UNIVERSE!

The *shiki tsukai* are "Keepers of the Seasons"—magical warriors pledged to defend the planet's natural order against those who would threaten it.

When 14-year-old Akira Kizuki joins the *shiki tsukai,* he knows that it'll be a difficult life. But with his new friends and mentors, he's up to the challenge!

*Special extras in each volume! Read them all!*